Mark my Word

my

A daily Devotional by

Reinhard Bonnke

edited by

Jeanne Halsey

365 daily Devotionals from the pen of
Missionary-Evangelist Reinhard Bonnke.
*"Much more than the average Daily Devotional,
this book will ignite a passion for lost souls,
motivate You to be a soul-winner."*
*"These are the 'power generators' of God:
the Cross of Calvary,
the Resurrection of Jesus Christ,
and the Holy Spirit Baptism."*

Featuring: a brief daily motivational message …
an inspiring Scripture verse for the day … where to find the Bible references …
a "Daily Power" phrase to carry you through the day … and more!

Presented to _____

by _____

on _____

Mark my Word
by Reinhard Bonnke
Edited by Jeanne Halsey

ISBN 3-935057-18-0

Editorial 1, Printing 1
©2001 by Full Flame GmbH
All rights reserved.

Unless indicated otherwise, all Scriptures are quoted from the

New King James Version of the Holy Bible,
©1999 by Thomas Nelson, Inc. All rights reserved; used by permission.

The Message by Eugene H. Peterson
©1995 published by NavPress All rights reserved; used by permission.

Today's Bible Reading is adapted by Jeanne Halsey

Daily Bible Reading Plan is compiled by Bob Phillips
©1992 by Harvest House Publishers All rights reserved; used by permission.

Cover Design by Isabelle Brasche
Cover Photos by Roland Senkel
Inside Photos by Peter van den Berg, Rob Birkbeck, Roland Senkel and Tom Henschke

Contact:

Reinhard Bonnke
Christ for all Nations
The Ministry of Evangelist Reinhard Bonnke

P.O. Box 590588 • Orlando, Florida 32859-0588 • USA
P.O. Box 25057 • London, Ontario N3C 6A8 • Canada
Postfach 60 05 74 • 60335 Frankfurt am Main • Germany
250 Coombs Road • Halesowen • West Midlands • B62 8AA • UK
P.O. Box 13010 • Witfield 1467 • Republic of South Africa
P.O. Box 10899 • Ikeja • Lagos • Nigeria
P.O. Box 51121 • Nairobi • Kenya

Published by:

Full Flame GmbH
Postfach 60 05 95 • 60335 Frankfurt am Main • Germany
www.fullflame.com

Printed in China

Preface

"One young man in his teens came to me one day and said that the Bible is too old and has no meaning anymore for the present modern day. I directed him to look at the sun in the bright morning sky. "Has the sun lost it's power? Does it not shine and shed warmth upon the earth – do we say the sun is cold because it is 'old?'"

II Timothy 3:16-17, tells us that *"All Scripture is God-breathed and is useful for teaching, rebuking, correcting and training in righteousness, so that the man of God may be thoroughly equipped for every good work."* The Holy Bible affects human beings so strongly because "all" the Bible is "God-breathed." It's more than a collection of moral principles; it's more than a good book; it's an inspired record, God's book. The prophets related what they saw and heard in human language, but their message came directly from God. Therefore, you can **Mark every Word** of your bible and live by it!

I am, first and foremost, an evangelist, a soul-winner. God has given me a fire that burns in my heart, one that simply refuses to go out. Therefore the way I view life is always filtered through that fire. If you want that same kind of fire to burn inside your bones, then you have got the right book! This is much more than a "daily devotional" that might give you some sort of a "sweet lift" to your morning – this book should daily ignite a passion for lost souls that will motivate you throughout your day and throughout your life!

My staff and I have deliberately designed this book to be a fast, intense, penetrating daily study that will help keep your focus on the Lord Jesus Christ, and continually remind you that, as Christians, our Number One Job is to reach the lost with the Good News! These are the "power generators" of God: the Cross of Calvary ... the Resurrection of Jesus Christ ... and the Holy Spirit Baptism. As often as possible – even while dealing with "practical issues" of daily life – you will be infused with God's purpose for your life, and given encouragement to fulfill the ministry which He has given you.

Reinhard Bonnke

Introduction

God has given us His Word, the Bible, so that we can understand Him better and grow strong in our faith. When you start reading it regularly, you will quickly discover that the Bible is a **lifeline** and a fool-proof **guidebook** for you.

The Word of God silences the accuser and routs doubts! Many people think they can base their faith on their feelings. The problem is that when their feelings plummet, their faith goes down with it! Your Christian faith is based on something far more solid than your feelings. It is based on what Jesus accomplished for us through His birth, life, death and resurrection. John 1:14 declares it so clearly when it says, *"And the Word became flesh and dwelt among us ..."*

It is through God's precious Word that your faith becomes strengthened and anchored ... your footsteps receive His light in the dark times of life ... your outlook becomes positive and upward when your spirit is tempted to look down and feel defeated ... your daily walk with the Lord becomes personal and relevant as you apply His precepts and principles to your life.

The Bible is a book you can completely rely on to tell you the truth about God ... and about yourself. It does not "contain" the Word of God ... it **is** the Word of God for you! As Jesus said, *"Heaven and earth will pass away, but my words will never pass away ... "* (Matthew 24:35).

God has given us **two** "witnesses" to reassure us of His love, acceptance, healing, forgiveness and daily provision ... and these two witnesses are the Word of God (the Bible) and the Spirit of God.

As you read through this volume day by day – my sincere prayer for you can be found in the words that Paul the Apostle prayed for the Ephesians ... *"I ask that your minds may be opened to see his light, so that you will **know** what is the hope to which he has called you; to **know** how rich are the wonderful blessings he promised you; and how **very great** is his **power** in you."* (Ephesians 1:18-19)

Helpful Tips

Read each day out loud. Not only **seeing** the words but **hearing** them – thus **planting** them in your heart as well as your mind – gives purpose and power to your daily motivation.

Make your own quick notes and mark passages as you read along. Often referring back to a particular day which really ministered to you – and having that date noted in your own handwriting – is one of the tools you can use to allow God to give His best to you ... *"that ye may look upon it"* (Numbers 15:39-40).

Each day's reading has several key self-help components:

- The "daily commentary/teaching" from Evangelist Bonnke's own writings.
- A daily Scripture passage that been specifically selected for each day.
  (You may want to consider memorizing key verses that speak to your heart!)
- A "daily Power Affirmation!" – for you to speak out loud and claim as a guide-post power-phrase to lift your focus and empower your footsteps.
- "Mark my Word" cross-reference guide – where the Biblical foundation for each day day can be read in context with greater detail – along with related passages for further study.
- A daily "through the entire Bible" reading plan. By faithfully following this, you will read through the entire Bible **plus** read the Book of Psalms **twice** in one year. It is so important to make sure your are getting your "daily bread" from the Word of God.

The wind of the Holy Spirit
is not sent to us to cool us down,
but to fan the flame.

To wait on God is an Old Testament concept.
The last ones that waited were the 120 in the upper room.
Now God waits on us. Green means GO.
When the light turns green,
you do not need a permit from the
"Secretary of Transportation" –
You just GO.

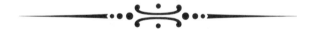

We shouldn't burn out for Jesus, but burn on!

God First

What better way to start a New Year than with a fresh commitment to put God first in your life! "Prioritizing God" sounds simple, but the pressures of our lives try very hard to push Him out of the way … and sometimes we find ourselves in that difficult place of suddenly stopping, re-evaluating our lives, and realizing that we've somehow lost that all-important "first love." Professor Eugene Peterson wrote it this way in his paraphrase of Romans 12: *"Take your everyday, ordinary life – your sleeping, eating, going-to-work, and walking-around life – and place it before God as an offering. Embracing what God does for you is the best thing you can do for Him. Don't become so well-adjusted to your culture that you fit into it without even thinking. Instead, fix your attention on God. You'll be changed from the inside out. Readily recognize what He wants from you, and quickly respond to it. Unlike the culture around you, always dragging you down to its level of immaturity, God brings the best out of you, develops well-formed maturity in you."*

Jesus demonstrated this sense of priority even as a young child – at the age of 12, he astounded His parents by stating: *"Did you not know that I must be about My Father's business?"* Later, in His ministry, He reiterated: *"I **must** work the works of Him Who sent Me."* There was no question about it – Jesus' first priority was pleasing His Father. Of course, the First Commandment is this: *"You shall have no other gods before Me."* Right back in Moses' time, learning to put God first was a **required priority.** The Second Commandment reveals further how important He wants to be in our lives: *"You shall not make for yourself a carved image … you shall not bow down to them nor serve them; for I, the Lord your God, am a jealous God."* Putting **anything** – careers, financial achievement, even relationships – ahead of God constitutes making "an idol" of it … and our "jealous God" warns strictly against it.

Make a covenant right now: "Lord, I want to always put You first in my life, in everything I do. Enable me, by Your Holy Spirit, to be consistent in this choice. Thank You!" When this prayer comes straight from your heart, then God's part of the equation is to respond to you with His strength and ability.

Today's Scripture

But seek first the Kingdom of God and His righteousness, and all these things shall be added to you.

(Matthew 6:33)

Daily Power!

Today I stand on God's promise that He will never leave me or forsake me … therefore I whole-heartedly put my trust in Him!

Today's Bible Reading

Genesis 1:1-31 through 2:1-25; Matthew 1:1-25 through 2:1-12; Psalm 1:1-6; Proverbs 1:1-6

Mark my Word
(for further study):

Exodus 20:1-17; Joshua 1:5; Matthew 6:25-34; Luke 2:49; John 9:4; Romans 12:1-2; Revelation 2:1-7

Today's Scripture

My food is to do the will of Him Who sent Me, and to finish the work.
(John 4:34)

Daily Power!

The Great Commission empowers me to be His evangelist. I am committed to fulfilling His will.

Today's Bible Reading

*Genesis 3:1-24
through 4:1-26;
Matthew 2:13-23
through 3:1-6;
Psalm 2:1-12;
Proverbs 1:7-9*

Mark my Word
(for further study):

*Mark 16:15-20;
John 4:34-38;
8:32; 17:17;
Ephesians 1:13;
Colossians 1:3-5*

Reason for Living

Because evangelism is my reason for living, it is also my favorite topic. The evangelist is a man with a driving urgency, not a man with two minds. The Gospel — and nothing else on Earth — matters: neither fame, money, earthly pleasures, nor life itself. Jesus had a total attraction for the wretched. It led Him to the Cross. He would bring His salvation and healing touch to broken lives, no matter what.

I believe in preaching a straightforward message – a Gospel that speaks of sin, salvation, healing, and discipleship. I do this with the heartfelt conviction that **it is preaching the Word of God that brings revival.** Nothing more – nothing less. *"God's Word is Truth ... You shall know the truth, and the truth will set you free"* ... *"In Him you also trusted, after you heard the Word of Truth, the Gospel of your salvation ... We give thanks to the God and Father of our Lord Jesus Christ, praying always for you, since we heard of your faith in Christ Jesus and of your love for all the saints, because of the hope which is laid up for you in Heaven, of which you heard before in the Word of the Truth of the Gospel."*

There has never been revival without aggressive evangelism. The first time I witnessed thousands running forward to respond to the call of salvation, God opened my eyes ... and I actually saw an invisible, mighty wave of Holy Spirit-power arrive in the stadium (this was in Africa). A mass baptism in the Holy Spirit – accompanied by many mighty miracles – took place. I wept like a boy, and vowed to the Lord that, in obedience, I would move across all of Africa to bring the vision to pass. I reasoned that if God could do that to ten thousand people, He could do it to four hundred fifty million.

I have a simple goal, which perfectly describes evangelism:
Heaven full – Hell empty!

God is with you and me – not because we have great faith – but because He has committed Himself irrevocably. Faith is not just for the possible – that is not faith at all. The mightiest resource in the universe is the Arm of God. The Lord of the Harvest **will** send forth His laborers, which includes you and me.

Perfectly certain

Another great way to start a New Year is to have assurance of salvation. When you are saved, you should know it. Otherwise, how can you be a witness for Christ? The Bible speaks clearly and positively … it does not stammer. When you read it, you become certain. Martin Luther once said, "The Holy Spirit is no skeptic." He writes no doubts. The promises of God are **Yes** and **Amen**, not **No** and **Maybe**. The Gospel trumpet sounds no faltering note.

When an earthquake shook the Philippian jail and all who were in it, the jailor cried out, *"What must I do to be saved?"* Paul did not reply, "Well, what do you think? Do you have any ideas?" He made a firm statement of fact: *"Believe on the Lord Jesus Christ, and you will be saved, you and your household."* The Gospel is God's message, not Christian opinion … and it is **yours** today!

What are the two greatest things God ever did? The Bible tells us that He created the Heavens and the Earth. Could anything possibly equal that – making our wonderful world, with its oceans, mountains and rivers, and filling the Heavens with stars? In fact, God did do something else that was far more difficult. We call it the "work of redemption." Creation cost God nothing – but that next task cost Him everything.

At Creation, God blessed us with the energies of Life. Then He blessed us with the gift of redemption, adding new life to ordinary life. Millions of people around the world enjoy it. They are jubilant. They exclaim and sing, "I am redeemed!" They cannot keep quiet about this wonderful gift that God has given them. Therefore, my friend, today I encourage you: **rejoice in your salvation!**

Today's Scripture

Believe on the Lord Jesus Christ, and you will be saved, you and your household.
(Acts 16:31)

Daily Power!

Reading God's Word is a constant source of assurance that I am saved and I know it. His Word says it — "God is not a man that He should lie."

Today's Bible Reading

Genesis 5:1-32 through 7:1-24; Matthew 3:7-17 through 4:1-11; Psalm 3:1-8; Proverbs 1:10-19

Mark my Word
(for further study)

Numbers 23:19; Acts 16:1-40; I Corinthians 1:17-20

JANUARY

4

Today's Scripture

I know Whom I have believed and am persuaded that He is able to keep what I have committed to Him until that day.

(II Timothy 1:12)

Daily Power!

When I repent and believe, and come to the Lord and Savior Jesus Christ, He receives me and I am cleansed in His precious Blood!

Today's Bible Reading

Genesis 8:1-22
through 10:1-32;
Matthew 4:12-25;
Psalm 4:1-8;
Proverbs 1:20-23

Mark my Word
(for further study)

Luke 19:10;
John 6:37;
Acts 2:38-39;
II Timothy 1:12

Salvation is not Speculation

The genius who made the first electric dynamo, Michael Faraday, was not only a master of all the sciences, but also a Christian. In 1867 when he was dying, his friends asked him what his speculations about life after death were. "Speculations?" he asked in surprise. "Speculations! I have none. I am resting on certainties!" Faraday's favorite Bible verse was: *"I know Whom I have believed and am persuaded that He is able to keep what I have committed to Him until that day."* He had no reservations about Biblical truth.

Some people argue that it is presumptuous to declare we are saved, but that is false modesty in the light of so much Scriptural evidence. When Christ confronts you with the question of your need, you should not respond, "I want to have my questions answered and to give my view of salvation." Instead, you must repent and believe! Being saved is not a casual experience, something you would hardly notice. When you repent and believe, and come to the Lord and Savior Jesus Christ, He receives you and you are cleansed in His precious Blood!

"Repent, and let every one of you be baptized in the Name of Jesus Christ for the remission of sins, and you shall receive the gift of the Holy Spirit. For the promise is to you and to your children, and to all who are afar off, as many as the Lord our God will call."

Take these two statements made by Christ Jesus Himself: *"All that the Father gives Me will come to Me, and the one who comes to Me I will by no means cast out"* and *"For the Son of Man has come to **seek and to save** that which was lost."* To you, that means when you give Christ your trust in His gift of salvation, He honors it, even to the Throne of the God the Father.

Spiritual Need

People need the Gospel, and their need creates a need in the heart of God: He **needs** to send us with the Gospel! He knows we must be born-again, and He can't just sit down on His Throne and do nothing about it. That would be completely contrary to all He has ever done.

"Whoever calls on the Name of the Lord shall be saved. How then shall they call on Him in Whom they have not believed? And how shall they believe in Him of Whom they have not heard? And how shall they hear without a preacher? And how shall they preach unless they be sent? ... So then faith comes by hearing, and hearing by the Word of God."

God knows our need, and is under compulsion to meet it. Likewise, if we – who are made in God's image – know about the hungry in the world, we **need** to do something about it. Their need creates in us a need to help the needy. If you and I have plenty, then we cannot merely stand by and watch our neighbors die of starvation. The same is true of spiritual food. Our spiritual need lays a compulsion on the heart of God – and our attitude toward others should be the same.

What should we be doing to fulfill that need in God's heart? The same that Jesus did – which was also a fulfillment of Isaiah's prophecy: *"The Spirit of the Lord God is upon Me, because the Lord has anointed Me to **preach** Good Tidings to the poor; He has sent Me to heal the broken-hearted, to **proclaim liberty** to the captives, and the opening of prison to those who are bound, to proclaim the acceptable year of the Lord, and the day of vengeance of our God; to **comfort** all who mourn, to **console** those who mourn in Zion, to give them beauty for ashes, the oil of joy for mourning, the garment of praise for the spirit of heaviness; that they may be called trees of righteousness, the planting of the Lord, that He may be glorified"* (emphasis added).

Today's Scripture

I must work the works of Him Who sent Me while it is day; the night is coming when no man can work.

(John 9:4)

Daily Power!

My desire is to fulfill that compulsion which God has placed within my heart: to reach out to the unreached, to tell the untold, the minister the Gospel of Jesus Christ to everyone I meet.

Today's Bible Reading

Genesis 11:1-32 through 13:1-4;
Matthew 5:1-26;
Psalm 5:1-12;
Proverbs 1:24-28

Mark my Word
(for further study)

Isaiah 6:1-3; 55:11;
Luke 4:18;
John 9:4;
Romans 10:13-18

6

The World's Need

Imagine if Abraham or Moses suddenly arrived back from the past, or perhaps Mohammed or Buddha – what would that do for the world? Well, none of them will come, so it is idle to speculate. But as we enter the third millennium, millions are looking for a great global leader. They even hopefully consult the stars, looking for a New Age under a super-personality to bring accord between the races, peace among the nations, and the rich caring for the poor. Is it only sentimental fantasy?

The wish seems so common: "Oh, for a great cosmic king and all-powerful leader to rule the rulers when they are unruly!" There is always a war somewhere, injustice, people being slaughtered or oppressed. The feeling there should be a single mind guiding the nations in the ways of wisdom and prosperity is like an instinct for something we have lost.

Age after age, we have seen "great men" rise to power, exerting their philosophical influence through political maneuvering and military strength … only to fall again, leaving a legacy of bloodshed, economic ruin, corruption, tyranny. Humanists **think** they have the answers to Mankind's need, but they are overlooking the essential element of the "God-shaped space" that resides in the heart of Man. Fill that space with alternatives – wealth, fame, pleasure, power – and Man is still left empty and unfulfilled.

All of Life's great experiences are pinpointed in the Bible. It is not for nothing that it is read. The Book of Judges describes a nation without a leader. After Israel settled in the Promised Land, there were two centuries of turmoil, anarchy and civil war. The Book explains why: *"In those days, there was no king in Israel, and every man did what was right in his own eyes."* This sounds so familiar, doesn't it? Today we stand in peril of repeating the same mistakes made by the children of Israel those thousands of years ago. Let us always endeavor to promote Jesus Christ – the True King on the Throne!

Today's Scripture

And I will establish My covenant between Me and you and your descendants after you in their generations, for an everlasting covenant, to be God to you and your descendants after you.
(Genesis 17:7)

Daily Power!

Everything I need to know about Life has already been written in God's Book of Life.

Today's Bible Reading

Genesis 13:5-18 through 15:1-21; Matthew 5:27-48; Psalm 6:1-10; Proverbs 1:29-33

Mark my Word
(for further study)

Genesis 17:7; Judges 17:6; 18:1; 19:1; 21:25

Only Jesus!

This Jesus! Nobody else had ever dared make such an amazing claim to provide "living water" – and fulfill it. He would ascend to glory where Creation began, and change the order of things. Something not known before would surge from Heaven to Earth. He called it *"the promise of the Father."* That promise is for **you** today!

The Promise – Out of over eight thousand promises in God's Word, the designation of **the Promise** makes it stand singularly and significantly alone. Christ made it His own promise. The Father's gift to Him is His gift to us, as John the Baptist said:

"I did not know Him, but He Who sent me to baptize with water said to me, 'Upon Whom you see the Spirit descending, and remaining on Him, this is He Who baptizes with the Holy Spirit.' And I have seen and testified that this is the Son of God."

There is a price we pay to receive that promise – but the price is well worth its cost … and it could never compare to the price which Jesus paid for **us**: His life. *"Whoever desires to come after Me, let him deny himself, and take up his cross, and follow Me."* Later, when His own disciples asked Him about "sharing His glory," He responded, *"You will indeed drink the cup that I drink, and with the baptism I am baptized with you will be baptized."*

When we allow Jesus into our lives, He makes us new from the inside out: *"Therefore, if anyone is in Christ, he is a new creation; old things have passed away; behold, all things have become new."* Today, allow that "living water" to infuse you with His love, joy and strength, down into the deepest part of your heart.

Today's Scripture

You shall receive power when the Holy Spirit has come upon you; and you shall be witnesses to Me in Jerusalem, and in all Judea and Samaria, and to the end of the Earth.
(Acts 1:8)

Daily Power!

The Father's gift to Jesus is also a gift to me!

Today's Bible Reading

Genesis 16:1-16
through 18:1-19;
Matthew 6:1-24;
Psalm 7:1-17;
Proverbs 2:1-5

Mark my Word
(for further study)

Mark 8:34; 10:39;
Luke 24:44-53;
John 1:1-37;
Acts 1:1-14;
II Corinthians 5:17

8

Jesus never changes

Jesus healed multitudes – that was His mission. He came to heal as well as to save. He did not come from Glory to Earth for only those people who happened to be alive during that period in history. He did not come to bring relief merely to a few thousand people. That was only the beginning: *"Then He healed many who were sick with various diseases, and cast out many demons, and He did not allow the demons to speak because they knew Him … And again He began to teach by the sea. And a great multitude was gathered to Him, so that He got into a boat and sat in it on the sea; and the whole multitude was on the land facing the sea. Then He taught them many things by parables."* The Bible says it was what *"Jesus **began** to do."* By His deeds, He showed us what He wanted to do, so that we can see what He was – and still is – like. He came to heal **them** so that He could heal **you** and **me**.

People living in the days of Jesus' earthly ministry possibly thought of Jesus more as a Healer than anything else. He set out to heal. That was Jesus. He didn't wait for the sick to come to Him – He often went to them. The apostle Peter actually said that Jesus went around for that very purpose. Healing was a major part of His mission, and Jesus said God sent Him to do those very works.

If a man spends eight years or more studying to become a doctor, when he has finished his studies, he will open a surgery to treat sick people. It would be ridiculous for a doctor not to practice after all his efforts to qualify. We read in the Book of Matthew, *"He Himself took our infirmities and bore our sicknesses."* That is a quotation from the prophet Isaiah about the Crucifixion. Christ bore your pains and your sins in His own Body on the Cross. If Jesus died for you, it is not too much to expect Him to heal you.

Today's Scripture:

Jesus went about all Galilee, teaching in their synagogues, preaching the Gospel of the Kingdom, and healing all kinds of sickness and all kinds of diseases among the people.
(Matthew 4:23)

Daily Power!

I know that Jesus included my healing in His purpose on Earth, so I accept His gift with thanksgiving.

Today's Bible Reading

Genesis 18:20-33 through 19:1-38; Matthew 6:25-34 through 7:1-14; Psalm 8:1-9; Proverbs 2:6-15

Mark my Word
(for further study):

Matthew 4:23; Mark 1:34; 4:1-9; John 5:17; 9:3-4; Acts 1:1-9; 10:38

The Faith Factor

The Bible was written for people with no real faith. Faith is not "believing what we know isn't true" nor "Believing something for which there is no evidence." That is foolishness.

But if we have no faith, **reading the Bible produces it.** And if we have **some** faith, we get more the same way. There's no mystique about it. We are born believers, having faith every day in our doctors and bankers, in our spouses and bosses. Without this natural faith, we could not function. Faith is possible to everybody … including you!

Your brain is the "doubt-box." Of course people say, "Seeing is believing." But if you can prove it, faith is unnecessary! Not seeing is no reason for not believing. Nobody sees radiation, but we know its effects. Nobody sees God, but millions see His effect in their lives. **Faith is a decision.** Make that decision irrevocable today!

Faith, like wiring, carries power … but is not power. It links us to the Power Source – God in Heaven. Many people seek power through thousands of theories and methods. Some Christian believers also seek the power of God by dubious processes, like extra-long prayer or touching "sacred" relics. But the mystic realms are not where the disciples found power. It is available on Earth. Christ's death and resurrection made available all the Divine power we could ever need. It is the simple faith or ordinary people that touches Christ, not mysterious spirituality. Christ said, *"I am the Way, the Truth, and the Life. No man comes to the Father except through Me."* He is the only Mediator between God and Man, and for that office, He paid the infinite price. Never underestimate the power of your faith because of His sacrifice.

Today's Scripture

Blessed are those who have not seen and yet have believed.
(John 20:29)

Daily Power!

*Faith is possible to everybody …
including me!*

Today's Bible Reading

*Genesis 20:1-18
through 22:1-24;
Matthew 7:15-29;
Psalm 9:1-12;
Proverbs 2:16-22*

Mark my Word
(for further study):

*John 14:6; 20:24-30;
I Timothy 2:5*

The Faith Fuse

Faith has neither bulk nor weight, for it is what you **do**. Jesus spoke of *"faith as small as a mustard seed,"* referring to something tiny but with huge potential. Perhaps today, He might speak of faith as a fuse. Tiny as it is, it transmits the awesome power generated in power stations to our homes. Without it, every appliance is useless, unable to draw from that power.

Our faith – however small we think it may be – can accomplish **great** things: *"Another parable He put forth to them, saying, 'The Kingdom of Heaven is like a mustard seed, which a man took and sowed in his field, which indeed is the least of all the seeds; but when it is grown it is greater than the herbs and becomes a tree, so that the birds of the air come and nest in its branches.'"*

As believers, we know what we believe and Who we believe. **Believing tests us.** Taking God's Word at face value, accepting its divine authority, we plug into the very Source! Faith is the vital link. By it, the energies of Heaven flow into the world ... and into your life. *"Believe on the Lord Jesus Christ, and you will be saved, you and your household."*

The greatness of God, the work of Christ, of the Word of God, are all there ... but without faith – as small as a fuse wire – none of that greatness avails. The circuit is broken. And once connected, the fuse itself cannot help but show the effects of the power surging through it. It warms up! Faith makes us dynamic, exuberant, excited! Allow God's fuse of faith to activate your life today. *"What does it profit, my brethren, if someone says he has faith but does not have works? Can faith save him? ... Thus also faith by itself, if it does not have works, is dead. But someone will say, 'You have faith, and I have works.' Show me your faith without your works, and I will show you my faith by my works."*

Today's Scripture

If you have faith as a mustard seed, you will say to this mountain, "Move from here to there," and it will move; and nothing will be impossible for you.
(Matthew 17:20)

Daily Power!

Today I take God's Word at face value, accepting its divine authority, and plugging into the very Source of Life.

Today's Bible Reading

Genesis 23:1-20 through 24:1-51; Matthew 8:1-17; Psalm 9:13-20; Proverbs 3:1-6

Mark my Word
(for further study)

Matthew 13:31-32; 17:14-21; Luke 17:5-10; Acts 16:38; James 1:14-19

The Hands of Jesus

When Jesus walked on Earth and delivered people from the oppression of Satan, that old deceiver watched Him. The blind saw and cripples walked … Christ was destroying the works of the devil systematically. Satan ground his teeth with rage and plotted to destroy the Lord Jesus Christ. He inspired evil men to crucify Christ. He gloated as they nailed down those wonderful hands of mercy. "Those hands will give me no more trouble," he thought. "It is all over!' What a mistake Satan made! The very Blood he caused to be spilled now breaks the stranglehold of Satan upon men and women everywhere, especially for you and me!

"And in the midst of the seven lamp-stands One like the Son of Man, clothed with a garment down to the feet and girded about the chest with a golden band … He laid His right hand on me, saying to me, 'Do not be afraid; I am the First and the Last. I am He Who lives, and was dead, and behold, I am alive forevermore. Amen. And I have the keys of Hades and of Death.'"

An atheist once challenged me on a television program, "I do not believe that there is any power in the Blood of Jesus. The Blood of Jesus has been around for two thousand years, and if there was any power in it – as you claim – the world would not be in such a sorry state."

I replied, "Sir, there is also plenty of soap around, yet many people are still dirty. Soap doesn't make anybody clean by just being around, not even if he works in a soap factory. If you want to know what soap can do – you have to **take it and apply it personally**. Then you will see! That is how it is with the Blood of Jesus. It is not enough to know about the Blood, sing about it, or preach about it. I now challenge you, sir," I said, "apply the Blood of Jesus to your sinful life, and you will join hundreds of millions of people all over the world who sing and say: 'There is power, power, wonder-working power, in the Blood of the Lamb!'"

Today's Scripture

How much more shall the Blood of Christ, Who through the eternal Spirit offered Himself without spot to God, cleanse your conscience from dead works to serve the living God.

(Hebrews 9:14)

Daily Power!

The Blood of Jesus has broken every stranglehold Satan has tried to establish over my life.

Today's Bible Reading

*Genesis 24:54-67 through 24:1-16;
Matthew 8:18-34;
Psalm 10:1-15;
Proverbs 3:7-8*

Mark my Word
(for further study)

*Hebrews 9:14;
I John 1:7;
Revelation 1:9-20*

Jesus is real

If Jesus is real, why do we live as if He did not exist? If there is a Father in Heaven, why do we behave as if we were orphans? If there is a Savior, why do we cringe in fear and misery? If there is a Healer, why don't we ask Him for healing? If Christ is offering Life in all its fullness, why do we scratch and peck around in the dust like chickens? Jesus says, *"Do not be afraid; only believe."*

If things go wrong, they can also go right! If the devil can be effective, how much more can God! Faith is supposed to prove its worth in times of great need – but for so many believers, that is precisely when it comes to a halt. For them, faith only works in "blessed Christian meetings." To put it figuratively, they wear their life preservers only so long as they are on the ship, and toss them off as soon as they fall into the sea. How ridiculous can you get! Let us embrace the living reality of Jesus Christ in our lives today!

Faith may follow a process like this:

(1) **Believing something is true.**
Believing "there is a God" is not enough –
the devil believes the same thing – but it is a start.
(2) **Believing a person is genuine.**
Many believe that Jesus was a "good man" …
but He claimed to be much more: the Savior of the world!
(3) **Believing in God's power.**
Many believed in Christ's healing power …
but didn't make Him Lord and Savior.
(4) **Believing as trust.**
Trust makes faith personal –
we simply trust people we feel won't fail us.
(5) **Believing in Christ.**
This is real faith. It is complete surrender,
letting Him take over every area of your life.

Today's Scripture

For the law of the Spirit of life in Christ Jesus has made me free from the law of sin and death.
(Romans 8:2)

Daily Power!

I live my life in the fullness of Christ Jesus, and I am an overcomer through Him.

Today's Bible Reading

*Genesis 26:17-35 through 27:1-46;
Matthew 9:1-17;
Psalm 10:16-18
Proverbs 3:9-10*

Mark my Word
(for further study)

*Mark 5:36;
Romans 8:1-17;
Galatians 4:1-7;
James 2:19*

God's universal Health Scheme

Jesus Christ is the Great Physician, on call day and night. His surgery never closes, and you don't have to wait for an appointment. He specializes in all kinds of troubles you may encounter – whether sickness of the soul, afflictions of the body, or the ills of society – and there are no fees! We all enjoy good health … when we have it! Unfortunately, so many people get up in the morning feeling run down, and start the day already exhausted, which was never God's idea. I trust this isn't you! The Gospel of Jesus Christ is the "national health scheme" for every nation on Earth, and the Bible is its textbook. Somebody said that God meant our bodies to last, with care, a lifetime.

Healing originated with God – it wasn't **our** idea. At the beginning of the Bible, when nobody had ever thought of such a thing, He healed people … and that was four thousand years ago! *"So Abraham prayed to God; and God healed Abimelech, his wife, and his female servants."* Nobody suggested healing to God, or begged Him for it. He did it because it was His nature … He **loved** doing it!

If there is something you don't like doing, you keep quiet about it. But if you enjoy doing something – perhaps a hobby or a sport – you devote time to it and generally talk about it too. God didn't keep quiet about healing – He couldn't! His heart was full of compassion. He not only talked about it, but **did** it as well.

The first page of the Bible says, *"Then God saw everything that He had made, and indeed it was very good."* The last page says, *"There shall be no more death, nor sorrow, nor crying … no more pain."* Things began very well, and they will end that way. Make that your choice today!

Today's Scripture

I am the Lord Who heals you.
(Exodus 15:26)

Daily Power!

Jesus Christ is my Great Physician, on call day or night. I know He hears me and will answer when I call.

Today's Bible Reading

Genesis 28:1-22 through 29:1-35; Matthew 9:18-38; Psalm 11:1-7; Proverbs 3:11-12

Mark my Word
(for further study)

Genesis 1:1-31; 20:7; Exodus 15:26; Revelation 21:1-8

14

Streams in the Desert

"If anyone thirsts, let him come to Me and drink. He who believes in Me, as the Scriptures as said, out of his heart will flow rivers of living water."

"Rivers of living water!" Not bottles, but **rivers** – fresh, lively, sparkling, abundant, unending. Some people live for what comes out of a bottle … but Jesus wants you to experience a fresh, vibrant "river." Television provides the highlights of Life for millions of people, just watching others live or pretending to live; even for children, who forget how to play.

Remember: people are always "going to" live – after "things change," after working hours, when they have money, when they get married, retire, go on holiday, whatever. Jesus came to give you Life **now**. No waiting – wherever you are, whatever you are doing. **He makes Life live.**

New water, new wine: *"And no one puts new wine into old wineskins or else the new wine will burst the wineskins and be spilled, and the wineskins will be ruined. But new wine must be put into new wineskins, and both are preserved."*

God wrote His plan for Israel in the wilderness across a blackboard forty years wide. The Israelites did not have to drink stale, flat water from skins – the Lord opened bubbling streams from a rock. The Temple drink offering was a celebration in memory of that wilderness water. Jesus, however, gave it a new and glorious meaning, a symbol of the outpouring of the Holy Spirit for you and me … and that symbol is a precious reminder to you today that God has made a provision for your life of fresh, lively, sparkling, abundant, unending waters of refreshment and restoration. Let that river flow in you today!

Today's Scripture

I have come that they may have Life, and that they may have it more abundantly.

(John 10:10)

Daily Power!

God has made a provision for my life of fresh, lively, sparkling, abundant, unending waters of refreshment and restoration!

Today's Bible Reading

Genesis 30:1-43 through 31:1-16; Matthew 10:1-25; Psalm 12:1-8; Proverbs 3:13-15

Mark my Word
(for further study)

Exodus 17:1-7; Numbers 20:1-13; Luke 5:37-38; John 4:3-30; 10:9-11

Finding God

We will only find God if we truly want Him. As God says in the Bible: *"I love those who love Me, and those who seek Me, find Me"* … *"Surely you shall call a nation you do not know, and nations who do not know you shall run to you, because of the Lord your God, and the Holy One of Israel, for He has glorified you. Seek the Lord while He may be found, call upon Him while He is near."*

And He makes this cast-iron promise: *"I know the plans I have for you … plans to prosper you and not to harm you, plans to give you hope and a future. Then you will call upon Me and come and pray to Me, and I will listen to you. You will seek Me and find Me when you seek Me with all your heart."*

At the point of our deepest need, the Good News of Jesus Christ cuts in! Jesus saw His life as a rescue mission. He said that He had come *"to seek and to save what was lost."* He also said that His death was no accident – because He had come to die: *"The Son of Man did not come to be served, but to serve, and to give His life as a ransom for many."*

Is "peace" our deepest need? No, although Christ too has provided that – "Peace I leave with you, My peace I give to you; not as the world gives do I give to you. Let not your heart be troubled, neither let it be afraid" – but **the Good News of Jesus Christ is our deepest need.** The Gospel encompasses all the unrest, all the heartache, all the loneliness, pain and despair, the sin and corruption that drives us wild … and offers instead the plan which God had in mind for us all along: **a rightful relationship with Him,** wherein all of our needs are satisfied. Make that your strongest heart-beat today – that you are always in right relationship with Christ, because **then** you can change the world!

Today's Scripture

"I know the plans I have for you," declares the Lord, *"plans to prosper you and not to harm you, plans to give you hope a future."*
(Jeremiah 29:11-13; NIV)

Daily Power!

My daily goal is to be in right relationship with Christ, because then I can change the world!

Today's Bible Reading

Genesis 31:17-55 through 32:1-12;
Matthew 10:26-42 through 11:1-6;
Psalm 13:1-6;
Proverbs 3:16-18

Mark my Word
(for further study)

Proverbs 8:17;
Isaiah 55:5-6;
Jeremiah 29:11-13 (NIV);
Mark 10:45;
Luke 14:27; 19:10

16

God's Identity

It is a striking thing that God's identity is linked to men. He was first known through the life of Abraham, and was called *"the God of Abraham."* The world's ideas about God came first from seeing what sort of man Abraham was. His life portrayed his God, and served as a recommendation for Him.

When Jacob first fled from home and from the murderous threats of Esau, he referred to the Lord as *"the God of his fathers, Abraham and Isaac."* That is how he identified God – by how their God had shaped their lives. This brought a sense of awe upon Jacob. He resolved that one day, their God would be his God. He didn't feel that could be a reality until his own life reflected his God. If the name of Jacob was to be associated with his fathers' God, he wanted to maintain the reputation of that God.

Evangelism means that somebody will say, "I believe in my mother's God" or "I believe in Paul's God" or "I believe in Jean's God." People talk about presenting the Gospel "in a nutshell" – but it can actually only be presented in a person. The Gospel is more than a formula for getting to Heaven when you die. The Gospel offers life, not just a life-belt. The essence of evangelism is to show what God is like.

"But you are a chosen generation, a royal priesthood, a holy nation, His own special people, that you may proclaim the praises of Him Who called you out of darkness into His marvelous light."

Make that the cry of your heart today: "God, I want to be your **bold** evangelist, pointing the way to life in Christ Jesus!"

Today's Scripture

Therefore, since we have such hope, we use great boldness of speech.
(II Corinthians 3:12)

Daily Power!

I believe that the essence of evangelism is showing what God is like – that means that every day of my life, I am representing Him to the best of my ability, through His power and compassion.

Today's Bible Reading

Genesis 32:13-32 through 34:1-31;
Matthew 11:7-30;
Psalm 14:1-7;
Proverbs 3:19-20

Mark my Word
(for further study)

Genesis 28:10-22;
Acts 4:13-31;
II Corinthians 3:12;
I Peter 2:9

Revival is Work

If we want New Testament revival, we need to study the New Testament pattern to be sure of what to expect. If we take the Book of Acts as the true ideal, then Acts also reveals the "formula." It is absolutely clear: **there was no other method than the preaching of the Gospel.** This is clearly stated in I Corinthians: *"It pleased God through the foolishness of the message preached to save those who believe."* They prayed, asking God to bless their evangelism, not for Him to do the task He had given to them.

People pray, "Do it again, Lord." But **we** should "do again" what the Early Church Christians did. When we do what they did, we shall get what they got. The preached, witnessed and worked as if it all depended on **them** – and prayed as if it all depended on **God**. They depended on God, and God depended on them. Oh, that God can depend on you and me!

The early Christians were unceasing in their witness: *"Day after day, in the temple courts and from house to house, they **never stopped** teaching and proclaiming the Good News that Jesus is the Christ."* Paul's witness in Ephesus caused the whole city to riot. No wonder! He said, *"I … taught you publicly and from house to house. For three years I did not cease to warn everyone night and day with tears."* Even slaves found ways to preach Christ. Timothy is seen as a bishop today, but Paul told him to do the work of an evangelist, not just pray for revival.

Revival is a state of mind, not a time of year. Revival comes from people whose hearts are so hungry for God **on a daily, personal basis** that they transmit their passion for God to others – especially the unsaved, who wonder, "What makes that person so different? What does he (or she) have that I don't have … and I need?" Make a revival mind-set yours today!

Today's Scripture

*Go **ye** into all the world and preach the Gospel to every creature.*
(Mark 16:15; emphasis added)

Daily Power!

I am committed to doing the work of evangelism, not just background preparation of prayer and financial support, but to put my own self into reaching the world for Christ!

Today's Bible Reading

Genesis 35:1-29 through 36:1-43; Matthew 12:1-21; Psalm 15:1-5; Proverbs 3:21-26

Mark my Word
(for further study)

Mark 16:15; Acts 5:42, 20:20, 31; I Corinthians 1:21

The silent Planet

Why do we need prayer? In the beginning, Adam and Eve did not pray in the sense in which most of us understand prayer today. God and Man seemed to enjoy almost family openness: *"God created Man in His own image … male and female He created them. Then God blessed them, and said, 'Be fruitful and multiply' … The Lord God planted a Garden eastward in Eden, and there He put the Man whom He had formed … The Tree of Life was also in the midst of the garden, and the Tree of the Knowledge of Good and Evil … So when the woman saw that the Tree was good for food, that it was pleasant to the eyes, and a Tree desirable to make one wise, she took of its fruit and ate. She also gave to her husband with her, and he ate … And they heard the sound of the Lord God walking in the Garden in the cool of the day, and Adam and his wife hid themselves from the presence of the Lord God among the trees of the Garden."*

Then the party broke up. Relations became strained and distant. C.S. Lewis described this world as "the silent planet" – silent toward Heaven. Earth hung in space like a spiritual "black hole" which gave no light. The Psalmist said: *"The Lord looks down from Heaven on the sons of men to see if there are any who understand, any who seek God. They have turned aside, they have together become corrupt; there is no one who does good, not even one."*

Why should we believe that the Almighty Creator of the Universe is even remotely interested in what's going on inside our hearts? Because the Bible emphatically says: *"When you pray, go into your room, and when you have shut the door, pray to your Father Who is in the secret place; and your Father Who sees in secret will reward you openly."* Prayer is a big subject in the Bible, because it is important to God. Today – make the commitment (afresh and anew) to make prayer an Important part of your life too … and then you just watch and see what God will do for you!

Today's Scripture

And Jesus, when He came out, saw a great multitude and was moved with compassion for them because they were like sheep not having a shepherd. So He began to teach them many things.

(Mark 6:34)

Daily Power!

The Word tells me that God invites me to meet Him through prayer ... therefore, I commit to being one who prays.

Today's Bible Reading

Genesis 37:1-36 through 38:1-40; Matthew 12:22-45; Psalm 16:1-11; Proverbs 3:27-32

Mark my Word
(for further study)

Genesis 1:26-28; 2:8-10; 3:6-8; Psalm 14:2-3; Matthew 6:6; Mark 6:34

Blood different from all others

Our blood is ordinary, but the Blood of Jesus is Holy Blood. There is power in the Blood of Jesus because no man who ever lived had Blood like His. The Blood of Jesus is holy simply because the Bible calls it precious, but there are also some other very interesting factors. Everybody inherits blood group factors at conception … Jesus did not. Normally a blood test can prove whether or not a particular man was the father of a child. The blood of a child and of his true father can be checked scientifically for some genetic connection.

Fifteen types of human blood groups have been noted, including a number of groupings that occur only in rare families. In his book, "Hematology", Dr. James V. Linman says, "A single system may involve one or several antigens or blood group factors. An infinite number of combinations is possible, and it seems likely that a person's precise blood type is as individually specific as are his fingerprints." With Jesus, there was a new situation: **He had no earthly father!** His Blood could not be grouped because it was singular. It was independent of any genetic inheritance. The father of Jesus was … the Father in Heaven! The Bible is very careful to explain this.

God inspired Luke, *"the beloved physician,"* to tell us the facts, which he probably learned from Mary, the mother of Christ. She could speak without embarrassment to a doctor, so Luke gives us this report: *"Then Mary said to the angel, 'How can this be, since I do not know a man?' And the angel answered her and said to her, 'The Holy Spirit will come upon you, and the power of the Highest will overshadow you; therefore, also, that Holy One Who is to be born will be called the Son of God.'"*

What an awesome sense of heritage and history we carry in our hearts … knowing that this same Blood flows through your spirit today … and Jesus Christ lives **big** in you through the power of His shed Blood!

Today's Scripture

For as many as are led by the Spirit of God, these are sons of God.
(Romans 8:14)

Daily Power!

I believe that the precious, holy Blood of Jesus now flows within my spirit!

Today's Bible Reading

Genesis 39:1-23 through 41:1-16; Matthew 12:46-50 through 13:1-23; Psalm 17:1-15; Proverbs 3:33-35

Mark my Word
(for further study)

Luke 1:34-35; Romans 8:14; Colossians 4:14

JANUARY

20

Today's Scripture

Therefore, brethren, having boldness to enter the Holiest by the Blood of Jesus, by a new a living way which He consecrated for us, through the veil, that is, His flesh, and having a High Priest over the House of God, let us draw near with a true heart in full assurance of faith, having our hearts sprinkled from an evil conscience and our bodies washed with pure water.
(Hebrews 10:19-22)

Daily Power!

The Blood of Jesus is my secret of divine power!

Today's Bible Reading

Genesis 41:17-57 through 42:1-17; Matthew 13:24-46; Psalm 18:1-15; Proverbs 4:1-6

Mark my Word
(for further study)

Matthew 19:26; Luke 3:38; John 1:14; I Corinthians 15:45; Hebrews 10:5; 19:22

Divine Blood Type

Mary and Joseph were engaged, but had not yet come together as husband and wife. As a virgin, Mary conceived by a miracle of God. Therefore Christ did not have blood group factors from Joseph or Joseph's ancestors. Jesus Christ was the only begotten of the Father. With regard to Mary's blood type, we know that a woman can bear a child which has a blood group completely incompatible with her own. Studies of what is known as the "Rhesus factor" have also shown that a mother can have "Rh-positive" blood and her baby "Rh-negative." The mother's blood supports the unborn child through the placenta, which also prevents her blood entering the veins of her baby, unless some kind of damage causes a leak. **The Blood of Jesus was His own Divine Blood ... and this is the secret of its power!**

Only one other man ever had blood that was not genetically received: Adam, the first man, mentioned as *"of God"* – that is, a special creation without any ancestor. The Bible calls Jesus *"the second Adam."* His body, like the first Adam's, was specially *"prepared"* as the Bible says. God caused Mary to bear a Son without the normal biological necessities, for nothing is impossible for God.

Birth without sexual partnership – or parthenogenesis – is known in nature. "It is not understood why such creatures, such as water-fleas and rotifer, reproduce their kind without male and female, while others do not," said Professor John Maynard-Smith (as reported in the Daily Telegraph, June 4, 1990). Nonetheless, the birth of Christ was supernatural, very different from any natural parthenogenesis. What is your "spiritual blood-type"? As a born-again child of God, you too can claim the redemptive blood-type of a believer, an adopted **heir** of the Heavenly Father!

Proven Signs

Christians are calling for Christ's return ... and we know that prayer will be answered any day. Why are we sure? There is every reason!

Christ came the first time exactly as the Bible predicted ... so He will surely come the second time as the Bible says. The Bible is the only Book that has ever predicted the future and proved accurate. The Lord said, *"I am watching to see that My Word is fulfilled."*

Bible prophecy was fulfilled to the hilt by Christ's first advent. The Magi (the "wise men" of Christmas fame) came a thousand miles and found Jesus at Bethlehem, where the Bible said He would be. The Bible prophets had spoken how He would be born and live, and how He would die: His hands pierced, His clothes made a lottery, His grave being *"with the wicked and the rich,"* and so on. One man, John the Baptist, knew about Him from Scripture, and that He was about to appear on the scene. Before Jesus stepped into public life, John identified Him as *"He Who should come."*

With all these unmistakable, proven signs of His first coming, we can watch the Biblical signs for His Second Coming with perfect assurance that He will indeed fulfill His promise! And our part is to continue *"gathering the harvest"* until He comes!

"My food is to do the will of Him Who sent Me, and to finish His work. Do you not say, 'There are still four months and then comes the harvest'? Behold, I say to you, lift up your eyes and look at the fields, for they are already white for harvest! And he who reaps receives wages, and gathers fruit for eternal life, that both he who sows and he who reaps may rejoice together."

Today's Scripture

Thrust in Your sickle and reap, for the time has come for You to reap, for the harvest of the Earth is ripe.

(Revelation 14:15)

Daily Power!

I am watching for Christ's return, completely confidant that He will fulfill His promise.

Today's Bible Reading

*Genesis 42:18-38 through 43:1-34;
Matthew 13:47-58 through 14:1-12;
Psalm 18:16-36;
Proverbs 4:7-10*

Mark my Word
(for further study)

*Isaiah 53:9;
Jeremiah 1:12;
John 4:34-36;
Revelation 14:15*

22

Today's Scripture

Jesus of Nazareth, a Man attested by God to you by miracles, wonders, and signs which God did through Him in your midst, as you yourself also know.

(Acts 2:22)

Daily Power!

As a believer, I accept that my every-day life is going to be filled with the miraculous – those "signs" that point others to Jesus Christ.

Today's Bible Reading

Genesis 44:1-34 through 45:1-28; Matthew 14:13-36; Psalm 18:37-50; Proverbs 4:11-13

Mark my Word
(for further study)

Acts 2:22; 5:12-14; 6:8; 8:13; 9:11; 15:12

Miracle Territory

New Testament believers did not go around searching and probing "to get a miracle." They lived on miracle territory! They were in the Kingdom of God, and they perceived the miracle-working hand of God in every situation. Believers understood every-day Christianity to be miraculous – miracles through and through. That theme is common in the letters of the apostle Paul.

In the very first days of the Early Church, miracles abounded: miracles of salvation (imagine if **your** church suddenly had to accommodate three thousand new members in one day!) … miracles of healing … miracles of fellowship (how inexplicable it must have appeared to onlookers to see slaves and masters embracing and sharing all!) … miracles of finances, and more. Just read the first five chapters of the Book of Acts to witness "everyday" miracles.

Miracles caught the attention of the authorities – and they frightened them, because they could not understand how they could be: *"What shall we do to these men? For indeed, that a notable miracle has been done through them is evident to all who dwell in Jerusalem, and we cannot deny it."* But for all their displeasure, punishment and denials, they could not stop the flow of the power of God – nor the boldness of the apostles in the Early Church!

Regrettably, what was normal then is not normal now. So much emphasis has been placed on finding new methods for miracles that it sounds as if it were all a profound secret. I want to remove the mystery and get back to the "simplicity that is in Christ." We shall look at a miracle, and then see something greater! Then let **you** and **me** see miracles in our own lives!

Miracle Conditions

In Matthew 14, we read about a wonderful miracle, which helps us to understand how miracles happen. First, understand that the "miracle conditions" **began** while Peter was still in the boat. Suddenly, **he** became different. One minute, panicking, his hair standing on end … the next minute, daring to do what no mere man had ever done: *"And when the disciples saw Him walking on the sea, they were troubled, saying, 'It is a ghost!' And they cried out for fear. But immediately Jesus spoke to them, saying, 'Be of good cheer! It is I, do not be afraid.' And Peter answered Him and said, 'Lord, if it is You, command me to come to You on the water.'"*

Peter found things different when he was different. Some people accept things as they are, and then blame what they are on where they are. However, we know that when Christ comes into someone's life, then Heaven works things out. Situations can be changed: *"So He said, 'Come.' And when Peter had come out of the boat, he walked on the water to go to Jesus. But when he saw that the wind was boisterous, he was afraid; and beginning to sink he cried out, saying, 'Lord, save me!' And immediately Jesus stretched out His hand and caught him, and said to him, 'O you of little faith, why did you doubt?' And when they got into the boat, the wind ceased. Then those who were in the boat came and worshipped Him, saying, 'Truly You are the Son of God!'"*

If we look more carefully at this story of Peter, we shall see something ever greater than Peter's circumstances changing. The water looked exactly the same. But **Peter had changed** – with his eyes fixed on Jesus, the sea billows still rolled, but Peter walked over them. Jesus saves us – our household, ourselves, and the things around us. Miracles begin within you, and then affect your surroundings. The sea threatened Peter, opening its foaming mouth to swallow him, but Peter made it an open thoroughfare when Jesus called him to come. Listen for that voice in your heart today … if you hear Him calling out to you to do anything … step out of your boat in obedience and move towards Him … you can because the path has been cleared for your journey today.

Today's Scripture

Jesus looked at them and said to them, "With men this is impossible, but with God all things are possible."

(Matthew 19:26)

Daily Power!

I choose to change, to line up with God and His Word, and see miracles happen in my life!

Today's Bible Reading

Genesis 46:1-34 through 47:1-31; Matthew 15:1-28; Psalm 19:1-14; Proverbs 4:14-19

Mark my Word
(for further study)

Matthew 14:22-33; 19:26

Sickness isn't God's Plan

Sickness in God's good world is like weeds growing among wheat. But make no mistake – God did not sow the weeds: *"An enemy has done this."* God sent Jesus, Who *"went about doing good and healing all who were oppressed by the devil, for God was with Him."* It was the Creator's protest against the sabotage of His work by the devil.

God planted cures in nature, which medical research keeps finding. Those cures are ours today. But the God Who heals naturally also heals supernaturally. Scripture denies that sickness is God's will, and it credits healings to God. Today His hand touches far more people than many realize. Throughout the world, many supernatural healings take place every year, proving that *"Jesus Christ is the same yesterday, today, and forever."*

When Jesus came, He offered to heal people. We read in John's Gospel that He performed some of His miracles without being specifically asked. Without anybody suggesting it, He went to the Pool of Bethesda where there were hundreds of afflicted people. He approached one paralyzed man and asked him if he wished to be healed. The man didn't even say, "Yes," but Jesus healed him anyway. Later, He saw a blind man, and without even asking him what he wanted, Jesus restored his sight. That's Jesus. That was Jesus yesterday … and that is Jesus today!

Jesus placed an importance on medicine – *"Those who are well have no need of a physician, but those who are sick"* – then He promptly set about healing people! When you learn to work **with** God for your healing – whether He chooses to work through doctors or through His own divine power – then you understand how much He loves you, and how He truly wants you to *"prosper and be in health, even as your soul prospers."*

Today's Scripture

God anointed Jesus of Nazareth with the Holy Spirit and with power, Who went about doing good and healing all who were oppressed by the devil, for God was with Him.

(Acts 10:38)

Daily Power!

Today I choose to sign up for God's Divine Health Plan. I resist the enemy and his seeds of destruction, and I accept God's ability in me to walk in physical health, even as my soul prospers!

Today's Bible Reading

Genesis 48:1-22 through 49:1-33; Matthew 15:29-39 through 16:1-12; Psalm 20:1-9; Proverbs 4:20-27

Mark my Word
(for further study)

Matthew 13:24-30; Mark 2:17; John 5:1-47; 9:1-41; Acts 10:34-48; Hebrews 13:1-25; III John 2

Avoid past Mistakes

A king in Israel was never God's plan for His people – He wanted His people to be ruled by His law planted in their hearts, accountable to Him. He established judges and priests to help the people, but they looked around, saw their neighboring nations with their glittering kings and princes … and wanted the "outward show" over the inward knowledge. Doesn't that sound familiar to what our society is like today? We look to "handsome, entertaining leaders" rather than those with quiet integrity. Modern statistics reveal that, historically, the **tallest** of political candidates usually wins the election – is that a valid criterion when good character and leadership qualities are really the issue?

Many years after entering the Promised Land, the Israelites had a king, and the nation became powerful and affluent. But rebellion by the king's own treacherous son drove him into exile. The son was killed, and the throne was vacant. Again came anarchy: *"All the people were at strife throughout all the tribes of Israel."* But the lesson of the bitter past had been learned and they knew the answer: *"Now therefore why speak ye not a word of bringing the king back?"*

Those episodes in the Scriptures pointed to yet another: Christ before Pontius Pilate. Pilate asked Jesus, *"You are a King then?"* Jesus answered, *"You are right in saying I am a King. For this reason I was born, and for this came I into the world, to testify to the truth."* Pilate said to the Jews, *"Here is your King!"* But they shouted, *"Take Him away! Crucify Him! We have no king but Caesar."* Pilate then asked, *"Shall I crucify your King?"* And again the chief priests answered, *"We have no king but Caesar."* In their blindness, they chose Caesar, a foreign oppressor. Within their lifetime, Caesar destroyed Israel as a nation. The fury of the Roman operation still pollutes the history of that empire. Is our world at risk for another such oppressive leader to rise and take over, to dominate the economy, the government, our very lives? The Bible tells us that answer: **Jesus Christ will return!**

Today's Scripture

Worthy is the Lamb Who was slain to receive power and riches and wisdom, and strength and honor and glory and blessing!
(Revelation 5:12)

Daily Power!

I need only one King in my life – Jesus Christ, the only begotten Son of God Almighty.

Today's Bible Reading

*Genesis 50:1-26
through Exodus 2:1-10;
Matthew 16:13-28
through 17:1-9;
Psalm 21:1-13;
Proverbs 5:1-6*

Mark my Word
(for further study)

*II Samuel 13 through 19;
Matthew 27:11-26;
John 18:37; 19:14-15;
Revelation 5:12*

26

"Even so, come, Lord Jesus!"

The world has no king, only warring leaders. It was so in Israel – every man did what was right in his own eyes. Isaiah said, *"All we like sheep have gone astray; we have turned every one to his own way."* We are all *"the children of disobedience"* or *"the sons of the rebellion."* "But I haven't done those great sins!" self-righteous people protest. The Bible replies, *"Those who practice such things are deserving of death, not only do the same but also approve of those who practice them."* When we condone governments who encourage sin – passing laws to permit abortions … ousting public prayer because of a perverted understanding of the true meaning of "separation of Church and State" … dishonoring our elders by spending and wasting their savings … vilifying those who speak out against homosexuality … and so many other sociopolitical issues – we fall into the same trap that brought about the fall of the Roman Empire and many other "great" civilizations. Compromise is the door to destruction.

World religious leaders, like the secular authorities, only tell us how to help ourselves. We know what we should do – but doing it is another thing! We want strength, not advice. Religions are an added burden, laying down dogmas and rules. We want a Deliverer-King, a Savior. Jesus laid down His life – not rules. We cannot redeem ourselves, but Christ is the world's Redeemer! A new age needs new people … and Christ creates *"new creatures"*! The Bible story shows that David took his throne again … and so will Jesus Christ, *"great David's greater Son."* Christ declared He would come back, and He will! Everything He ever said turned out to be true – it is impossible for this one promise not to be true also. For two thousand years, the tens of millions of the Church of Christ have expected His return. The doctrine has taken many forms, but Scriptures teach the personal, visible presence of Christ on Earth. This is the key-hope of every Christian creed. The last prayer of the Bible is, *"Amen! Come, Lord Jesus!"* Make that your prayer today.

Today's Scripture

And the Spirit and the Bride say, "Come!" And let him who hears say, "Come!" And let him who thirsts, come. Whoever desires, let him take the water of life freely.

(Revelation 22:17)

Daily Power!

Each day, as I follow Him, Jesus is making me a new creation in Him.

Today's Bible Reading

Exodus 2:11-25
through 3:1-22;
Matthew 17:10-27;
Psalm 22:1-18;
Proverbs 5:7-14

Mark my Word
(for further study)

Isaiah 53:5;
Luke 1:17;
Romans 2:32;
II Corinthians 5:17;
Revelation 22:17

The golden Gift

Faith in Christ is different than any other kind of faith. It is not found in the Old Testament. In the New Testament, the word used means believing **into** Christ, suggesting movement. Faith **in** Christ means moving close to Him in trustful love. It is an embrace ... and He extends His arms to you today.

This kind of loving embrace between Man and his Maker comes only through Christ. Nobody in the Old Testament days could think of such a thing. God was Spirit – another kind of Being, too awesome to be approached except with fear and trembling: *"The hour is coming, and now is, when the true worshippers will worship the Father in spirit and truth, for the Father is seeking such to worship Him. God is Spirit, and those who worship Him must worship in spirit and truth."* Yet one inspired book in the Old Testament Scriptures touches the heart of a new experience: the Song of Songs, a lyric of love that gathers up all its words of supreme love in one phrase: *"I am my beloved's and my beloved is mine."* This was an attitude towards God that nobody understood, until Christ came. Aren't you glad that you can live and walk in a full understanding of how much He loves you!

Faced with His reality, ordinary people in the Gospel suddenly knew He was the Savior, a swift revelation followed by complete commitment: *"However, when He, the Spirit of truth, has come, He will guide you into all truth; for He will not speak on His own authority, but whatever He hears He will speak; and He will tell you things to come. He will glorify Me, for He will take of what is Mine and declare it to you."* No longer was faith for the rare individual, as in the Old Testament. Somehow Calvary does what the awesome manifestations of Sinai could not do. Jesus is the great faith-creator. He said Himself, *"No man comes to the Father except through Me."* He doesn't point to "a way" – **Christ is the Way!**

Today's Scripture

Jesus said to him, "I am the Way, the Truth, and the Life. No one comes to the Father except through Me."
(John 14:6)

Daily Power!

By faith, I respond to Christ's welcoming embrace. I gladly live and walk in a full understanding of how much He loves me.

Today's Bible Reading

Exodus 4:1-31 through 5:1-21; Matthew 18:1-22; Psalm 22:19-31; Proverbs 5:15-21

Mark my Word
(for further study)

Song of Solomon 6:1-3; John 4:23; 14:1-21; 16:13

Today's Scripture:

"I am the Alpha and the Omega, the Beginning and the End," says the Lord, "Who is and Who was and Who is to come, the Almighty."
(Revelation 1:8)

Daily Power!

I have a present-tense God and He has given me present-tense faith.

Today's Bible Reading

Exodus 5:22-23
through 7:1-24;
Matthew 18:23-35
through 19:1-12;
Psalm 23:1-6;
Proverbs 5:22-23

Mark my Word
(for further study)

Matthew 8:1-4;
Hebrews 13:8
(the Message);
James 1:6-7;
Revelation 1:4, 8

A present-tense Faith

A leper in the New Testament saw something about Christ that few others have seen: *"When He had come down from the mountain, great multitudes followed Him. And behold, a leper came and worshipped Him, saying, 'Lord, if You are willing, You can make me clean.' Then Jesus put out His hand and touched him, saying, 'I am willing; be cleansed.' Immediately his leprosy was cleansed."* Meeting Jesus, this leper stated, *"If You will, You can make me clean."* Not "If You **can**, You **will** …" but "If You **will**, You **can**!" The Bible was not written to tell us what God **can** do – we **know** God is Almighty – the Bible tells us what He **will** do.

It's easy to believe that God did things long ago … but past-tense faith is hollow unless it transfers to today. John wrote of faith in three tenses: past, present and future. He said, *"Grace and peace to you from Him Who **is**, and Who **was**, and Who **is to come** … and from Jesus Christ, Who is the faithful witness."* What He will be, He is now and always has been!

"Jesus doesn't change – yesterday, today, tomorrow, He's always totally Himself." Healing is a part of Jesus' nature – therefore, to be consistently Himself, He **will** heal. The issue then becomes our faith – or lack of it (also known as "doubt"). *"Ask boldly, believingly, without a second thought. People who 'worry their prayers' are like wind-whipped waves. Don't think you're going to get anything from the Master that way."* So don't let doubt interfere with what you **know** about the nature of God!

The God Who created the universe didn't go into retirement when He was done. What He did then shows us what He is now, and always will be: creative, active and good. Creation was the first and greatest of all miracles … so what's the problem with God healing deaf ears or blind eyes? Yet too many have a "used-to-be" God, anchored in history. **We have a present-tense God and He's given us a present-tense faith!**

Aspects of the Holy Spirit

There are many different expressions for the baptism of the Holy Spirit: being baptized in holy fire ... endued with power ... anointed with the oil of God ... immersed in the Spirit ... filled with the Spirit ... walking, praying, living in the Spirit ... our bodies being temples of the Holy Spirit ... having another Comforter besides Christ Himself. These are sketches, but color and details have to be added. The Bible is a picture gallery of the Holy Spirit in operation: it portrays signs, wonders and miracles ... men looking as if **they had been with Jesus** ... the world turned upside down ... people coming to "know the Lord," enjoying a new experience. Not just religious enthusiasts, church-goers – but a new breed with vibrant faith. Don't you enjoy having that vibrant faith percolating in you!

Paul says that, *"Even when we were dead in trespasses,* [God] *made us alive together with Christ* [by grace you have been saved]*"* and that we are *"strengthened with all might, according to His glorious power, for all patience and long-suffering with joy."* The Lord Jesus Christ Himself promised it that we would receive power. I liken baptism of the Holy Spirit to a household appliance that comes with a built-in electric cord. Unless you plug it into the power-source, the appliance does not function. All its potential is there – it may even carry a famous brand-name – but it must be connected to the power-source to achieve its fullest purpose. As recipients of God's free gift of salvation, we have been "branded" as His children ... so now, let us come off the shelf of self-reliance or the closet of timidity, and allow the Holy Spirit to energize us by His power.

As a born-again believer, you are special – you are a saint in His eyes – and the baptism in the Spirit is Christ's next major experience for you. Jesus alone made it possible when He died, and rose and sat down at the right hand of the Majesty on High. What a gift! Receive that gift today! You will never be the same again.

Today's Scripture

If you then, being evil, know how to give good gifts to your children, how much more will your Heavenly Father give the Holy Spirit to those who ask Him!

(Luke 11:13)

Daily Power!

Today I claim the gift of the Holy Spirit as my own. I yield myself to that gift that changes me into His likeness and empowers me with His strength and ability.

Today's Bible Reading

Exodus 7:25 through 9:1-35; Matthew 19:13-30; Psalm 24:1-10; Proverbs 6:1-5

Mark my Word
(for further study)

Matthew 3:11; Luke 3:16; 11:13, 24-49; John 14:16; Acts 1:8; Romans 8:26; I Corinthians 6:19; Galatians 5:25; Ephesians 2:5; 5:18; Colossians 1:11

God's infinite Blood

There is a vast difference between the first Adam and the second Adam: *"The first man was of the Earth, made of dust; the second man ... from Heaven."* Adam's sin-contamination runs in the veins of us all ... but it did not run in the veins of Jesus. His Blood is holy. The Bible declares that **Christ's Blood is actually the Blood of God.** The Book of Acts speaks of *"the Church of God, which He purchased with His own Blood."* How can that be, seeing that God is Spirit? A spirit has no flesh and blood. The answer is simple: *"The Word became flesh and dwelt among us."*

In the womb of the Virgin Mary, Godhood and Manhood became one. The Blood of Jesus is the Blood of God the Son. One individual's blood may legally be shed for one other man – but the Blood of Jesus Christ has no such limitation. God's infinity is involved. The Blood of the Son of God has *"grace to cover all my sin,"* and the sin of the whole world.

God demonstrated the enormous capacity of the blood when Israel left Egypt. The Israelites had to slay and eat the Passover lamb; but if a family was too small, they could share the lamb with another family. This is a lovely picture of Jesus – the Lamb of God too great for one household. He was the Lamb too great for merely the apostles at the Last Supper. John later wrote: *And He Himself is the propitiation for our sins, and not for ours only but also for the whole world";* and then, later in visions, he saw *"a great multitude that no one could count, from every nation ... they have washed their robes and made them white in the Blood of the Lamb."*

How we thank God that His Blood flows through your veins! It cleanses you from your unrighteousness ... it renews your body, mind and soul ... it empowers you to do God's work ... and it is ours to freely share with the world, pointing them to the Cross where Jesus died and shed His Blood for them too.

Today's Scripture

Let us hold fast the confession of our hope without wavering, for He Who promised is faithful.
(Hebrews 10:23)

Daily Power!

I have been freed from the contamination of sin because the precious Blood of Jesus Christ now flows within me!

Today's Bible Reading:

Exodus 10:1-29
through 12:1-13;
Matthew 20:1-28;
Psalm 25:1-15;
Proverbs 6:6-11

Mark my Word
(for further study)

Exodus 12:4;
John 1:14; 4:24;
Acts 20:28;
I Corinthians 15:47;
Hebrews 10:23;
I John 2:2;
Revelation 7:9, 14

Knowing God

Above all else, know the Lord. How easy it is to ask the wrong person for the things we need! But we do not usually ask a plumber for medicine, or a doctor to repair a water pipe. **Know Who God is!** *"[God] grant you, according to the riches of His glory, to be strengthened with might through His Spirit in the inner man, that Christ may dwell in your hearts through faith; that you, being rooted and grounded in love, may be able to comprehend with all the saints what is the width and length and depth and height – to know the love of Christ which passes knowledge; that you may be filled with all the fullness of God."*

Do not address a vague "somebody somewhere up there in the stratosphere," with no idea of Who He is or how He might react. Do not be like the liberal preacher who thought of God as "a kind of oblong blur" … or like the Athenians with an altar *"to the unknown god."* Some people even talk of "seeking the unknown." That kind of mystical nonsense is like begging from any passerby, hoping to chance on a billionaire. But it is better to **know** a billionaire! To recognize God's true identity always encourages more intelligent and more effective praying. God is our Father.

What kind of reaction can we expect if we treat God as an "oblong blur"? The Almighty has made almighty efforts to tell us about Himself, even sending His own Son, Jesus Christ. To ignore what He says involves a deliberate and dangerous resolution to remain in ignorance – exactly what we might expect when the devil influences us. To brush aside the greatest spiritual knowledge ever revealed is suicidal! Even God Himself can do nothing more for us then. People question, "Why – if God is all-powerful – does He not do this or that?" But God is not only all-powerful, but He is also all-wise, holy, and just. Furthermore, He has His own prior plans, not likely to be changed for one of our impulses. You do not ask a surgeon performing an operation to make you a cup of tea. We must at least flow in the direction of the divine stream. Jump into the reality of Christ alive in you today!

Today's Scripture

Then Moses said to God, "Indeed, when I come to the children of Israel and say to them, 'The God of your fathers has sent me to you,' and they say to me, 'What is His Name?' what shall I say to them?" And God said to Moses, "I am who I am."
(Exodus 3:13-14)

Today's Bible Reading

Exodus 12:14-51 through 13:1-16; Matthew 20:29-34 through 21:1-22; Psalm 25:16-22; Proverbs 6:12-15

Daily Power!

My Heavenly Father is all-wise, all-knowing, all-powerful, all-loving, holy, just, compassionate. He is I am who I am … the Beginning and the End.

Mark my Word
(for further study):

*Exodus 3:13-14;
Acts 17:22-23;
Ephesians 3:14-21*

It is a crime to bend God's exclamation mark
into a question mark.

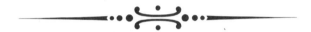

The church that is not saving the lost is lost itself!

These are the power generators of God:
The cross of Calvary!
The resurrection of Jesus Christ!
The Holy Spirit Baptism!

The Principles of Power

If Christianity is to progress, we must follow the Divine way. Christ knew that the world would expand – there are now sixty times more people alive than when He was here. He expected that all the world would hear His quiet words spoken so long ago in an obscure Roman province, not by normal propaganda methods, but by His power. Because the world hovers between spiritual life and death, utmost consideration must be given to anything that can secure the destinies of precious people.

Just as in the wilderness, Jesus was tempted to misuse divine powers when He had been filled with the Holy Spirit … so others are likely to be tempted in the same way. The temptation springs from pride, which corrupts our sincere motives for the power gifts, and produces flamboyant behavior and egotistical display. Jesus was tempted to throw Himself off the pinnacle of the Temple. One thing to be taken to heart is that the supernatural is not always sensational. We can attract personal admiration by our gifts, but our job is to set people's eyes on Jesus. When Paul and Barnabas were offered worship at Lystra, they were horrified, running among the people to assert that they were not divinities.

"And as Moses lifted up the serpent in the wilderness, even so must the Son of Man be lifted up, that whoever believes in Him should not perish but have eternal life" … "When you lift up the Son of Man, then you will know that I am He."

Jesus said that this generation seeks a sign. Sensation always has a market. We can exploit a situation and use the gifts of God for our own advantage. Simon Magus wanted the Holy Spirit in order to bolster his prestige. Uzza died for his presumption in putting his hand upon the ark of testimony. If anyone says, "I would like the gift of healing" or some other gift, the proper response is, "Why?" Motive is vital. Be certain your motives are Christ-centered.

Today's Scripture

In the same way that Moses lifted the serpent in the desert so people could have something to see and then believe, it is necessary for the Son of Man to be lifted up – and everyone who looks up to Him, trusting and expectant, will gain a real life, eternal life.
  (John 3:14-15; the Message)

Daily Power!

The supernatural is not always sensational … Our job is to set people's eyes on Jesus.

Today's Bible Reading

Exodus 13:17-22 through 15:1-18; Matthew 12:23-46; Psalm 26:1-12; Proverbs 6:16-19

Mark my Word
(for further study)

I Chronicles 13:10; Matthew 4:1-11; 12:39; John 3:14-15; 8:28; Acts 8:9, 19; 14:8-18

2

The divine Imperative

What God **is** is what He **must** do. God cannot be what He is and not do it. If He is Love, He must love somebody. If He is a Savior, He must save. He must heal, because He has revealed Himself to be a Healer.

In the Gospel of John, this comes out in the imperatives of Jesus. When Jesus said, *"You must be born again,"* He meant that He Himself must do it for us. We cannot rebirth ourselves. Only God can bring such a thing about. The apostle James declared, *"He chose to give us birth through the word of truth."* Rebirth comes by the Word of truth – the Gospel. If the world is to be saved, the people must hear the Gospel. If they hear the Gospel, then somebody must preach it. That is a command for you and for me to fulfill.

Redemption is like creation – nobody thought of it but God. It never crossed anyone's mind, not even that of the wisest person who ever lived. There are many religions in the world, but none of them offers redemption. People believe in many different gods, but not one of them is a redeemer. There are many holy books, but only one of them brings us the Good News of Redemption: the Bible.

Some religions promote attaining peace … others promise wealth and favor … some encourage self-improvement – but all of these are empty promises when they do not address the ultimate question: "What happens after death?" Only God answered that, through His Son: *"For God so loved the world that He gave His only begotten Son, that whoever believes in Him should not perish but* **have everlasting life.***"*

Jesus Christ is the Redeemer who gives eternal life. And this is our responsibility today, yours and mine: to spread the news of the Redeemer to the lost world.

Light Reflectors

"The Christian's main business is evangelism" – that means it is **our** business. It is important that evangelism remains important. It is important for the countries evangelized **and** for the countries evangelizing.

When Paul was in Troas, he preached all night. A young man called Eutychus fell out of a window, and Paul restored him to life. We read, *"There were many lamps in the upper room where they were gathered together."* Well, there are many lamps among us ... I trust. The virgins in the parable of the Bridegroom all had lamps (the same Greek word, *lampas*), but half of the lamps had gone out. That doesn't mean the lamps had "half-gone out" – that means that half of them were not even lit! *"Then the Kingdom of Heaven shall be likened to ten virgins who took their lamps and went out to meet the bridegroom. Now five of them were wise, and five were foolish. Those who were foolish took their lamps and took no oil with them, but the wise took oil in their vessels with their lamps ... And at midnight a cry was heard, 'Behold, the bridegroom is coming; go out to meet him!' Then all those virgins arose and trimmed their lamps ... The bridegroom came, and those who were ready went in with him to the wedding, and the door was shut. Afterward the other virgins came also, saying, 'Lord, Lord, open to us!' But he answered and said, 'Assuredly, I say to you, I do not know you.'"*

We can't be half-alight! We either shine or are a patch of shadow. I wonder if fifty-fifty is a general average among Christians. Half the virgins were asleep and unprepared. So was Eutychus – and look what happened to him! People who go to sleep on the job, whose lamps have gone out because they had no oil – people like this are bound to fail! Perhaps that is why we read: *"Wake up, O sleeper, rise from the dead, and Christ will shine on you."* **Today** is a good day to make sure your life is awake and prepared for whatever God has for you!

Today's Scripture

If then your whole body is full of light, having no part dark, the whole body will be full of light, as when the bright shining of a lamp gives you light.

(Luke 11:36)

Daily Power!

Father, my prayer is that my lamp may be completely filled with your Spirit, and that I may be Your light shining in my world today.

Today's Bible Reading

*Exodus 17:8-16 through 19:1-15;
Matthew 22:34-46 through 23:1-12;
Psalm 27:7-14;
Proverbs 6:27-35*

Mark my Word
(for further study)

*Matthew 25:1-13;
Luke 11:36;
Acts 20:7-12;
Ephesians 5:1-20*

Unlocked Doors

The most famous escape-artist of all was Harry Houdini, a show business notable. Police would lock him up in a cell and – as they walked away, he would follow them … already loose within seconds. Except once. Half an hour went by and Houdini still was fuming over the lock. Then a policeman came and simply pushed the door open. The door had never been locked! Houdini was fooled, trying to unlock a door which had already been unlocked.

Likewise, Christ has gone right through the castle of Giant Despair. He has the keys of death and Hell, and He has opened the gates. So why are millions sweating, trying every trick to get out of their evil habits and bondages? They join new cults or old heathen religions, hear new theories, go to psychiatrists. But why? Jesus does set men free. He does it all the time.

Dialogue? The Gospel is not open to modification. It is mandatory, a royal and divine edict. Some systems and theories of deliverance are bondages in themselves, full of life-long duties and demands. Only Jesus saves and calls us to Liberty. I remember a man who told me that he also was a "spiritual counselor." However he didn't believe that Jesus Christ is the Son of God, nor that the Bible is the Word of God. I wondered, therefore, how this so-called counselor helped anybody. "Do they come to you, and then go away with broken hearts?" I asked.

"Oh no," he assured me, "I just calm them down."

I looked him in the eye and said, "Mister, a man on a sinking ship needs more than a tranquilizer. Don't calm him down. He is going down already. When Jesus comes to a man in a shipwreck, He doesn't throw him a Valium pill and say, 'Perish in peace.' He reaches down His nail-scarred Hand, grips him, lifts him and says to him, 'Because I live, you will live also.'" **This** is the Gospel of Jesus Christ that **must** be preached. Jesus **is** the Savior of our world. This message is life, peace and health for spirit, soul and body. Speak it boldly today!

Today's Scripture

Because I live, you will live also. At that day you will know that I am in my Father, and you in me and I in you.
(John 14:19-20)

Daily Power!

The Gospel of Jesus Christ must be preached.

Today's Bible Reading

Exodus 19:16-26 through 21:1-21; Matthew 23:13-19; Psalm 28:1-9; Proverbs 7:1-5

Mark my Word
(for further study)

John 14:19-20; Matthew 16:19; Matthew 18:18

Terrible Truth

In a hospital, a doctor is meeting with one of her patients. She has some bad news to tell him: he only has a few weeks to live. The Bible has similar news to tell us. It has both good news and bad news for us – starting with the bad news.

The problem of suffering and evil does not stop on our TV screens. It is easy to point the finger at the stories we see on the news and say, "That's the problem with the world today!" Instead, the problem is much closer to home – the problem is actually in our own hearts.

The Bible is not just honest about human suffering and evil in the world – it forces us to be honest about ourselves too. Jesus pinpointed this when He said: *"From the inside, from a person's heart, come the evil ideas which lead him to do immoral things, to rob, kill, commit adultery, be greedy, and do all sorts of evil things."* Jesus used a simple, rather old-fashioned word to describe what has gone wrong with us: the word "sin."

Originally, the word "sin" was used by archers to describe what had gone wrong when their arrows had not hit the bulls-eye. To sin means to miss the mark of what God intended us to be. One part of the Bible says this: *"All have sinned and fall short of the glory of God."* This makes sense. We have all done things we feel ashamed of. We have all hurt other people … and ourselves.

But the Bible goes even further. It says that sin is a negative bias, a force that constantly spoils our best aims. It is not just that we occasionally do wrong things, but there is a deep problem inside, like cancer, that makes us go wrong. The question you and I asked ourselves is: how can sin – the cancer – can be cured? There *is* an answer, one we can learn from God's own Word … and it comes in the form of our Savior, and it's made possible through His shed Blood! Thus the song writer of old penned the words, "What can wash away my sin? Nothing but the Blood of Jesus!" Walk in the fullness of that cleansing flow today!

Today's Scripture

For all have sinned and fall short of the glory of God.
(Romans 3:23)

Daily Power!

The sin of my heart has already been addressed by the cleansing Blood of Jesus. I have free access to that Blood whenever I repent of my sins.

Today's Bible Reading

Exodus 21:22-31 through 23:1-13, Matthew 24:1-28; Psalm 29:1-11; Proverbs 7:6-23

Mark my Word
(for further study)

Mark 7:20-22; Romans 3:22-24

6

Read the Bible

Know God, His ways, His counsel, His character! All His attributes are laid open in His Word. Read it! This is the secret of so many Christians' wonderful faith and confidence – their path to God guided by Scripture. *"Now to Him Who is able to do exceedingly abundantly above all that we ask or think, according to the power that works in us, to Him be glory in the Church by Christ Jesus to all generations, forever and ever. Amen."*

Learn to know God – He already knows you: *"I will give you the treasures of darkness and hidden riches of secret places, that you may know that I, the Lord, Who call you by your name, am the God of Israel … I have even called you by your name; I have named you, though you have not known Me. I am the Lord, and there is no other; there is no God besides Me."*

The Book of James – largely about prayer – speaks of God's goodness as always shining like the sun: *"Every good gift and every perfect gift is from above, and comes down from the Father of lights, with Whom there is no variation or shadow of turning."* We know that James was picturing a sundial, which registers the sun's movement by its shadow. When there is no shadow, it is noon, because the sun is at the zenith and casts no shadow. God never casts a shadow because He is always at the zenith. He never varies, changes, or declines. For everybody, He is always the same prayer-answering God.

Some people have learned to "pray the Bible" – that is, they read the richness of the Word and make it their personal prayer. For instance, I might pray this way: "I shall let patience have its perfect work in me, Reinhard, that I may be perfect and complete, lacking nothing. And if I lack wisdom, I shall ask of God, Who gives to all liberally and without reproach, and it shall be given to me." Combining your prayers with God's Word is one of the most powerful, effective weapons you can ever utilize!

Today's Scripture

But let him ask in faith, with no doubting; for he who doubts is like a wave of the sea driven and tossed by the wind.

(James 1:7)

Daily Power!

It is my desire to know God better and better each day, so I will seek Him in His Word, the Bible, where His nature and character are clearly written.

Today's Bible Reading

Exodus 23:14-18 through 25:1-40;
Matthew 24:29-51;
Psalm 30:1-12;
Proverbs 7:24-27

Mark my Word
(for further study)

Isaiah 45:3-5;
Ephesians 3:20-21;
James 1:4-7, 17

The Heart-Interest of God

Alfred, Lord Tennyson, only told half the truth when he wrote: "More things are wrought by prayer than this world dreams of." The other half is this: more things are not handled in prayer than this world dreams of. We live dangerously, leaving many important matters out of our prayers. Unanswered prayers are usually the ones that were never prayed – *"Until now, you have asked nothing in My Name; ask, and you will receive, that your joy may be full"* – but interceding for the salvation of the nations receives immediate attention: *"Now this is the confidence that we have in Him, that if we ask anything according to His will, He hears us. And if we know that He hears us, whatever we ask, we know that we have the petitions that we have asked of Him."* It touches the heart-interest of God: *"God, be merciful to us and bless us, and cause Your face to shine upon us, that Your way may be known on Earth, Your salvation among all nations. Let the peoples praise You, O God; let all the peoples praise You. Oh, let the nations be glad and sing for you! For You shall judge the people righteously, and govern the nations on Earth."*

Right now, my friend, pray this prayer of repentance and renewing of conviction:

"My Heavenly Father, I yearn to feel Your heart, to see what Your eyes see, to have greater compassion for the lost and dying of my world today. Forgive me when I've been careless or thoughtless, and neglected my daily intercession for the lost. Renew in me Your very fire of salvation – that gift which I've received and treasure – and rekindle in me a passion for souls that drives me to my knees. I know this is Your heart … now make it mine. In the Name of my beautiful Savior and Lord, Jesus Christ. Amen."

I know the Holy Spirit has heard your heart-felt prayer today and I know He will speedily answer by His Holy Spirit. More than ever before … become an intercessor **today!**

Today's Scripture

It is Christ Who died, and furthermore is also risen, Who is even at the right hand of God, Who also makes intercession for us.
(Romans 8:34)

Daily Power!

Interceding for the salvation of the nations touches the heart-interest of God, that's where I choose to put my heart also.

Today's Bible Reading

Exodus 26:1-37 through 27:1-21; Matthew 25:1-30; Psalm 31:1-8;
Proverbs 8:1-11

Mark my Word
(for further study)

Psalm 67:1-7; John 16:24; Romans 8; I John 5:14

We need a Deliverer

Israel rejected their greatest Son, their true King … and, by and large, the world does the same. The world today is leaderless, shepherdless, without a King. Where are we, and where can the world turn for true authority? As individuals, we find that unless God rules our lives, the devil will. The Bible simply states the obvious when it declares the whole world is led by the devil, and we need a Deliverer!

Christ left His imprint, but is like a "King-in-exile." The world wants to manage its own affairs – to them, He is the "absentee Lord." People want only people to help them.

"For since the creation of the world His invisible attributes are clearly seen, being understood by the things that are made, even His eternal power and Godhead; so that they are without excuse, because, although they knew God, they did not glorify Him as God, nor were thankful, but became futile in their thoughts, and their foolish hearts were darkened. Professing to be wise, they became fools, and changed the glory of the incorruptible God into an image made like corruptible man … And even as they did not like to retain God in their knowledge, God gave them over to a debased mind, to do those things which are not fitting."

When Jesus made His official entry into the capital of Jerusalem, He wept, saying, *"How often I have longed to gather your children together as a hen gathers her chicks under her wings, but you were not willing. Look, your house is left desolate to you."* Christ's great apostle Paul described things similarly: *"They did not think it worthwhile to retain the knowledge of God, He gave them over to a depraved mind and worshipped and served created things rather than the Creator."* Let us choose our Deliverer wisely!

Today's Scripture

And Jesus came and spoke to them, saying, "All authority has been given to Me in Heaven and on Earth. Go therefore and make disciples of all the nations, baptizing them in the Name of the Father, and of the Son and of the Holy Spirit, teaching them to observe all things that I have commanded you; and lo, I am with you always, even to the end of the age." Amen.
(Mark 28:18-20)

Daily Power!

Jesus Christ is my present-day Deliverer.

Today's Bible Reading

Exodus 28:1-43; Matthew 25:31-46 through 26:1-13; Psalm 31:9-18; Proverbs 8:12-13

Mark my Word
(for further study)

Matthew 23:37-38; Mark 28:18-20; Romans 1:20-32

Jesus the King

What will Jesus do when He is King? We can judge that by His First Coming – it altered the destiny of nations. His Second Coming will do all that, and more. He is the Prince of Peace. The first time, He lived in obscurity, never wrote a book, and died seemingly as a victim of political intrigue – but nobody has affected the world like He has. His next appearance will not be as a humble Babe in a manger. He wore no halo then, but He declared His return would be *"in power and great glory."* It will shake and re-shape the world. *"See, your King comes to you!"*

"And I heard a loud voice from Heaven saying 'Behold, the Tabernacle of God is with men, and He will dwell with them, and they shall be His people. God Himself will be with them and be their God. And God will wipe away every tear from their eyes; there shall be no more death, nor sorrow, nor crying. There shall be no more pain, for the former things have passed away.' Then He Who sat on the Throne said, 'Behold, I make all things new.'"

Knowing Jesus Christ as our King makes our lives very, very different. Being a follower of His doesn't mean that we suddenly become "super-people," raised far above the ranks of ordinary men. Rather, being His follower means *"becoming fishers of men," "forsaking worldly pleasures and distractions"* and *"taking up His Cross to follow Him."*

Whatever shape the world takes – the rise and fall of empires, *"wars and rumors of wars,"* technology and sociological "progress" – you and I have this great assurance: **Our King, Jesus Christ, not only lives in our hearts today, but His Kingdom is yet coming to this Earth!** That's a great promise, isn't it!

Today's Scripture

And he who does not take his cross and follow after Me is not worthy of Me. He who finds his life will lose it, and he who loses his life for My sake will find it.
(Matthew 10:38-39)

Daily Power!

I will be a world-shaper and world-shaker because I follow in the footsteps of My King, Jesus Christ.

Today's Bible Reading

Exodus 29:1-46 through 30:1-10; Matthew 26:14-46; Psalm 31:19-24; Proverbs 8:14-26

Mark my Word
(for further study)

Matthew 4:19; 10:38-39; 16:24; 21:5; Revelation 21:1-8

Today's Scripture

Jesus said to her, "Did I not say to you that if you would believe you would see the glory of God?"
(John 11:40)

Daily Power!

Because I believe, I know I will see the glory of God!

Today's Bible Reading

Exodus 30:11-39 through 31:1-18; Matthew 26:47-68; Psalm 32:1-11; Proverbs 8:27-32

Mark my Word
(for further study)

John 11:17-44; Romans 12:2; I Corinthians 1:18-25; Philippians 3:13-14; James 2:23

Breakthrough Faith

Unbelief sees today's miracles as suspect. People say, "Bible miracles were real, but today's are spurious" or "Today's tongues cannot be the same as at Pentecost. God answered prayer then, but now it's coincidence." How did Jesus reply to this pessimism? *"If you would believe, you would see the glory of God."* Rationalization is one of the biggest excuses: "Well, he wasn't really sick in first place" or "The medication had done its work, it was just a matter of time before the results showed up" or "She is in remission." The Bible clearly tells us that all people are "spiritually blind" until their eyes are opened by the truth of God's Word, often at that miracle-moment called salvation: *"For the message of the cross is foolishness to those who are perishing, but to us who are being saved it is the power of God … Has not God made foolish the wisdom of this world? … Because the foolishness of God is wiser than men, and the weakness of God is stronger than men."*

People often pray, "Use me, O Lord" … but do nothing. You cannot wait to "feel" faith, for it isn't a feeling. You simply **do** what should be done when you know that you can't succeed unless God helps you. The whole Bible is written to break down unbelief and build up our trust in God: *"Be not conformed to the world, but transformed by the renewing of your mind … And Abraham believed God and … he was called the friend of God … Forgetting those things which are behind, and reaching forth unto those things which are before, I press toward the mark."*

We talk of "big believers" with "great faith" … but some event inspired and encouraged them. They took their opportunity, changed their attitude … and believed. **Faith is a leap into the light, not into the darkness.** Believing is like a child standing where it is not safe but without any fear because his father is waiting to catch him. He falls on purpose to be caught! Jesus never commended people – He commended their faith. Be a Believer!

Down-to-Earth Faith

God has done something about the evil and suffering in our world. Over two thousand years ago, He sent His Son into one of the world's worst trouble spots: Palestine. He grew up to become a carpenter, living in a country occupied by foreign troops.

Surrounded by violence, poverty and disease, Jesus spent His life bringing the love of God to ordinary people. He healed the sick. He taught people to love those who hated them. He showed people how much God loved them. He turned the minus of their lives into a glorious plus: *"How God anointed Jesus of Nazareth with the Holy Spirit and with power, Who went about doing good and healing all who were oppressed by the devil, for God was with Him."*

But Jesus also made some powerful enemies. In the end, the politicians fixed it for Him. He was arrested, beaten up and handed over to the occupation troops. They took Him to the local killing ground and put Him to death. If there had been TV then, it might have made the evening news: *"And we were witnesses of all things which He did both in the land of the Jews and in Jerusalem, Whom they killed by hanging on a tree."*

Some people say that the Christian faith is out of touch with reality. But the life and death of Jesus show that this simply cannot be true. A real Jesus was pinned with real nails to a real piece of wood and shed real blood. The cross was a terrifying, bloody execution. It was as down-to-earth as you can get: *"Him God raised up on the third day, and showed Him openly ... and He commanded us to preach to the people, and to testify that He is Who was ordained by God to be Judge of the living and the dead."*

Christianity does not turn a blind eye to human suffering. Like the bulletins we see on the news, Jesus' crucifixion shows us that something has gone terribly wrong with the human race. But unlike them, it also shows us that there is a solution. It tells us that God has done something to change it all! That's His promise to you and to me today.

Today's Scripture

All authority has been given to Me in Heaven and on Earth. Go therefore and make disciples of all the nations, baptizing them in the Name of the Father and of the Son and of the Holy Spirit, teaching them to observe all things that I have commanded you; and lo, I am with you always, even to the end of the age.
(Matthew 28:18-20)

Daily Power!

A real Jesus was pinned with real nails to a real piece of wood and shed real blood ... and He did this all for me!

Today's Bible Reading

Exodus 32:1-35 through 33:1-23; Matthew 26:69-75 through 27:1-14; Psalm 33:1-11; Proverbs 8:33-36

Mark my Word
(for further study)

Matthew 27:1-66; 28:1-20; Acts 10:38-42

12

The Secret of Revival

The Early Church was alive and lively, always in action. That is what *"passing from death to life"* meant for them. They lived … they quickened … they revived! The secret of true revival is in the Word: *"Your Word has given me life."* People often try to learn what revival is by studying past revivals, special seasons in the previous century or two. **We** have chosen to call these events "revivals." Then we look at them to see what a revival is. This is a circular process, and begs the question – examining and going by the New Testament model is safer.

The saying goes: "Every revival springs from prayer." Obviously this is assumed, for Christians pray and must have prayed before any revival. **In actual fact, there is no evidence of anyone praying for revival in the New Testament.** The famous prayer, *"O Lord, revive Your work!"* was an **Old Testament prayer**. Nevertheless, God answered and revived His work — the answer to that prayer was **Jesus** and **Pentecost**. When Peter preached in the first Pentecostal meeting ever held, he saw what had never before been seen on Earth in all the history of Israel. Something happened on that day that Elijah, Isaiah or Jeremiah never saw: Three thousand people repenting and being saved. Only the revived can pray revival prayers; the dead pray dead prayers. **Revival comes through the revived.** Let you and I be "the revived"!

Each one is given grace, a gift … and when that has been done, the Lord plants each one in the Church. God gives only the gifted to the Church. We are nothing until He does a work in us. But everyone is a gift because everyone has his or her gift. The parable of the Sower says, *"The sower sows the Word"* – He plants in you what He wants planted in the world.

Today's Scripture

Grant to Your servants that with all boldness they may speak Your Word, by stretching out Your hand to heal, and that signs and wonders may be done through the Name of Your holy Servant Jesus.

(Acts 4:29-30)

Daily Power!

*O God, let **your** revival come through me, because I claim the promises of one who has been revived!*

Today's Bible Reading

*Exodus 34:1-35 through 35:1-9;
Matthew 27:15-31;
Psalm 33:12-22;
Proverbs 9:1-6*

Mark my Word
(for further study)

*Psalm 68:18; 119:50;
Habakkuk 3:2;
Mark 4:14;
John 5:24;
Acts 4:29-30;
Ephesians 4:7,
I John 3:14*

A Witness to the Light

13

To dispel the darkness, it is no use arguing with it – just switch on the light! Polemic is no substitute dynamic for truth and the Holy Spirit. No amount of darkness can put out the light of a single candle.

I noticed an interesting thing in John's Gospel. Jesus said that John was *"a burning and shining lamp."* Earlier in John, we read, *"And the light shines in the darkness, and the darkness did not comprehend it. There was a man sent from God, whose name was John. This man came for a witness, to bear witness of the Light, that all through him might believe."* It struck me that if the light was already shining, why was John needed? When the sun rises, we all know about it and don't need anybody to testify that it is daylight. The answer is" *"He was not that Light, but was sent to bear witness of that Light."* Is a witness necessary? Does that mean that God **needs** you and me? **Yes!**

What is God's command to us about being lights to the world? First, He exhorts us to be "available" light: *"You are the light of the world. A city that is set on a hill cannot be hidden. Nor do they light a lamp and put it under a basket, but on a lamp stand, and it gives light to all who are in the house. Let your light so shine before men, that they may see your good works and glorify your Father in Heaven."* Then He encourages us to be sure our light is "good": *"The lamp of the body is the eye. If therefore your eye is good, your whole body will be full of light. But if your eye is bad, your whole body will be full of darkness. If therefore the light that is in you is darkness, how great is that darkness!"* **Let your good light shine today!**

Today's Scripture

For it is the God Who commanded light to shine out of darkness, Who has shone in our hearts to give the light of the knowledge of the glory of God in the face of Jesus Christ.
(II Corinthians 4:6)

Daily Power!

I am a single candle burning in the darkness – a light that no man can put out because it is God's light shining through me!

Today's Bible Reading

Exodus 35:10-35 through 36:1-38; Matthew 27:32-66; Psalm 34:1-10; Proverbs 9:7-8

Mark my Word
(for further study)

II Samuel 22:29; Matthew 5:14-15; 6:22-23; John 1:1-14; 5:35; II Corinthians 4:6

14

Light vs. Darkness

What is *"a witness to light"*? If you look into the sky on a clear night, the moon is shining. Men have been to the moon, and they know it has no light of its own. Also, also space around the moon is in pitch-blackness. We all know, of course, that the moon only reflects the light that comes from the sun. If the sunlight passes through space to reach the moon, why is all the sky dark around the moon?

The answer is – as famed fictional detective Sherlock Holmes, would say, "Elementary, my dear Watson!" – **Light is invisible.** You only know light is there at all when it strikes an object.

Space is completely empty. There is nothing there to catch the light from the sun, until it reaches the moon. Actually, space is full of light but it looks dark. **This universe is full of God.** He is *"the Father of lights,"* and all light comes from Him. But millions walk in profound darkness. How can that be? **How can people walk in spiritual darkness when the whole universe is steeped in the light of God?**

"The lamp of the body is the eye. If therefore your eye is good, your whole body will be full of light. But if your eye is bad, your whole body will be full of darkness. If therefore the light that is in you is darkness, how great is that darkness!"

Jesus commanded us: *"Let your light so shine before men, that they may see your good works and glorify your Father in Heaven."* Later, Paul the apostle reminded us: *"But we all, with unveiled face, beholding as in a mirror the glory of the Lord, are being transformed into the same image from glory to glory, just as by the Spirit of the Lord."* Let us choose to be reflectors of God's light in a world of darkness.

Today's Scripture

I am the light of the world. He who follows Me shall not walk in darkness, but have the light of life.

(John 8:12)

Daily Power!

Without Christ in my life, I have no light. But because He infuses me with His light, not only do I reflect His light, but I can be a source of light and life in the darkened world around me.

Today's Bible Reading

Exodus 37:1-29 through 38:1-31; Matthew 8:1-20; Psalm 34:11-22; Proverbs 9:9-10

Mark my Word
(for further study)

Matthew 5:16; 6:22-23; John 5:19; 8:12; James 1:17

Who is the Holy Spirit?

As much as we may wish for it, the Lord does not send publicity by Heavenly mail to tell us Who He is! The works performed by His Spirit are seen on Earth. **The Holy Spirit is a Person – He is God in action.** Creation came as *"the Spirit of God was hovering over the face of the waters."*

When God chose His servants, the power of the Holy Spirit rested upon them: *"See, the Lord has called by name Bezalel ... and He has filled him with the Spirit of God ... and He has put in his heart the ability to teach" "The Lord raised up a deliverer for the children of Israel ... the Spirit of the Lord came upon [Onthiel], and he judged Israel."*

After these judges, the prophet Samuel guided an entire nation for a lifetime. How? *"Holy men of God spoke as they were moved by the Holy Spirit."* The prophet Micah testified, *"But truly I am full of power by the Spirit of the Lord."*

These are portraits of the Holy Spirit. This is that Spirit Whom Christ promised: the Spirit of wisdom and knowledge, creative, empowering, healing – the Spirit of strength, confidence and virtue. Jesus **is** the Holy Spirit – the One Who never leaves us: *"And I will pray the Father, and He will give you another Helper, that He may abide with you forever – the Spirit of truth, Whom the world cannot receive, because it neither sees Him nor knows Him; but you know Him, for He dwells with you and will be in you. I will not leave you orphans; I will come to you."*

God's power is not a kind of "super-charge" for people already gifted with great personality and drive but is for those who **need** it, the weak and the unknown. Isn't it great to have that dynamic working in **your** life!

Today's Scripture

He gives power to the weak, and to those who have no might He increases strength.
(Isaiah 40:29)

Daily Power!

I am a chosen servant of God, empowered by His Holy Spirit, filled with His wisdom and knowledge, strength, confidence and virtue!

Today's Bible Reading

Exodus 39:1-43 through 40:1-38;
Mark 1:1-28;
Psalm 35:1-16;
Proverbs 9:11-12

Mark my Word
(for further study)

Genesis 1:2;
Exodus 35:31-32, 34;
Judges 3:9-10;
Isaiah 40:29;
Micah 3:8;
John 14:16-18;
II Peter 1:21

16

Today's Scripture

Now when they saw the boldness of Peter and John, and perceived that they were uneducated and untrained men, they marveled. And they realized that they had been with Jesus.

(Acts 4:13)

Daily Power!

It's not by might nor by power, but by My Spirit, says the Lord.

(Zechariah 4:6)

Today's Bible Reading

Leviticus 1:1-16 through 3:1-17; Mark 1:29-45 through 2:1-12; Psalm 35:17-28; Proverbs 9:13-18

Mark my Word
(for further study)

Zechariah 4:6; Acts 2:14-21; 4:1-31; 17:1-34; I Corinthians 4:1-21

Christ's secret Weapon

The world two thousand years ago was a wild place. It was a place of bloodshed, uncontrolled passions, and fanatical hatreds. Its chief pleasures were immorality, idolatry, indulgence, and – worst of all – cruelty. The crowds considered it a wonderful day's outing to listen to the shrieks of tortured and dying people. The disciples had to take the Gospel to that world ... and the Gospel centred on the cruelty suffered by Jesus. It was also a place of much learning. The influences of the great Greek thinkers were strong, and new ideas were eagerly sought. The disciples offered no radical "new" ideas ... but only the story of a crucified Messiah. Peter, James, John, Simon, and Thomas were unsophisticated, untutored – they even spoke with a Galilean accent! ... the very opposite of city elegance. What hopes had Christianity, left in the hands of a few rough-handed, unscholarly fishermen, men jealous of one another and full of doubts? So – thinking of these men and their world – from the start, the Gospel looked doomed to fail. Twelve local men – who had never travelled fifty miles in their lives – were to go into all the world – the Roman world! – and conquer its conquering armies, shake the emperor on his throne, and convert the wild tribes on its borders.

"But Peter, standing up with the eleven, raised his voice and said to them, 'Men of Judea and all who dwell in Jerusalem, let this be known to you, and heed my words. For these are not drunk, as you suppose, but this is what was spoken by the prophet Joel: And it shall come to pass in the last days, says God, that I will pour out My Spirit on all flesh ... And it shall come to pass that whoever calls on the Name of the Lord shall be saved.'" No doubt Jesus **did** anticipate those twelve becoming a world force, but He trusted twelve men – sons of toil, some of them almost peasants – to provide the vital first link between Him and the mighty Church to come. Christ's secret was the empowerment by the Holy Spirit on the Day of Pentecost. Well, what are you afraid of? You are already empowered by the Holy Spirit!

Unusual Miracle Conditions

In the miracle story from Matthew 14, it was Christ Himself Who put the disciples where they were — He **made** the disciples get into the boat and go on ahead of Him to the other side: *"Immediately Jesus made His disciples get into the boat and go before Him to the other side, while He sent the multitudes away. And when He had sent the multitudes away, He went up on the mountain by Himself to pray … But the boat was now in the middle of the sea, tossed by the waves, for the wind was contrary."* Yet the boat was buffeted by the waves because the wind was against it. So troubles may arise **when** we are – or even **because** we are – doing God's explicit will but we must give God time and let Him work things together for good. That is true for you and me.

Jesus, in fact, was in charge. He had seen them struggling out on the Sea of Galilee while He was up on the hillside. Don't worry – the Lord has good eyesight! God does not guarantee us everlastingly calm seas and prosperous voyages. Even Paul was shipwrecked three times. The disciples were fighting the elements in one of those lumbering boats of their day, for the very reason that was where God wanted them! Many people feel disillusioned about this very thing. They do what is right, yet suffer for it. But we need not worry. The trouble which comes when God puts us where He wants us – is "a miracle in the making"! The stormy winds of Galilee were the first component for a wonder for Peter and his companions.

Why do we think miracles should only occur in "optimal" conditions (such as a vibrant Christian church service)? We usually need a miracle when we're in the direst of problems! Never put limits on God for when He is "allowed" to touch your life with His miracle-power!

Today's Scripture

Therefore, having been justified by faith, we have peace with God through our Lord Jesus Christ, through Whom also we have access by faith into this grace in which we stand, and rejoice in hope of the glory of God. And not only that, we also glory in tribulations, knowing that tribulation produces perseverance; and perseverance, character; and character, hope.
(Romans 5:1-4)

Daily Power!

Jesus is in charge of my life, and He will be with me every time the storms of life threaten to overcome me.

Today's Bible Reading

Leviticus 4:1-35 through 5:1-19; Mark 2:13-28 through 3:1-6; Psalm 36:1-12; Proverbs 10:1-2

Mark my Word
(for further study)

Matthew 14:22-36; Mark 6:45-52; Romans 5:1-4

18

Today's Scripture

And we know that all things work together for good to those who love God, to those who are the called according to His purpose.

(Romans 8:28)

Daily Power!

I know that troubles may arise, even when I am doing God's will, but I rely on Him to work things together for His glory and my good.

Today's Bible Reading

Leviticus 6:1-30
through 7:1-27;
Mark 3:7-30;
Psalm 37:1-11;
Proverbs 10:3-4

Mark my Word
(for further study)

Job 5:7;
Psalm 91:14-16;
Mark 6:47-48;
Romans 8:28

We all need Miracles

Difficulties don't always indicate we are doing God's will – sometimes they show us we are doing our own wills. We land ourselves with problems. For that matter, *"Man is born to trouble, as the sparks fly upward"* – this is "natural" in our fallen world. Also, there is a devil.

Whether a situation is our fault or not, we all need a miracle sometime or other. Difficulties arise for all of us at times – perhaps in health, occupation, marriage, family, or some other area of our lives. Some people find their sins and failures rattling around behind them, the skeletons getting out of the closet! Like the disciples in their boat, we can sit amid waves of worry, conjuring up haunting specters – even the sudden appearance of Jesus was part of the disciples' fears! They needed a miracle – nothing less would do!

God wants His children to live within the guidelines of His Book … then we would never "need" miracles to help us out of our problems. But because our human nature is so sin-ridden, our own stubborn pride is so prevalent, and our enemy is doing his utmost to sabotage us, our need for supernatural intervention is strong. And because Christ came to redeem us – which includes access to His divine power – we have a "right" to be miracle-recipients! *"Because he has set his love upon Me, therefore I will deliver him; I will set him on high, because he has known My Name. He shall call upon Me, and I will answer him; I will be with him in trouble; I will deliver him and honor him. With long life I will satisfy him, and show him My salvation."*

Thank God, He did not intend for you and me to live our lives without miracles. His original plan was that, even after you have done your best, you will still be dependent upon Him to meet your needs.

Longing for God

From the beginning of human existence, there has been a natural longing for God to manifest Himself in unshadowed reality. The universal cry is for God to convince the world that He is God: *"Why the big noise, nations? Why the mean plots, peoples? Earth-leaders push for position, demagogues and delegates meet for summit talks ... Heaven-throned God breaks out laughing ... So, rebel-kings, use your heads; upstart-judges, learn your lesson; worship God in adoring embrace, celebrate in trembling awe. Kiss Messiah! Your very lives are in danger, you know; His anger is about to explode, but if you make a run for God – you won't regret it!"* Even the ungodly demand hard evidence of God, and scoff, "He isn't apparent" – as in Psalm 10: *"The wicked man says to himself, 'God has forgotten; He covers His face and never sees.'"* A similar situation troubled the Psalmist himself, who asked, *"Why, O Lord, do You stand far off? Why do You hide Yourself in times of trouble?"* Indeed, the wish for God to prove Himself is implicit in many Psalms, and the frequent plea is: *"Let God arise, let His enemies be scattered!"*

The ways in which it was hoped that God might reveal Himself were closely linked to the culture and outlook at the time. Israel, a small, beleaguered nations, visualized God as a mighty Warrior coming to champion their cause. Even in Christian times, thoughts of how God might awe the world have varied considerably, as have ideas about what Christians should do to bring it about.

Renewal has come to the Church at various times throughout the Christian era, but it has taken different forms, some of which have appeared strange. It has been said that the history of America is the history of religious revivals. However, God was not simply inactive for seventeen hundred years, until the Evangelicals came along. Jesus said, *"I will build My Church,"* and despite everything that has taken place since He made that statement, He has steadily continued to do just that. Be Christ's Church today!

Today's Scripture

The fool has said in his heart, "There is no God" ... Oh, that the salvation of Israel would come out of Zion! When the Lord brings back the captivity of His people.
(Psalm 14:1, 7)

Daily Power!

I am a part of God's Church-building, Kingdom-populating army.
Our motto is:
"Heaven full, Hell empty!"

Today's Bible Reading

Leviticus 7:28-36 through 9:1-6;
Mark 3:31-35 through 4:1-25;
Psalm 37:12-29;
Proverbs 10:5

Mark my Word
(for further study)

Psalm 2:1-12 (the Message); 10:1-18; 14:1-7; 68:1; Matthew 16:18

The King and His Kingdom

We hear about radical politicians, but there has never been one yet who reversed the ways of the world with its materialism and godlessness. Yet when Paul and Silas went to Thessalonica, the unbelieving Jews said, *"These who have turned the world upside down have come here too."* Unbelief had damaged their eyesight. But for their distorted vision, they would have seen that the world was already upside down – before the arrival of Paul and Silas. That's why they had come: to put it the right way up! *"Where do wars and fights come from among you? Do they not come from your desires for pleasure that war in your members? … Do you not know that friendship with the world is enmity with God? Whoever therefore wants to be a friend of the world makes himself an enemy of God."*

We are so used to the world, despite the warning of Scripture that the world is an enemy of God. Its standards are the opposite of everything God wants. Money is priority number one. People with money are at the top, the privileged elite. The rest may grovel in the dust. Big business crushes ordinary people. Achieve greatness by standing on everybody else's shoulders, and you will be honored and envied. The trials of ordinary people do not touch the world's "greats."

But the Kingdom of God is a Kingdom of reversed principles and priorities. Jesus said, *"Many who are first will be last, and the last first."* The Lord puts the people last whom the world puts first. **First in the Kingdom of Christ are the poor in spirit** – not those who are laughing all the way to the bank with fat profits. **Then come those who mourn** – not those with a permanent (probably fake) grin on their faces. **Next on the list of blessed are the meek** – not those who walk all over others to get to the front: *"The humble shall upstage the proud."* **Blessed are those who hunger and thirst for righteousness** – not those who change their politics to win votes. **Blessed are the merciful** – not the vengeful, the retaliators. **Blessed are the pure in heart** – not the devious. Then follow **the peacemakers** – not the war makers – and **the persecuted** – not the compromisers. Let your life be an instrument to usher in the Kingdom of God.

Today's Scripture

Humble yourselves in the sight of the Lord, and He will lift you up.

(James 4:10)

Daily Power!

I desire to be God's most humble servant.

Today's Bible Reading

Leviticus 9:7-23 through 10:1-20; Mark 4:26-41 through 5:1-20; Psalm 37:30-40; Proverbs 10:6-7

Mark my Word
(for further study)

Mark 10:31; Acts 17:16; James 4:1-10

Using your Parachute

Two skydivers jump from a plane at 15,000 feet. Both are wearing parachutes. One of them folds his arms, ignores the rip-cord, and says to himself, "I'm perfectly safe because of my parachute." He is still saying these words as he hits the ground at one hundred miles-per-hour, smashing into a million pieces. The other skydiver knows he will be safe only if he actually does something. He pulls the rip-cord and lands safely.

You and I may **know** about the Christian faith. You and I may **respect** Jesus and agree that what He did on the Cross is the answer to our deepest needs. But until you and I actually **ask** for His help and commit our lives to Him, it is like falling with a closed parachute. We need to take urgent action. We need to pull the rip-cord while there is still time!

The rip-cord is this: *"Believe on the Lord Jesus, and you will be saved."* There is nothing else you or I can do. We cannot save ourselves – we can only throw ourselves on what Jesus achieved for us on the Cross. He has done everything that we need.

"Nor is there salvation in any other, for there is no other name under Heaven given among men by which we must be saved."

How do we know this is true? We can stake our lives on the promises given to us in the Bible and proved in real life by hundreds of millions of Christians:

"The Lord upholds all those who fall … Jesus is able to keep you from falling and to present you before His glorious presence without fault and with great joy … He is also able to save to the uttermost those who come to God through [Jesus]."

Although your life may sometimes feel like it is spinning out of control, you can draw on the assurance that the Holy Spirit is never farther away than your next prayer.

Today's Scripture

Now to Him Who is able to keep you from stumbling, and to present you faultless before the presence of His glory with exceeding joy, to God our Savior, Who alone is wise, be glory and majesty, dominion and power, both now and forever. Amen.
(Jude 24-25)

Daily Power!

Every day, I am "upheld by the right hand of God."
(Isaiah 41:13; paraphrased)

Today's Bible Reading

Leviticus 11:1-47 through 12:1-8;
Mark 5:21-43;
Psalm 38:1-22;
Proverbs 10:8-9

Mark my Word
(for further study)

Psalm 145:14;
Acts 4:12; 16:31;
Hebrews 7:25;
Jude 24-25

Riches of Assurance

Many people want assurance of salvation to register in their feelings. This is a common mistake which often has a disastrous outcome. God never said that your emotions would be the test of your salvation. Assurance is not dependent on your psyche, but on His eternal Word. Although the human soul is a masterpiece of creation, it was made to fluctuate with experience, registering ups and downs, being glad or being sad, according to your state of mind … **even after you are saved**. Saved people do not have ever-smiling faces, like plastic masks, but they have entered God's original plan for their lives and have no need to consult their emotions to determine whether they are saved or not.

So, salvation is embedded in the rock of the eternal Word. Jesus stated: *"Heaven and Earth will pass away, but My words will never pass away."* This is the *"cleft in the rock"* to which you must flee whenever Satan attacks you with doubts. You are saved because the Word of God says you are. Whatever I feel, my conviction remains unshakable.

The first Christians were not uncertain. Scripture says that they were *"abounding in hope,"* having *"abundance of joy"* and *"abundance of grace."* *"Abounding"* means enough and some to spare, a surplus, like the twelve baskets of food left over after Jesus fed the five thousand. Assurance of salvation is not over-confidence, but a deep, settled peace which fills your soul in moments when the devil whispers doubts.

Paul described Christians in Colosse as having *"all riches of the full assurance."* Riches of assurance! That word "riches" in the original Greek is "ploutos", the root of the word "plutocrat," which means "somebody who reigns by his wealth." I do not mind being a spiritual plutocrat, being **wealthy in confidence in God**. The letter to the Hebrews speaks of *"full assurance,"* and in Thessalonica, they had *"much assurance,"* literally, "much fullness." That is the true fullness, being rich in faith towards God.

Today's Scripture

Let Your people be clothed with righteousness, and let Your saints shout for joy.
(Psalm 132:9)

Daily Power!

I am rich in the assurance that Christ Jesus has cleansed me from all sin and clothed me in His righteousness.

Today's Bible Reading

Leviticus 13:1-59;
Mark 6:1-29;
Psalm 39:1-13;
Proverbs 10:10

Mark my Word
(for further study)

Psalm 132:9;
Matthew 14:15-21;
24:35;
Romans 5:17;
II Corinthians 8:2;
Colossians 2:2; 6:11;
10:22;
I Thessalonians 1:5

The Power comes with the Task

We need God-power … God needs Man-power. The usual ratio is ninety-nine percent God-power to ten-percent Man-power. From the dawn of history, when Joshua stood on the borders of a whole land to be conquered, God said, *"I will be with you."* With the task is given the means – the ability, the wisdom, and, most of all, the unseen but moving power of God, working secretly or openly – in the souls of people or in visible miracles.

We can only do what we have power to do. If God asks us to do more than is in our power, He makes up for the deficiency! We do what we can … and God does what we can't. Whatever we do on this planet is limited by the power available. In past centuries, power was only physical strength, muscle power. They built the pyramids, dug the great canals of Suez and Panama, and cut roads through the mountains … all by brawn. The Seven Wonders of the ancient world are examples of brawn power. Now we have a thousand modern wonders brought into being by new power sources, not brute strength. **Nothing is impossible when the right kind of power is operating.** Jesus said, *"You shall receive power when the Holy Spirit has come upon you; and you shall be witnesses to Me … to the end of the Earth."* The Church has too often trusted scholarship, erudition, genius, logic, and philosophy. But Paul said, *"God has chosen the foolish things."* If we are to evangelize the world by cerebral methods, we will never do it. That has been tried for centuries. But real Church growth has been brought about by the simple message of the Gospel touching people from all walks of life.

God promises that you will never be given too much to bear, that you won't be asked to do more than you are capable to do with His help. Not only in your speech – *"Praying … that utterance may be given to me, that I may open my mouth boldly to make know the mystery of the Gospel"* – but also in your actions be a **doer** today in every way that He leads you!

Today's Scripture

We are fools for Christ's sake, but you are wise in Christ! We are weak, but you are strong! You are distinguished, but we are dishonored.
(I Corinthians 4:10)

Daily Power!

I agree with the Psalmist David:
"O Lord, open my lips, and my mouth shall show forth Your praise".
(Psalm 51:15)

Today's Bible Reading

Leviticus 14:1-57;
Mark 6:30-56;
Psalm 40:1-10;
Proverbs 10:11-12

Mark my Word
(for further study)

Joshua 1:5;
Psalm 51:15;
Acts 1:8;
I Corinthians 1:27;
Ephesians 6:18-20

24

The Promise of Power

In Matthew 10 and Luke 9, we have the first limited commissioning of the twelve disciples for a pilot-mission which took place while Jesus was still on Earth, a miniature project to exemplify the full-scale operation that was to follow after the empowering of Pentecost. It explains to us what the power of Pentecost was going to be:

"And when He had called His twelve disciples to Him, He gave them power over unclean spirits, to cast them out, and to heal all kinds of sickness and all kinds of diseases ... These twelve Jesus sent out and commanded them, saying, 'Do not go into the way of the Gentiles, and do not enter a city of the Samaritans. But go rather to the lost sheep of the house of Israel. And as you go, preach, saying: The Kingdom of Heaven is at hand. Heal the sick, cleanse the lepers, raise the dead, cast out demons. Freely you have received, freely give ... He who receives you receives Me, and he who receives Me receives Him Who sent Me.'"

Today's Scripture

Rejoice because your names are written in Heaven.

(Luke 10:21)

Daily Power!

Thank You for giving me the gift of Your Holy Spirit as my continual Source of Power!

Today's Bible Reading

Leviticus 15:1-33
through 16:1-28;
Mark 7:1-23;
Psalm 40:11-17;
Proverbs 10:13-14

Mark my Word
(for further study)

Matthew 10:1, 5-8, 40;
Luke 9:2; 10:18-19

Luke chapter 9 gives a similar account of this first commissioning – *"He sent them to preach the Kingdom of God, and to heal the sick"* – with Luke chapter 10 recounting the commissioning of seventy-two others: *"Then He said to them, 'The harvest truly is great, but the laborers are few; therefore pray the Lord of the harvest to send out laborers into His harvest. Go your way; behold, I send you out as lambs among wolves.'"* Then the Word reports: *"Then the seventy returned with joy, saying, 'Lord, even the demons are subject to us in Your Name!' And He said to them ... 'Behold, I give you the **authority** [KJV: **power**] to trample on serpents and scorpions, and over all the power of the enemy, and nothing shall by any means hurt you. Nevertheless, do not rejoice in this – that the spirits are subject to you – but rather rejoice because your names are written in Heaven.'"*

So long as Jesus was there with them, they had power ... but when He left, they had **another** Comforter and Power Source: the **Holy Spirit**. He is your same Power Source today!

The Acts of the King

If Christ Jesus did no more than continue doing what He did when He first appeared on Earth, what a happier world it would be! One man who personally knew Jesus said, *"He went about doing good, and healing all who were oppressed of the devil, for God was with Him."* *"Doing good"* meant that Jesus did things nobody else ever did. To multitudes, His very presence brought certainty of forgiveness and healing. He lifted the fallen, delivered the devil-possessed, and championed the oppressed. His graciousness and understanding overwhelmed people. His words created astonishment.

Crowds thronged Him, and immediately wanted to put Him on the throne. Instead, He let His enemies put Him on the Cross. He came as a Savior, not as a Caesar. He was the Redeemer, not a rebel leader. He lived the most extraordinary life, an inspiration to other good lives. His enemies took it as the end when He expired on the Cross – it was, in fact, the beginning. They were dealing with Somebody like nobody had ever before encountered. He conquered death, rose from the tomb robed in immortality, ascended to God, and left the promise that every eye would see Him again.

At the onset of His ministry, He told everyone what He was going to do: *"And He was handed the book of the prophet Isaiah 'The Spirit of the Lord is upon Me, because He has anointed Me to preach the Gospel to the poor; He has sent Me to heal the broken-hearted, to proclaim liberty to the captives, and recovery of sight to the blind, to set at liberty those who are oppressed; to proclaim the acceptable year of the Lord' And He began to say to them, 'Today this Scripture is fulfilled in your hearing.' So all bore witness to Him, and marveled at the gracious words which proceeded out of His mouth."* He fulfilled every prophecy, every promise. When later He promised He would return for His own, He will make good on that promise too. This is our King Jesus!

Today's Scripture

Jesus went about all Galilee, teaching in their synagogues, preaching the Gospel of the Kingdom, and healing all kinds of sickness and all kinds of diseases among the people. Then His fame went throughout all Syria; and they brought to Him all sick people who were afflicted with various diseases and torments, and those who were demon-possessed, epileptics, and paralytics; and He healed them.
(Matthew 4:23-24)

Daily Power!

Because Christ Jesus lives in me, I can do the same things which He did!

Today's Bible Reading

Leviticus 19:29-34 through 18:1-30; Mark 7:24-37 through 8:1-10; Psalm 41:1-13; Proverbs 10:15-16

Mark my Word
(for further study)

Isaiah 61:1-2; Matthew 4:23-24; Luke 4:18-22; Acts 10:34-48

26

Today's Scripture

Jesus Christ the same, yesterday, today and forever.

(Hebrews 13:8)

Daily Power!

I rejoice in that my Lord and Savior Jesus Christ is as alive today as He was in Bible days, and He is my Healer today, just as He was then.

Today's Bible Reading

Leviticus 19:1-37 through 20:1-21; Mark 8:11-38; Psalm 42:1-11; Proverbs 10:17

Mark my Word
(for further study)

Malachi 3:6; 4:2, Hebrews 13:8

We read, *"Jesus Christ the same yesterday, today and forever."* Jesus is alive, just as ready to heal now as He ever was. He is not like the moon which has phases, sometimes showing a darkened portion. He is *"the sun of righteousness risen with healing in His wing."* What Jesus was, He is – constantly and forever: *"For I am the Lord, I do not change."*

Miracles are part and parcel of the Gospel of Jesus Christ, not something added on as an afterthought. He said, *"I have come to **preach** the Gospel to the poor"* – He did that, and He was very popular among the poor people of His day (and largely unpopular with the wealthy, ruling class). He said, *"I have come to **proclaim** liberty to the captives"* – He did that, releasing bonds of sickness and even death. He said, *"I have come to **give** sight to the blind"* – He did that, many times, both in physical healings, and in opening spiritual eyes to God's truths. He said, *"I have come to **set at liberty** those who are oppressed"* – He did that, delivering demon-possessed people. All the things He said He would do – from miracle healings to life-changing teaching – He did them. From start to finish, Christianity is supernatural, beginning as resurrection life and power. Healings demonstrate the essential truths of Christianity, and show us Jesus as He really is. If we look back, we see that what Jesus was then … He is now.

If we look forward, we see that He will be what He was. He is not **becoming** great, He **is** great! He is **now** at the height of His greatness. He always was and will always be the Healer and the Savior. Jesus Christ is our great Redeemer!

The Banner of God

Roman soldiers used ensigns for signaling in battle, occasionally per-fuming them with oils and decorating with flowers. Jews considered these ensigns to be spiritually offensive. Nowadays, we do not regard ceremonial objects with the same appreciation or revulsion as did the Romans or Jews of centuries gone by, but we can learn a lot by under-standing how people revered banners in Bible times: *"You have given a banner to those who fear You, that it may be displayed because of the truth."*

When exiled in Egypt, the Hebrews had no banner, were anonymous, unorganized, and without distinction. As slaves, they had no identifi-cation, no flags and no rights. When the tribes finally escaped, they were as refugees, united only in huddled fear, a mixed rabble. Only Moses and Aaron kept them together – and even then, some of them probably suspected them of being religious fanatics – and the families clung to each other for mutual support. The first few days were criti-cal. Then murderous bands of Amalekite plunderers began to harry their flanks, picking off stragglers and stripping them of their meager belongings. Joshua had to muster what men and arms he could. It was a pitiful show, since they do not have so much as a rag raised on a pole to rally them. However, Moses had his own bare hands to raise to the God of Heaven … and the Amalekites were routed. Moses pro-claimed, *"Hands were lifted up to the Throne of the Lord. The Lord will be at war against the Amalekites from generation to generation."*

God gave Israel a name and nationhood, but no national symbol. Moses surveyed Joshua's Israelite force – primitive but victorious, undistinguished by a single fluttering pennant or token, an army with-out pageantry – and said, *"Yahweh Nissi – the Lord is my banner."* He replaced heraldry by reality. Later, Israelite tribes each adopted its own standard. When Joshua welded together Israel's first real army on Canaan's soil, a formidable figure confronted him, whom Joshua attempted to challenge. The response was, *"As Commander of the Army of the Lord I have now come."* That Heavenly Commander-in-Chief needed no ensign and never lost a battle! And He is your Chief today!!

Today's Scripture

Then all this assembly shall know that the Lord does not save with sword and spear; for the battle is the Lord's, and He will give you into our hands.
(I Samuel 17:47)

Daily Power!

As the old Sunday School song goes, "I'm in the Lord's army!"

Today's Bible Reading

Leviticus 20:22-27 through 22:1-16;
Mark 9:1-29;
Psalm 43:1-5;
Proverbs 10:18

Mark my Word
(for further study)

Exodus 17:15-16;
Joshua 5:14;
Psalm 60:4

The true Banner

If ever Israel can be said to have displayed a national symbol, it is in the events described in Numbers 21: *"The Lord said to Moses, 'Make a snake and put it up on a pole; anyone who is bitten can look at it and live.' So Moses made a bronze snake and put it up on a pole."* It was a strange standard indeed. But in that lost wilderness, God's own True Banner was first displayed. Today, it is the greatest symbol in the world: the Cross. The link is made clear in the New Testament: *"Just as Moses lifted up the snake in the desert, so the Son of Man must be lifted up."* Isaiah said, *"Raise a banner for the nations. The Lord has made proclamation to the ends of the earth: 'See, your Savior comes!'"*

"Therefore the people came to Moses, and said, 'We have sinned, for we have spoken against the Lord and against you; pray to the Lord that He take away the serpents from us.' So Moses prayed for the people. Then the Lord said to Moses, 'Make a fiery serpent, and set it on a pole; and it shall be that everyone who is bitten, when he looks at it, shall live.' So Moses made a bronze serpent, and put it on a pole, and so it was, if a serpent had bitten anyone, when he looked at the bronze serpent, he lived." ... *"And as Moses lifted up the serpent in the wilderness, even so must the Son of Man be lifted up, that whoever believes in Him should not perish but have eternal life."*

Paul seems to have been thinking in such terms when he wrote, *"Before your very eyes Jesus Christ was clearly portrayed as crucified."* He uses a word based on the Greek: "grapho" – "to write" or "to inscribe." It has been translated "to placard." The Cross of Christ is the sign writing of Almighty God on the billboards of history. Our banner is no mere arbitrary artistic design, but the Lord Himself, visible to all, riveted to that wooden "pole," exhibiting forever His unrestrained love, the living banner of a dying Savior. We set Him forth, the crucified One and through Him we conquer. Today, go and conquer for Christ!

Today's Scripture

And I, if I am lifted up from the Earth, will draw all peoples to Myself.
(John 12:32)

Daily Power!

The Cross of Jesus Christ is my enduring symbol of hope, salvation, healing.

Today's Bible Reading

Leviticus 22:17-33 through 23:1-44; Mark 9:30-50 through 10:1-12; Psalm 44:1-8; Proverbs 10:19

Mark my Word
(for further study)

Numbers 21:7-9; Isaiah 62:10-11; John 3:14; 12:32; Galatians 3:1

To each Generation

Christ's Great Commission is not a scrap of paper, blown to our feet from centuries ago. It is Jesus, standing in the midst of His Church forever, saying, *"Go ... lo, I am with you."* Suppose Jesus said that to you personally – would you take more notice of it? Just imagine you had a vision of the Lord in your church, like John experienced on Patmos ... or Jesus spoke to everybody, saying, *"Go into all the world and preach the Gospel to every creature ... and these sings will follow those who believe"* – what would you do? Would you continue living with a business-as-usual attitude? Or would you press on more urgently to witness for Christ?

If anyone wonders whether the Great Commission is "relevant" today, they may as well ask if plowing and harvesting are releva-nt ... or if getting out of bed is! "Relevant" is not the word. The task is urgent. It is sup-posed to be our existence! The name "Chris-tian" devel-oped because it easily identified believers – they were the people who always talked about Christ. The Christian's business is not busyness, but witness. Witnessing is the commerce of the people of the King-dom of God.

The written commands of Christ in Scripture are just as immediate as if He had spoken to us personally in a vision. The Great Commission is "our baby," and our work in this task is not optional. The Lord does not ask, "Would you mind helping Me? I would like to invite you." He says: *"You did not choose Me, but I chose you and appointed you that you should go and bear fruit, and that your fruit should remain."* Jesus was not talking about the call to salvation, but rather of the call to service. We do not serve at our discretion. The Great Commission is like a draft call-up, not a suggestion for our consideration. We are not to go for the sake of going, but for the sake of being sent by Jesus. In fact, Christ's command is much more than that – Jesus turns us into witnesses. He changes our nature by His Spirit within us. He did not tell say, "Go witness" – He said, *"Be witnesses!"* It was a creative word. He chose **you** and then made **you** a light-bearer.

Today's Scripture

If then your whole body is full of light, having no part dark, the whole body will be full of light, as when the bright shining lamp gives you light.

(Luke 11:36)

Daily Power!

The Great Commission is like a draft call-up, not a suggestion for our consideration.

Today's Bible Reading

Genesis 1:1-13;
Mark 16:14-20;
Psalm 96:1-11;

Mark my Word
(for further study)

Matthew 28:16-20;
Luke 11:36;
John 15:16

You must be plugged in
before you can be switched on!

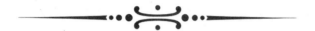

Jesus does not choose us because of what we are,
but because of what He makes of us.

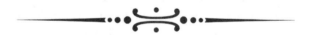

Why does God use one minister more than another?
When you have two stoves,
one hot and the other cold –
which one will you use to make a cup of tea?

Sin in the 21ˢᵗ Century

When looking for a cure for sin, we need to understand the disease. How does sin work in our world?

"Therefore, just as through one man sin entered the world, and death through sin, and thus death spread to all men, because all sinned … Nevertheless, death reigned from Adam to Moses, even over those who had not sinned according to the likeness of the transgression of Adam, who is a type of Him Who was to come … For if by the one man's offense death reigned through the one, much more those who receive abundance of grace and of the gift of righteousness will reign in life through the One, Jesus Christ."

Towards the end of the 19ᵗʰ century, humanists believed that Mankind had finally come of age. They said we were too mature to make war, and that scientific progress would guarantee a wonderful, peaceful future for the human race. At heart, human beings were essentially good. We had evolved into higher beings – emerging from the jungle by an evolutionary law that guarantees "the survival of the fittest."

However, this sort of optimism and faith in human progress has suffered a number of severe setbacks. In 1867, the Swedish chemist, Alfred Nobel, invented a new high explosive which he named "dynamite." He was convinced that dynamite had made war too horrible ever to happen again – but he quickly discovered that there was no shortage of buyers for his new explosive. He went on to make a vast fortune from his invention. At the end of his life, he left the profits to fund the five Nobel Prizes. These include the Nobel Peace Prize – paid for by the sale of high explosives! Just as the Bible says, *"And the way of peace they have not known."*

Man with all his ingenuity, cannot **make** peace, cannot **find** peace, cannot **know** peace … apart from that *"perfect peace"* which only comes from God through Christ Jesus: *"You will keep him in perfect peace whose mind is stayed on You because he trusts in You."* Let the peace of Christ envelope you today.

Today's Scripture

Peace I leave with you, My peace I give to you; not as the world gives do I give to you. Let not your heart be troubled, neither let it be afraid.
(John 14:27)

Daily Power!

My heart rejoices in God's promise: And the Word became flesh and dwelt among us, and we beheld His glory, the glory as of the only begotten of the Father, full of grace and truth.
(John 1:14)

Today's Bible Reading

Leviticus 24:1-23 through 25:1-46; Mark 10:13-31; Psalm 44:9-26; Proverbs 10:20-21

Mark my Word
(for further study)

Isaiah 26:3; John 1:14-17; 14:27; Romans 3:17

World-wide Sin

The First World War shattered the optimism of many people about human progress, but some tried to cling on by calling it "the war to end all wars." However, the 20th century went on to become the most murderous in history. Adolph Hitler even used the "law of the survival of the fittest" as a justification for the Holocaust – slaughtering those **he** considered unfit to survive.

"I will set Egyptians against Egyptians, everyone will fight against his brother, and everyone against his neighbor, city against city, kingdom against kingdom. The spirit of Egypt will fail in its midst, I will destroy their counsel."

The genocides and wars caused by people such as Hitler, Stalin and Pol Pot have killed off any optimism about human goodness or the future of the human race. And as optimism has shriveled up, it has left our culture with nothing to believe in.

"And you will hear of wars and rumors of wars … For nation will rise against nation, and kingdom against kingdom. And there will be famines, pestilences, and earthquakes in various places."

This is just a glimpse of how sin has done its devastating work in the world during the 20th century. But how does it affect us at the personal level? We must not only consider the cultural ramifications of world-wide sin … we must look into our own individual hearts, to see where sin has eroded basic human goodness – or the Christ-like nature we long to have – and learn how we can overcome – that is, root out – sin, and be washed clean and fresh, and have something good to contribute to our world!

Turning your life over to Jesus Christ – exchanging your sinful nature for His purity – is the best decision you can ever make! Now walk in the fullness of that decision today!

Today's Scripture

Wash me and I shall be whiter than snow.
(Psalm 51:7b)

Daily Power!

Exchanging my sinful nature for the purity of Jesus Christ is the best decision I will ever make.

Today's Bible Reading

Leviticus 25:47-54 through 27:1-13;
Mark 10:32-52;
Psalm 45:1-17;
Proverbs 10:22

Mark my Word
(for further study)

Psalm 51:1-19;
Isaiah 19:1-4;
Matthew 24:6-7

The World depends on us

People cannot see the light of invisible things until somebody else catches it and reflects it. The sun's rays would not be seen on Earth but they radiate the molecules of the atmosphere, the dust and moisture. The sun fills millions of miles with light … but there is no trace of it until it is reflected. The moon sails in invisible sunlight, and passes on enough light for us to find our way.

The apostle Paul talked about *"the King eternal, immortal, invisible."* The light of God is constant, brilliant. It is never intermittent. But who sees it? People walk in darkness. The stark fact is that the only light they will ever see is reflected light. Just as John was *"a burning and shining lamp,"* a witness to the light – so are believers. We are commanded to *"walk in the light,"* for if we don't, there will be no light. The world depends upon light reflectors – that's you and me! If our Gospel is hidden, it is hidden to those who are lost.

The Psalmist knew what it meant to *"walk in the light"*: *"For You have delivered my soul from death. Have You not kept my feet from falling, that I may walk before God in the light of the living?"* Jesus encouraged His disciples to persevere in "walking in the light": *"A little while longer the Light is with you. Walk while you have the Light, lest darkness overtake you; he who walks in darkness does not know where he is going. While you have the Light, believe in the Light, that you may become sons of Light."* Walking in the light is **active** – "waiting on God" is passive. To "wait on God" for His light to shine on us is an Old Testament concept. The last one who "waited" were the one hundred and twenty in the Upper Room. Now God waits on US. Green means "Go"! When the light turns green, you do not need a permit from the "Secretarial Department of Traffic and Transportation" – you just "Go"! Remember this command: *"But be doers of the Word, and not hearers only, deceiving yourselves."*

Today's Scripture

The Lord is not slack concerning His promise, as some count slackness, but is longsuffering toward us, not willing that any should perish but that all should come to repentance.
(II Peter 3:9)

Daily Power!

Lord, make me like John the Baptist – to be a constant, burning lamp, a shining witness to those who walk in darkness.

Today's Bible Reading:

*Leviticus 27:14-34 through Numbers 1:1-54;
Mark 11:1-25;
Psalm 46:1-11;
Proverbs 10:23*

Mark my Word
(for further study)

*Psalm 56:13;
John 12:35-36;
II Corinthians 4:3-6;
I Timothy 1:7;
James 1:22;
II Peter 3:9;
I John 1:7*

4

Today's Scripture

In Him was life, and the life was the light of men.
(John 1:4)

Daily Power!

I choose to have an open face to the world, so that people may see the glory of God in me.

Today's Bible Reading

Numbers 2:1-34
through 3:1-51;
Mark 11:27-33
through 12:1-17;
Psalm 47:1-9;
Proverbs 10:24-25

Mark my Word
(for further study)

Exodus 34:35;
Malachi 4:2;
John 1:1-4;
II Corinthians 3:13;
James 1:17

In Exodus and II Corinthians, we learned that the face of Moses shone with the glory of God, but he veiled his face. The reason he veiled it was not humility (humble as he was) – it was because the glory would fade, and he knew it would be a bad thing if the superstitious people of Israel saw the glory disappearing. They would draw wrong conclusions from the diminishing effect. So he veiled his face altogether so that they would not know whether his face was shining or not whenever God gave Him audience. *"But whenever Moses went in before the Lord to speak with Him, he would take the veil off until he came out; and he would come out and speak to the children of Israel whatever he had been commanded. And whenever the children of Israel saw the face of Moses, that the skin of Moses' face shone, then Moses would put the veil on his face again, until he went in to speak with Him … Unlike Moses, who put a veil over his face so that the children of Israel could not look steadily at the end of what was passing away."*

Paul's point is that the light of God – His glory – in the Christian age does not fade. It is permanent. We can have an open face to the world, so that people may see the glory of God in us.

James makes a similar statement: *"Every good gift and perfect gift is from above, and comes down from the Father of lights, with Whom there is no variation or shadow of turning."* As the New International Version puts it, God *"does not change like shifting shadows."* The sun causes a shadow as it turns, and the shadow moves. You see that on a sundial, and that is how we know the time. When there is no shadow, the sun is directly overhead at its zenith. In fact, God never casts a shadow at all, because He is always at the zenith. And He never shifts from that perfect position. The light of God is ceaseless, not temporary, and always fully on. *"But to you who fear My Name, the Sun of Righteousness shall rise with healing in His wings."*

The Power of the Blood

There is power and redemption for everyone in the Blood of Jesus Christ. A Buddhist told me that she could not understand how that could be. "Maybe," she said, "one man could die for a hundred, or at most, for a thousand … but never for all Mankind."

Not only Buddhists, but people of many religions find the teaching of forgiveness through the Blood of Jesus revolutionary. People generally expect to pay for their sins, either now or in some other existence. The Christian revelation is the glorious fact that **Jesus has paid it all.** Our doubts are traitors when they prevent us from proving the power of Christ's cleansing Blood.

"I have been crucified with Christ; it is no longer I who live, but Christ lives in me; and the life which I now live in the flesh I live by faith in the Son of God, Who loved me and gave Himself for me. I do not set aside the grace of God, for if righteousness comes through the law, then Christ died in vain."

"Therefore let it be known to you, brethren, that through this Man [Jesus] *is preached to you the forgiveness of sins,"* announced the apostle Paul. True forgiveness is as substantial as the Cross on which Christ bought it. None of us can understand forgiveness unless we're taught by experience. If the joy of it could be communicated, some would consider it too wonderful to be true. You can be assured, however, that divine forgiveness is not a fairy tale or wish fulfillment. It rests on a rock-solid foundation, on the historic fact of Jesus Christ's redemptive sacrifice. He suffered *"the just for the unjust, that He might bring us to God."* The Cross was no fiction. Real Blood fell on real ground. And this real Blood brings real cleansing to real sinners – and for you and me! – and does much more besides.

Today's Scripture

God demonstrates His own love toward us, in that while we were still sinners, Christ died for us.
(Romans 5:9)

Daily Power!

Because there is power and redemption for everyone in the Blood of Jesus Christ ... there is power and redemption for me in the Blood of Jesus Christ!

Today's Bible Reading

Numbers 4:1-49 through 5:1-31; Mark 12:18-37; Psalm 48:1-14; Proverbs 10:26

Mark my Word
(for further study)

Acts 13:38; Romans 5:9; Galatians 2:20-21; I Peter 3:18

Today's Scripture

By this we know that we know Him, if we keep His commandments.
(I John 2:3)

Daily Power!

My Heavenly inheritance has been guaranteed by the Holy Spirit of God.

Today's Bible Reading

Numbers 6:1-27
through 7:1-89;
Mark 12:38-44
through 13:1-13;
Psalms 49:1-20;
Proverbs 10:27-28

Mark my Word
(for further study)

Matthew 11:25;
Acts 2:36; 15:8; 17:31;
Ephesians 1:13-14; 4:30;
I John 2:3; 5:20

Ringing Confidence

The whole New Testament rings with confidence. Peter spoke positively when preaching in Jerusalem, *"Let all the house of Israel know assuredly, that God has made that same Jesus ... both Lord and Christ."* He later brought the news about the conversion of the Gentiles and said that *"God ... acknowledged them by giving them the Holy Spirit."* The Ephesians received the *"earnest"* (guarantee) of their spiritual inheritance and were *"sealed"* with the Holy Spirit. What a contrast to nervous indecision! The Corinthians were told: *"Now we have received, not the spirit of the world, but the Spirit Who is from God, that we might know the things that have been freely given to us by God."*

Any doctrine which leaves you guessing about your soul's salvation is completely out of harmony with the New Testament. Paul told the skeptics of Athens: *"[God] has appointed a day on which He will judge the world in righteousness by the Man Who He has ordained. He has given assurance of this to all by raising [Jesus] from the dead."* You do not have to guard your salvation as if it would disappear if you were careless. The Lord preserves your soul! The only one who wants you to doubt your salvation is ... Satan himself, who stands to lose you from his evil grip!

If you want even more proof, read the epistles of John. In one short letter, he uses two Greek verbs normally translated "know" forty-two times, like this: *"Now by this we **know** that we **know** Him, if we keep His commandments ... By this we **know** that we are in Him ... And we **know** that the Son of God has come and has given us an understanding, that we may **know** Him Who is true; and we are in Him Who is true, in His Son Jesus Christ. This is the true God and eternal life."*

This does not make Christians "know-it-alls." Salvation does not depend on your intelligence or analysis of abstract theological concepts. In fact, Jesus rejoices because He can say to His Father in Heaven, *"I thank You, Father, Lord of Heaven and Earth, that You have hidden these things from the wise and prudent and have revealed them to babes."* God has revealed these things to you!

The Forerunner

The crowds had more than once wanted Jesus to be King and conquer the much-hated Roman armies of occupation in the land of the Jews, but He refused. His servants did not fight to make Him an earthly Lord – He had a new way. Nailed and helpless, Jesus conquered the Roman commander in charge of the squad of soldiers assigned to carry out executions. Within three hundred years, Rome itself had been conquered – not by the jackbooted feet of military forces – but by the bleeding feet of this Man hanging there. The last pagan emperor, Julian, tried to restore the old worship of the gods, but the tides released by Christ's death were too powerful; Julian cried out in agony, "Oh Galilean, You have conquered!" The Cross stands fast, an *"anchor of the soul."* This figure of speech is found in Hebrews: *"This* [hope] *we have as an anchor of the soul, both sure and steadfast, and which enters the Presence* [behind] *the veil, where the Forerunner has entered for us,* [even] *Jesus."*

There is a seagoing picture from those ancient days. A ship comes into harbor, but cannot draw too near the shore in the darkness. So a sailor – called the "forerunner" – gets into a boat with an anchor and a line connecting ship and anchor. As he rows, the line linking anchor and ship is played out. Eventually, the forerunner's boat reaches the shore, and the seaman secures the anchor on land. In the morning, the ship needs no sails. The crew of the ship begins to wind in the anchor cable. However, it is not the anchor which moves but the ship. Slowly the vessel is winched towards the shore.

Your "Forerunner" is Jesus, Who has entered through the veil and made fast your anchor. Your salvation is secure like the anchor ashore whom the crew cannot see. Christ is no longer visible to you ... He is "ashore" in glory, and **you are attached, by faith, to glory by Him.** Day by day, the cable is shortening and pulling you nearer and nearer to your Forerunner. Eventually you will reach Heaven's shore ... and what will you see? Your Forerunner waiting to greet you, because where He is, there you may also be. Faith links you already and will bring you to Him at last. **That faith is your assurance.**

Today's Scripture

This hope we have as an anchor of the soul, both sure and steadfast, and which enters the Presence behind the veil.
(Hebrews 6:19)

Daily Power!

To "see and believe" means to see Jesus tasting death for every man ... and for me.

Today's Bible Reading

Numbers 8:1-26 through 9:1-23; Mark 13:14-37; Psalm 50:1-23; Proverbs 10:29-30

Mark my Word
(for further study)

John 14:3; Hebrews 6:19-20

Strategic Weaponry

Christians have a world to reclaim and regain for God. The enemy has brought about vast destruction, death and wickedness. Prayer opens up God's Armory with its superior weapons. If we think we do not need to pray, we do not know what we are up against! If we think we can manage on our own achievements, we simply make ourselves the devil's laughing stock. **Prayerless means defenseless.** Cleverness and science are a feather duster against a tank. The limitless greatness of the Cross is needed against the cosmic evil.

Prayer and intercession cast out the entrenched enemy, violate his borders, and retake lost territory. The devil hates this kind of prayer. Praying is not "meditative, retiring breathing" … "the still dews of quietness till all our strivings cease" (from the hymn, "Dear Lord and Father of Mankind," by J.G. Whittier). It is Heaven's militancy! It is not a muttered litany, but a high "C" soul-shriek! Prayer is an aggressive multi-purpose weapon put in our hands by God to overcome every kind of Satanic resistance. The man who prays overleaps human limits. Believers are authorized to go to the counter of Heaven's Supply Store for superhuman resources.

"God is strong, and He wants you strong. So take everything the Master has set out for you, well-made weapons of the best materials. And put them to use so you will be able to stand up to everything the Devil throws your way. This is no afternoon athletic contest that we'll walk away from and forget about in a couple of hours. This is for keeps, a life-or-death fight to the finish against the Devil and all his angels … Pray long and hard."

The mental image here is a far cry from the old man with meekly folded hands – it's much more like seeing **warrior** who is well armed and ready for combat! Picture yourself that way today … well-armed, equipped and ready to do battle in the Name of the Lord!

Today's Scripture

*And when you pray, do not use vain repetitions as the heathen do. For they think they will be heard for their many words. Therefore do not be like them. **For your Father knows the things you have need of before you ask Him.***

(Matthew 6:7-8; emphasis added)

Daily Power!

"The man who prays overleaps human limits" – that's me! "Believers are authorized to go to the counter of Heaven's Supply Store for superhuman resources" – that's my right!

Today's Bible Reading

Numbers 10:1-36 through 11:1-23; Mark 14:1-21; Psalm 51:1-19; Proverbs 10:31-32

Mark my Word
(for further study)

Matthew 6:1-15; Ephesians 6:10-13, 18 (the Message)

The new and living Way

The coming of Christ was the beginning of the end for the devil. The spiritual advance goes on today. The armies of God form a new race of men and women – a holy nation, born-again, presenting the Word of God with faith and power: *"Be prepared. You're up against far more than you can handle on your own. Take all the help you can get, every weapon God has issued, so that when it's all over but the shouting you'll still be on your feet. Truth, righteousness, peace, faith, and salvation are more than words. Learn how to apply them. You'll need them throughout your life. God's Word is an* **indispensable** *weapon. In the same way, prayer is essential in this ongoing warfare. Pray long and hard. Pray for your brothers and sisters. Keep your eyes open. Keep each other's spirits up so that no one falls behind or drops out."*

We have new access to God, a new method of operation and new authority *"by a new a living way"* through Christ Jesus! Victory is assured! *"The creation itself also will be delivered from the bondage of corruption into the glorious liberty of the children of God ... For we are saved in this hope."* Why live as if we were not on speaking terms with the Lord? He dwells with us. We are not mere neighbors, living with a brick wall between us. The Lord has broken down the middle wall. We have been *"brought near by the Blood of Christ."* The Christian life means "life with God," with everything centered on Him, God-oriented. The Holy Spirit gives us *"utterance"* to get through to God.

Christ's model prayer ends with: *"For Yours is the Kingdom and the power and the glory."* God's is the power – ours is the prayer. Prayer is necessary, not just "nice" – it is a vital part of the equation. Ezekiel the prophet pictures the currents of the Spirit as waters to swim in. The Lord provides the waters, but you do the swimming. Without prayer, you are not "in the swim" at all! So go ahead and jump in today ... the water is flowing ... and the answers from Heaven are on the way!

Today's Scripture

And they overcame him by the Blood of the Lamb, and by the word of their testimony, and they did not love their lives to the death.
(Revelation 12:11)

Daily Power!

I am a member of the army of God, part of a new race of men and women – a holy nation, born-again, presenting the Word of God with faith and power.

Today's Bible Reading

Numbers 11:24-35 through 13:1-33;
Mark 14:22-52;
Psalm 52:1-9;
Proverbs 11:1-3

Mark my Word
(for further study)

Ezekiel 47;
Matthew 6:13;
Acts 2:4;
Romans 8:21, 24;
Ephesians 2:13; 6:13-18
(the Message);
Hebrews 10:10

10

The Climax of Time

Christ's coming is the climax of all time. Historians have said they find no pattern in the events of the past … but there is. The true way to see history is through the Bible. It points to a unifying plan, which will bring everything together and make sense of it all. Christ is returning!

The very moment Jesus left the Earth, God sent even angelic messengers urgently to reassure and impress upon His followers that He had not gone for good. *"This same Jesus, Who has been taken from you into Heaven, will come back, in the same way you have seen Him go into Heaven."* That promise chimes like a glockenspiel of bells throughout Scriptures, and has rung in the Christian church for twenty centuries. The apostle Paul described what being a Christian meant, saying it was *"to wait for God's Son from Heaven, Whom He raised from the dead."*

Starting at the beginning of the New Testament, we find that the first three books – the Gospels of Matthew, Mark and Luke – point to Christ's coming and His Kingdom. It is emphasized in stories and plain teaching, including whole chapters – Matthew 24 through 26, Luke 21, Mark 13. Christ taught us to pray about it in His famous "Sermon on the Mount": *"Thy Kingdom come, Thy will be done on Earth as it is in Heaven."* The fifth Christian book, Acts, telling us how Christianity spread, includes sermons by apostles in which they preached the truth of Christ's return.

These are more than just dry data from an old book. These are **true signs** that not only did He come the first time as the Book said He would … but **Christ will come again, just as He said!** What a tremendous promise that is for you and me!

Today's Scripture

Then they will see the Son of Man coming in a cloud with power and great glory. Now when these things begin to happen, look up and lift up your heads, because your Redemption draws near.

(Luke 21:27-28)

Daily Power!

With great joy do I await Your Second Coming, Lord Jesus!

Today's Bible Reading

Numbers 14:1-45 through 15:1-16;
Mark 14:53-72;
Psalm 53:1-6;
Proverbs 11:4

Mark my Word
(for further study)

Matthew 6:7-15;
Luke 21:27-28;
Acts 1:11;
I Thessalonians 1:10

Bought back

The Bible speaks of our being *"redeemed with the precious Blood of Christ,"* which means that we were "bought back" by Jesus. By following Satan and sin, Man sold himself to the devil and had to be redeemed. When Jesus paid for our redemption with His precious Blood, does that mean that the Blood was paid to Satan? No, definitely not!

The price for our salvation was paid into the Court of God's Justice, as Hebrews 9 indicates:

"And according to the law almost all things are purified with blood, and without shedding of blood there is no remission. Therefore it was necessary that the copies of the things in the Heavens should be purified with these, but the Heavenly things themselves with better sacrifices than these. For Christ has not entered the Holy Places made with hands, which are copies of the true, but into Heaven itself, now to appear in the presence of God for us; not that He should offer Himself often, as the high priest enters the Most Holy Place every year with blood of another – He then would have had to suffer often since the foundation of the world; but now, once at the end of the ages. He has appeared to put away sin by the sacrifice of Himself. And as it is appointed for men to die once, but after this the Judgment, so Christ was offered once to bear the sins of many. To those who eagerly wait for Him, He will appear a second time, apart from sin, for salvation."

The Lord paid the full price. The divine currency for our salvation was not in His pocket, but flowed in His veins! There was no question of negotiation, discount, rebate, or bargaining! Jesus gave the last drop of His heart's Blood for us. Therefore our salvation cannot be challenged by anyone on Earth, in Heaven or under the Earth, not in time nor in eternity! Because of the Blood of Jesus, **You are irrevocably saved!** Praise Him for that today!

Today's Scripture

And as it is appointed for men to die once, but after this the judgment; so Christ was offered once to bear the sins of many. To those who eagerly wait for Him, He will appear a second time, apart from sin, for salvation.
(Hebrews 9:27-28)

Daily Power!

He paid a debt He did not owe, I owed a debt I could not pay.

Today's Bible Reading

Numbers 15:17-41 through 16:1-40;
Mark 15:1-47;
Psalm 54:1-7;
Proverbs 11:5-6

Mark my Word
(for further study)

Hebrews 9:16-28;
I Peter 1:18-19

MARCH

12

Today's Scripture

But now in Christ Jesus you who once were far off have been brought near by the Blood of Christ.

(Ephesians 2:13)

Daily Power!

I bear the Blood-mark of Jesus Christ with both pride and humility.

Today's Bible Reading

Numbers 16:41-50 through 18:1-32; Mark 16:1-20; Psalm 55:1-23; Proverbs 11:7

Mark my Word
(for further study)

Leviticus 8:23; Ephesians 2:13

The Mark of the Blood

I can explain one of the most thrilling, often overlooked truths about the Blood of Jesus. It marks those who trust in Jesus Christ, and distinguishes them from everybody else. The first mark is **internal**, the sign of inner cleansing. When a sinner calls on the Name of the Lord to be saved, and takes Jesus Christ personally as his Savior, the Blood of Jesus does a deep and thorough work. We are clean in soul and mind, conscious, subconscious or unconscious. Every evil image is thrown down. No more nightmares about Hell and judgment, but divine visions and dreams. It is wonderful to dream about Jesus! Our past has gone and God remembers it no more. There is no need to keep digging it up and asking again for forgiveness. God never recalls it. This, however, does not mean that we are already "spiritually perfected Christians." As we feed on the Word of God, we will be led by the Holy Spirit from dimension to dimension.

The next mark is **external**. I can explain it through the Bible – it was foreshadowed in the Old Testament and fulfilled in the New Testament. In the Old Testament we read: *"Moses slaughtered the ram and took some of its blood and put it on the lobe of Aaron's right ear, on the thumb of his right hand and on the big toe of his right foot."* This is the New Testament fulfillment: after Jesus has cleansed us inwardly from all our sins by His Blood, an outward mark is impressed upon us. Just as there was one drop of blood upon the right ear, on the thumb and on the big toe, so the born-again believer is blood-marked. Of course, this is not a sign on our physical body, but **one which both Heaven and Hell can discern**. When God's people walk through the streets, the demons can spot them. I imagine one evil spirit calling to another, "Can you see over there? That one has the Blood-mark of Jesus on his ear, toe and thumb. He belongs to Jesus Christ! Don't try to touch him – it's too dangerous. Dare to touch him … or you will have a legion of angels to contend with!" You are marked by the Blood of Jesus Christ!

"Typical Revival"

The 18th century saw the birth of what has been called "evangelical Christianity," although evangelical truths have always been woven into the tapestry of Christian faith. Evangelicalism arrived on the religious scene with extraordinary marks, and for nearly two centuries, powerful emotional and physical occurrences – such as prostration, anguish of soul, and outcries – were part of the responses that accompanied the new evangelism. Special times such as these are identified as "revival."

Today, revivals are being idealized. They are considered to be "God, and the Christian faith, at their peak." A revival atmosphere, in the classic sense, is sought as the sign of a God-blessed Church. Some preachers minister as "revivalists" – itinerants fostering revival-type reactions, warmth and fire, in churches. A revival, such as is recorded in the work of Wesley, is taken as the answer to the ancient cry of the soul for God to come forth from the *"hiding places of His power."* Israel cried out for God to display His reality by destroying their enemies … but now Christians cry out for God to draw them to Himself. The motivation is different – but "revival" is the desired response.

Did you know the word "revival" does not appear in the Bible? There are numerous references to people who are "revived" from illness or death, or when a nation's broken spirit was "revived" by new trust in God … but the term "revival" is a man-made expression. Perhaps we put too much emphasis on our constructions … and not enough trust in God and His mercy?

The accounts of the times of Wesley, Whitefield, Edwards, Evans, and others fill many people with longing. Stories of these times are told repeatedly today, and prayer has increased for a true manifestation of divine power. However, despite intercession, the decades of the 20th century have seemed increasingly different from the revival times of the 19th century – in Western countries, at least. The reason why "revival tarries" is usually held to be the deficient lives of Christians. What an indictment! We want to be God's instruments of bringing revival to this world!

Today's Scripture

I indeed baptize you with water unto repentance, but He Who is coming after me is mightier than I, Whose sandals I am not worthy to carry. He will baptize you with the Holy Spirit and fire.
(Matthew 3:11)

Daily Power!

O Lord, send Your revival … and start the work in me.

Today's Bible Reading

Numbers 19:1-22 through 20:1-29; Luke 1:1-25; Psalm 56:1-13; Proverbs 11:8

Mark my Word
(for further study)

Matthew 3:1-17

14

All Prayer

Turn over each page of the New Testament and mark every prayer reference ... then you will see how prayer is emphasized. In the first Gospel alone, there are forty-one references, and two hundred thirty throughout the New Testament, some of them extensive, with ten different words for prayer. We read about *"praying always with **all** prayer."* Different methods, forms, moods – all of them available for Man to use against the devil.

"Now it came to pass, as He was praying in a certain place, when He ceased, that one of His disciples said to Him, 'Lord, teach us to pray, as John also taught his disciples.' "So He said, 'When you pray, say: Our Father in Heaven, hallowed be Your Name. Your Kingdom come, Your will be done on Earth as it is in Heaven. Give us day by day our daily bread. And forgive us our sins, for we also forgive everyone who is indebted to us. And do not lead us into temptation, but deliver us from the evil one.'"

Some texts use one special word – like a hammer to drive the nail in deeply – the adverb *"without ceasing"* (in Greek: ektenes, adialeiptos), which comes only six times in Scripture and only about prayer, as if this were the one thing never to let up:

"Prayer was made without ceasing of the church unto God for him" ... *"Without ceasing I make mention of you always in my prayers"* ... *"We give thanks to God always for you all, making mention of you in our prayers, remembering without ceasing your work of faith"* ... *"We also thank God without ceasing"* ... *"Pray without ceasing."*

Jesus Himself taught that *"men always ought to pray and not lose heart."* That becomes His charge to you today! Pray ... and don't lose heart!

Today's Scripture

Pray without ceasing.
(I Thessalonians 5:17)

Daily Power!

I am charged by Jesus Christ Himself to always pray and never to lose heart.

Today's Bible Reading

Numbers 21:1-35
through 22:1-20;
Luke 1:26-56;
Psalm 57:1-11;
Proverbs 11:9-11

Mark my Word
(for further study)

Luke 11:1-4; 18:1;
Acts 12:5;
Romans 1:9;
Ephesians 6:18;
I Thessalonians 2:13;
5:17;
II Timothy 1:3

Equipped with Power

Jesus never sent His disciples out without equipping them with **power**: *"And Jesus came and spoke to them, saying, 'All **authority** [power] has been given to Me in Heaven and on Earth. Go therefore and make disciples of all the nations, baptizing them in the Name of the Father and of the Son and of the Holy Spirit, teaching them to observe all things that I have commanded you; and lo, I am with you always, even to the end of the age.' Amen."* ... *"And He said to them, 'Go into all the world and preach the Gospel to every creature. He who believes and is baptized will be saved; but he who does not believe will be condemned. And these signs will follow those who believe: in My Name they will cast out demons; they will speak with new tongues; they will take up serpents, and if they drink anything deadly, it will by no means hurt them; they will lay hands on the sick, and they will recover.'"*

The "signs" were **power signs**. We are commissioned to only one kind of ministry: **a power-sign Gospel!** *"Jesus came and stood in the midst of them, and said to them, 'Peace be with you.' When He had said this, He showed them His hands and His side. Then the disciples were glad when they saw the Lord. So Jesus said to them again, 'Peace to you! As the Father has sent Me, I also send you.' And when He had said this, He breathed on them, and said to them, 'Receive the Holy Spirit.'"*

The Father sent His Son in the power of the Holy Spirit ... and Christ never anticipated that we would go to the nations with anything less! A power ministry is not merely a "possibility" – it is the **only one** Jesus envisioned! It is normal experience for those who go in Christ's Name ... by definition. It is our ministry, together, today!

Today's Scripture

*"As the Father has sent Me, I also send you."
And when He had said this, He breathed on them, and said to them, "Receive the Holy Spirit."*
(John 20:21-22)

Daily Power!

*The precious Holy Spirit is as near my next breath – and I **know** He is breathing on me.*

Today's Bible Reading

*Numbers 22:21-41
through 23:1-30;
Luke 1:57-80;
Psalm 58:1-11;
Proverbs 11:12-13*

Mark my Word
(for further study)

*Matthew 28:18-20;
Mark 16:15-18;
John 20:21-23*

MARCH

16

Pentecost gave us Keys

The Christian age is the power age. In the Old Testament, we read of the God of wonders performing marvels at the Red Sea, and under Elijah and Elisha. But not much more stands out in the thirty-nine books of the Old Testament … except as Holy Spirit power fell on occasion upon a few individuals and the prophets. Then Jesus gave Peter the keys of the Kingdom of Heaven! Those keys are not jangling from Peter's belt at his post beside the Pearly Gates – the keys are the Gospel of Christ crucified and the Holy Spirit. He opened the Kingdom … and today we have the same keys. Peter saw what nobody on Earth had ever seen: three thousand people in one day turning in repentance and being born again by the Holy Spirit. Then the apostles went out and put the power of those keys to the test. The dead were raised, the deaf, blind and crippled restored to full health, multitudes turned to Christ and a new thing arose in the world: the Church of Jesus Christ.

Pentecost is the giving of the Holy Spirit to the world in manifest form. It is God at work in the physical and material world. We only know of one form of the Spirit, and that is in manifestation. There is no "resting" Spirit, no Spirit in quiescence. The essence of Pentecost is the moving of the Spirit – the mighty wind from Heaven and the flaming tongues of fire. The Holy Spirit is only known at work. There is no Spirit without movement, any more than there is a wind without movement. A wind that doesn't blow isn't a wind at all. Wind is never quiet, or just an atmosphere. The Holy Spirit is a gale, and nobody can stand still in a force-eight gale and talk politely about the atmosphere! Where the Spirit is there is action, the miraculous – God in operation!

Any talk of "miracles as belonging to the past" denies the very purpose and nature of the Gospel, as well as the character of the Holy Spirit. The Spirit is sent to work in this world. Deny the miraculous, the power of the Holy Spirit – and you deny what Christianity is supposed to be: God's power in action in the present age of living men and women. That makes this age the Christian age. Perhaps we ought to call this the Holy Spirit age – let us live in this age to the fullest!

Today's Scripture

And I will give you the keys of the Kingdom of Heaven, and whatever you bind on Earth will be bound in Heaven, and whatever you loose on Earth will be loosed in Heaven.

(Matthew 16:19)

Daily Power!

Thank You, Father, for your Holy Spirit's power at work in my life today!

Today's Bible Reading

Numbers 24:1-25 through 25:1-18; Luke 2:1-35; Psalm 59:1-17; Proverbs 11:14

Mark my Word
(for further study)

Matthew 16:19

God's own Banner and Bow

When Noah saw the Earth desolated by the Flood, he must have been traumatized. Afterwards, whenever the skies grew dark overhead, he would need reassurance. God said, *"I have set My rainbow in the clouds, and it will be the sign of the covenant between me and the Earth."* The rainbow is the flag of God, the seven-colored royal standard. No icon, no regimental colors and no imperial symbol could match that!

"O Lord my God, in You I put my trust … My defense is of God, Who saves the upright in heart. God is a just Judge, and God is angry with the wicked every day. If He does not turn back, He will sharpen His sword, He bends His bow and makes it ready; He also prepares for Himself instruments of death, He makes His arrows into fiery shafts … I will praise the Lord according to His righteousness, and will sing praise to the Name of the Lord Most High."

The word "bow" in Genesis 9:13 (where it is translated "rainbow") is the same Hebrew word as for a bow which is used to shoot arrows – a weapon of war … but what a weapon, spanning the whole horizon! What mighty arrows it must shoot when God goes into battle against the devil! *"The Lord will march out like a mighty Man, like a Warrior He will stir up His zeal; with a shout He will raise the battle cry and will triumph over His enemies."*

The rainbow is not a mere phenomenon of natural beauty, but a divine reminder of God's archery. The divine graphics span the whole Bible, for when we reach the book of Revelation, we read. *"A rainbow … encircled the throne … From the throne came flashes of lightning."* God's mighty arrows. No wind can blow a rainbow away and no devil can switch it off. The battle truly belongs to the Lord. You may suffer life's storms, when ominous blackness fills your skies, but that arching splendour of prismatic color in the rain cloud, seen with your mortal eyes, is the objective standard of God to reassure you. It is a sign of God's love bent to the world and to you. Receive His love today!

Today's Scripture

For the weapons of our warfare are not carnal but mighty in God for pulling down strongholds.
(II Corinthians 10:4)

Daily Power!

The rainbow is far more than a trick of light and water – it truly is God's promise.

Today's Bible Reading

Numbers 26:1-51;
Luke 2:36-52;
Psalm 60:1-12;
Proverbs 11:15

Mark my Word
(for further study)

Genesis 8:13;
Psalm 7:1-17;
Isaiah 42:13;
Revelation 4:3-5

18

Today's Scripture

The Spirit Himself bears witness with our spirit that we are children of God.

(Romans 8:16)

Daily Power!

What a privilege it is to call my wonderful Heavenly Father, "Daddy!"

Today's Bible Reading

*Numbers 26:52-65 through 28:1-15;
Luke 3:1-22;
Psalm 61:1-8;
Proverbs 11:16-17*

Mark my Word
(for further study)

*Matthew 22:29;
Romans 8:16;
Galatians 4:3-7;
II Peter 1:4*

The Spirit of God

After you have believed what the Word of God says about the certainty of your salvation through Jesus Christ – and **only after** – the Holy Spirit becomes active in your life: *"It is the Spirit Himself bearing witness with our spirit that we are children of God."* Note that the Bible uses the word "spirit" twice, once with a capital letter – denoting God's Spirit – and once with a small letter – denoting the human spirit. God's Spirit witnesses to your human spirit that you **are** a child of God. You received a divine nature, and your new heart tells you God is your Father. Then you have a close relationship with Him and cry, *"Abba, Father!"* This settles the matter completely, because then even your feelings will adjust to the testimony of the Holy Spirit within you.

"When the fullness of time had come, God sent forth His Son, born of a woman, born under the Law, to redeem those who were under the Law, that we might receive the adoption as sons. And because you are sons, God has sent forth the Spirit of His Son into your hearts, crying out, 'Abba, Father!' Therefore you are no longer a slave but a son, and if a son, then an heir of God through Christ."

The key is that after repentance and faith, you **believe** the Word of God ... or you can never even start being sure of your salvation. It says that God calls you His child – so you can be certain He is your Father ... and all other believers are your brothers and sisters. This puts the whole Family of God together, without distinction or discrimination by race, or wisdom, or age, or education, on Earth or in Heaven. Glory be to God!

If people try to show off their learning by posing weighty problems, supposedly to display their "intellectual honesty," Jesus simply says they *"are mistaken, not knowing the Scriptures nor the power of God."* Logic cannot possibly embrace the dimension of eternal salvation which comes from the mind and heart of God. You cannot put God in a test tube. Let the Word of God be your Guide today.

Scripture Dynamite

What did Jesus preach? Jesus talked about Himself. On the Emmaus road, walking with Cleopas and a friend, He explained to them, going throughout the Scriptures, the *"things concerning Himself"* – all His teaching goes back to Himself. For example, after He had left Nazareth and begun His wonderful ministry, the Gospel of Luke tells us that Jesus returned one day and went into the synagogue. For twenty years He had attended that very synagogue faithfully every week. The custom was to allow men who were known to read the Scriptures, and perhaps comment on them afterward. Naturally, when Jesus was present at the synagogue again, He was invited to do this. The Gospel message was found in the Old Testament – in fact, the Old Testament is full of the Gospel! Luke tells us that Jesus read from Isaiah: *"The Spirit of the Lord is upon Me, because He has anointed Me to preach the Gospel to the poor, He has sent Me to heal the broken-hearted, to proclaim liberty to the captives and recovery of sight to the blind, to set at liberty those who are oppressed, to proclaim the acceptable year of the Lord."*

No doubt, many in the synagogue knew that passage by heart, for those words had been read for eight hundred years. The scroll of the Scriptures was handed back, the synagogue leader took it with great reverence, kissed it, and put it away, to be forgotten until the next week. But suddenly, that scroll seemed to become a stick of dynamite: the Word on the lips of Jesus produced effects alright – it awakened the drowsy congregation! He showed them that the Word was about Himself. There are seven distinct statements in that verse and they all apply to Him, as well as to the present. *"Today,"* He dared to announce, *"this Scripture is fulfilled in your hearing."* Thus He declared Himself to be the Anointed One – the Christ, the One to perform all those promised exploits. Proclaim liberty! Do not preach for effects, for pulpit display, or to charm, excite, or scare folk. Do not preach to calm people down. You can preach for all kinds of effects, but Jesus simply announced liberty. He proclaimed, that day in the synagogue, that the Jubilee had begun. He showed them what a true Jubilee would be: deliverance! It would be a Jubilee – not merely for Israel – but for the whole world. A Jubilee for you … and for those to whom you speak the Gospel!

Today's Scripture

And He began to say to them, "Today this Scripture is fulfilled in your hearing." So all bore witness to Him, and marveled at the gracious words which proceeded out of His mouth.
(Luke 4:21-22)

Daily Power!

The Gospel of Jesus Christ on our lips will produce spiritual dynamite.

Today's Bible Reading

*Numbers 28:16-31 through 29:1-40;
Luke 3:23-38;
Psalm 62:1-12;
Proverbs 11:18-19*

Mark my Word
(for further study)

*Isaiah 61:1-2;
Luke 4:18-22*

20

Yesterday, today, forever

Here is an example of Christ's consistency from Luke's Gospel, when Jesus raised a young man from the dead in the village of Nain, the son of a widow: *"And when He came near the gate of the city, a dead man was being carried out, the only son of his mother; and she was a widow ... When the Lord saw her, He had compassion on her and said to her, 'Do not weep.' Then He came and touched the open coffin, and those who carried him stood still. And He said, 'Young man, I say to you, arise.' So he who was dead sat up and began to speak. And He presented him to his mother."* We read that Jesus had compassion on the weeping mother. In the same region, the great prophets Elijah and Elisha had both also raised mothers' sons from the dead. That was eight hundred years before.

Now notice this: in each case, the Bible says that Elijah and Elisha gave the sons back to their mothers ... and **Jesus did exactly the same**. He raised the young man from death and gave him back to his mother. Christ knew the Scriptures, and it was His pointed way of showing what He had just done for this grieving mother, He had done long before for other mothers. It was He Who raised those two sons from death! Jesus had been around in Israel long before His birth in Bethlehem, and had worked – by His Holy Spirit – through Elijah and Elisha.

Eight centuries then made no difference to His power or compassion ... and two millennia since have made no difference to His power or compassion now! Generation after generation have experienced Christ's healing touch. We recognize His fingerprints, His typical way of working. He is like the noon-day sun and never switches off. His powerful sunlight kills the virus of evil.

Two millennia have passed since He left Earth and ascended to the Father ... but that makes no difference to His power or compassion in your life today or in mine! Our healing is based in His resurrection power! **He is alive!**

Today's Scripture

The Spirit of the Lord is upon Me because He has anointed Me to preach the Gospel to the poor; He has sent Me to heal the broken-hearted, to proclaim liberty to the captives and recovery of sight to the blind, to set at liberty those who are oppressed, to proclaim the acceptable year of the Lord.

(Luke 4:18-19)

Daily Power!

I yield myself to be the tool that God uses to show His compassion to all people.

Today's Bible Reading

Numbers 30:1-16
through 31:1-54;
Luke 4:1-30;
Psalm 63:1-11;
Proverbs 11:20-21

Mark my Word
(for further study)

I Kings 17:1-24;
II Kings 4:1-44;
Luke 4:18-19; 7:11-17

Allergic to God?

Sin causes a catastrophic breakdown in relationships. We can see this breakdown all around us: violence in the streets … child abuse … hatred between people of different races and nationalities … corruption … marriages that are wounded and killed by one or both partners. One Hollywood actress said, "I have found that divorce lawyers – not diamonds – are a girl's best friend."

The final casualty in this chain of breakdown is our relationship with God. Cut off from God, we feel the pain of separation from Him. For many people, life has no meaning or purpose. This is not how God planned it. He created us to live in a relationship of love with Him. But instead, we have run away and hidden from God, as if we were allergic to Him:

"Then the eyes of both of them were opened, and they knew that they were naked; and they sewed fig leaves together and made themselves coverings. And they heard the sound of the Lord God walking in the Garden in the cool of the day, and Adam and his wife hid themselves from the presence of the Lord God among the trees of the Garden."

Jesus put it like this: *"Light has come into the world, but men loved darkness instead of light."* Lost in the darkness, far from home, what hope is there for us? It is important to review these questions not only to see where God has brought us **from** – the hopeless, filthy depths of sin – and so we are better equipped to offer His light of hope and salvation to the world still lost in the darkness today.

"In Him was life, and the life was the light of men. And the light shines in the darkness and the darkness did not comprehend it."

Let the light of Christ Jesus fill your heart – and shine from you today!

Today's Scripture

Even the righteousness of God, through faith in Jesus Christ, to all and on all who believe.
(Romans 3:22a)

Daily Power!

I choose to remember where I came from — my former life of sin — so that I ever have a thankful heart that Christ Jesus saved me … and so I continue to offer God's light of hope and salvation to the world still lost in darkness.

Today's Bible Reading

Numbers 32:1-42 through 33:1-39;
Luke 4:31-44 through 5:1-11;
Psalm 64:1-10;
Proverbs 11:22

Mark my Word
(for further study)

Genesis 3:7-8;
John 1:4; 3:19;
Romans 3:22

How to rout Doubt

Paul's feelings in Corinth were of weakness and trembling, and even fear for his mortal life. Nevertheless he **knew** God was with him. He was often *"cast down,"* he said, and *"despaired even of life,"* but it left his assurance of hope absolutely unaffected. Do you know that the devil can bring on lying feelings? If he does not succeed in confusing you with lying words, he resorts to depressing your emotions. However, remember the Bible's warning that Satan is the father of lies – he is a master at the game. Some people feel saved one day and not the next, but the day after that it seems as if their salvation has come back. **All feelings!** If you do not believe Satan's lying words, do not believe the lying feelings he gives you either.

What should you do? The answer is: **Go to the Word of God. Find a Scripture like John 5:24 ... and read it over and over again!** The Word is your birth certificate. God says you are His child, you have eternal life, and that Word is never wrong. You will not be lost. You just believe it, and believe it you must!

A little boy had received Jesus as his Savior at Sunday School. His teacher had hammered John 5:24 into him, and he had underlined it in his New Testament. That night he got into bed, read his Bible, prayed and switched off the light. Then the devil came bringing doubts, suggesting that he was not saved. The boy quickly switched on the light and read John 5:24 again. He was happy that the Bible had not changed! It still said he **possessed** eternal life. Once more he switched off the light, and again doubt came back. This time, he said, it was as if it came from under his bed. Once more he switched on the light, and turning again to John 5:24, held his New Testament under the bed and said, "Look. devil, if you don't believe me, then read it for yourself: **I have passed from death to life.** I am a child of God!" In simple, child–like faith – accept that promise as yours today!

Today's Scripture

He who hears My Word and believes in Him Who sent Me has everlasting life, and shall not come into judgment, but has passed from death into life.

(John 5:24)

Daily Power!

I walk by faith, not by feelings.

Today's Bible Reading

Numbers 33:40-56 through 35:1-34; Luke 5:12-28; Psalm 65:1-13; Proverbs 11:23

Mark my Word
(for further study)

John 5:24; 8:44; I Corinthians 2:3; II Corinthians 1:8; 4:9

Jesus' Imperative

When Jesus said, *"You **must** be born again,"* it meant that He also had to say almost immediately, *"The Son of Man **must** be lifted up."* He used the same word, **must**. Our need becomes His need to meet our need.

Jesus lived under a constant sense of the imperative will of God. He **must** save because we need to be saved. He said, *"I have other sheep"* – sheep that **must** be saved. *"I **must** bring them also."*

"If a man has a hundred sheep, and one of them goes astray, does he not leave the ninety-nine and go to the mountains to seek the one that is straying? And if he should find it, assuredly, I say to you, he rejoices more over that sheep than over the ninety-nine that did not go astray. Even so it is not the will of your Father Who is in Heaven that one of these little ones should perish."

This revelation of God becomes our basis for both faith and evangelism. The God of the Bible – our Lord Jesus Christ, the changeless One – will never let us down. You and I go at His bidding with our hands in His … and we introduce Him to a weary world.

Jesus "infected" the apostle Peter with this urgent need to reach the lost: *"The Lord is not slack concerning His promise, as some count slackness, but is longsuffering toward us, not willing that any should perish but that all should come to repentance."*

Let me remind you that the initiative is not with us – it is with God. Behind everything is the moving Spirit of God. That being the case, we are either relevant … or irrelevant to what God is doing. Oh, let us strive to always be relevant to what God is doing in the world today!

Today's Scripture

And as Moses lifted up the serpent in the wilderness, even so must the Son of Man be lifted up, that whoever believes in Him should not perish but have eternal life.

(John 3:14-15)

Daily Power!

My Heavenly Father desires a true relationship with me, therefore He sent His Very Best that I might enter into that relationship with a pure heart.

Today's Bible Reading

Numbers 36:1-13 through Deuteronomy 1:1-46; Luke 5:29-39 through 6:1-11; Psalm 66:1-20; Proverbs 11:24-26

Mark my Word
(for further study)

Matthew 18:10-14; John 3:1-21; 10:7-18; II Peter 3:9

Our highest and noblest Task

Paul the apostle, persecuted for his Lord, was one day brought up from a foul-smelling dungeon under the king's palace, with his wrists sore because of the iron manacles, and appeared in court. He lifted his hands, fetters clinking, and preached Christ to the proud and noble assembly in their splendor of purple and gold. They were destined to be remembered – but only because Paul stood before them that day. Their prisoner – a little Roman Jew from Tarsus – immortalized **them**.

Claudias Lysias, the centurion … governor Felix … Ananias, the high priest … Tertullus the orator … Drusilla, wife of Felix … Procius Festus … King Agrippa and Queen Bernice – it sounds like the role-call of some high-society soirée. These names probably would not have survived into history but for Luke writing about them in telling of the trials of Paul and the acts of the Early Church. While Paul spoke, he was changing the future of Europe and the whole world. Smelling of the prison, Paul's great heart was breaking in compassion for them – kings, companions, courtiers, and all. He concluded his defense by saying, *"I pray God that not only you, but all that are listening to me today may become what I am, except for these chains."*

Today, we are called to address the "great and mighty" of our world. We reach the small and obscure because they are always more open to hear the loving truths of the Gospel. But we must also purpose to reach those in authority: *"I will speak of Your testimonies also before kings and will not be ashamed."* Boldness and obedience are keys to such witness: *"You will be brought before governors and kings for My sake, as a testimony to them and to the Gentiles. But when they deliver you up, do not worry about how or what you should speak. For it will be given to you in that hour what you should speak; for it is not you who speak, but the Spirit of your Father Who speaks in you."*

This is the lot of God's servants even today. Preaching the Gospel of Jesus Christ – and thus building His eternal Kingdom – is a higher and nobler task than any other. I invite you to join me in this splendid mission of the King of kings and the Lord of lords!

Today's Scripture

To open their eyes, in order to turn them from darkness to light, and from the power of Satan to God, that they may receive forgiveness of sins and an inheritance among those who are sanctified by faith in Me.
(Acts 26:18)

Daily Power!

I am dedicated to preaching the Gospel of Jesus Christ, and thus building His eternal Kingdom. This is a higher and nobler task than any other.

Today's Bible Reading

Deuteronomy 2:1-37 through 3:1-29;
Luke 6:12-38;
Psalm 67:1-7;
Proverbs 11:27

Mark my Word
(for further study)

Psalm 119:46;
Matthew 10:18-20;
Acts 26:1-32

John's Problem

John the Baptist had a similar problem to those of the prophets Jonah and Elijah: he preached the fire of judgment, saying, *"You brood of vipers! Who warned you to flee from the coming wrath? … The ax is already at the root of the trees, and every tree that does not produce good fruit will be cut down and thrown into the fire … His winnowing fork is in His hand to clear His threshing floor and to gather the wheat into His barn, but He will burn up the chaff with unquenchable fire."* That is so much like the preaching of the fiery Elijah that it sounds ironic when Luke adds, *"With many other words John exhorted the people and preached the Good News to them"*! "Hell fire" equals "Good News"?

John later saw Jesus at work and saw no flaming judgments fall. He sent to ask Jesus if he had identified the wrong man as Messiah. Jesus sent back the messengers to describe the mercies of God among the afflicted and dying, and to deliver a message: *"Blessed is the man who does not fall away on account of Me."*

How do you and I judge the man who rapes and murders children? Deserving of judgment … or of mercy? How do we act towards the prostitute who lures men into depravity and deadly diseases? Eligible for hell-fire to cleanse away her sin … or a helping hand extended to redeem? If it were up to us – human beings – we would have wiped out our entire species years ago! But God continually loves us human beings, and He pours out His compassion and mercy upon us generation after generation. It is He Who inspires the heart of the evangelist to shine the Good News into a dark and filthy world – and that is yours and mine!

MARCH

25

Today's Scripture

Jesus answered and said to them, "Go and tell John the things you have seen and heard: that the blind see, the lame walk, the lepers are cleansed, the deaf hear, the dead are raised, the poor have the Gospel preached to them. And blessed is he who is not offended because of Me."
(Luke 7:22-23)

Daily Power!

I want my life to be a representation of the merciful compassion which Christ exhibited so freely throughout His life, even to His death.

Today's Bible Reading

Deuteronomy 4:1-49;
Luke 6:39-49
through 7:1-10;
Psalm 68:1-18;
Proverbs 11:28

Mark my Word
(for further study)

Luke 3:7-18; 7:22-23

26

Increasing Faith

If we have no real faith, reading the Bible produces it. If we have some faith, we get more the same way. We don't acquire faith first and bring it to Scripture. Scripture encourages faith: *"Faith comes by hearing the Word of God."* Many who don't believe, don't read the Bible. They are sick … and leave the medicine with the bottle tightly corked. People without faith should be "warned" that if they open the Bible, they are likely to finish up as believers!

The Bible brings us to the Cross. People do not start moving mountains until they've been to Mount Calvary. They couldn't move even a molehill – or a mole. Real faith doesn't start at the university – but we'll have less if we go there without any! If we have not been to where Christ saves, not even a Doctor of Theology will do. The starting pistol is fired at the *"green hill far away outside the city wall."* From there, we tread on and on towards the mark of the high calling of God in Christ. Walking in doubt is like going back to a Victorian-age, London "pea-souper" fog. We need radar … and faith provides it in this world of uncertainty: *"The righteousness of God is revealed from faith to faith; as it is written, 'The just shall live by faith.'"* Believe God! It is Life's greatest adventure.

"And the apostles said to the Lord, 'Increase our faith.' So the Lord said, 'If you have faith as a mustard seed, you can say to this mulberry tree: Be pulled up by the roots and be planted in the sea, and it would obey you.'"

I want to offer knowledge and experience across the area of faith as widely as I can. Whether people are well along the road, or just beginning, or haven't even started … I want to come alongside them and share treasures with them I have collected over a lifetime. And as you grow in your walk with the Lord … I want you to go and do the same. Your faith is too precious to hide … **share** it as often as you can … and **show** it by the way you live today and every day.

Today's Scripture

I press toward the goal for the prize of the upward call of God in Christ Jesus.
(Philippians 3:14)

Daily Power!

Dear Lord, this is my prayer: give me opportunity today to share my faith for Your glory.

Today's Bible Reading

Deuteronomy 5:1-33 through 6:1-25;
Luke 7:11-35;
Psalm 68:19-35;
Proverbs 11:29-31

Mark my Word
(for further study)

Luke 17:5;
Romans 1:17; 10:17;
Philippians 3:14

The Secretary of the Trinity

I once heard someone say that the Holy Spirit is the "Secretary of the Trinity." When I thought about it, I had to agree. A secretary's work is to communicate the decisions of the Board to the people concerned. And now, after you have received Jesus as your Savior, the Holy Spirit immediately swings into action. A "registered letter" arrives, as it were, at the door of your heart with the something like the following message:

Dear _____ (put your own name here),

I have been advised by the Father and the Son to inform you that your sins are forgiven and blotted out; pursuant to Colossians 2:14 – *"Having wiped out the handwriting of requirements that was against us, which was contrary to us. And He has taken it out of the way, having nailed it to the Cross."* Furthermore, I have been instructed to let you know that your name has been written in the Lamb's Book of Life in Heaven; see Luke 10:20b – *"Rejoice because your names are written in Heaven."* I am to exhort you to be faithful unto death; Revelation 2:10 – *"Do not fear any of those things which you are about to suffer. Indeed, the devil is about to throw some of you into prison, that you may be tested, and you will have tribulation … Be faithful until death, and I will give you the crown of life"* – and because an incorruptible crown and inheritance is waiting for you in Heaven; I Peter 1:3-5 – *"Blessed be the God and Father of our Lord Jesus Christ, Who according to His abundant mercy has begotten us again to a living hope through the resurrection of Jesus Christ from the dead, to an inheritance incorruptible and undefiled and that does not fade away, reserved in Heaven for you, who are kept by the power of God through faith for salvation ready to be revealed in the last time."* Finally, I am to urge you to be strong in the Lord and in the power of His might (see Ephesians 6:10).

Yours most faithfully and ever-abidingly (see John 14:16),
on behalf of the Trinity, the **Holy Spirit**

Today's Scripture

The Spirit Himself bears witness with our spirit that we are children of God.

(Romans 8:16)

Daily Power!

My "love letter" from God is engraved upon my heart.

Today's Bible Reading

*Deuteronomy 7:1-26 through 8:1-20;
Luke 7:36-50 through 8:1-3;
Psalm 69:1-18;
Proverbs 12:1*

Mark my Word
(for further study)

*Luke 10:20;
John 14:16;
Ephesians 6:10;
Colossians 2:4;
I Peter 1:3-5;
Revelation 2:10*

Introduction to the Holy Spirit

Multitudes have been baptized in the Holy Spirit in our Gospel crusades, regularly witnessing mighty manifestations of the power and love of God. I desire to explain the understanding I have gained from these events we've been so deeply involved. My final authority has been Scripture. Certainly experience has helped me grasp the things of the Spirit, but as Peter wrote, God *"has given to us all things that pertain to life and Godliness."* Scripture validates experience.

In sharing my understanding of the things of the Spirit, I try to show that my conclusions were arrived at through the Word, illuminated by what I have seen. There are many alternative views. Variations are sure to exist, unless a Standard Authority is accepted and agreed upon to judge all such teachings. Experience itself varies, but the Scriptures do not. There is a natural appetite to hear things God has done, and a tendency to draw primarily from experience – the Word is often regarded only as a backup, if used at all. This "anecdote theology" is not new. There are theories of revival, for example, which have been claimed as being based purely on studies of what has happened in the past. I was concerned about this approach … and I determined that my grounds must be the Word. That is where I stand. Our pneumatology (the things of the Spirit) had to be subject to the judgment of what the Word says. This was wholesome discipline. I have made this study as thorough as possible, to the best of my ability.

Experience must be challenged by Scripture – experience must not challenge Scripture nor adapt Scripture to what "happens to happen." Nevertheless, you will see that I illustrate my teaching with things God has been doing in our evangelistic crusades. Among Christians who pray for and support the nation-shaking campaigns of *Christ for all Nations*, there is obviously a considerable variety of viewpoints on many doctrines, including that of the Holy Spirit. I offer this exposition of the Word as a contribution to the understanding of the work of the Holy Spirit – I pray that it ministers to you.

Today's Scripture

Come near to Me, hear this: I have not spoken in secret from the beginning; from the time that it was, I was there. And now the Lord God and His Spirit have sent Me. Thus says the Lord, your Redeemer, the Holy One of Israel; I am the Lord your God, Who teaches you to profit, Who leads you by the way you should go.
(Isaiah 48:16-17)

Daily Power!

Holy Spirit, teach me Your truths.

Today's Bible Reading

Deuteronomy 9:1-29 through 10:1-22;
Luke 8:4-21;
Psalm 69:19-36;
Proverbs 12:2-3

Mark my Word
(for further study)

Isaiah 48:16-17;
II Peter 1:3

Our Mission is Compassion

Elijah was the scourge of Baal, of Jezebel and her pathetic husband, King Ahab. Jesus did not come as a scourge – He bared His own back to the scourge, not ours. He showed to us the ultimate reality behind the universe: a heart beating with infinite longing and concern over every one of His creatures. In fact, the more sunken in the pit the people were, the more He bled for them. That kind of love is the true Spirit of evangelism.

You and I know people are going to Hell, and if we care about them, we should warn them. But we should warn them as if they were our own children walking on the brink of an active volcano. Hatred should be not present in our preaching. Our mission is compassion. Because Hell opens its mouth to devour sinners, we should feel the greater anxiety for their souls. We can't gloat in satisfaction and shout for joy over sinners in Hell. Warnings are one thing – threats another. *"How shall we escape if we neglect to great a salvation, which at the first began to be spoken by the Lord, and was confirmed to us by those who heard Him; God also bearing witness both with signs and wonders, with various miracles, and gifts of the Holy Spirit, according to His own will."*

Jonah found it difficult to preach. He enjoyed preaching wrath, but knew that God did not enjoy being angry. God is long suffering (eternally patient): *"The Lord is longsuffering and abundant in mercy, forgiving iniquity and transgression."*

"For God is my witness, how greatly I long for you all with the compassion of Jesus Christ. And this I pray, that your love may abound still more and more in knowledge and all discernment, that you may approve the things that are excellent, that you may be sincere and without offense till the day of Christ."

With the compassion of Jesus Christ as our motivation, you and I should joyfully present the Gospel to the world!

Today's Scripture

But He was wounded for our transgressions, He was bruised for our iniquities; the chastisement for our peace was upon Him, and by His stripes we are healed.
(Isaiah 53:5)

Daily Power!

I am filled with the fruit of the Spirit: love, joy, peace, longsuffering, kindness, goodness, faithfulness, gentleness, self-control.
(Galatians 5:22; paraphrased)

Today's Bible Reading

Deuteronomy 11:1-32 through 12:1-32;
Luke 8:22-39;
Psalm 70:1-5;
Proverbs 12:4

Mark my Word
(for further study)

Numbers 14:18; I Kings 16:1-34; 18:1-46; 19:1-21; 21:1-29; II Kings 9; Isaiah 53:5; Jonah 3:1-10; Galatians 5:22; Philippians 1:8-10; Hebrews 2:3-4

30

Today's Scripture

For we do not wrestle against flesh and blood, but against principalities, against powers, against spiritual hosts of wickedness in the heavenly places.
(Ephesians 6:12)

Daily Power!

When it feels like I'm living my life "behind enemy lines," I remember that Christ Jesus came to rescue me from the power of the enemy.

Today's Bible Reading

Deuteronomy 13:1-18 through 15:1-23;
Luke 8:40-56 through 9:1-6; Psalm 71:1-24;
Proverbs 12:5-7

Mark my Word
(for further study)

Genesis 1:28;
Matthew 4:8-10;
John 12:31; 14:30; 16:11;
Romans 1:21;
Ephesians 2:2;
Colossians 1:21;
I John 5:19

Under Attack!

Think of what happens to a country at war – in some cases, it is totally cut off from the outside world. No more commerce or trade, no more mail or telephone conversations. Much the same thing happened when the human race surrendered to sin and the devil. We were cut off from the outside world – from God, from the world of the Spirit. Demonic forces occupied this world and dominated our attitudes. Divine power lines were severed and a permanent spiritual blackout occurred.

Originally, God put Man in charge to manage this world – *"Then God blessed them, and said, 'Be fruitful and multiply; fill the Earth and subdue it; have dominion over the fish of the sea, over the birds of the air, and over every living thing that moves on the Earth'"* – but we were a pushover to sin and the devil swayed people, even as Rasputin swayed the Czar of Russia. The Bible makes this clear:

"The whole world lies under the sway of the wicked one" … *"Our foolish hearts were darkened"* … *"The prince of the power of the air … now works in the sons of disobedience"* … *"Alienated and enemies in your mind by wicked works."*

Three times, Jesus called the devil *"the ruler of this world."* When the devil offered the kingdoms of this world to Christ, Jesus did not contest the devil's ability to do so: *"Again, the devil took Him up on an exceedingly high mountain, and showed Him all the kingdoms of the world and their glory. And he said to Him, 'All these things I will give You if You will fall down and worship me.' Then Jesus said to him, 'Away with you, Satan! For it is written: you shall worship the Lord your God, and Him only you shall serve.'"* Therefore, since he has cut off our rightful communication with God, it is up to us to learn how to re-establish those lines and not let them be severed again! Make your **connection** to God today … keep it strong all day long!

"Classic Revival"

An isolated, late example of a "classic revival" – with physical and deeply emotional revivalist effects – took place in 1949 on the islands of Harris and Lewis in the Hebrides. Duncan Campbell, who described it as, "God entering the field," led it. With the dawning of the third millennium, the longing for a repeat of the times of classic or traditional "revival" grips millions. The glorious and exciting vista of the anticipated revival fills the wide screen of the whole world, and is no longer limited to a particular church or local renewal. The need for revival on that kind of international scale is urgent enough.

Prayer is made that the divine fire which burned in Welsh villages or similar communities will girdle the globe, remembering that, *"With God, all things are possible."* It would change everything. No more struggle and constant effort, discouragement and ongoing sacrifice, constant witnessing and endless prayer … but brilliant Gospel success.

I believe a "lack of revival" in our world today begins with individuals recognizing that we have, perhaps, become like the church of Ephesus: *"I know your works, your labor, your patience, and that you cannot bear those who are evil. And you have tested those who say they are apostles and are not, and have found them liars; and you have persevered and have patience, and have labored for My Name's sake and have not become weary. Nevertheless, I have this against you, that **you have left your first love**. Remember therefore from where you have fallen, repent and do the first works."* Remember that great joy you experienced when first you received Jesus as **your** Savior? Are we so selfish that we cannot desire to freely share that joy with others who have never heard? Is "revival" to refresh the saved – or to reach the lost, to rescue those who are "dead in their sins"? Let us strive to see revival happen in our lifetime!

Today's Scripture

And it shall come to pass afterward that I will pour out My Spirit on all flesh; your sons and your daughters shall prophesy, your old men shall dream dreams, your young men shall see visions. And also on My menservants and on My maidservants I will pour out My Spirit in those days.
(Joel 2:28-29)

Daily Power!

I believe that the need for revival on an international scale is urgent, and so I will obey my Father's commands to bring that revival to pass.

Today's Bible Reading

Deuteronomy 16:1-22 through 17:1-20;
Luke 9:7-27;
Psalm 72:1-20;
Proverbs 12:8-9

Mark my Word
(for further study)

Joel 2:28-32;
Revelation 2:1-7

Our brain is the doubt-box

A fuse that works will feel the power first.

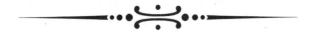

Don't confuse, don't refuse, but check your fuse!

God's Counter-Attack

Just as in wartime, countries have secret agents and the means of maintaining contact with them, so the Lord has His men and women and keeps in contact with them. Amos the prophet said, *"Surely the Lord does nothing, unless He reveals His secret to His servants, the prophets"* – men like Enoch, Noah, Abraham, Moses, Elijah, Daniel, Isaiah. The whole nation of Israel was to have been God's ally against the occupying enemy from Hell … but they failed to perceive His plan and comply with it.

The Lord revealed one great secret to His servants, the prophets – namely, that there was to be an invasion of Fortress Earth from the outside. And it took place – Christ came to the shores of Satan's usurped dominion, proclaiming the Kingdom of God and displaying its power: *"If I cast out demons with the finger of God, surely the Kingdom of God has come upon you."*

"What then shall we say to these things? If God is for us, who can be against us? … Who shall separate us from the love of Christ? Shall tribulation, or distress, or persecution, or famine, or nakedness, or peril, or sword? As it is written, 'For Your sake we are killed all day long; we are accounted as sheep for the slaughter.' Yet in all these things we are more than conquerors through Him Who loved us. For I am persuaded that neither death nor life, nor angels nor principalities nor powers, nor things present nor things to come, nor height nor depth, nor any other created thing, shall be able to separate us from the love of God which is in Christ Jesus our Lord."

That means that you **can** come out from beneath Satan's ruthless grip and be freed to walk unencumbered with God! So stand up and walk in that liberty … today!

Today's Scripture

You are of God, little children, and have overcome them, because He Who is in you is greater than he who is in the world.
(I John 4:4)

Daily Power!

I've been enlisted in God's army, ready to fight against the enemy!

Today's Bible Reading

Deuteronomy 18:1-22 through 20:1-20;
Luke 9:28-50;
Psalm 73:1-28;
Proverbs 12:10

Mark my Word
(for further study)

Amos 3:7;
Luke 11:20;
Romans 8:31-39;
I John 4:4

2

How to become a true Intercessor

A true intercessor must have some standing with both parties – God and the lost. We know people … but we must also know God! Abraham was a good example of someone who knew God. The cities of Sodom and Gomorrah had become morally perverted … God proposed to remove them, but said, *"Shall I hide from Abraham what I am doing?"* When Abraham learned that these two cities were listed for destruction, he took up their case with God … and went a long way along the road to saving them. He was qualified – because he knew God and the cities. He was called "the friend of God." Why? *"Abraham believed God, and it was credited to him as righteousness, and he was called God's friend."* Believers – I do not mean "unbelieving so-called believers, full of doubts, asking clever questions" – but men and women of living faith, who know the Lord … are the King's friends at Court, His confidantes, people to whom He listens and with whom He wants to cooperate. *"But you are My servant, whom I have chosen, the descendants of Abraham My friend … I have taken you from the ends of the Earth … and said, 'You are My servant, I have chosen you and have not cast you away; fear not, for I am with you, be not dismayed, for I am your God. I will strengthen you, I will help you, I will uphold you with My righteous right hand."* These people whom He honors are to be His intercessors.

That is what Scripture means by "a friend." Jesus said, *"I no longer call you servants … Instead, I have called you friends, for everything that I learned from My Father I have made known to you."* A friend-intercessor will have the mind of the Lord, Who tells us nothing for mere interest but for us to pray about it. A "word of knowledge" is not necessarily for public consumption, but often for private prayer. God reveals what He will do to those who clamor for His will to be done. **Pray today** – and ignite a fresh fire and inner desire to **do God's will** in every way!

Today's Scripture

You are My friends if you do whatever I command you. No longer do I call you servants, for a servant does not know what his master is doing; but I have called you friends … You did not choose Me, but I chose you and appointed you that you should go and bear fruit, and that your fruit should remain, that whatever you ask the Father in My Name He may give you.

(John 15:14-16)

Daily Power!

As I am learning more and more about God and His character, I desire to become His friend – one to whom He listens and with whom He wants to cooperate.

Today's Bible Reading

Deuteronomy 21:1-23 through 22:1-30; Luke 9:51-62 through 10:1-12; Psalm 74:1-23; Proverbs 12:11

Mark my Word
(for further study)

Genesis 18:1-33; II Chronicles 20:7; Isaiah 41:8-10; John 15:14-16; James 2:23

God's Property

We human beings look after our property and protect it. You can be absolutely sure that God looks after His property too. We cost God too much for Him to neglect and lose us. We were *"bought at a price,"* even the precious Blood of Jesus. When Jesus takes over, He saves and keeps us. As long as we follow Him, He will not allow repossession of His property by unclean spirits: *"He who dwells in the shelter of the Most High will rest in the shadow of the Almighty"* ... *"They overcame him by the Blood of the Lamb and by the Word of their testimony; they did not love their lives so much as to shrink from death."* This is the glorious and perfect protection which the Lord gives His children, free of charge.

"'No weapon forged against you will prevail, and you will refute every tongue that accuses you. This is the heritage of the servants of the Lord, and this is their vindication from Me,' declares the Lord." No curse can be fastened on you, and no witchcraft can harm you. *"Like a flitting sparrow, like a flying swallow, so a curse without cause shall not alight."*

We serve a mighty God ... not a struggling God Who might lose battles sometimes. He cannot be blackmailed nor forced to compromise with the devil. He could never go into partnership and share His right–of–possession of you with any evil spirit. Follow Jesus and you are wholly the Lord's. Reinhard Bonnke lives with this assurance – I am marked by the Blood of Jesus, and nobody can pluck me from His hand. Satan cannot kidnap my soul. It is hidden with Christ in God, which is a safe in a strongroom, and bears the seal–mark of the Blood. You too are marked by the Blood of Jesus.

Today's Scripture

For you were bought with a price; therefore glorify God in your body and in your spirit, which are God's.
(I Corinthians 6:20)

Daily Power!

What a joy to be able to shout: "I am God's property!"

Today's Bible Reading

Deuteronomy 23:1-24 through 25:1-19; Luke 10:13-37; Psalm 75:1-10; Proverbs 12:12-14

Mark my Word
(for further study)

Psalm 91:1; Proverbs 26:2; Isaiah 54:17; I Corinthians 6:20; Colossians 3:3; Revelation 12:11

4

Family is a divine Purpose

Today's Scripture

For in Him we live and move and have our being.

(Acts 17:28)

Daily Power!

God has no grand-children. I am His because I chose Him myself, and He chose me.

Today's Bible Reading

Deuteronomy 26:1-19
through 27:1-26;
Luke 10:38-42
through 11:1-13;
Psalm 76:1-12;
Proverbs 12:15-17;

Mark my Word
(for further study)

Psalm 68:6;
Luke 17:21;
Acts 17:28

In Acts 16, Paul told the Philippian jailer: *"Believe on the Lord Jesus and you will be saved, **and your household.**"* His household? There would be more under his roof than today's proverbial "nuclear family with 2.3 children." There would be his wife, adult sons and their wives, daughters, servants, slaves, and possibly grandparents. Could his faith save their souls? We may as well ask if a father's cup of coffee could satisfy his family! **The household could be saved, but each one must believe on the Lord Jesus.** Nobody can be saved second-hand through his father or mother. God has no grandchildren. But this phrase – *"you and your household"* – did mean something, it was no casual, throwaway line. Behind it lay Paul's understanding of the purposes of God spelled out in the Scriptures. He knew that in Scripture, "family" is a Divine purpose – almost what the whole world is all about, mentioned above three hundred times. Paul had much to say about "the household" in his letters.

Family is God's idea. He created the Family, and fathered the Family of Man. "He sets the solitary in families." That is His blessing. He never intended separation, isolation and individualism. Modern individualism is not a product of Bible teaching, but came from the Descartes philosophy of "I think, therefore I am." We might say that Family's roots are in the very nature of God as Father, Son and Holy Spirit. The Family reflects God more than an individual life.

The perfection of God's glory needs the whole *"household of God."* God made families because unity is necessary for all Creation … and prayer for our family has the ear of God. We were made for interdependence with one another and mutual responsibility – **we are** *"our brother's keepers."* We came from Him, and that can never change. Everything is forever united in Him as normal. "In Him we live and move and have our being." Jesus prayed, *"That they all may be one, even as We are one,"* because there had been a rupture of unity which Christ came to rectify and restore. That one-ness for which Christ prayed would not be artificial, imposed. It would bring back the real for you and me, and put things as they were meant to be.

The Objective of our Work

The nine men who wrote the Christian Scriptures of the New Testament all spoke of Christ's return, and to them it was clear that it was that hope which gave meaning to their faith and an objective for their work. The main writer, Paul, went into much detail: how Christ would appear … what He would do … what the state of the world would be. He wrote more than three pages of his great letter to the church in Corinth, chapter 15, and made the return of Jesus the keystone of the future. Here are some of his words:

"Christ died for our sins according to the Scriptures. He rose again the third day according to the Scriptures. As in Adam, all die, even so in Christ, shall be made alive, but every man in his own order. Christ the Firstfruits; afterward they that are Christ's at His coming."

When he was preaching to the intellectuals in Athens – then the greatest city of learning on Earth – he said, *"God has appointed a day in the which He will judge the world in righteousness, by that Man Whom He has ordained; whereof He has given assurance to all men, in that He has raised Him from the dead."*

John was closer to Christ than anybody, and he rested his hope on Christ's return. He wrote: *"We are now the sons of God, and it does not yet appear what we shall be; but we know that, when He shall appear, we shall be like Him, for we shall see Him as He is."* Furthermore, John wrote the Book of Revelation – or "the Apocalypse" – with twenty-one chapters of prophecy concerned with Christ's return as Lord of lords. It ends with the words of Jesus: *"He that testifies these things says, 'Surely I come quickly.'"*

This is God's promise to you, and to me!

Today's Scripture

Now Christ is risen from the dead, and has become the firstfruits of those who have fallen asleep. For since by man came death, by Man also came the resurrection of the dead. For as in Adam, all die, even so in Christ, all shall be made alive.
(I Corinthians 15:20-22)

Daily Power!

I claim this promise: "Now I am a child of God, and it has not yet been revealed what I shall be, but I know that when Christ is revealed, I shall be like Him, for I shall see Him as He is."
(I John 3:2; paraphrased)

Today's Bible Reading:

Deuteronomy 28:1-68;
Luke 11:14-36;
Psalm 77:1-20;
Proverbs 12:18

Mark my Word
(for further study)

Acts 17:31; I Corinthians 15:1-58; I John 3:1-3; Revelation 22:20

6

Today's Scripture

Whoever drinks of the water that I shall give him will never thirst. But the water that I shall give him will become in him a fountain of water springing up into everlasting life.

(John 4:14)

Daily Power!

I need God to forgive me, to bring me home and restore the relationship He has always wanted to have with me.

Today's Bible Reading

Deuteronomy 29:1-29 through 30:1-20;
Luke 11:37-54 through 12:1-7;
Psalm 78:1-31;
Proverbs 12:19-20

Mark my Word
(for further study)

Luke 8:11-15; 12:19-20; 23:1-56; 24:1-53;
John 4:14

Searching in Darkness

Some people see no hope in any direction – tragically, they give up and sink into despair. Others try to escape from it all. As one person observed, "People can't stand too much reality – that's why we have soap operas!"

Longing for real life, some people get tangled in a web of destruction – often in the most common and obvious snares, such as drugs or drink. These addictions have never solved one single problem … but have created millions. Those who cannot live **without** drugs and drink also cannot live **with** them. They produce only a chemical dream, a mirage in a waterless desert: *"Now the ones that fell among thorns are those who, when they have heard, go out and are choked with cares, riches and pleasures of life, and bring no fruit to maturity."*

Others become addicted to the pursuit of success. Their diaries get fuller, their bank accounts fatter, their cars faster – but they never catch up with happiness. Like mountaineers, millions of people display enormous courage, determination and ingenuity to get to the top … but they find only emptiness when they get there: *"And I will say to my soul, 'Soul, you have many goods laid up for many years; take your ease; eat, drink, and be merry.' But God said to him, 'Fool! This night your soul will be required of you; then whose will those things be which you have provided?'"*

Meanwhile, in today's "religious supermarket," many people are hypnotized by the bright, shiny brands of "do-it-yourself salvation." The shelves are crowded with New Age products: pyramid power … hypnotherapy … transcendental meditation … white magic – all of them are a sham, and some of them are lethally dangerous. They offer nothing that can reach the heart of the human problem: *"Those by the wayside are the ones who hear; then the devil comes and takes away the Word out of their hearts, lest they should believe and be saved."*

You need more than a cheap solution or a quick fix – **you need peace with God**. You need Him to forgive you, to bring you home, restore you to the relationship He has always wanted to have with you.

Faith is a Venture

One morning, Jesus walked along the shingled edge of Lake Galilee and beckoned to a few local fishermen. He said, *"Follow Me!"* … and at that moment, everything began for them. "Everything" before had only been fish … and then it became people, action, and changing world history, with ever-increasing faith and effects. Jesus did not call them – nor you, nor me – to switch off smiles and wear sackcloth, to turn folk into stick-in-the mud people. He wasn't so conventional Himself! The disciples caught His bubbling spirit, which challenged the stuffy establishment. He showed them new things – especially faith and love – and by them, they conquered the world.

The primary truth about God is that He is the Deliverer, the Emancipator, and the Savior. He is God only to the free. **Faith is a venture that turns Life into an adventure.** Doubts get us nowhere. They are mooring ropes. Believing God means we cast off, like ships designed for riding the high seas and going somewhere. Faith inspires – doubt paralyzes. Faith says, *"I can do all things through Christ Who strengthens me"* – unbelief does nothing. Faith in God is exciting – unbelief is depressing.

"If you abide in My Word, you are My disciples indeed. And you shall know the truth, and the truth shall make your free." We become what we were born to be only when we are "born-again" by faith in Christ Jesus. *"If the Son sets you free, you will be free indeed."* The world's greatest Book on freedom is the Bible. The very idea of freedom came from the Bible, not from Greece or Rome. Read it! Remember God made the first free nation ever seen on Earth – Israel – and He wants to put a sense of liberty in our very souls. God opposes tyranny. The Gospel makes us the freeborn sons of God. *"For this reason we also, since the day we heard it, do not cease to pray for you, and to ask that you may be filled with the knowledge of His will in all wisdom and spiritual understanding, that you may walk worthy of the Lord, fully pleasing Him, being fruitful in every good work and increasing in the knowledge of God."* Go – and walk in your Godly freedom today … in Jesus' Name!

Today's Scripture

Therefore if the Son makes you free, you shall be free indeed.
(John 8:36)

Daily Power!

Today I walk in the freedom given me by Christ Jesus my Lord.

Today's Bible Reading

*Deuteronomy 31:1-30 through 32:1-27;
Luke 12:8-34;
Psalm 78:32-55;
Proverbs 12:21-23*

Mark my Word
(for further study)

*Matthew 4:19;
John 8:36;
Philippians 4:13;
Colossians 1:9-10*

8

Motivation

The world cannot see what motivates Christians to shine brightly in a darkened place. In ignorance, they only see Christians as "religious enthusiasts" or "religion pushers," "Bible punchers" or "religious freaks." Unbelievers are like sheep who can't understand why human beings listen to music. Jesus told us that the Holy Spirit is not given to the world. That makes unbelievers basically different, almost alien, as if they were from Mars.

However, one candle is lit from another candle. The fire – the light of God – is transmitted. That is why we are here. Paul the apostle spent only a few days introducing the Gospel to the people of Thessalonica ... but a little later in a letter to them, Paul congratulated their enthusiasm, saying, *"Your faith in God has become known everywhere."* Faith lights the lamps that show the way. "Send the light!"

We begin, perhaps, with no faith – a minus. But at the Cross, the flame of faith leaps into our hearts, bringing the Holy Spirit, salvation and forgiveness. At that place, Christ's infinite work is accomplished, and faith makes it ours. We believe and receive. The Holy Spirit translates all Jesus did for us into our personal experience. We are the lights of the world. The world likes to think religion is dying, but in vast areas of the world, the death rattle is heard in the throat of secularism. As Christ is to Resurrection, godlessness is to death – they are both synonyms. People are not finding satisfaction in what mere governments can do, and are turning to the things of the Holy Spirit. That is the situation. Have faith – be filled with the Spirit – and burn for God! Let the seven-branched lamp standard be ablaze! "If you believe, and I believe, and we together strive; the Holy Spirit will come down, and nations will revive."

Today's Scripture

Every time we think of you, we thank God for you. Day and night you're in our prayers, as we call to mind your work of faith, your labor of love, and your patience of hope in following our Master, Jesus Christ, before God our Father. It is clear to us, friends, that God not only loves you very much but also has put His hand on you for something special. When the Message we preached came to you, it wasn't just works. Something happened in you. The Holy Spirit put steel in your convictions.
(I Thess. 1:5-8; the Message)

Daily Power!

I have faith, I am filled with the Spirit, and I burn for God!

Today's Bible Reading

Deuteronomy 32:28-52; Luke 12:35-59; Psalm 78:56-64; Proverbs 12:24

Mark my Word
(for further study)

I Thessalonians 1:8

Daily Bread

Prayer is an important topic in the Word of God. The apostle Paul often uses a word meaning "keep at it, persevere, be a stayer, show stamina, stick at it, keep awake!" Translate these texts like that yourself:

"Continue earnestly in prayer, being vigilant in it" ... *"Continue steadfastly in prayer"* ... *"We will give ourselves continually to prayer"* ... *"Pray in the Spirit on all occasions with all kinds of prayers and requests ... Be alert and always keep on praying for all the saints."*

The way Jesus speaks of prayer is not quite like some mighty suppose. He said, *"Ask, and it will be given to you. Seek. Knock."* These words are in the Greek present indicative: "be asking, be seeking, be knocking." But elsewhere He used a different tense (aorist) indicating a single, completed action: *"Give us this day our daily bread."* Ask once, but ask every day. *"Give us this day"* – ask for each day's need daily. That is how God likes it ... we don't "have faith" for everything for a whole year – that would be arrogant! – but we come to Him as children over and over, asking for the Bread of Life – the Holy Spirit – daily, not once forever. We always receive every day!

The concept of "daily bread" was first seen with the newly-liberated Israelites in the wilderness: *"Then the Lord said to Moses, 'Behold, I will rain bread from Heaven for you. And the people shall go out and gather a certain quota every day, that I may test them, whether they will walk in My law or not.'"* From that day to this, God has been **testing us** to see if we have faith in Him on a **daily** basis. And so it is with prayer – we must be faithful on a daily basis to participate in prayer with God.

Today's Scripture

Praying always with all prayer and supplication in the Spirit, being watchful to this end with all perseverance and supplication for all the saints.

(Ephesians 6:18)

Daily Power!

It is my privilege as a child of God to come to Him every day, with the open-hearted expectation of a child, knowing that my Father loves me!

Today's Bible Reading

Deuteronomy 33:1-29;
Luke 13:1-21;
Psalm 78:65-72;
Proverbs 12:25

Mark my Word
(for further study)

Exodus 16:1-5;
Matthew 6:11; 7:7;
Acts 6:4;
Ephesians 6:18;
Colossians 4:2

God hears Prayer

Scripture consistently declares that prayer will **always** be heard: *"Your Father knows the things you have need of before you ask Him"* ... *"Everyone who asks receives, and he who seeks finds, and to him who knocks it will be opened"* ... *"This is the assurance we have in approaching God; that if we ask anything according to his will, He hears us. And if we know that He hears us – whatever we ask – we know that we have what we asked of Him."*

Have you ever tried someone's telephone number again and again, without getting through to that person? After awhile you wonder, "Did I write that number down correctly?" But our Heavenly Father has our number – right down to the very number of hairs on our heads: *"But the very hairs of your head are all numbered"* – and He cares intimately about you! *"Or what man is there among you who, if his son asks for bread, will give him a stone? Or if he asks for a fish, will he give him a serpent? If you then, being evil, know how to give good gifts to your children, how much more will your Father Who is in Heaven give good gifts to those who ask Him!"*

When you call on God – when you "dial up His number" – you will **never** get a busy signal or a phone that just rings with no answer: *"Give ear, O Lord, to my prayer; and attend to the voice of my supplications. In the day of my trouble I will call upon You, for You will answer me"* ... *"He shall call upon Me, and I will answer him; I will be with him in trouble, I will deliver him and honor him"* ... *"Then you shall call, and the Lord will answer; you shall cry, and He will say, 'Here I am'"* ... *"Call to Me, and I will answer you, and show you great and mighty things, which you do not know."* I believe that it was even God Who originated the idea of "call waiting": *"It shall come to pass that **before** they call, I will answer; and while they are still speaking, I will hear."*

Today's Scripture

Now this is the confidence that we have in Him, that if we ask anything according to His will, He hears us. And if we know that He hears us, whatever we ask, we know that we have the petitions that we have asked of Him.
(I John 5:14-15)

Daily Power!

I have confidence that each time I call on my Heavenly Father, He is always "at home" – He always hears me when I pray.

Today's Bible Reading

Deuteronomy 34:1-12 through Joshua 2:1-24;
Luke 13:22-35 through 14:1-6;
Psalm 79:1-13;
Proverbs 12:26

Mark my Word
(for further study)

Psalm 86:7; 91:15;
Isaiah 58:9; 65:24;
Jeremiah 33:3;
Matthew 6:8; 7:8-11;
10:40; I John 5:14-15

"The Spirit yearns"

The important principle of faith is: Christ Jesus is alive in me. Many wait for the Spirit to move, but He must move in the direction they want. The moving of the Spirit is not just in our feelings. There's a strange and neglected verse in James: *"The Spirit that dwells in us lusts to envy."* The word "lusts" is the same as "yearns." The Holy Spirit within us conflicts with fleshly desire, urging us into service for Him.

Let us look at Ephesians: *"For by grace you have been saved through faith – and that not of yourselves, it is the gift of God."* Faith is a mutual act between God and me. There are two spirits in opposition: the spirit of the devil, and the Spirit of God. They both pressurize us. First, we read of *"the spirit who is now at work in those who are disobedient,"* then we read that when we are saved: *"We are ... created in Christ Jesus to do good works."* When we do His will, do His good works, it is by His grace. We can't pride ourselves on it. The glory is all the Lord's.

Perhaps you notice that Jesus never commended **people**, but He commended their **faith**. If we have small faith, don't worry ... everybody starts there – or with no faith at all! Even the apostles were called, *"Little faiths."* If you are dissatisfied with yourself, God made you that way. *"The Spirit within us yearns."* He plans to strengthen us.

If you consider yourself to be a poor believer, there can be a breakthrough. The whole Bible is written to break down unbelief and build up your fortifications of trust in God. You may study it intellectually for doctrine or for prophecy, but its central objective is to bring **you** the peace of perfect rest in God.

Today's Scripture

For by grace you have been saved through faith, and that not of yourselves; it is the gift of God.

(Ephesians 2:8)

Daily Power!

The central objective of God's Word is to bring me into the peace of perfect rest in God.

Today's Bible Reading

Joshua 3:1-17 through 4:1-24; Luke 14:7-35; Psalm 80:1-19; Proverbs 12:27-28

Mark my Word
(for further study)

Ephesians 2:2, 8, 10; James 4:5

Today's Scripture

He who speaks with other tongues does not speak to men but to God.
(I Corinthians 14:2)

Daily Power!

*The baptism of the Holy Spirit is **essential** for successful Christian life.*

Today's Bible Reading

*Joshua 5:1-15
through 7:1-15;
Luke 15:1-32;
Psalm 81:1-16;
Proverbs 13:1*

Mark my Word
(for further study)

*Acts 2:1-4;
II Corinthians 14:2*

Power!

Power! That is the essence of the Gospel. A powerless Gospel preacher is like an unwashed soap salesman. Singing "There is power in the precious Blood of the Lamb" ... and then having to fast and pray for a month to get power does not add up. At the beginning of my Christian life, I had an experience of the Holy Spirit coming into my life which I believe was as great as that of any disciple on the Day of Pentecost. It seemed to me that the God Who fills Heaven and Earth crowded into my soul.

"When the Day of Pentecost had fully come, they were all with one accord in one place. And suddenly there came a sound from Heaven, as of a rushing mighty wind, and it filled the whole house where they were sitting. Then there appeared to them divided tongues, as of fire, and one sat upon each of them. And they were all filled with the Holy Spirit and began to speak with other tongues, as the Spirit gave them utterance."

Peter managed to stand up and preach, but the physical effects of my baptism in the Spirit would certainly have been too much for me to stand and preach immediately, as tremendous as my empowering was for later service. I will tell you how it happened to me ... but I ought to say that nobody should think that God ever gives the Spirit in exactly the same way to everyone.

It happened like this: I was a boy of eleven in Germany when my father told me about special prayer meetings for the baptism in the Holy Spirit. Ever eager for the things of God, I begged him to take me along. A missionary from Finland was visiting the church, and he explained the truth of the baptism in the Holy Spirit. We had just knelt down when the power of God began to pour into and over me. Joy unspeakable filled my heart, and I began to speak in other languages, as the Spirit gave me *"utterance."* It was like a Heavenly fountain opening up within me – it is still flowing today! It was one of the most precious events in my life – and one I trust you too have experienced.

Apply the Blood

In the entire Bible, no blood except the Blood of Jesus is called precious. Millions of animals have been slaughtered to atone for sin, but their blood was not precious. The Old Testament sacrifices of Israel were simply poured away at the sides of the altars – powerless.

Suppose you have a table with a big stain on its surface. When visitors come, you cover the stain with a tablecloth so that nobody will notice it. The stain is covered … but not removed. This is the meaning of the Old Testament word atonement – "covered." The rivers of blood of millions of sacrificial animals were not able to "take away" sin, but only to cover it for awhile. That is the reason why John the Baptist was so excited when he saw Jesus come to the River Jordan, and cried: *"Behold! The Lamb of God Who takes away the sin of the world!"*

Jesus' Blood works "under the tablecloth" and behind every one of our façades. It tackles the root sins and problems of all people who put their faith in Jesus Christ. The Blood of the Lamb of God alone has value and power to save. His sacrifice was sufficient for you and me – for all men, women, boys, and girls, no matter how old they are. The apostle Peter is the one who called the Blood of Jesus "precious" – *"But with the precious Blood of Christ, as of a lamb without blemish and without spot"* – because he personally witnessed the crucifixion and death of his Best Friend. He saw with his own eyes the life-blood of his Master pour out of His body. Peter **knew** the true value of the precious Blood of Jesus – and that is what you and I must learn to value and honor today.

Today's Scripture

In Him we have redemption through His Blood, the forgiveness of sins, according to the riches of His grace.
(Ephesians 1:7)

Daily Power!

I accept the completed sacrifice which Jesus Christ became for me, and I acknowledge His precious Blood activated on my behalf … he is my Lamb of God.

Today's Bible Reading

Joshua 7:16-26 through 9:1-2;
Luke 16:1-18;
Psalm 82:1-8;
Proverbs 13:2-3

Mark my Word
(for further study)

John 1:29;
Ephesians 1:7;
I Peter 1:19

Today's Scripture

God is not a man that He should lie, nor a son of man that He should repent. Has He said, and will He not do? Or has He spoken, and will He not make it good?
(Numbers 23:19)

Daily Power!

Whenever I wonder what the nature of God may be, I need only look into His Word to see His consistent character and heart.

Today's Bible Reading

Joshua 9:3-27 through 10:1-43; Luke 16:19-31 through 17:1-10; Psalm 83:1-18; Proverbs 13:4

Mark my Word
(for further study)

Genesis 20:1-18; Numbers 23:19; Isaiah 55:6-12

God's unchanging Heart

God works by prompting prayer. When God wants to do a certain thing, He inspires prayer that He may do it – He only works that way. In Genesis 20, we read the first healing story recorded in Scripture: the prayer of Abraham brought forgiveness and healing to the whole household of the Philistine chief, Abimelech. However, this was not Abraham's idea – it was the Lord's idea from the start. He told Abimelech to ask Abraham to pray for him to be healed. He inspired Abraham to pray, and inspired Abimelech to expect Abraham's prayer to be answered. It was all of God. And by healing a heathen family, God had committed Himself – He could never again be any different.

The Lord had revealed what He was, and He could not go back on it. God shows Himself by His deeds, and His deeds do not stand in contrast to His nature. God may not copy His own deeds. He never repeats Himself, for He has an infinite store of new approaches and plans. He has shown Himself to be the Healer … and that healing is what He wants to do.

God's reliability and trustworthiness are undoubted, and what He says to the just, He also says to the sinner: *"Seek the Lord while He may be found. Call upon Him while He is near. Let the wicked forsake his way, and the unrighteous man his thoughts; let him return to the Lord, and He will have mercy on him; and to our God, for He will abundantly pardon … So shall My Word be that goes forth from My mouth; it shall not return to Me void, but it shall accomplish what I please, and it shall prosper in the thing for which I sent it."*

Never forget: what His deeds demonstrate is the unchanging heart and character behind them. He has the same love, the same will He always had, and His deeds cannot violate His character.

Samson and Christ

If we need anybody back in our world today, it is Jesus Christ! Nations could relax, peace and security would be realized. This is the wonderful thing about Christ – He is *"the Coming One."* This shows what He really is.

The Book of Judges refers to Israel without a king. It told us that God raised up deliverers. One deliverer was Samson … and there was a strange reaction to his prowess. Israel leaders, in cowardly fear of their oppressors, tried to betray Samson. In the end, he actually did fall into the hands of Israel's enemies. They blinded him and set him to hard labor in prison. But there was a final "curtains down" last scene, where Samson saw a way to crush the leadership of the enemy, even though it meant losing his own life. But he was not afraid. The day came … and he made one final and supreme effort – and smashed the power of Israel's foes! In doing so, he forfeited his own life.

It is an allegory. The world's Deliverer – Jesus Christ – like Samson, was betrayed and bound. Then, like Samson, by His death, Christ brought deliverance. He broke the power of evil and of the devil on the Cross. He defeated the enemy, Satan, once and for all.

The Samson story has another episode. To betray him, they bound him hand and foot. Then when his enemies came upon him, he rose and broke the bonds like ropes of sand. It is a Bible pictorial of Christ being bound, immobilized with nails through His feet, and finally shut up in the silence of the tomb. But Christ the Deliverer broke every bond and fetter, mocked the powers of Hell, and rose triumphantly back to God Who sent Him!

Today, you and I can identify with Christ Jesus, our Deliverer!

Today's Scripture

For God in all His fullness was pleased to live in Christ, and by Him God reconciled everything to Himself. He made peace with everything in Heaven and on Earth by means of His Blood on the Cross.
(Colossians 1:19-20)

Daily Power!

My Redeemer, my Deliverer, Christ Jesus, lives in me today!

Today's Bible Reading

Joshua 11:1-23 through 12:1-24; Luke 17:11-37; Psalm 84:1-12; Proverbs 13:5-6

Mark my Word
(for further study)

Judges 13:1-25 through 15:1-20; Colossians 1:19-20

Today's Scripture

*Your Kingdom come,
Your will be done, on
Earth as it is in Heaven.*
(Matthew 6:10)

Daily Power!

*My true heart's desire is
to be "wise," therefore,
I am a soul-winner.*

Today's Bible Reading

*Joshua 13:1-33
through 14:1-16;
Luke 18:1-17;
Psalm 85:1-13;
Proverbs 13:7-8*

Mark my Word
(for further study)

*Psalm 2:12;
Proverbs 11:30;
Isaiah 9:6;
Matthew 6:10;
Mark 16:15;
Luke 19:10; 24:46-48;
Acts 2:14-39*

"Kiss the Son"

The apostle Peter, preaching the first Christian sermon, said, *"Him has God the Father exalted to be a Prince and a Savior."* Jesus Christ took that office when He ascended. To carry out the work, He must return. It can only be accomplished on Earth. That was always God's purpose.

As difficult as it was for the disciples to understand, Jesus was born to die. They feared – and probably hated – the religious leaders and the Romans who put Jesus to death … but they quickly learned that even His death was part of His plan: *"Thus it was necessary for the Christ to suffer and to rise from the dead the third day, and that repentance and remission of sins should be preached in His Name to all nations, beginning at Jerusalem. And you are witnesses of these things."* From that understanding, they learned to extend forgiveness and reconciliation, even with those who persecuted them. This they could do because they respected and honored the Kingship of Christ Jesus, and walked in their responsibilities to carry out His assignment to them: *"Go into all the world and preach the Gospel to every creature."*

The everlasting King is poised on the threshold – *"the government shall be upon His shoulder."* He will take over global responsibilities. No power on Earth or Hell can prevent it! Psalm 2 warns the nations: *"Kiss the Son, lest He be angry and you perish from the way when His wrath is kindly but a little."* When He comes, the whole world in every corner will know. With all power in Heaven and Earth, He will remove from His Kingdom everything that offends. His coming is as sure as the dawn.

How do you and I know Christ is returning? Christians everywhere are praying, "Even so, come Lord Jesus. Thy Kingdom come!" … and that prayer will be answered any day now! And while we are waiting His return, we obey His command: "Occupy until I come!" – which means we don't just sit around waiting for Him to return … but we continue doing the work of the Kingdom, which is winning souls! *"He who wins souls is wise."* That should be your description and mine today!

History in Advance

This is the time of ripening for the final harvest. Both wheat and tares fill the field. Satan can see that his opportunities are slipping away – it is now or never for him. So the greatest display of wickedness, lawlessness and degradation is ahead. But believers have more to think about than mere survival – there are likely to be persecutions, and no doubt blood will flow – our thoughts, however, are on triumph and conquest for Jesus. The build-up of enemy forces is being more than matched by an ever-increasing measure of the Holy Spirit: *"When the enemy comes in, like a flood the Spirit of the Lord will lift up a standard against him."* The greatest outpouring, the greatest anointing of God's power ever known, is coming upon us. Past revivals will seem as nothing when Pentecost breaks upon the entire Church. We already get glimpses of it – the battle of the anointed against the anti-anointed. We now know what it means in Revelation chapter12: *"And they overcame him by the Blood of the Lamb, and by the word of their testimony, and they did not love their lives to the death."* That showdown is fully described:

"So the great dragon was cast out, that serpent of old, called the Devil and Satan, who deceives the whole world; he was cast to the Earth, and his angels were cast out with him. Then I heard a loud voice saying in Heaven, 'Now salvation, and strength, and the Kingdom of our God, and the power of His Christ have come, for the accuser of our brethren, who accused them before our God day and night, has been cast down."

Bible prophecies like these are not alterable. They are history written in advance! When the devil is out to trouble the world, God will trouble the devil. God will do what He said He would, even to the dot on the last "i." Hallelujah! We rejoice! We know! The future is settled beforehand, and the last hour is determined, with its very glorious conclusion. And this is the period we are now entering!

Today's Scripture

They defeated him through the Blood of the Lamb, and the bold word of their witness. They weren't in love with themselves; they were willing to die for Christ.
(Revelation 12:11; the Message)

Daily Power!

God will do what He said He would, even to the dot on the last "i".

Today's Bible Reading

Joshua 15:1-63;
Luke 18:18-43;
Psalm 86:1-17;
Proverbs 13:9-10

Mark my Word
(for further study)

Isaiah 59:19;
Revelation 12:9-11

Today's Scripture

The time is fulfilled, and the Kingdom of God is at hand. Repent and believe in the Gospel.

(Mark 1:15)

Daily Power!

Sharpen my understanding, O Lord, so that I may desire only what you desire, and not what is the desire of Man.

Today's Bible Reading

Joshua 16:1-10 through 18:1-28; Luke 19:1-27; Psalm 87:1-7; Proverbs 13:11

Mark my Word
(for further study)

Psalm 7:5; 35:23; 44:23; 59:4-5; 144:5-6; Isaiah 64:1; Mark 1:15

"God entering the Field"

Duncan Campbell's famous "revival"-related expression, "God entering the field," portrays a solo performance given by the Lord, a display of such dramatic effectiveness that the Godly stand aside in awe. It would fulfill the longing of the Psalmist, *"Part Your Heavens, O Lord, and come down ... Send forth lightning and scatter the enemies; shoot Your arrows and rout them."*

One of the first points one notes about revivalist literature is that references are mainly to the Old Testament. This may be because the New Testament presents a picture of God already at work – hope fulfilled rather than desired. For example, in the 1998 "Heart-Cry For Revival" Conference in Lancaster, Pennsylvania, United States of America, seeking Scriptural backing, Wesley L. Duewell turned to Isaiah 64: *"Oh, that You would rend the Heavens and come down, that the mountains would tremble before You! As when fire sets twigs ablaze and causes water to boil, come down to make Your Name known to Your enemies and cause the nations to quake before You!"* This verse from Isaiah is a typical text calling on God to take new, unprecedented action – it is an appeal for a divine visitation. Isaiah's words are used to express a similar prayer for revival, for God to rend the Heavens today and "move in revival power." It pictures God excelling Himself.

Something here should be carefully noted. Isaiah's words adopted for revival imply the belief that God works at higher or lower levels of power, that His presence fluctuates in His dealings, and that there are periods when He lies low. The assumption is that He can be stirred to manifest Himself, by prayer. That was certainly how the psalmists thought of Him! They even cry, *"Awake, O Lord! Why do You sleep?"* This needs some qualifying. The Psalms themselves do not record these utterances as faith prayers. On the contrary, they are invariably complaints that God is not doing the things He could! Let us commit to being where God wants us to be, when He wants us to be there, so we can fulfill our part in bringing the Gospel to the world today.

The "impossible" Jesus

People talk of Christianity but forget that – at the heart of it – is this greatest hope: Christ's Second Advent. We can't pick and chose the bits we like and still call it Christianity. We know He is coming back because He was raised from the dead. He rose ... so He will come. Paul said so when he was preaching in Athens to the most brainy people around! It was the kind of absolute logic they liked. Peter also said, *"In His great mercy, He has given us new birth into a living hope through the resurrection of Jesus Christ from the dead, until the coming of the salvation in the last time."*

Jesus made many tremendous promises, which He has kept. His promise to rise from the dead – nobody could take it. It was "impossible," and they couldn't think He meant it. But He did ... and He walked out of the tomb. **Jesus deals in impossibilities.** *"You are the God Who does wonders."* He came out of the grace ... so coming from Glory is no problem.

"For Christ has not entered the holy places made with hands, which are copies of the true, but into Heaven itself, now to appear in the presence of God for us; not that He should offer Himself often, as the high priest enters the Most Holy Place every year with blood of another – He then would have had to suffer often since the foundation of the world; but now, once at the end of the ages, He has appeared to put away sin by the sacrifice of Himself. And as it is appointed for men to die once, but after this the judgment, so Christ was offered once to bear the sins of many. To those who eagerly wait for Him, He will appear a second time, apart from sin for salvation."

Christ died and came back, so now He lives – He should manage it! Fantastic? Yes, but not fantasy, nor "truth stranger than fiction." This event was planned from Adam. It is where history is going. If not, then history is going nowhere at all. With great joy, you and I hold onto that tremendous promise: knowing that Christ Jesus is coming again for us!

Today's Scripture

Blessed be the God and Father of our Lord Jesus Christ, Who according to His abundant mercy has begotten us again to a living hope through the resurrection of Jesus Christ from the dead.
(I Peter 1:3)

Daily Power!

I enjoy being connected to the God Who does wonderful works: "Many, O Lord my God, are Your wonderful works which You have done; and Your thoughts toward us cannot be recounted to You in order."
(Psalm 40:5; paraphrased)

Today's Bible Reading

Joshua 19:1-51 through 20:1-9; Luke 19:28-48; Psalm 88:1-18; Proverbs 13:12-14

Mark my Word
(for further study)

*Psalm 40:5;
Hebrews 9:24-28;
I Peter 1:3*

Our God-given Rights

We know Christ is coming back because He belongs here. He is *"the Man, Christ Jesus."* He was born here … ate here and grew here … breathed here and lived here … was tempted just as we are – but never sinned. He was falsely accused here … tried and convicted here … beaten and reviled here … shamed and despised here … and He shed His Blood here. He rose again in the same body in which He died on the Cross, but renewed and immortal. The Son of Man is tied to this world of men, forever, incorruptible, the Resurrection and the Life!

He has two homes – Earth and Heaven … with us, and with the Father. He went to God because He came from God … He will come back here because He came from here. *"In My Father's House are many mansions; if it were not so, I would have told you. I go to prepare a place for you. And if I go and prepare a place for you, I will come again and receive you to Myself; that where I am, there you may be also."* He belongs to God and belongs to us. As He loved the Father, He went to Him … and because He loves us, He will come to us. When the new Heaven and Earth come, He will belong to both.

People talk of rights – we have no rights except what God gives. The greatest right is our claim on Jesus Christ: *"God so loved the world that He gave His only Son"* … *"the unspeakable gift."* We own Him like God owns Him, Earth as much as Heaven. *"Unto us, a Child is born, and unto us, a Son is given."* He said, *"I am among you as He that serves."* He put Himself under obligation to us by His incredible grace. One of our God-given rights is to see Him here on Earth. That is our inviolable privilege: *"Every eye shall see Him"*!

Today's Scripture

For unto us a Child is born, unto us a Son is given; and the government will be upon His shoulder. And His Name will be called Wonderful, Counselor, Mighty God, Everlasting Father, Prince of Peace. Of the increase of His government and peace there will be no end.
(Isaiah 9:6-7)

Daily Power!

My greatest claim is that God Himself gave me His very Best – His "unspeakable Gift" – in His Son Jesus Christ.

Today's Bible Reading

Joshua 21:1-45 through 22:1-20; Luke 20:1-26; Psalm 89:1-13; Proverbs 13:15-16

Mark my Word
(for further study)

Isaiah 9:6-7; Luke 22:27; John 3:16; 4:42; 14:2-3; II Corinthians 9:15; Revelation 1:7

Intercession Results

After a crusade meeting, a lady came to me and told me how she had been "molested by evil spirits for many years," and how she despaired of her life. I was moved by what she said, and I promised to pray for her. When I reached my hotel room, the Lord told me to fast and pray for her – I did so. The next day, I was praying for her with all of my heart, when at noon, I suddenly experienced a breakthrough. The glory of the Lord filled my soul, and the Holy Spirit said to me, "It is done."

That evening, I met the lady again. Before I could say anything, she reported with shining eyes, "God has done the miracle! Today at noon, I experienced a mighty deliverance in my home." What God does on a small scale, He will also do on the largest.

Moses was perhaps the greatest intercessor (before Christ). After he led the Israelites out of Egypt – a feat wrought miraculously by the mighty hand of God – the children of Israel dared to complain about their newfound freedom in the wilderness: "We don't have enough food … We don't have enough water … We are vulnerable out here … We want to go back to Egypt!" Again and again, God was disturbed by these ungrateful former-slaves, and threatened to destroy them and their ingratitude … and again and again, Moses prevailed with God not only to spare them, but to provide for them generously and miraculously. Intercession is not made because someone deserves God's mercy, but because He is kind and loving and generous.

What needs are there in your own life that you need intercessory prayer for? Remember: *"You have not because you ask not."* There is no embarrassment in asking a fellow-believer to pray with you – that's a privilege for both of you … that's bound to bless the two of you!

Today's Scripture

Now this is the confidence that we have in Him, that if we ask anything according to His will, He hears us. And if we know that He hears us, whatever we ask, we know that we have the petitions that we have asked of Him.
(I John 5:14-15)

Daily Power!

It is the believer's privilege to pray for each other.

Today's Bible Reading

*Joshua 22:21-34 through 23:1-16;
Luke 20:27-47;
Psalm 89:14-37;
Proverbs 13:17-19*

Mark my Word
(for further study)

*John 16:22-24;
I John 5:14-15*

Move by Feelings of Concern

A true intercessor is moved by feelings of concern. The story in Exodus 32 is a strange episode, but shows us the heart of a true intercessor. Moses was angry over Israel's idolatry. Israel had escaped from Egypt after a fantastic display of omnipotence that would make God seem physically near. Above them towered Mount Sinai, with the *"cloud of God's glory"* concealing Moses, who had ascended to speak with God. The people thought he had deserted them. Their simple minds were soaked in the superstitions of Egypt and its gods … and so they made a golden calf to lead them back to Egypt.

The Lord said He would put an end to them because of this appalling lapse, and begin a new nation through Moses. Moses' first reaction was to send swordsmen to rid Israel of the ringleaders … then his pity overcame his anger, and he besought God to save the nation that God called *"a stiff-necked people."* Moses countered by calling them *"**Your** people,"* and pleaded, *"Oh, these people have committed a great sin … Yet now, if You will forgive their sin – but if not, I pray, blot me out of Your Book."* Here, words failed him, such was the force of his compassionate outburst. He offered to die as an atonement for Israel's sin – his offer was turned down because only the Son of God could atone for sin. But this is an example of true intercession.

This proposal was unsolicited. Moses had not been pushed into it. He had brought this rabble of tribes to nationhood like a woman bringing a child into the world. They broke his heart, but he still defended them from the inevitable disaster of their own folly. *"Greater love has no one than this, than to lay down one's life for his friends."* Do you have an unsaved friend or relative who can exasperates you and tries your patience to the limit? **Pray for them!** They really don't need a piece of your mind … they really need some prayers from your heart.

Today's Scripture

I am the Good Shepherd; and I know My sheep, and am known by My own … I lay down My life for the sheep. And other sheep I have which are not of this fold, them also I must bring, and they will hear My voice; and there will be one flock and one Shepherd. Therefore My Father loves Me, because I lay down My life that I may take it up again. No one takes it from Me, but I lay it down of Myself. I have power to lay it down, and I have power to take it again.
(John 10:14-18)

Daily Power!

Father, take me out of my "comfort zone" and put me in a place where Your heart of compassion beats in my own, giving me stronger feelings of concern for the lost.

Today's Bible Reading

Joshua 24:1-33; Luke 21:1-28; Psalm 89:38-52; Proverbs 13:20-23

Mark my Word
(for further study)

Exodus 32;
John 10:14-18; 15:13

Believers who didn't see Miracles

The idea that God disappeared is an old fear of unbelief. Israel participated in the Exodus, and saw His glory and knew it was all true. But within months, they became mistrustful. They wanted something to see … and made a golden calf – to lead them back into slavery! Unbelief always leads to slavery. Faith means freedom.

However, they all lost their passports and visas of faith in God, and never crossed the border into the Promised Land – with two exceptions: Caleb and Joshua, who held onto their faith and entered in. Unbelief is that old. It is neither clever nor modern. Eve doubted. From that moment for her and us, it is a satanic nonsense and foolishness that never did anybody any good. If we are to deal with God, how on Earth can it be but by trusting Him? What trust is He likely to have with those who give Him the cold shoulder or pretend He doesn't even exist? He owes us nothing, and if that is the way we want it, that is the way He will let it be: *"Since they did not think it worthwhile to retain the knowledge of God, He gave them over to a depraved mind."*

After the death of Joshua, very few ever saw a miracle until Christ came, except under Elijah and Elisha. In fact, very little happened that was supernatural. Yet men and women displayed amazing faith. Jesus spoke of them and said, *"Blessed are those who have not seen and yet have believed."* They read the Scriptures, and believed the God of the Exodus could not fail them and would work on their behalf. He did! David, for example, never saw a miracle, and had only the sketchiest experience of the supernatural – yet he went ahead in that total expectation of Divine help. Today, three thousand years later, his faith is still a model for us. Stand firm in your faith today!

Today's Scripture

If you abide in My Word, you are My disciples indeed. And you shall know the truth, and the truth shall make you free.
(John 8:31-32)

Daily Power!

The truth of God's Word lives in my heart, lighting my path eternally.

Today's Bible Reading

*Judges 1:1-36
through 2:1-9;
Luke 21:29-38
through 22:1-13;
Psalm 90:1-17
through 91:1-16;
Proverbs 13:24-25*

Mark my Word
(for further study)

*Exodus 32:1-35;
John 20:29;
Romans 1:28*

Today's Scripture

That which is born of the flesh is flesh, and that which is born of the Spirit is spirit.

(John 3:6)

Daily Power!

The world may wobble around me, but I am centered on the Solid Rock, Christ Jesus.

Today's Bible Reading

Judges 2:10-23
through 3:1-31;
Luke 22:14-34;
Psalm 92:1-16
through 93:1-5;
Proverbs 14:1-2

Mark my Word
(for further study)

Genesis 3:3-4;
Proverbs 14:33-34;
John 3:1-21;
Romans 12:2

An eccentric World

God is our center, not this world. People say that we Christians are eccentric. An eccentric object wobbles around a point that is off-center ... but that is what the Bible calls "the world"! It is not believers – evangelists, witnesses, Christians – who are eccentric ... but the world! The world wobbles as it revolves around itself ... but the believer is centered on God.

When people in the Church talk about making the Gospel relevant, they usually mean that we need to show that the Gospel has something in common with the world of industry, entertainment or commerce. They have it backward! The question is not whether the message can be related to this world – but whether the world is willing to relate to the message of the Cross. Too bad for the world if it is not, for it **will** be judged at the Cross. If the world is not relevant to the Gospel, then the world is drifting ... it has no anchor. *"And do not be conformed to this world, but be transformed by the renewing of your mind, that you may prove what is that good and acceptable and perfect will of God."*

The mistaken belief that "Church and State should be separate" is not a new idea – because the enemy has been trying to put people ahead God in importance since the beginning of time: *"Then the serpent said to the woman, 'You will not surely die. For God knows that in the day you eat of it, your eyes will be opened, and you will be like God, knowing good and evil.'"* But God's Word proclaims, *"Wisdom rests in the heart of him who has understanding, but what is in the heart of fools is made known. Righteousness exalts a nation."*

Another thing I hear people say is, "Evangelists answer questions the world is not asking." Thank God for that! We are **giving answers**, ready for when the world decides to ask the right questions. Because it is asking all the wrong questions, any answers would be equally wrong. Purpose in your heart to be ready with God's answers to every situation in life.

God made Families

The unity working in the very heart of Creation makes prayer for a family viable. God wants families saved. The entire Old Testament is the story of God's family-work, particularly the concentration on one family. It exemplifies His thoughts. He chose Israel from the days of Abraham and Sarah, and the tribes of Jacob, and kept their generations recognizable.

They didn't make themselves notable. They were slippery material, and tended to blend into the heathen nations around where their identity would be lost – but their indifference showed even more God's Family determination! Despite themselves, He made Israel distinguished in racial character. After four thousand years, Israel is the most distinct single family on Earth, however widely scattered. No other race suffered such persecutions and attempts at genocide … because no other race was so personal to God. The Nazi star upon their clothing was, in fact, a testimony by their enemies of their unbreakable Family relationship. Captivity, loss of homeland, Jewish dispersion … nothing ever affected it – for Israel is God's sign to the world of His Family design and purpose!

Isaiah pointed this out: *"But now, thus says the Lord, Who created you, O Jacob, and He Who formed you, O Israel: 'Fear not, for I have redeemed you; I have called you by your name; you are Mine … For I am the Lord your God, the Holy One of Israel, your Savior; I gave Egypt for your ransom, Ethiopia and Seba in your place. Since you are precious in My sight, you have been honored, and I have loved you … Fear not, for I am with you; I will bring your descendants from the east and gather you from the west … Bring My sons from afar and My daughters from the ends of the Earth – everyone who is called by My Name, whom I have created for My glory; I have formed him, yes, I have made him.'"* Like a family named after the father, Israel bore God's name, **Isra – El**. "El" is basic Hebrew for the Deity. Today, wear your true name – "Christian" – with pride!

Today's Scripture

Fear not, for I have redeemed you, I have called you by your name, you are Mine. When you pass through the waters, I will be with you, and through the rivers, they shall not overflow you. When you walk through the fire, you shall not be burned, nor shall the flame scorch you; For I am the Lord your God.
(Isaiah 43:1-3)

Daily Power!

Being a member of the Family of God is a centuries-old honor and privilege.

Today's Bible Reading

Judges 4:1-24 through 5:1-31;
Luke 22:35-53;
Psalm 94:1-23;
Proverbs 14:3-4

Mark my Word
(for further study)

Isaiah 43:1-28

26

Concentrated Care

"As for your nativity, on the day you were born your navel cord was not cut, nor were you washed in water to cleanse you; you were not rubbed with salt nor wrapped in swaddling cloths. No eye pitied you, to do any of these things for you, to have compassion on you; but you were thrown out into the open field, where you yourself were loathed on the day you were born. And when I passed by you and saw you struggling in your own blood, I said to you in your blood, 'Live!' ... I made you thrive like a plant in the field, and your grew, matured and became very beautiful." Ezekiel 16 describes the concentrated care of God for Israel like finding a newborn child *"cast out on the open field,"* which He saved, nursed and nourished to become a beautiful woman. This parable typified God's intentions with the whole of Humanity. When He brought the world and its inhabitants into existence, He did not walk away and leave us to our own devices, not even when we deliberately broke away. The Creator-creature bond can never be annulled. No matter how far we draw away, our existence is dependant on Him. *"If I make my bed in Hell, behold, You are there."* The link between Creator and His creatures may be stretched as slender as a spider's thread, but cannot be broken. He is always sensitive of us.

How often do we think that we are alone in this world, and it is always an uphill struggle to try to find where God must be hiding. It is important for you to know that the concentrated care which God lavishes on you – whether or not you realize it, whether or not you recognize His hand active and moving in your life, whether or not you acknowledge His tender touch – is what He gives because He **wants to**, not because you deserve it. His love for you is without limit ... and His gift of salvation – that all-important point where your estrangement from Him is erased and you are drawn close to His heart – is given freely.

Today's Scripture

Where can I go from Your Spirit? Or where can I flee from Your presence? If I ascend into Heaven, You are there; if I make my bed in Hell, behold, You are there. If I take the wings of the morning, and dwell in the uttermost parts of the sea, even there Your hand shall lead me, and Your right hand shall hold me.

(Psalm 139:7-10)

Daily Power!

Thank You God, You are always with me.

Today's Bible Reading

Judges 6:1-40;
Luke 22:54-71
through 23:1-12;
Psalm 95:1-11
through 96:1-13;
Proverbs 14:5-6

Mark my Word
(for further study)

Hebrew 13:5;
Psalm 139:7-10;
Ezekiel 16:1-14

Jesus – God and Man

We know Jesus is coming back because He is one of us – just like you and me! We read in Hebrews 2: *"Inasmuch then as the children have partaken of flesh and blood, He Himself likewise shared in the same, that through Death He might destroy him who had the power of death, that is, the devil."* He belongs to the Family of Man, and He will not desert His family, nor stay away forever.

Some foolishly teach that Jesus Christ was once an archangel – but an angel doesn't have our nature. We read, *"He took not on Him the nature of angels, but of Abraham."* Also, an angel doesn't have the Divine nature. Angels are neither real Man nor real God.

Jesus Christ was fully human, conceived by God but born of a woman. It was His intention to live a full life, just as humans do, so that He could more readily identify with us. If His sole purpose was to be a sacrifice for our sins, He could have been crucified as an infant. But He chose to endure all the heartaches and hardships that we do … because of His great compassion for us. *"For we do not have a High Priest Who cannot sympathize with our weaknesses, but was in all points tempted as we are, yet without sin."* Jesus was the Son of Man **and** the Son of God.

But *"there is one Mediator between God and men, the Man Christ Jesus."* A mediator has links to both parties. An angel representing neither God nor us could not be a link. This is the only Mediator – like Jacob's ladder – set up between Heaven and Earth. Jesus binds Heaven and Earth, God and Man, deity and flesh, together in Himself. His presence on Earth will be the most natural thing of all. This is the great hope to which we cling!

Today's Scripture

But we see Jesus, Who was made a little lower than the angels, for the suffering of death, crowned with glory and honor, that He, by the grace of God, might taste death for everyone.
(Hebrews 2:9)

Daily Power!

Because Christ Jesus became flesh-and-blood like me, I will reign with Him in Heavenly places!

Today's Bible Reading

*Judges 7:1-25
through 8:1-17;
Luke 23:13-43;
Psalm 97:1-12
through 98:1-9;
Proverbs 14:7-8*

Mark my Word
(for further study)

*I Timothy 2:5;
Hebrews 2:5-14; 4:2*

Jesus in the real World

Who was Jesus? The Bible tells us that He was *"God with us"* – that God *"became a Human Being and, full of grace and truth, lived among us."* In other words, Jesus showed us God getting involved in the real world. He got His hands dirty … He got His hands nailed to a Cross! And He did it so that we could be set free from the power and devastation of sin.

When Roman prisoners were marched out to be crucified, they carried the crossbeam on their shoulders. With their arms tied to the beam, they walked, bent double, to the place of execution. That is how Jesus must have walked through the streets of Jerusalem to the execution hill called "the place of the skull." *"Then the soldiers of the governor took Jesus into the Praetorium and gathered the whole garrison around Him. And they stripped Him and put a scarlet robe on Him. When they had twisted a crown of thorns, they put it on His head, and a reed in His right hand. And they bowed the knee before Him and mocked Him, saying, 'Hail, King of the Jews!' Then they spat on Him, and took the reed and struck Him on the head. And when they had mocked Him, they took the robe off Him, put His own clothes on Him, and led Him away to be crucified."*

It was as if He was carrying a banner – a giant sign – proclaiming an awful truth in a language the whole world could understand and never forget. The crossbeam carried by Jesus speaks of our human minus or negative – the failure and sin that lies in the heart of us all.

The Cross shows us God's incredible response to human suffering. God Himself entered into our suffering, and took our sin on Himself. Jesus – although He was completely innocent and without sin – was made to be "sin for us." As one of the first Christians put it: *"While we were still sinners, Christ died for us."*

On that hill, Jesus put the crossbeam of our sin and wickedness across the upright. He changed our human **minus** into God's **plus**. Jesus released the power of God's mercy, forgiveness and healing to anyone who would come to Him and simply ask for it. That means you!

Today's Scripture

God demonstrates His own love toward us, in that while we were still sinners, Christ died for us.

(Romans 5:8)

Daily Power!

On the Cross of Calvary, Jesus changed my human minus into God's plus. He released the power of God's mercy, forgiveness and healing to me if I would come to Him and simply ask for it.

Today's Bible Reading

Judges 8:18-35 through 9:1-21; Luke 23:44-56 through 24:1-12; Psalm 99:1-9; Proverbs 14:9-10

Mark my Word
(for further study)

Matthew 27:27-56; Romans 5:8; II Corinthians 5:21

Saints in Lights

Look at them! What a blaze of glory glitters down the endless stream of redeemed humanity! Here is one of the firsts: a beautiful woman, Mary, once torn apart inwardly by seven devils; she sat with heartbreaking longing and love near His empty tomb, as His everlasting worshipper: *"Now when He rose early on the first day of the week, He appeared first to Mary Magdalene, out of whom He had cast seven devils."* Here is Peter – Jesus had to work so hard on him to make anything of him, but now he is resplendent in divine light: *"Blessed be the God and Father of our Lord Jesus Christ, Who according to His abundant mercy has begotten us again to a living hope through the resurrection of Jesus Christ from the dead."* And here is Paul, who persecuted Him: *"But the Lord said to him, 'Go, for he is a chosen vessel of Mine to bear My Name before Gentiles, kings and the children of Israel."* The thief who mocked Him ... Zacchaeus, who received a heart of gold at Jesus' touch. The trail of light passes down the long centuries: dedicated lovers of Jesus – martyrs, apostles, saints, people who praised God while their fingers burned like tapers, evangelists, pastors, missionaries, humble workers, the faithful, you ... Jack and Jennifer, Bob and Louise ... and even me.

He saved a poor sinner like me! Here we are now, and one day we shall be there with the saints in light, the triumphs of His grace, drawn from all tribes, all ethnic groups, all social ranks ... and all bathed in His glory. Adulterers, homosexuals, thieves, liars, perverts, witches, murderers, addicts, Satanists, the covetous, the idolaters, the unclean, the sophisticated and unsophisticated side by side, the learned and the simple hand in hand – all washed in the Blood of Jesus! Such is the population of the Kingdom of God! This is the glory of the King, the Church of the Living God, the City of God, the Bride of the Lamb. *"Look, ye saints, the sight is glorious!"* Rejoice today, that your name is written in the Lamb's Book of Life!

Today's Scripture

O God, You are my God; early will I seek You; my soul thirsts for You, my flesh longs for You in a dry and thirsty land where there is no water. So I have looked for You in the sanctuary, to see Your power and Your glory. Because Your loving kindness is better than life, my lips shall praise You, thus I will bless You while I live; I will lift up my hands in Your Name.
(Psalm 63:1-4)

Daily Power!

I am privileged to be counted among God's saints who have gone before – Peter, Paul, Mary, and more – and to worship at the Throne of God together with them.

Today's Bible Reading

Judges 9:22-57 through 10:1-18; Luke 24:13-53; Psalm 100:1-5; Proverbs 14:11-12

Mark my Word
(for further study)

Psalm 63:1-11; Mark 16:9; Acts 9:15; I Peter 1:3

Christ's great Commission

It was impossible to act on the Great Commission before the Day of Pentecost. Jesus had told His disciples to wait. **Then** things started to happen! The evangelism that took place on that one day produced the Church. But … what is the Church? Are we clear about its nature and its purpose? The Church is an extension of the compassion of the Lord Jesus, an extension of His comfort, His healing, His goodness. *"Jesus of Nazareth … went about doing good and healing all who were oppressed by the devil."* That is what we should be doing!

The Church is His body, we are told. God has no arms but ours with which to embrace this pitiable world. Love is His supreme characteristic. I feel that we are only His body to the degree or extent that we show clear evidence of His compassion. A loveless Church is no church at all. The love of God which was personified in Jesus needs to be personified in the Church. *"Let this mind be in you which was also in Christ Jesus."* The Church is the current evidence of what we read of Jesus in the Gospels. If I dare say it: the Church is His love-child, the embodiment of His Spirit of sonship.

The Church is to be a continuation of the Day of Pentecost. The purpose of evangelism is not to turn the Church into an ecclesiastical advertising agency or a society for propagating its own existence. It burst into view on the Day of Pentecost speaking in tongues, with prophecy and fire! If the Church isn't like that – no fire, no tongues, no prophecies, no evangelism, no bold preaching of Christ and the Resurrection, no triumphant certainty and promise – how can any rational person identify it as the same Church? Who would recognize its visage as that of the Church in Jerusalem in AD 30 without the power and manifestation of the Spirit? We are left with the natural processes of success, organization, intellectual abilities, human wisdom, prowess, and energies. Those assets – relied upon alone – leave the Church an empty shell. You don't need to belong to **that** "church" … but to the living Church of Christ!

Today's Scripture

For as the body is one and has many members, but all the members of that one body, being many, are one body, so also is Christ … Now you are the body of Christ, and members individually.
(I Corinthians 12:12, 27)

Daily Power!

Christ will be magnified in my body, whether by life or by death.
(Philippians 1:20)

Today's Bible Reading

*Judges 11:1-40
through 12:1-15;
John 1:1-28;
Psalm 101:1-8;
Proverbs 14:13-14*

Mark my Word
(for further study)

*Acts 10:30;
I Corinthians 12:12, 27;
Colossians 1:18;
Philippians 1:20; 2:5*

The Gospel is not an alternative,
it is God's ultimatum.

The Bible is the constitution of the Kingdom of God.

Unity is not uniformity

God's lively Stones

The five "gifts" listed in Ephesians – apostles, prophets, teachers, evangelists, and pastor-teachers – are given to meet the aim of building up the body of Christ. The purpose is made clear in Paul's first letter to the Corinthians: *"To each one the manifestation of the Spirit is given for the common good."* He names again three of the same gifts – apostles, prophets and teachers – but in place of evangelists and pastors, he refers to those who work miracles, have the gifts of healing, speak with tongues, and interpret. He continues saying that the Church is built up (edified) by prophecy and tongues. All these gifts are given to believers for the benefit of their fellow-believers, to build up the unity of the Church. There are no dead stones, only living stones, equipped to serve.

The whole theme of Ephesians is not what "we are," but what **"He is."** It is Christ – not church offices – with which we should be concerned. God at work in us and through us, by Him and for Him. He is *"the fullness of Him who fills everything in every way."* He does not evangelize, but expects us to do so … by His endowment. We are His voice, His hands and His feet – when we are His. He has not ceased to be active – He is the fullness filling us, filling the Church, and making it what it is. And behind everything … is the gift of His grace. What a treasure we have within us – called to be "Jesus with skin on" to the world, and completely equipped to fulfill His assignment!

Later in Ephesians, Paul enumerated the equipment needed to be effective soldiers in God's army … and then he tells us that even soldiers receive promotions: *"For which I am an **ambassador** in chains, that in it I may speak boldly, as I ought to speak."* If we aspire to greatness in God's Kingdom, then we must decide that bold speaking is our requirement … as we shake off the centuries of "downtrodden, pseudo-humble, so-called Christianity" that has paralyzed believers down through the ages. Walking with God's own authority to clearly (and boldly) speak the **truth** to the world in Christ's Name … with His love … is your opportunity and divine responsibility! Walk in that authority.

Today's Scripture

Coming to Him as to a Living Stone, rejected indeed by men, but chosen by God and precious, you also, as living stones, are being built up a spiritual house, a holy priesthood, to offer up spiritual sacrifices acceptable to God through Jesus Christ.
(I Peter 2:4-5)

Daily Power!

Thank You, Father, that You have established me as one of Your lively stones in the Kingdom!

Today's Bible Reading

Judges 13:1-25 through 14:1-20;
John 1:29-51;
Psalm 102:1-28;
Proverbs 14:15-16

Mark my Word
(for further study)

I Corinthians 12:1-31; 14:1-39;
Ephesians 1:23; 6:1-24

Today's Scripture

Speak, Lord, for Your servant hears.
(I Samuel 3:9)

Daily Power!

I am eternally grateful, Father, that You have chosen me to be your beloved child.

Today's Bible Reading

Judges 15:1-20 through 16:1-31; John 2:1-25; Psalm 103:1-22; Proverbs 14:17-19

Mark my Word
(for further study)

I Samuel 3:1-21; Luke 6:12-17

Hardly Supermen

The twelve disciples were anything but supermen. How did Jesus choose His apostles? In the Book of Luke, we read: *"Now it came to pass in those days that He went out to the mountain to pray, and continued all night in prayer to God. And when it was day, He called His disciples to Himself; and from them He chose twelve whom He also named apostles: Simon, whom He also named Peter, and Andrew his brother; James and John; Philip and Bartholomew; Matthew and Thomas; James the son of Alphaeus, and Simon called the Zealot; Judas the son of James, and Judas Iscariot who also became a traitor. And He came down with them and stood on a level place with a crowd of His disciples and a great multitude of people from all Judea and Jerusalem, and from the seacoast of Tyre and Sidon, who came to hear Him and be healed of their diseases."*

Jesus prayed *"all night"* before He selected His disciples. Usually it is thought that through the night, God dropped the name of each apostle one by one into the mind of the Lord – "You should pick Bartholomew, Matthew, Thaddeus …" – and that the Lord made a list of Divinely nominated and approved characters. Perhaps He took one hour over each one of them to establish that He had got it right. *"He prayed all night"* means – so experts propose – twelve hours, one hour for each apostle!

Now I dare to ask: was that **really** what He did – to ask for guidance to choose men with just the right calibers and potentials, men whose greatness God could see beforehand? Were they to be people whom a judge of character would designate for high office? Or was Jesus, in fact, wrestling with that as a temptation – to choose men whose natural capacities would prove to be adequate, men with distinguished and noble qualities – the great, the brilliant, the influential, the mighty? I can imagine that it could be so. It could have been twelve hours of prayer struggling between the natural way of the world (to plan success by appointing gifted men) … and God's way. If that is the case, do you think God would have chosen **you** or **me**? Let us believe, together, that each of us has His divine calling engraved in our hearts … and let us treasure and thank Him for that calling today.

Jonah – the reluctant Evangelist

When you read through the Bible, beginning at Genesis, you will find nothing said about evangelism until you get to the little Book of Jonah – a book that stands out from the rest of the Bible. It is almost the evangelist's vade mecum — a personal handbook for daily use.

Though most people are acquainted with Jonah, many (including some Christians) don't believe the story presented in this book – they think there's "something fishy" about the story of Jonah! However, Jesus and His contemporaries regarded it a history, not as a fable or even a parable. And whoever wrote down the story of Jonah knew how to write. This small book deserves our close attention.

"This is an evil generation. It seeks a sign, and no sign will be given to it except the sign of Jonah the prophet. For as Jonah became a sign to the Ninevites, so also the Son of Man will be to this generation … The men of Nineveh will rise up in the judgment of this generation and condemn it, for they repented at the preaching of Jonah, and indeed a greater than Jonah is here."

The prophet Jonah lived about eight hundred years before Christ. He heard the call of God to go to Nineveh, the last capital city of the Assyrian Empire. It stood on the River Tigris, six hundred miles as the crow flies due east from where Jonah lived. Instead of going to Nineveh, however, Jonah bought passage on a ship to Tarshish – that is, going west – in the other direction. He was desperate to get away from his obligation … Nineveh was the **last place** he wanted to go!

Have you ever been in that place – where God asked you to do something for Him, to go somewhere for Him … and you just didn't want to do it? I know I have! Yet I have found that every time I stepped out in faith to obey Him, His mercy was always there to lead and guide me: *"In You, O Lord, I put my trust … For You are my Rock and my Fortress; therefore, for Your Name's sake, lead me and guide me."* If God is asking you to step out in faith to do something today … just say "Yes" and let Him lead you and guide you … today!

Today's Scripture

Salvation is of the Lord.
(Jonah 2:9b)

Daily Power!

Lord, every day let my prayer be: "Where You lead me, I will follow."

Today's Bible Reading

*Judges 17:1-13
through 18:1-31;
John 3:1-21;
Psalm 104:1-23;
Proverbs 14:20-21*

Mark my Word
(for further study)

*Psalm 31:1-3;
Jonah 1:1-17
through 4:1-11;
Matthew 12:38-42*

4

Going down

When we read about Jonah, note the way his flight is described. Jonah chapter 1 says he went **down** to Joppa … then he went **down** into the ship … and then went **down** into the ship's hold. Then when a storm came, the sailors threw Jonah **down** into the sea, and a great fish swallowed him up, and he went **down** into the belly of the big fish. He then prayed, saying to the Lord, *"You hurled me into the deep. I went down to the moorings of the mountains."* When the fish vomited Jonah and God spoke, the text says, *"Jonah arose."* Going to preach when God sends us is elevating – we arise!

Let's have a little sympathy for Jonah: Nineveh **really did** have a fearsome reputation! One or two of their kings were decidedly brutal, some of the worst to ever walk the Earth. They took pleasure in atrocities and cruelties so monstrous that they shock us even today. If I were to describe them, likely you wouldn't sleep tonight … and if you did, it would be the stuff of nightmares! Jonah certainly didn't relish the thought of a confrontation with men like that. How could a foreigner hope to preach against them and come out alive?

Of course, he did eventually go … and Nineveh actually repented of its wicked ways. Jonah's preaching seems to have been effective. Yet Jonah was perturbed by the end-results. He wanted to see the judgment of God fall on Nineveh … and who could blame him? He had warned the city that God was about to destroy it. Their wickedness had reached the ears of God, and judgment was what they deserved. But the city repented, and God withheld His judgment (at least for a period of time – less than two hundred years later, Nineveh was **totally** destroyed).

Sometimes you and I feel like God is calling us to impossible tasks – but take heart: **your God is the God of the impossible!**

Today's Scripture

Jesus said to him, "If you can believe, all things are possible to him who believes."

(Mark 9:23)

Daily Power!

My constant assurance is that, on my own strength, I cannot succeed … but with God, all things are possible!

Today's Bible Reading

Judges 19:1-30 through 20:1-48; John 3:22-36 through 4:1-3; Psalm 104:24-35; Proverbs 14:22-24

Mark my Word
(for further study)

Jonah 1:1-17; Matthew 19:16-22; Mark 9:14-29

Seven Rules of Prayer

(1) Ask in faith in God. We cannot ask too much and blow a fuse by overloading the demand on divine help. **Ask!** That is Christ's **command,** so you cannot be outside the will of God by as king … but you can "tie His hands" if you do not ask.

(2) Do not come apologetically in case you are asking inappropriately or outside God's will. Our job is to ask anyway, and let God decide how to act. We have made it such a mark of high piety to ask "only for what God wants" that it contradicts what Jesus said: *"Ask whatever you wish."* God allows mature believers free choice over large areas of their lives – and blesses what they decide.

(3) Forgive as God forgives you: *"And whenever you stand praying, if you have anything against anyone, forgive him, that your Father in Heaven may also forgive you your trespasses."*

(4) Do not pray *"to be heard of men,"* but with sincerity. Remember: God is full of grace.

(5) Pray in the Name of Jesus. Since we are in Christ, one with Him, when we pray in the Name of Jesus, we are speaking with Christ's merits imputed to us. Use common sense.

(6) Cherish the Word of God. Notice the balance of this sentence: *"If … My words remain in you, ask whatever you wish, and it will be given you."* The Psalmist wrote: *"If I had cherished sin in my heart, the Lord would not have listened."* Treasure the Word of Christ; do not cherish iniquity.

(7) Deal with obstacles to answered prayer. James warns why many times we may not be heard: *"He who doubts … should not think he will receive anything from the Lord"* … *"When you ask, you do not receive because you ask with wrong motives, that you may spend what you get on your pleasure."* Wisdom in prayer is essential.

Apply these guides to your prayer life and see for yourself how prayer really does **change things!**

Today's Scripture

But love your enemies, do good, and lend, hoping for nothing in return; and your reward will be great, and you will be sons of the Most High. For He is kind to the unthankful and evil world.

(Luke 6:35)

Daily Power!

I am obedient to Christ's command – "Ask!" – so I spend valuable time every day in prayer.

Today's Bible Reading

Judges 21:1-25 through Ruth 1:1-22; John 4:4-42; Psalm 105:1-15; Proverbs 14:25

Mark my Word
(for further study)

Psalm 66:18; Matthew 5:23-24; 21:22; Mark 11:25; Luke 6:35-37; 18:10-14; John 14:13; 15:7; 16:23; James 1:6-7; 4:3

Perfect Wisdom

Jesus prayed: *"Not My will, but Yours be done."* We are not all-wise and do not make perfect petitions. If we had the management of omnipotence (unlimited power), we would soon make a mess of things. God, however, will not be persuaded to do what is folly – not even to please somebody. His answers are wiser than our prayers, even His **"No!"**

It used to be taught that when King Hezekiah prayed for longer life and God gave him another fifteen years – *"Thus says the Lord, the God of David your father, 'I have heard your prayer I have seen your tears, surely I will heal you … And I will add to your days fifteen years."* It was taught that this was actually **against** God's will, because during those fifteen years, Manasseh, Hezekiah's wicked son, was born; later, for over fifty years, Manasseh led the nation into wickedness. But in fact, if Hezekiah had died without a son, the Davidic line as chronicled in Matthew chapter one would have come to a premature end. This teaching does not ring true.

In Christ's "family tree," there are princes and criminals, prostitutes and warriors, kings and idolaters – and so there are in every family tree. From generation to generation, God is constantly seeking those who will turn their hearts toward Him: Noah found His favor in the midst of sin … Abraham turned away from the false gods of Ur … Rahab the harlot helped save the people of Israel … Ruth left the idols of Moab and married Boaz, to become grandparents of David the king … and onward. Only God knows: *"The heart is deceitful above all things, and desperately wicked; who can know it? I, the Lord, search the heart, I test the mind, even to give every man according to his ways, according to the fruit of his doings."* God does nothing against His will – even His "long-term" will – because He knows the end from the beginning, and **never** makes a mistake. Therefore … you can **pray on** with Godly confidence … for your prayers are not being said in vain!

Today's Scripture

Remember the former things of old, for I am God, and there is no other; I am God, and there is none like Me, declaring the end from the beginning, and from ancient times things that are not yet done, saying, "My counsel shall stand, and I will do all My pleasure."

(Isaiah 46:9-10)

Daily Power!

My God is infallible. Whenever I pray, He weighs my requests against His plan-without-time, and then answers accordingly.

Today's Bible Reading

Ruth 2:1-23 through 4:1-22; John 4:43-54; Psalm 105:16-36; Proverbs 14:26-27

Mark my Word
(for further study)

II Kings 20:1-21; 21:1-26; Isaiah 38:1-22; 46:9-10; Jeremiah 17:10; Matthew 1:1-17; Luke 22:42

Prepare your Family

The minds of children – indeed all of us – need protection. But we have a full set of spiritual armor: *"Put on the whole armor of God that you may be able to stand against the wiles of the devil ... Stand therefore, having girded your waist with truth, having put on the breastplate of righteousness, and having shod your feet with the preparation of the Gospel of peace; above all, taking the shield of faith with which you will be able to quench all the fiery darts of the wicked one. And take the helmet of salvation, and the sword of the Spirit, which is the Word of God."*

That is why every father in Israel was commanded to teach the children around their table the words of the covenant of God: *"These words which I command you today shall be in your heart. You shall teach them diligently to your children, and shall talk of them when you sit in your house, when you walk by the way, when you lie down, and when you rise up."*

The need is underlined in the Bible by the tragic fact that not every Godly man had Godly children ... which usually ended in tragedy. The high priest Eli and the prophet Samuel both had heartbreaking sons: *"Now the sons of Eli were corrupt; they did not know the Lord ... Therefore the sin of the young men was very great before the Lord, for men abhorred the offering of the Lord"* ... *"Now it came to pass when Samuel was old that he made his sons judges over Israel ... But his sons did not walk in his ways; they turned aside after dishonest gain, took bribes and perverted justice."* When our children do not follow Godly ways, they can bring whole nations to ruin. God had appointed His priests and judges to rule His people Israel, but when Samuel's sons became godless, the people began to clamor for a different way of government – which ultimately brought Israel back into the wilderness of godlessness. Training our children to walk in Godly ways – and then helping them maintain that walk into their adult years – is more important than just for our own satisfaction, because it works closely with God's ultimate plan: that our families will be shining examples of Godly living in a world filled with darkness and anarchy.

Today's Scripture

Point your kids in the right direction – when they're old, they won't be lost.
   (Proverbs 22:6; the Message)

Daily Power!

Help me to set a Godly example to the world, and to be a Godly person always.

Today's Bible Reading

I Samuel 1:1-28 through 2:1-21; John 5:1-23; Psalm 105:37-45; Proverbs 14:28-39

Mark my Word
(for further study)

I Samuel 2:12, 17; 8:1-3; Proverbs 22:6; Ephesians 6:10-17

First Generation

Today's Scripture

Let us eat and be merry, for this my son was dead and is alive again; he was lost and is found.

(Luke 15:23-24)

Daily Power!

I will be a consistent example of Godly living to my children and to my community.

Today's Bible Reading

I Samuel 2:22-36
through 4:1-22;
John 5:24-47;
Psalm 106:1-12;
Proverbs 14:30-31

Mark my Word
(for further study)

Deuteronomy 30:19;
Luke 15:11-32;
Romans 6:23; 10:9-10

God has no grandchildren. We teach our children to know God, understand His Word, walk in righteousness – and we believe our well-taught children will return to God, and in the promise that our households will be saved through our witness. But there is no automatic guarantee that our children will follow after God – parents cannot choose to **make** their children righteous. As Godly parents, we must **train up** our children – we always **pray fervently for the salvation of our children** and our loved ones – but what decisions they make for themselves are up to them! That is "free will": *"I have set before you life and death, blessing and cursing; therefore choose life, that both you and your descendants may live."*

God cares so much for His children that He constantly seeks them, wooing them with love. But even the "best-raised" children can be stubborn and rebellious, wandering away from their Godly heritage. The perfect example is the Parable of the Prodigal Son: *"A certain man had two sons, and the younger said, 'Father give me the portion of goods that falls to me.' So he divided to them his livelihood. And not many days after, the younger son gathered all together, journeyed to a far country, and there wasted his possessions with prodigal living ... But when he came to himself, he said, 'I will arise and go to my father, and will say to him: Father, I have sinned against Heaven and before you ... Make me like one of your servants.' And he arose and came to his father. But when he was still a great way off, his father saw him and had compassion, and ran and fell on his face and kissed him ... 'For this my son was dead and is alive again; he was lost and is found.'"* I do not know of any Christian parents of wayward children who would not respond with joyful tears when their loved ones returned to God! As Christian parents, our responsibility is to **set a good, consistent example for our children** ... and then believe that the "attractions" of sin will be shown for their actual evil nature, and that our children will return voluntarily to a personal relationship with God. God has chosen children – all of them are "first generation."

The Logo of God's Love

The story of Jesus does not end with the Crucifixion. If it did, the Cross would be a symbol of crushing defeat and despair. The Good News is that Jesus not only destroyed the power of sin on the Cross, He also destroyed the power of death. On the third day, God raised Him back to life, triumphant over darkness, death and Satan: *"And behold, there was a great earthquake, for an angel of the Lord descended from Heaven, and came and rolled back the stone from the door, and sat on it … And the guards shook for fear of him, and became like dead men. But the angel answered and said to the women, 'Do not be afraid, for I know that you seek Jesus Who was crucified. He is not here, for He is risen, as He said. Come, see the place where the Lord lay.'"*

Jesus, the carpenter of Nazareth, turned the wood of the Cross into the Door to Life. That is the deep heart of the Good News: **The Cross has the power to transform us.** Minus is turned to plus, negative to positive. On the Cross, darkness changes to light, death to life, hate to love, chains to freedom, fear to faith, despair to joy, brokenness to wholeness … and Hell to Heaven!

Jesus is still alive! He is here today, to reverse every curse and to cancel Satan's evil work. Sinners are forgiven. The sick are made well. Broken relationships are restored. Against the power of Jesus on the Cross, the forces of evil will finally be defeated! This is why the Cross is the symbol or logo of the Christian faith. It belongs to Jesus alone. No founder or leader of another religion would dare to use this logo because it stands for something that they themselves have never done!

None of them has been crucified for the sins of the world. None of them has been raised from the dead. None of them can give us the help we so desperately need. Only Jesus is able to save us. As He said: *"I am the Way, the Truth, and the Life; no one goes to the Father except by Me."* Embrace the Cross of Jesus Christ – not as a symbol of death – but as God's transforming promise to turn negative into positive.

Today's Scripture

Let not your heart be troubled; you believe in God, believe also in Me. In My Father's House are many mansions; if it were not so, I would have told you. I go to prepare a place for you. And if I go and prepare a place for you, I will come again and receive you to Myself, that where I am, there you may be also.
(John 14:1-4)

Daily Power!

Only Jesus is able to save me. He said it: "I am the Way, the Truth, and the Life; no one goes to the Father except by Me."

Today's Bible Reading

I Samuel 5:1-21 through 7:1-17; John 6:1-21; Psalm 106:13-31; Proverbs 14:32-33

Mark my Word
(for further study)

Matthew 28:1-20; John 14:1-6

Releasing God's Power

The God Who loves us so completely is also the One Who holds ultimate power in the universe. He is the One Who created all things simply by calling them into being. The Bible also tells us that Jesus, as God's Son, is *"the radiance of God's glory and the exact representation of His being, sustaining all things by His powerful Word."*

Hanging on the Cross, Jesus appeared to be anything but powerful. Laughed at by the crowds, tortured by the soldiers, deserted by His friends, slowly bleeding to death, Jesus was utterly helpless. And yet it was at the Cross that the power of God was released! How can this be? *"With Him they also crucified two robbers … And those who passed by blasphemed Him, wagging their heads and saying, 'Aha! You Who destroy the temple and build it in three days, save Yourself and come down from the cross!' Likewise the chief priests also, mocking among themselves with the scribes, said, 'He saved others, Himself He cannot save. Let the Christ, the King of Israel, descend now from the cross, that we may see and believe.' Even those who were crucified with Him reviled Him."*

One way to picture it is through nuclear power. In every atom, positive and negative forces are held together in balance. But when the atom is split, positive splits from negative and power is released, either for destruction or for benefit. Something like this happened on the Cross. Hanging there, Jesus experienced in Himself two opposing forces – the negative of our sins, and the positive of God's love. Jesus was the holy, perfect Son of God, and yet on the Cross, He was made *"sin for us."* There He became the cosmic center where all evil and goodness met.

Finally, Jesus overcame evil, which split away, setting loose new powers of righteousness and resurrection. Evil, death, guilt, and fear are conquered, while the saving power of God's love is released for everyone who asks for it. Within three days, this new power swung into action, when Christ gloriously and triumphantly rose from the dead. Jesus Christ is alive today – isn't that great news! Go out and share that Good News with someone you love today!

Today's Scripture

For He made Him Who knew no sin to be sin for us, that we might become the righteousness of God in Him.

(II Corinthians 5:21)

Daily Power!

*God – Who created all things simply by calling them into being, Who holds ultimate power in the universe – **God loves me!***

Today's Bible Reading

I Samuel 8:1-22 through 9:1-27; John 6:22-42; Psalm 106:32-48; Proverbs 14:34-35

Mark my Word
(for further study)

Mark 15:27-32; II Corinthians 5:21; Hebrews 1:3

The tingling Impule

I was just a young boy when I received the baptism of the Holy Spirit, but soon after that initial experience, I was in a service which my father was leading in a church in North Germany. There was nothing very wrong I wanted to do … but I began to get an impulse during prayer to do something I thought my father would not like. Inexplicably, I could not stop thinking about a woman on the opposite side of the church. This feeling grew stronger and stronger – not just in my head, it seemed to be all over me. I tingled with this feeling more and more, like steadily increasing voltage. I tried to push it out, but the tingling current became stronger. "I shall have to do it!" I spoke to myself. "But what will she say … and what will Father do?" So I crouched down behind the seats, and step–by–step, moved across to her. Then I whispered, "I want to pray for you."

She looked at me and answered, "All right – pray for me!" I put my hand on this grown woman … and something happened: the current in my body seemed to jolt right out into her.

At that point, Father couldn't help but notice. He asked, "Reinhard, what are you doing?"

The lady responded for me, "Reinhard put his hand on me, and I felt the power of the Lord go through me … and look! I am well! I am healed!" At that time, I did not know the spiritual principles behind this healing: if we are obedient, there is enough power from God. I still had to learn that lesson and many like it.

Many times we hear others' awe-inspiring visitations and revelations. They are exciting … but often leave folks feeling downcast because they have had nothing like it. They think they must be inferior to these God-used people. I want you to know the truth about the Holy Spirit: He is for all Christian workers, not only for those who happen to have had some rare and fantastic moments. Many will be like new people when they discover these truths – I trust this is true for you too.

MAY

11

Today's Scripture

You shall receive power when the Holy Spirit has come upon you.
(Acts 1:8)

Daily Power!

By the power of the Holy Spirit working in me, I expect to be a miracle-worker!

Today's Bible Reading

*I Samuel 10:1-27 through 11:1-15;
John 6:43-71;
Psalm 104:1-43;
Proverbs 15:1-3*

Mark my Word
(for further study)

Acts 1:1-8; 2:1-47

Today's Scripture

Remember, our Message is not about ourselves; we're proclaiming Jesus Christ, the Master. All we are is messengers, errand runners from Jesus for you.

(II Corinthians 4:6; the Message)

Daily Power!

Christianity is the Holy Spirit in action, making the Word of God happen.

Today's Bible Reading

I Samuel 12:1-25 through 13:1-22; John 7:1-29; Psalm 108:1-13; Proverbs 15:4

Mark my Word
(for further study)

John 14:6; Acts 1:5, 8; II Corinthians 4:6

When the Spirit comes

There is a promise we are so familiar with that we may have lost sight of its tremendous wonder … for it is one of the most impossible and fantastic expectations that any person could ever entertain: *"You shall be baptized with the Holy Spirit … you shall receive power when the Holy Spirit has come upon you."* Could this really happen in the 20th century? It did for me. I can't think of anything more wonderful for humans than that. It means being filled with God. It isn't "getting high" on God – a sort of euphoric, giddy happiness without substance. The Holy Spirit is not a super drug, tranquilizer or stimulant. He doesn't come to give us an emotional "trip" – but make no mistake about it: His presence is heart-moving. God sends His power into the tough situations of life. He is the original Life-Force meant for us all. Over the years, fresh enlightenment has burst upon me. It is all so wonderful! God wants me to share it with the whole world in my preaching.

When people talk of Christianity as a world religion, they are quite wrong. A religion is a system … and Jesus left no system. **Real Christianity is actually Divine power in action!** Christian truth can't just be written down like so many facts or definitions. Christian truth is alive. You can't draw a picture of a man and say, "That's him!" – and you can't write Christianity down and say, "That's it!" The breath of God animates the Gospel, or it is a dead body of truth instead of living truth. Jesus said, *"I am the Way, the Truth, and the Life."* That is how I know it and preach it.

But let us try to define Christianity in up-to-date terms: **It is the Holy Spirit in action, making the Word of God happen.** We must be able to show people that the Gospel is what it claims to be. When a champion athlete stands on the track, we don't need to argue to prove he is world-class. Just fire the starting pistol! That is what I do – the Gospel of Christ is alive, so I go into a stadium and let the Gospel do its own thing. Everybody can see it is alive. That is what the Holy Spirit does. Believe me when I tell you that what I have witnessed the power of the Gospel do in a stadium filled with thousands, it can do in your heart that is filled with a desire to receive all the God has for you!

Demystifying Faith

There are some odd ideas about faith. Faith is not "believing what you know isn't true" nor "believing something for which there is no evidence." That's foolish. The Bible is a book about faith … and the elementary fact is that faith is built-in. We are born believers. If you think you have no faith – try not believing in anything or anybody, your spouse, doctor, bank, boss, or banker. There are no guarantees – we put our lives into the hands of surgeons … we trust drivers of trains, cars, and planes … we eat food prepared by total strangers – without thinking of faith. But that's what it is.

Faith is a kind of immune system filtering out fears that otherwise would paralyze all activity. When it fails, we develop all kinds of phobias and compulsions. Jesus said not to have phobia but faith. Stop using this faculty of faith, and you would never get out of bed in the morning or step outside. You would fancy the sky might fall down. In this world, a million cobra-troubles are coiled to strike, but we carry on, usually quite regardless and confident. The Bible says, *"God has dealt to every man the measure of faith."* Christ said, *"Only believe,"* because we can.

Getting married is one of the best illustrations of faith I know. Did any bride or bridegroom ever imagine the other was perfect? Yet they commit themselves to each other for life, for better or worse. One bride refused to repeat the words "I take thee for better for worse," retorting "I only take him for worse. I know he'll never be better." She still went ahead, confident … but not optimistic!

There is no mystique about faith. Perhaps little children are the biggest believers. Many a time I've lifted a child in my arms, but not one ever screamed for fear of falling. Jesus Himself carried a child as an illustrated sermon. He said the child carried a passport to the Kingdom of God. Faith doesn't come by murdering common sense. It isn't a peculiar psychology developed with great effort by bizarre "saints" in isolated caves, living on bread and water. It isn't peculiar at all. It is natural. Doubt is peculiar – irrational, in fact. It is the only thing that ever surprised Jesus. **Walk in Faith!**

Today's Scripture

God has dealt to each one a measure of faith.
(Romans 12:3)

Daily Power!

Faith is natural, doubt in irrational.

Today's Bible Reading

I Samuel 13:23 through 14:1-52; John 7:30-53; Psalm 109:1-31; Proverbs 15:5-7

Mark my Word
(for further study)

Mark 5:36; Luke 8:50; Romans 12:3

Character Test

Today's Scripture

*The path of the just
is like the shining sun,
that shines every brighter
unto the perfect day.*
                (Proverbs 4:18)

Daily Power!

*Faith is a perfectly
ordinary thing that
makes us outstanding in
the eyes of God.*

Today's Bible Reading

*I Samuel 15:1-35
through 16:1-23;
John 8:1-20;
Psalm 110:1-7;
Proverbs 15:8-10*

Mark my Word
(for further study)

*Proverbs 4:18;
Hebrews 11:1-40*

People often confuse faith and virtue. Faith is there. Faith is just faith. Virtue is developed. Faith doesn't come, as does learning the piano grade by grade. People talk about "big believers," as if believing came in sizes like suit jackets. We can have faith even when we know we are not very good. Sinners can have faith – otherwise they could never be saved! Nobody is good … but Christ taught us that **all** can believe. He commended some people for their faith – but they were foreigners, quite ignorant of doctrine. The Bible does the same. In Hebrews chapter 11, it has a "Roll of Honor," listing heroes and heroines of great faith. They are remembered not for valor or kindness, but for their complete reliance upon God. Faith is a perfectly ordinary thing that makes us outstanding in the eyes of God. Scripture states, *"Without faith it is impossible to please God."* By faith, it is possible to please God … and faith is possible to everybody.

We are what we believe. We had better watch what we do believe. We make that decision, and it makes us in fact. Some believe in UFOs, or that the Earth is alive, or in voices from the dead – perhaps they just want to be different. There are a million things to believe … but God is supreme. We are focused on believing in God. That is what I believe in believing. Surveys show that practically everybody believes in God – some sort of God, somewhere. The question is: what sort?

Believing tests us. The kind of God we believe in is a window into our soul – believing in Christ, or Karl Marx, for example. Following a faith that only demands a few prayers – what does that say about us? Minimum-effort religions can be quite popular – small demands, big following – cheap faith for worth-nothing people. Jesus Christ asks everything: *"Give Me your heart."* A broad religion is an easy road, but gets narrower and leads to nowhere. Hold fast to this truth: **Your faith in Christ is a narrow road that gets wider and goes somewhere.**

Miracles and Skepticism

Miracles today are always suspect. "Tongues couldn't be the same tongues as on the Day of Pentecost" … "Angels were real then, but they are hallucinations now" … "Bible miracles were real miracles and today's are spurious" … "They will be real in the millennium, but never now!" … "God actually answered prayer in Bible days, but now it is all coincidence and exaggeration" … "There was real revival two hundred years ago, but the quality is missing today." The critics think people don't even pray like they used to do, and all the greatest men and women of God lived yesterday: "There were giants in the Earth in those days, but Christians now are all pygmies." Oh Unbelief, how ancient and intransigent thou art! As Jesus said, *"O ye of little faith! … How long must I be with you?"*

When Jesus went to the grave of Lazarus and began to show what He was about to do, telling them to remove the stone blocking the mouth of the tomb, Martha was shocked, protesting, *"Lord, by this time he smells. He has been dead four days!"* His reply still comes ringing in all our ears, rattling against our impervious pessimism like welcoming rain on the hard wilderness:

"If you would believe, you would see the glory of God!"

Only doubt and you wouldn't move a molehill, never mind a mountain. That day, the God of the past performed the greatest wonder ever seen: Lazarus walked out of the grave.

The God of Moses and Elijah is not behind you, but ahead of you! You can't update Him. He has brought in the Kingdom age, the dispensation of the Holy Spirit. His message to you and me is loud and clear … *"All things are possible. Only believe!"*

Today's Scripture

Jesus said, "If? There are no ifs among believers. Anything can happen."
(Mark 9:23; the Message)

Daily Power!

I believe in my life that I will see the miraculous glory of God!

Today's Bible Reading

*I Samuel 17:1-58 through 18:1-4;
John 8:21-30;
Psalm 111:1-10;
Proverbs 15:11*

Mark my Word
(for further study)

*Matthew 6:30; 17:17;
Mark 9:23;
John 11:39-40*

Revival is here!

People have been brought up in Charismatic churches, but are still praying week in and week out, year in and year out: "Lord, send the old-time power." Send it? He already has! That is what Pentecost means – **the Holy Spirit has come.** They pray, "Lord, rend the Heavens" … but He has already done it! The Lord rent the Heavens – Jesus came and tore them open again like the veil of the Temple when He soared back to God. He tore them wider still when the Holy Spirit came on the Day of Pentecost. When Stephen, the first Christian martyr, had a vision moments before they stoned him, he said, *"Look! I see the heavens opened and the Son of Man standing at the right hand of God."* Praise God: the veil is rent … and no devil in Hell has a needle and thread big enough to stitch it up again!

An often-quoted passage of Scripture comes to mind: *"If My people who are called by My Name will humble themselves, and pray and seek My face, and turn from their wicked ways, then I will hear from Heaven, and will forgive their sin and heal their land."* The punctuation in this verse is actually quite important … and gives us directions to "getting revival." First, we who call ourselves Christian must **humble ourselves** – this means to recognize that without God, we can do nothing. Second, we must **pray and seek His face** – this means that we don't yell at God to "send a revival," nor do we seek His hand – the "signs and wonders" we're so certain are the main evidence of "revival" – but from that position of humility, we simply worship and adore Him, seeing Him for **Who** He is, not **what** He does. The third point – **turn from their wicked ways** – is perhaps the most difficult of all … yet it goes right back to where our priorities are supposed to lie: in pleasing God above all else, to make Him first in our lives. Then we read, *"I will hear from Heaven"* – which there has been a two-way conversation between us and God. Finally, God answers: *"I will forgive their sin and heal their land"* – which is His outpouring on both the long-time Christian and the brand-new seeker. Revival should never be bottled up inside the walls of our churches. **Together, let's take it to the people who need it!**

Today's Scripture

If My people who are called by My Name will humble themselves, and pray and seek My face, and turn from their wicked ways, then I will hear from Heaven, and will forgive their sin and heal their land.
(II Chronicles 7:14)

Daily Power!

Because I am filled with the Holy Spirit, I am "in revival" Now!

Today's Bible Reading

*I Samuel 18:5-30 through 19:1-24;
John 8:31-59;
Psalm 112:1-10;
Proverbs 15:12-14*

Mark my Word
(for further reading)

*II Chronicles 7:14;
Acts 7:56*

Geard to God

Relevance is a matter of position and focus. **You and I are only relevant when we relate to what the Holy Spirit is doing.** We are often told our ministry has to be "geared to the times." This is nonsense! **We are geared to God.** The machinery of Heaven is turning, wheels within wheels.

"And I will give you the keys of the Kingdom of Heaven, and whatever you bind on Earth will be bound in Heaven, and whatever you loose on Earth will be loosed in Heaven."

It is the machinery of Heaven – not of industry – that must be our concern. To be geared to the world means turning our Gospel into another form of materialism – just another way to rake in money and goods. What makes us relevant is not whether our message fits the situation – *"Do not be conformed to this world,"* the Bible tells us – but whether the situation corresponds to the truth of Christ. In fact, the world is of no importance if it does not relate to God.

This self-important, sin-filled world is destined to pass away, to be replaced by God's perfect order: *"Now I saw a new Heaven and a new Earth, for the first Heaven and the first Earth had passed away … There shall be no more pain, for the former things have passed away."*

You and I need to get our priorities right. We either get into the mainstream of revelation – the love of God for a wasted world – or we drift into a backwater filled with debris of theological controversy and church politics. Our priority must be the same as that of the Spirit.

Why is the Holy Spirit here? The Holy Spirit is given to make us witnesses … and His own work is to highlight the work of Christ and actuate it in human lives. If you want to move in the Spirit, you need to get into that kind of activity because that is what He is doing!

Today's Scripture

I beseech you therefore, brethren, by the mercies of God, that you present your bodies a living sacrifice, holy, acceptable to God, which is your reasonable service. And do not be conformed to this world, but be transformed by the renewing of your mind, that you may prove what is that good and acceptable and perfect will of God.
(Romans 12:1-2)

Daily Power!

It is my strong desire that I always be in the mainstream of what God is doing, that my heart is tuned to God's heart and I hear what He is saying to this fallen world today.

Mark my Word
(for further study)

Ezekiel 10:6; John 16:9-11; Acts 1:8; Romans 12:1-2; Revelation 21:1-7

Today's Bible Reading

I Samuel 20:1-42 through 21:1-15; John 9:1-41; Psalm 113:1-5 through 114:1-8; Proverbs 15:15-17

Today's Scripture

*Has not God made
foolish the wisdom of
this world? For since,
in the wisdom of God,
the world through
wisdom did not know
God, it pleased God
through the foolishness
of the message preached
to save those who
believe.*

(I Corinthians 1:20-21)

Daily Power!

*We do what we believe
– therefore, I believe in
preaching the Gospel of
Jesus Christ.*

Today's Bible Reading

*I Samuel 22:1-23
through 23:1-29;
John 10:1-21;
Psalm 115:1-18;
Proverbs 15:18-19*

Mark my Word
(for further study)

*Psalm 46:1;
John 20:29;
I Corinthians 1:21;
Hebrews 11:6;
James 2:19*

Faith pins Hope

Believing is not just brain cells in motion – there should be a response. Do we **do** what we believe? If we believe in seed, we plant it. A man who owns a plane but won't risk a trip is a contrary character. It will get him exactly nowhere. We may as well believe in Mickey Mouse as the Almighty if we don't expect Him to do anything. In his short epistle, James – the half-brother of Jesus, an upright and forthright character – made some hard-hitting remarks: *"You believe in one God? You do well, so do the devils, and they tremble."* Their theology was sound but useless – they were sham believers. He talked about them as lovers of money, impatient with God, and said that faith which doesn't work isn't faith. God is not a figure of theory or past history but *"a very present help."*

People say, "I'll believe it when I see it." No, they won't – they can't. You can only believe or have faith in what you **don't see**. What you see is fact, and is not up for believing. If you can prove it, faith doesn't come into it. Nobody believes two plus two equals four – they know so! But **God wants faith!** *"Without faith it is impossible to please God"* … *"Blessed are those who have not seen and yet have believed."* That's the way to get God's blessing – not by being so clever you believe nothing unless you can run your tape measure round it.

This was Paul's point when writing to the Corinthians. He was familiar with the great thinkers of Greece. They had discovered the certainties of mathematics. Reason worked for figures, so they imagined it would work for everything else – the meaning of Life, God, and the whole business of Life – God, Life, goodness, reality. They set thinkers off on a red herring trail that lasts to this day! Paul knew what had happened, and told the learned thinkers of Corinth: *"the world through wisdom did not know Him."* Faith is a personal relationship, not a mathematical relationship between numbers. You may know what God did, but you have to trust Him for tomorrow. There can be no guarantees.

The Eye to the Unseen

Faith is akin to love, a heart matter. We don't decide to fall in love after weighing all the pros and cons. Couples get married on trust, not on scientific evidence or conclusive logic. Faith is the eye to see the unseen. Physical optics are not the instruments to perceive God. He is a Spirit. Mortal eyes are too weak to discern *"the invisible God, the King eternal, immortal."* We have to deal with Him as He is. *"He who comes to God must believe that He is, and that He is a Rewarder of those who diligently seek Him."*

But there is a better way of seeing. Eyes can play tricks. Plato, the greatest of the Greek philosophers, said that nothing is ever actually how it looks to us. But Moses *"endured as seeing Him Who is invisible."* If we only believed what we **saw**, what would a blind man believe? Radio waves fill your room, but who would know without a receiver? God is invisible Spirit – it is as useless to argue and expect God to be what He isn't … as it is to expect the moon to be made of green cheese. *"Blessed are those who have not seen and yet have believed"* – they are on the track of truth!

Wanting a God they can see has led people to vast mistakes. People have made God in their own image, which the God of the Bible is certainly not! It led to idolatry, erecting images and icons. Today, some treat "the living Earth" as "God." They have a pretty big god … but the God of the whole Earth is rather bigger. That is where the Gospel steps into the picture – this God did become **visible**. He was *"made flesh and dwelt among us and we beheld His glory as of the only begotten Son of God."* That verse comes from John's Gospel, which is all about seeing. In the first chapter alone, there are eighteen references to seeing. John wrote about knowing as seeing. He wrote a letter beginning, *"That which we have heard, which we have seen with our eyes … the Word of Life."* John saw in Christ the Word of Life. Let others see that Word in your life today!

Today's Scripture

That which we have seen and heard we declare to you, that you also may have fellowship with us, and truly our fellowship is with the Father and with His Son Jesus Christ.
(I John 1:3)

Daily Power!

I do not need to see the Spirit of the living God to know He is within me.

Today's Bible Reading

I Samuel 42:1-22
through 25:1-44;
John 10:22-42;
Psalm 116:1-19;
Proverbs 15:20-21

Mark my Word
(for further study)

John 1:14; 20:29;
Colossians 1:15;
I Timothy 1:17;
Hebrews 11:27;
I John 1:1, 3

Today's Scripture

Nor is there salvation in any other, for there in no other Name under Heaven given among men by which we must be saved.

(Acts 4:12)

Daily Power!

Every day, I discover more of God's transforming power through my relationship with Jesus Christ.

Today's Bible Reading

I Samuel 26:1-25 through 28:1-25; John 11:1-53; Psalm 117:1-2; Proverbs 15:22-23

Mark my Word
(for further study)

John 14:6;
Acts 4:10-12;
Ephesians 1:3-14

Transforming Power

Since the Resurrection of Jesus, a wave of spiritual power has swept forward through the world and down the generations, bringing God's new life to everything it touches: the power of God's forgiveness, which sets us free … the power that enables us to forgive those who have hurt us … the power to resist what we know is wrong … the power of God's Spirit, Who brings us the new life of Jesus … the power of God's love, which fills us with love for Him and for others. *"Blessed be the God and Father of our Lord Jesus Christ, Who has blessed us with every spiritual blessing in the Heavenly places in Christ … In Him we have redemption through His Blood, the forgiveness of sins, according to the riches of His grace … In Him also we have obtained an inheritance."*

"Every spiritual blessing" – now what sort of spiritual blessing would you like to have active in your life? Some Christians desire "the power gifts" – prophecy, preaching, healing – active in their lives … while others want the "simple gifts" – love, joy, peace – to be predominant. Sometimes this is the difference between wanting to make an impact on the world … and wanting to stay happily in your "comfort-zone." Just remember: God's blessings are given to us to bless us, certainly, but also to make us a blessing!

How can we know this power for ourselves? How can we discover this love of God which is able to transform our lives? This is the question that seekers throughout the ages have asked … and there is only one Man Who has dared to answer it: *"I am the Way, the Truth, and the Life. No one comes to the Father, except through Me."* Jesus is the **only way** whereby our sins can be forgiven and our right relationship with God our Father re-established. His death on the Cross was the final sacrifice needed – nothing else is required. His resurrection was once-and-for-all proof that He is the Son of God. His Holy Spirit is our means of tapping into God's transforming power. Live in the fullness of that power today!

The Voice of Love

I have often wondered how Jesus sounded when He spoke. Once Jesus pronounced seven woes against certain cities. But I wonder, "What was His tone of voice?" I imagine Jesus spoke these judgments with a voice of sorrow. What love filled His voice, what tears filled His eyes, even when He went to Jerusalem to be rejected! His heart would show in His tone of voice. What kind of tone did those privileged people hear?

The Gospel of Luke records that they *"were amazed at the gracious words that came from His lips."* The Temple police were sent to arrest Jesus – they came back spellbound and disarmed. They said, *"No one ever spoke the way this man does."* How did Jesus sound when He cried, *"Father, forgive them for they do not know what they are doing"*?

D.L. Moody once spoke in London, England to an invited audience of a thousand or so "rationalists." The meeting was fiercely hostile, but Moody literally sobbed, with tears running down his beard, as he pleaded with them to turn to Christ. Suddenly, the meeting broke and hundreds turned to Christ. Those people were never the same again.

I don't mean that the Gospel should be turned into sob-stuff, a tear-jerker. The voice of Jesus did far more than stir people's emotions – their reaction was not tears, but joy. He told His disciples that He spoke to give them peace and joy. In fact, there was no pathos in the words or teaching of Jesus, nothing that people today would call "syrupy-sweet sentimentalism." The Gospel sound should be triumphant, certain, with a note of gladness!

This is, of course, a long way from – and in stark contrast to – the warning voice of Jonah in doomed Nineveh … but grace and truth came to light through Jesus Christ. **There is no bell that rings as loudly as love.** You and I should always speak with Christ-like words of love.

Today's Scripture

These things I have spoken to you, that My joy may remain in you, and that your joy may be full.

(Luke 15:11)

Daily Power!

Whenever I speak, I believe that my words will be triumphant, certain and glad, in keeping with the tone of the Gospel.

Today's Bible Reading

*I Samuel 29:1-11 through 31:1-13;
John 11:54-57 through 12:1-19;
Psalm 118:1-18;
Proverbs 15:24-26*

Mark my Word
(for further study)

*Jonah 3:1-5;
Matthew 23:37;
Luke 4:22; 15:11; 23:34;
John 7:46; 14:27; 15:11;
Revelation 2:1-29; 3:1-22*

Today's Scripture

For the wages of sin is death, but the gift of God is eternal life through Christ Jesus our Lord.

(Romans 6:23)

Daily Power!

I have made my choice to accept the gift of salvation.

Today's Bible Reading

II Samuel 1:1-27 through 2:1-11; John 12:20-50; Psalm 118:19-29; Proverbs 15:27-28

Mark my Word
(for further study)

Genesis 3:1-24; Romans 6:23

How Sin happened

When God first put Adam and Eve in the Garden of Eden, they did not know sin. When Satan tempted Eve and she succumbed, she learned about *"the knowledge of good **and** evil"* … which opened the door to sin. "Sin" is "doing evil in God's sight" or "separation from God" … but the opportunity to do good is also there. Adam and Eve were cursed in the Garden because of sin – that's when death, pain and sickness entered into the picture – and God Himself said, *"'Behold, the Man has become like one of Us, to know good and evil. And now, lest he put out his hand and take also of the Tree of Life, and eat and live forever' – therefore the Lord God sent him out of the Garden of Eden."* Because once-immortal Man now existed in a state of sin, he could **not** live forever that way – imagine an awful eternity steeped entirely in sin! It was God's decision to spare Man an endless separation from Himself … but He also knew there would be a terrible price to pay to mend that gulf: the life of His only begotten Son.

Every man is created in God's image, and within every man there exists a place that was fashioned **only for God**. So many spend their entire lives trying to fit other "things" into that God- shaped space. There is only One Who will fit there: our Lord and Savior Jesus Christ. *"For the wages of sin is death, but the gift of God is eternal life in Christ Jesus our Lord."* To accept or reject the gift of salvation – that cannot be decided by loving filled parents, nor legislated by churches, governments or societies – it must be individually chosen and acted upon. *"If you confess with your mouth the Lord Jesus and believe in your heart that God has raised Him from the dead, you will be saved. For with the heart one believes unto righteousness, and with the mouth confession is made unto salvation."* You can exhibit "on the outside" what appears to be God-like living – but it's what you believe **deep inside** your heart that makes the difference.

Godly Families

Not every Godly man in the Bible had Godly children, as typified by the high priest Eli and the prophet Samuel. But perhaps the most significant example of this sad truth was found in the life of Israel's greatest historical personality: King David. One of his sons, Absalom, murdered his brother, Amnon, for a treacherous act of rape and incest against his sister, Tamar. From this evil episode sprang another: when pampered Absalom tried to take the throne from David, resulting in the loss of his own life in the civil war he had begun. On his death-bed, King David learned yet another son had been killed in an attempt to illegally mount the throne. Tragedy followed tragedy … yet David was *"a man after God's own heart"*!

When news was brought to David that Absalom had been killed, he was beside himself, weeping, crying aloud, *"O my son Absalom – my son, my son Absalom – if only I had died in your place! O Absalom, my son, my son!"* David saw himself in his son. He himself had been treacherous, murdered a faithful and good man, and stolen his lovely and loved wife. He wrote a Psalm of public repentance – but he had set an unrighteous example … which Absalom followed. The pathos of David echoes to this day. *"If only I had died in your place"* – for it was with himself that the blame lay. David's complex character proved powerful in his family's attitudes. They needed greater exposure to the Law, the Words of God, as He commanded.

If we pray with our families, it is not enough. The means and method of God is the **Word of God**. It speaks louder than testimony. God is on our side when we set out to create families, and families of families. We are helping create the world Family of God named in Heaven and Earth. This is His focus and way. You purpose to follow and walk in the fullness of that truth every day!

Today's Scripture

Teach me Your way, O Lord, I will walk in Your truth; unite my heart to fear Your Name.
(Psalm 86:11)

Daily Power!

My family will follow my example more than my words – and I will strive to live by Your Word.

Today's Bible Reading

II Samuel 2:12-32 through 3:1-39; John 13:1-30; Psalm 119:1-16; Proverbs 15:29-30

Mark my Word
(for further study)

II Samuel 18:33; Psalm 86:1-17

From Zero to Ten

Throughout the Old Testament, the Divine method which God chose to select the leaders of His people was to choose nobodies, rejects: *"The base things of the world and things which are despised God has chosen, and the things which are not, to bring to nothing the things that are."* Jesus prayed … and came back to pick the most unlikely apostles – almost anybody! He bumped into young men without any qualities at all – other than very human character traits: impetuous Peter … his quieter brother Andrew … James and John, the hot-headed sons of Zebedee … rationalistic Thomas … sociable Philip … and thieving Judas.

When God chooses, it isn't important what we are – it's what He makes of us that counts. He chose an unlikely bunch of local men. One or two of them were picked only because they were relations – James and John were the sons of Salome, who is believed to be the sister of Mary the mother of Jesus. They had always known Him. Jesus took a stroll along the beach where local fishermen happened to be, and called them – it looked almost as if He picked the first young fellows He bumped into that morning.

When people are "no good" in Germany, those who constantly fail in their efforts in daily life, we call them "zeros." But these are the ones God is especially interested in! When Jesus calls a "zero" and the "zero" responds – he (or she) will soon find out that the Lord is the number one … and a zero next to a one equals **ten**! In other words: **Jesus gives value to every zero as long as He is the number one!** The worthless become highly valuable. This is the way God builds His Kingdom. So it was with the first disciples … and so it is today. I claim this as my own testimony too … and so should you! Make sure that Jesus Christ is **number one** in your life today!

Today's Scripture

According to my earnest expectation and hope that in nothing I shall be ashamed, but with all boldness, as always, so now also Christ will be magnified in my body, whether by life or death.
(Philippians 1:20)

Daily Power!

To my lowly zero, Jesus has added His glorious One – and now we are a "perfect ten"!

Today's Bible Reading

II Samuel 4:1-12 through 6:1-23; John 13:31-38 through 14:1-14; Psalm 119:17-32; Proverbs 15:31-32

Mark my Word
(for further study)

I Corinthians 2:8; Philippians 1:8

Witnesses, not Lawyers

It has become established practice that preachers should present the case for the defense of Jesus Christ. It has also been said that preachers are like lawyers in court. Ministers are supposed to be like barristers talking to congregations as if to a jury, arguing to get a verdict in the favor of Jesus. That approach looks so right, plausible and sensible. But is it? No, not at all! That is our human approach, trying to convey the Gospel message with the wisdom of words.

Jesus needs no defending. He is not a prisoner in the dock. His reputation does not depend on any jury. The time has gone when Jesus was dragged to the bar of Rome to be judged by Pilate. Today, Pilate stands at the bar of history and Jesus is His Judge. We are not supposed to be lawyers, but **witnesses**! Normally, a witness only describes what he or she has seen. Sometimes, however, a witness is a piece of evidence.

Perhaps a man has been cruelly attacked and injured. He appears in court to display himself, the damage and the injury. His injuries speak for themselves. He himself is a piece of evidence. We believers are not lawyers, attorneys or barristers in court pleading in defence of Jesus ... we are witnesses. Witnesses don't argue, plead, or make speeches. They simply speak the truth, stating what they know. When Peter preached on the Day of Pentecost, he said that the one hundred and nineteen standing with him were all *"witnesses of the resurrection."* In fact, not one of them had seen Christ's actual resurrection – yet that resurrection had **transformed** them. They were themselves alive with resurrection life, emboldened, certain, filled with the fire of God – they were evidence in themselves that Jesus was alive! If Jesus had still been dead, they wouldn't have been as people then saw them, but just as they had been before: cringing, slinking into the safety of a locked room for fear. Now, they were fearless ... and it was the turn of the crowd to be afraid, to be filled with fear and awe. Be certain you have that resurrection evidence alive in you today!

Today's Scripture

And they were all filled with the Holy Spirit and began to speak with other tongues, as the Spirit gave them utterance.

(Acts 2:4)

Daily Power!

Lord, make me bold to daily speak from my heart what You have done for me.

Today's Bible Reading

II Samuel 7:1-29
through 8:1-18;
John 14:15-31;
Psalm 119:33-48;
Proverbs 15:33

Mark my Word
(for further study)

Acts 2:1-32

26

Two Gifts

The Father gave us two gifts, both personal and equal. First, He gave us His Son … and then He gave us His Spirit. Jesus ranked the Spirit alongside Himself, describing Him as *"another Comforter."* He said it was better for the Spirit to come than for He Himself to remain with us in the flesh. The Holy Spirit's commission is to continue Christ's work of ministry on Earth. Jesus healed the sick, for example, and the Holy Spirit follows the pattern of Christ.

"Most assuredly I say to you, he who believes in Me, the works that I do he will do also; and greater works than these he will do, because I go to My Father … And I will pray the Father, and He will give you another Helper, that He may abide with you forever – the Spirit of truth, Whom the world cannot receive, because it neither sees Him nor knows Him; but you know Him for He dwells with you and will be in you."

How do we know Who the Spirit is? The Holy Spirit is God in action. Whenever there are supernatural operations, they are by the Spirit. All divine manifestations, such as the gifts, are always by the Spirit. When God moved on the world in the beginning, it was by His Spirit. *"The Spirit of God was hovering over the waters."* The Father's will is spoken by the Word, and performed by the Spirit. He executes the will of the Godhead.

The only Spirit Jesus promised us is the miracle Spirit, the Holy Spirit. There is no non-miracle Holy Spirit. To claim to possess the Holy Spirit and deny the very work which has always distinguished Him can only grieve Him. It is He Who began with the supreme physical wonder of creating the world. He doesn't change His nature. What He was, He is and always will be – God operating in the earthly sphere. *"I Am Who I Am."* The Holy Spirit Who made the world supernaturally should have no difficulty in continuing supernaturally. And that Holy Spirit is **your Friend** today!

Today's Scripture

I will ask the Father, and He will give you another Helper, that He may abide with you forever – the Spirit of truth, Whom the world cannot receive, because it neither sees Him nor knows Him; but you know Him for He dwells with you and will be in you.

(John 14:16-17)

Daily Power!

The Holy Spirit is God in action!"

Today's Bible Reading

II Samuel 9:1-13 through 11:1-27; John 15:1-27; Psalm 119:49-64; Proverbs 16:1-3

Mark my Word
(for further study)

Genesis 1:2; Exodus 3:14; John 14:12, 16-17

Many Baptisms?

John the Baptist, the Divinely-sent forerunner who introduced Christ, proclaimed a new era: *"Repent, for the Kingdom of Heaven is at hand."* The central core of that proclamation was the Messiah Who would baptize in the Holy Spirit. It was far greater than the restoration of Israel's greatness – it was nothing less than a cosmic change. John unfolded a map of the future, showing – not a river of water – but of fire! John used an earthly element – water – but Christ baptizes in a heavenly element – Divine Fire!

Jesus echoes the same words: *"John baptized with water, but in a few days you will be baptized with the Holy Spirit."* We should take note of the fact that Jesus did not baptize anybody with the Spirit while He was on Earth. John preached to people from *"all the land of Judea, and those from Jerusalem ... and* [they] *were all baptized by him in the Jordan River, confessing their sins."* It was to this random mass of people that John preached and declared, *"I indeed baptized you with water, but He will baptize you with the Holy Spirit."* John laid down no special qualifications except repentance.

Individuals can seek to be filled for themselves ... but one filling of the Spirit is not lasting or enough, and we need to keep coming for a repeat experience: "many fillings." If the whole Church was baptized forever on the Day of Pentecost, why are Christians supposed to seek many fillings? We might ask if anyone listening to John or Christ ever dreamed they meant such a thing. We can't direct you to a Scripture that argues for this point, because there is not a single word about "repeated fillings." Neither is there the slightest suggestion that there would be a distinct baptism exclusively for an elite band of early disciples by proxy for the Church of all time. Whether the Spirit comes at new birth or not, the first believers enjoyed a personal experience of the indwelling Spirit ... and nothing less than that is offered to all who have believed since the Day of Pentecost. Personally, I enjoy my *"times of refreshing"* in the Holy Spirit – and I'm sure you do too!

Today's Scripture

Repent therefore and be converted, that your sins may be blotted out, so that times of refreshing may come from the presence of the Lord.
(Acts 3:19)

Daily Power!

Jesus Christ baptizes in the Heavenly element of Divine Fire.

Today's Bible Reading

II Samuel 12:1-31;
John 16:1-33;
Psalm 119:65-80;
Proverbs 16:4-5

Mark my Word
(for further study)

Matthew 3:2, 11;
Mark 1:5, 8;
Acts 1:5; 3:19

28

Becoming a Child of God

Today's Scripture

Do not enter the path of the wicked, and do not walk in the way of evil. Avoid it, do not travel on it; turn away from it and pass on.

(Proverbs 4:14-15)

Daily Power!

I know that faith is not a feeling — it is an act.

Today's Bible Reading

II Samuel 13:1-39;
John 17:1-26;
Psalm 119:81-96;
Proverbs 16:6-7

Mark my Word
(for further study)

Proverbs 4:14-15;
Mark 1:15;
Romans 10:13

If you are ready to come to the Cross for the help you need, there are two steps you need to take now. The steps are called "repent" and "believe." As Jesus said, *"Repent and believe the Good News!"* What do these two steps mean?

Repent: This is another old-fashioned word, like the word "sin." It simply means "change your mind." Picture it like this: you have taken a wrong turn and you are driving further and further away from where you want to go. You need to stop, turn around completely, and start traveling in the right direction.

This will mean taking time to examine how you live. You will need to ask God's forgiveness for all that is wrong in your life – and ask Him to save you and set you free. Repentance means that you turn away from your sin to God. If you change your position, then Jesus will change your situation.

Believe: Faith is an act – not a feeling. You decide to believe. Every person alone for himself or herself can pull that "faith rip-cord of belief." If you do that now, the Lord will not delay by "investigating" your suitability, your worthiness, or your past. No matter who or where you are, in the nick of time as you repent and believe, the parachute opens – with a bang! – and you are safe, for real.

Jesus has never once failed, and He will not fail you either. Here and now, the rip-cord is in your hands by the promise of God. The Bible is clear about it: *"Everyone who calls on the Name of the Lord will be saved."* One believing call, in simple language which you would use in calling a friend for help, addressed to Jesus Christ for forgiveness and salvation, is the way the parachute of salvation opens. God Himself will intervene for you. He promised it. Pull the rip-cord quickly, wherever you are!

The new Way

The first Christians crossed the Bible landscape in an aura of prayer. They reveled in prayer, and with good reason. Their kind of praying was a new thing – using the authority of the Name of Jesus! The New Testament speaks of *"fellowship with the Father,"* but Israel did not pray, *"Our Father."* They had such a lofty conception of God that He seemed unapproachable, the Sovereign Lord of Hosts, mighty in battle, or, at best, *"a present help in trouble."* Only an elite band enjoyed God's company and intimate prayer life with Him.

Most knew God only second-hand, via a priest or prophet. In a sense, people called on the Lord in their own name: *"Lord, remember David!"* the Psalmist wrote, hoping for a personal favor. We can **try** to get God's attention on our own merits, but we will always fall short: *"But we are all like an unclean thing, and all our righteousnesses are like filthy rags"* … *"For all have sinned and fall short of the glory of God."* Because we are sin-infested, God cannot even **look** at us … unless our sins are covered over by the cleansing Blood of the Lamb of God.

"Most assuredly I say to you, he who believes in Me, the works that I do he will do also; and greater works than these he will do, because I go to My Father. And whatever you ask in My Name, that I will do, that the Father may be glorified in the Son. If you ask anything in My Name, I will do it."

And that brings us right back to where we started: we pray in the Name of Jesus, He Who enables us to even approach the holy Throne of God. That's your right and mine: **to speak, to pray, to act in Jesus' Name!**

Today's Scripture

Let us therefore come boldly to the Throne of Grace, that we may obtain mercy and find grace to help in time of need.

(Hebrews 4:16)

Daily Power!

My relationship with my Heavenly Father is determined by my relationship with His Son Jesus Christ, for it is He Who gives me use of His Name because of His sacrifice on Calvary.

Today's Bible Reading

II Samuel 14:1-33 through 15:1-22; John 18:1-24; Psalm 119:19-112; Proverbs 16:8-9

Mark my Word
(for further study)

Psalm 46:1; 132:1; Isaiah 64:6; John 14:12-14; Romans 3:10-23; Hebrews 4:16

Why God spoke

When we first read about Abraham, he was in the city of Ur of the Chaldees, with his father, Terah. Like all cities, it had an official god, and families had a shrine for their own household god, as India today with its millions of gods. However, a *"Most High God"* was acknowledged – and Abram heard His voice. It was a Divine breakthrough. It came from God's side, not Abraham's – God breaking through to Abraham.

God has shown concern for the world. When nobody sought Him, He sought them. Abraham was not seeking God … probably nobody was. He made Abraham aware of Who He was, and gave him simple instructions to leave Ur. He was not told where to go … but he set off. The Bible stresses that Abraham lived in tents, away from houses and streets. Why? To get paganism, city manners and customs flushed out of his system. Abraham had been born and bred in an idolatrous civilization. God was to purge him of everything except what He showed him. He showed him a destiny beyond his own interests and in the future of nations. God said, *"I will make you a great nation and I will bless you … and all peoples on Earth will be blessed through you"* – the first man of a New World order.

In Abraham's time, people everywhere lived for themselves, usually by fighting everybody else around. One day the nations will be judged. Christ painted a picture of a vast drama on the stage of the whole universe: the Parable of the Judgment of the Nations. They have to give account. God's eyes of concern run through the whole Earth. Why have we faith? To bless ourselves? To get wealth and be prosperous? If we have such faith, God gave it. But He enriches us to enrich others, to "pass it on." Politicians produce manifestos and agendas looking after their own corner of the world, but what is the purpose of the nation? Just to exist? No moral aims? Individuals have their own also, but what about their life-purpose? Abraham lived on that level. Let God's purpose be yours.

Today's Scripture

Do you see what we've got? An unshakable Kingdom! And do you see how thankful we must be? Not only thankful, but brimming with worship, deeply reverent before God.
(Hebrews 12:28; the Message)

Daily Power!

When nobody sought God, He sought them.

Today's Bible Reading

II Samuel 15:23-37 through 16:1-23; John 18:25-40 through 19:1-22; Psalm 119:113-128; Proverbs 16:10-11

Mark my Word
(for further study)

Genesis 12:2-3; Matthew 25:31-46; Hebrews 11:8-10; 12:28

God at Work

Some people who talk about "moving in the Spirit" seem to think and act as if **they** are the ones moving the Spirit. This is not Biblical: *"Who has directed the Spirit of the Lord, or as His counselor has taught Him?"*

Jesus was often criticized by authorities and religious leaders because He did not confine His ministry to "the elite," but rather, spent much of His time with sinners – prostitutes, criminals, moneylenders, beggars, the sick, the outcast. They just didn't understand the compassion that moved Him: *"What man is there among you who has one sheep, and if it falls into a pit on the Sabbath, will not lay hold of it and lift it out? Of how much more value then is a man than a sheep? Therefore it is lawful to do good on the Sabbath."*

God is not moving secretly. He has not suddenly shot off in some new and unexpected direction, only spotted by a few members of some spiritual elite. We still find God at work among people who are down: the sinful, the hopeless, the derelicts. **"Follow Jesus"** – that is a better expression that "moving in the Spirit." Follow Him … and you will go where He goes, doing good and healing all who are oppressed by the devil. Praise be to God!

Jesus Himself said, *"I don't do anything unless I've seen My Father do it … I don't say anything unless I've heard My Father say it … I simply imitate My Father"* (paraphrased). Having that Christ-like attitude – **that** is the Spirit of God moving in our hearts, and He utilizing our responsiveness to Him – **this** is the best equipment we can have to walk in this world and do the works of Him Who sends us. Make a choice to equip yourself today with all of your spiritual weapons, so you are ready to go into battle!

Today's Scripture

When Jesus heard that, He said to them, "Those who are well have no need of a physician, but those who are sick. But go and learn what this means, 'I desire mercy and not sacrifice. For I did not come to call the righteous but sinners to repentance.'"
(Matthew 9:12-13)

Daily Power!

I choose to follow Jesus in every action, every thought, every step of my daily life. I prefer to be a God-pleaser than to be a man-pleaser.

Today's Bible Reading

II Samuel 17:1-29;
John 19:23-42;
Psalm 119:129-152;
Proverbs 16:12-13

Mark my Word
(for further study)

Isaiah 40:13;
Matthew 9:12-13;
12:11-12;
John 5:19-23; 9:4;
Acts 10:38

God says:
Do not plan with that which is in your pocket,
but with that which is in my pocket.

God says:
For every deadline I will throw you a life line.

The church is not a pleasure boat, but a lifeboat –
from the captain to the cook
all hands on deck for saving souls!

Reason for Believing?

Not seeing is no reason for not believing. Nobody sees radiation – we simply wait for its warming and lighting effects. Nobody sees air (unless it's badly polluted) – we simply breathe it in and out. Nobody sees God – but millions find His effects in their lives every day! Things happen that can only be from Him. Even one prayer answered … one healing … one miracle … one deliverance from addiction – is evidence of Him. Two thousand years ago, this report was given: *"How God anointed Jesus of Nazareth with the Holy Spirit and with power, Who went about doing good and healing all who were oppressed by the devil, for God was with Him."* Peter testified to unmistakable evidence of God!

But it wasn't just one prayer answered, one miracle manifested … and all this taking place wasn't only two thousand years ago. **Today**, **millions** are healed, millions delivered, millions of prayers answered, millions have experiences which can only be attributed to Jesus Christ risen from the dead. *"Jesus Christ is the same yesterday, today and forever."* When I step on a platform in Africa, or India, or anywhere else, often – without any touch of mine – the blind begin to see, the deaf to hear, the dumb to speak, the cripples to walk, and those driven to madness by clinging spirits of evil are released. It is not psychology, for babies are healed, even in the womb. The greatest effect is deliverance from sin and guilt, and the transformation of people's attitudes and personalities – Jesus saves!

Why should we care what Jesus did two thousand years ago, **unless** it was written to give us inspiration and hope to what He can – and does – today? He taught with wisdom and insight that caught the attention of would-be intellectuals and philosophers and turned their hearts toward God. He ministered healing with compassion and authority – not to people who **deserved** to be healed, but simply because He cared so much for them that He desired to relieve their suffering. He sacrificed His very own life – not because they demanded His death – but because He was being obedient to His Father. There was no hypocrisy in Jesus two thousand years ago – and there is nothing but truth in Him today.

Today's Scripture

Jesus doesn't change – yesterday, today, tomorrow, He's always totally Himself.
   (Hebrews 13:8; the Message)

Daily Power!

I do not see God, but I feel His presence in my heart and I see His work in my life.

Today's Bible Reading

II Samuel 18:1-30 through 19:1-10; John 20:1-31; Psalm 119:153-176; Proverbs 16:14-15

Mark my Word
(for further study)

Acts 10:38; Hebrews 13:8

2

Faith or Chaos?

Today's Scripture

That you may be sons of your Father in Heaven; for He makes His sun rise on the evil and on the good, and sends rain on the just and on the unjust.

(Matthew 5:45)

Daily Power!

I take great comfort in knowing that my faith in God in based on His Word.

Today's Bible Reading

II Samuel 19:11-43 through 20:1-13; John 21:1-25; Psalm 120:1-7; Proverbs 16:16-17

Mark my Word
(for further study)

Psalm 97:7; Matthew 5:45

There is no substitute for faith in God. History rings the warning bells. Without the knowledge of the Lord God, nothing ever made sense. The ancients – even the most brilliant thinkers – produced the wildest ideas, superstitions, and speculations. Mystery clothed nature. They were sure of nothing, not even of the weather or the seasons. To "make" the sun rise, they worshipped it. To "make" it rain, they offered divine worship. Rivers had to be persuaded to run and not dry up. Everyone had his own god. *"Let all be put to shame who serve carved images, who boast of idols."*

Therefore, the prophets were raised up and inspired with a burning realization of God's reality and His will. The conception of God as the Father of all was unknown. Conflicts and family blood-feuds took place, and war was the glory of men. But Israel's prophets taught Israel not to fear the signs of the Heavens, to work and not to war. God would faithfully look after all His creatures. They should not worry about harvests, like the heathens around them. Jesus Himself clearly taught this: *"That you may be sons of your Father in Heaven; for He makes His sun rise on the evil and on the good, and sends rain on the just and on the unjust."*

It is easy to sit and watch TV, and casually say you don't believe in God. But the consequences are eternal. They fertilize corruption, bribery, violence, terrorism, and crime. Atheists claim they can live decent lives without believing in God, but they forget they got the very idea of decency from Christianity. Before Christ, it was a different story and a far crueler world. In fact, we don't know what is good and bad without faith in God. Nobody otherwise has ever agreed on the subject. A totally unbelieving world would be like a lunatic asylum taken over by its patients. If you don't trust God, you soon trust nobody. Resolve today to wear your faith in God like an emblem on your sleeve.

Wonderful Knowledge

The real point of the story of Jonah – and it speaks to every evangelist who ever went out to do God's work – is that he had preached judgment ... but no judgment came. That was just what he feared would happen. In fact, Jonah had never wanted to preach against the city – for the very reason that if his preaching were successful, God would change His mind about judgment! Afterwards, he protested, saying, *"O Lord, is this not what I said when I was still at home? That is why I was so quick to flee to Tarshish. I knew that You are a gracious and compassionate God, slow to anger and abounding in love, a God Who relents from sending calamity."*

Jonah had profound insight into the character of God. In all thirty-nine books of the Old Testament, this statement of the prophet stands out as something exceptional. **Jonah knew God had a heart of unparalleled goodness.** More than that, he knew that the mercies of the Lord extended beyond the borders of Israel into enemy territory, embracing even the Gentiles.

Few in Israel would have believed this could be true. In that age of spiritual darkness, only the Holy Spirit could have shown this to the prophet. He somehow knew God could be as gracious with Gentiles as with Israel, even with the worst sinners on Earth. That is why he went ... **and** why he didn't want to go. Part of him wanted this wicked nation to get what it really deserved ... but at the same time, he knew God was not like that. Jonah wanted vengeance ... but God was – and still is – a God of forgiveness.

You and I may look at our world with dismay and revulsion at the evidence of sin – greed, hatred, inequality – but when we choose to look at the world through God's eyes ... we see lost souls dying without Him, and our hearts are filled with compassion. Ask God to give you a fresh vision for souls today. Allow Him let you see others the way He sees them.

Today's Scripture

The Lord is very compassionate and merciful.
(James 5:11b)

Daily Power!

I know that God is gracious, even with the worst sinners on Earth, for He delivered me.

Today's Bible Reading

II Samuel 20:14-26 through 22:1-20;
Acts 1:1-26;
Psalm 121:1-8;
Proverbs 16:18

Mark my Word
(for further study)

Psalm 116:5;
Jonah 4:1-11;
James 5:11

4

Truth, and People who reflect it

The prophet-evangelist Jonah knew the compassion of God, but he had no compassion himself. Any man who stands up to speak of Christ knew very well what Jonah knew. It is common knowledge among the saved that God is loving, gracious, merciful, and compassionate. But do we personally harbor such feelings for the lost?

Jonah had none at all – he preached only out of duty or obedience. There could not be a more serious shortcoming for any evangelist or anybody who preaches the Word of God. Evangelism is not a matter of simply mouthing words of God's pitying love or spelling out theology. An evangelist's heart should beat in tune with the heartbeat of God, expressive of His heart's longings and compassion. The need in evangelism is twofold: the truth, and the people who reflect it. Some people say that "preaching the right thing" is enough – **it is not!** The Holy Spirit has a part in this, placing the missing ingredient in our own hearts: *"God has poured out His love into our hearts by the Holy Spirit, Whom He has given us."* The love of God in Christ is more than a piece of systematic theology, and it is meant to come alive in those who declare it. We can preach with tongues of fire when we have His fire in our hearts! How do you get those fires burning? **Get to know the Word of God for yourself.** It is God's Word to you!

Jonah was a rare preacher and prophet in that **he didn't want to succeed**. He hoped nobody in Nineveh would take notice of the message he preached. Yet even the king on his throne became alarmed about his sins and decided to do something about it. If we take the Word of God upon our lips, we should know what we are doing. **This is major firepower that no one should "play" with!** Ask God today to give you a fresh outpouring of His compassion for the lost.

Today's Scripture

Then Jesus, moved with compassion, stretched out His hand and touched him, and said to him, "I am willing; be cleansed."

(Mark 1:41)

Daily Power!

It is my daily prayer to be renewed and consumed by the same compassion which Jesus exhibited to a lost and dying world.

Today's Bible Reading

II Samuel 22:21-51
through 23:1-23;
Acts 2:1-47;
Psalm 122:1-9;
Proverbs 16:19-20

Mark my Word
(for further study)

Jonah 3:1-10;
Mark 1:40-45;
Romans 5:5

"Our Father"

We should all seek to perceive God's true position – He is infinitely superior to us. But the invitation to call Him "Father" brings Him close to us and makes Him approachable. Readers of the Book of Hebrews, still emerging from the old dispensation of the Law, had to be taken by the hand and led into this new relationship. They were told:

"Therefore, since we have a great High Priest ... Jesus, the Son of God ... let us then approach the Throne of Grace with confidence ... We have confidence to enter the Most Holy Place by the Blood of Jesus, by a new a living way opened for us through the curtain, that is, His body."

When Jesus taught His disciples to pray, it made them a new breed ... praying always and about everything. He told them, *"I tell you the truth, My Father will give you whatever you ask in My Name ... Ask and you will receive."*

In a way, to call on God is instinctive. Who does not – especially when in distress? There is a story told about an atheist who was fishing on a lake, when suddenly the "Loch Ness Monster" rose up out of the water and opened its jaws to swallow him. The atheist cried, "Oh God, help me!" Then he heard a Voice saying, "So now you believe in Me?" To which the atheist replied desperately, "Come on, give me a break! I didn't believe in the Loch Ness Monster either until a second ago!"

Christ taught us the right way to go about it – to pray in His Name. His mighty works mark a new road to God. He has opened Heaven's door. Enter! You will be received! That's a promise for you today.

Today's Scripture

Most assuredly I say to you, whatever you ask the Father in My Name He will give you. Until now you have asked nothing in My Name. Ask, and you will receive, that your joy may be full.
(John 16:23-24)

Daily Power!

My key to Heaven's door is to pray in the Name of Jesus.

Today's Bible Reading

II Samuel 23:24-39 through 24:1-25; Acts 3:1-26; Psalm 123:1-4; Proverbs 16:21-23

Mark my Word
(for further study)

John 16:23-24; Hebrews 4:14-16; 10:19-20

God is unusual

In the first chapter of Revelation, God revealed the nature of His Son, Jesus Christ, by twice referring to Him in three tenses: *"Grace to you and peace from Him Who is, and Who was, and Who is to come"* (verse 4) and *"'I am the Alpha and the Omega, the Beginning and the End,' says the Lord, 'Who is and Who was and Who is to come, the Almighty'"* (verse 8). These are unusual words, for it says: *"Who is to come,"* when we would have said, "Who will be" – the same verb, "to be." God uses it twice in *"Who was, and Who is,"* then switches to a different one and says, *"to come."* Anybody can see this is unusual. Why this peculiar way of putting it?

The reason is that God is **unusual.** He baffles grammar and syntax, and the language has to be pushed around when we speak of Him! Christ Himself was a mystery: *"No man knows the Son but the Father,"* and to talk about Him in ordinary language always leaves something out. When it comes to the Lord, human language is never good enough. The first Christians had to give new meanings to many words, and even coin new words, because Jesus did new things and was a new kind of Person. God Himself did not communicate about Himself with mere words, such as Mohammed's "Final Testament" or Joseph Smith's Mormon "Revelations." God simply presented Himself with His actions, and to describe Him we often need a bigger alphabet. It is like angel's music that needs a new notation. When we speak of God, we can lack the words and feel like the Queen of Sheba seeing Solomon's court: *"Not even half was told me."*

God never relied on mere words to inspire our faith in Himself. To show us Who and what He is, He **came**! *"The Word became flesh and dwelt among us and we beheld His glory, full of grace and truth."* Isn't it a wonderful privilege to be able to say: **"My God has come to live with me!"**

Today's Scripture

And the Word became flesh and dwelt among us, and we beheld His glory, the glory as of the only Begotten of the Father, full of grace and truth.

(John 1:14)

Daily Power!

I serve a most unusual God, Who does impossible things – He is great!

Today's Bible Reading

*I Kings 1:1-53;
Acts 4:1-37;
Psalm 124:1-8;
Proverbs 16:24*

Mark my Word
(for further study)

*I Kings 10:7;
Matthew 11:27;
John 1:14;
Revelation 1:1-20*

The continual Promise

"I am the Alpha and the Omega, the Beginning and the End ... Who is, and Who was, and Who is to come, the Almighty." A grammar teacher would notice that this sentence – this eternal promise from God – contains three verbs: *"am"* (from *"to be"*), *"was"* (also from *"to be"*) and *"to come."* Why did God change verbs? Why did He say He *"is coming"*? It means He is everlastingly breaking in upon us! We get the same thing in Matthew where Christ was called *"the coming One."* God isn't a will be God, and He is not a process becoming something later on. What He will be, He is now and always has been: the eternal unchanging One. He is already perfect. *"I am the Lord. I change not."*

Yes, but it is different for us as individuals. We are always finding something new in Him. Suppose you stand in the water at the edge of the River Thames. You are at the river ... yet the river keeps coming toward you. And the water we stand in today will be the same river that somebody else may stand in tomorrow further downstream as the waters flow. God is like that. We come to Him ... He is there ... and yet He keeps coming to us. He is not just "being God" somewhere – like the Sphinx, just being mysterious. *"We will come to you,"* Jesus said, and He never stops coming, not now nor ever.

The Old Testament prophet caught a glimpse of this: *"This I recall to my mind, therefore I have hope. Through the Lord's mercies, we are not consumed, because His compassions fail not. They are new every morning, great is Your faithfulness. 'The Lord is my portion,' says my soul, 'Therefore I hope in Him.' The Lord is good to those who wait for Him, to the soul who seeks Him. It is good that one should hope and wait quietly for the salvation of the Lord."* Later, Peter testified to this continual renewal of the presence of God: *"Repent therefore and be converted, that your sins may be blotted out, so that times of refreshing may come from the presence of the Lord."* **Our God never stops being and never stops coming to refresh you!**

Today's Scripture

Through the Lord's mercies, we are not consumed, because His compassions fail not; they are new every morning; great is Your faithfulness.
(Lamentations 3:22-23)

Daily Power!

Each day, when I meet my Lord, He is ever the same and always refreshing.

Today's Bible Reading

I Kings 2:1-46
through 3:1-3;
Acts 5:1-42;
Psalm 125:1-5;
Proverbs 16:25

Mark my Word
(for further study)

Lamentations 3:21-26;
Malachi 3:6;
Matthew 11:3;
Acts 3:19;
Revelation 1:8

Today's Scripture

Be filled with the Spirit.
(Ephesians 5:18)

Daily Power!

Christ is called the Baptizer because that is His constant work, His Heavenly Office.

Today's Bible Reading

I Kings 3:4-28
through 4:1-34;
Acts 6:1-15;
Psalm 126:1-6;
Proverbs 16:26-27

Mark my Word
(for further study)

Luke 3:16;
Acts 4:8;
Hebrews 13:8

He earned the Name

John the Baptist plainly announced the purpose of Christ: to baptize men and women in the Spirit. It would characterize Him, giving Him the Name of Baptizer, just as John was "the Baptist." Nobody can pretend that a single performance shows what we are. I once baked a cake, but it isn't typical of me … and I would need a lot of urging to attempt it again! They don't call me a baker because of my sole success – I would have to bake cakes **daily** to bear the name of baker! Christ is called the Baptizer because that is His constant work, His Heavenly office: the Baptizer in the Holy Spirit, *"the same yesterday, today, and forever."*

The Bible scholar, Ronald W. Foulkes, offered a more technical explanation: "There is a cliché, 'one baptism, many fillings,' but we should realize this is not Scriptural; the Biblical pattern and provision is for constant fullness. One is to go on being filled. The word 'filled' is in a verbal form known as 'ingressive aorist,' suggesting an entrance into a state of condition. It is clear that the Christian who is baptized does not enter into a transitory experience, but into an abiding condition of fullness. Luke elaborates on the effect when speaking of Peter; he describes him as one *'filled with the Holy Spirit,'* using the passive participle of the aorist tense, indicating a happening in process."

You will no doubt hear people talk about "one baptism, many fillings." Remember that these are the code-words of those who oppose the baptism in the Spirit with signs following. But if Charismatics or Pentecostals talk like this, we must ask some simple questions: "When someone says he or she has been baptized in the Spirit, how long does it last? A week? An hour? Six months?" … "Does the Holy Spirit leak away like power from a car battery?" … "Is the baptism with the Spirit only one drink which we need to be refreshed with again and again?" … "How do we know when the Spirit has gone and we need another renewal?" … "How long can we say, 'I am Spirit-filled'? What signs indicate when we are and when we are not?" These are questions to ask yourself, knowing that the Spirit Himself will give you the answers.

Faith is a Decision

The great Swiss theologian, Dr. Emil Brunner, summed up his thought in four words: "Faith is a decision." He took it from Jesus, Who always talked that way. He praised believers ... and blamed unbelievers. Just as we can see, hear, feel, taste, smell – we can **believe**. That is our "sixth sense" or faculty, spiritual eyesight, an ear to hear, or a hand to take God's blessing. Believing is not beyond anybody. "I'm not made that way," they plead, but we all **are**. Some think of faith as money – a good thing if you have some. Faith is not what you **have** but what you **do**. We can **all** rise to the heights – if we want to.

Paul, the master apostle, understood that everyone has faith, but some are more proficient at its use than others: *"Receive one who is weak in the faith, but not to disputes over doubtful things. For one believes he may eat all things, but he who is weak eats only vegetables. Let not him who eats despise him who does not eat, and let not him who does not eat judge him who eats, for God has received him ... For if we live, we live to the Lord; and if we die, we die to the Lord. Therefore, whether we live or die, we are the Lord's."*

Who wants unbelief? It is a blind alley, the way to "no land, no water, and no love." To get out of it, turn around. Or in Bible language, *"repent"* – decide to believe instead of not believing. Doubt is deadly. Choose to live. *"Repent and believe the Gospel."* Faith produces good works, but good works don't produce faith – just as milk produces butter, but butter does not produce milk.

> Faith, mighty faith the promise sees
> And looks to that alone
> Laughs at impossibilities
> And cries, "It shall be done."

Today's Scripture

Therefore let us not judge one another anymore, but rather resolve this, not to put a stumbling block or a cause to fall in our brother's way.
(Romans 14:13)

Daily Power!

Today, I choose to live in Christ, active in faith and strong in believing.

Today's Bible Reading

*I Kings 5:1-18 through 6:1-38;
Acts 7:1-29;
Psalm 127:1-5;
Proverbs 16:28-30*

Mark my Word
(for further study)

Romans 14:1-13

The Size of Faith

Today's Scripture

Having then gifts differing according to the grace that is given to us, let us use them; if prophecy, let us prophesy in proportion to our faith.

(Romans 12:6)

Daily Power!

If I have faith as small as a microchip, I can still move mountains!

Today's Bible Reading

I Kings 7:1-51;
Acts 7:30-50;
Psalm 128:1-6;
Proverbs 16:31-33

Mark my Word
(for further study)

Isaiah 40:31;
Luke 17:5-6;
Romans 12:6

The apostles said to the Lord, *"Increase our faith."* Christians have wanted that ever since – faith in bulk! What was the reply of Jesus? *"If you have faith as small as a mustard seed, you can say to this mulberry tree, 'Be uprooted and planted in the sea,' and it would obey you."* That must have puzzled the apostles. They wanted **big** faith, but He spoke of the smallest thing they knew. He did not refer to the mustard seed because it was **very small** – the issue was the contrast between massive faith … and small (but living) seed. He wanted to hammer home that faith is never a matter of size. **Size** is the wrong word. Faith has neither bulk nor weight. What shape is a thought? **"Believing"** is what you **do** – an **action** – not a substance. Scripture speaks of the *"proportion of faith"* – it is proportionate to the job at hand, linked to the need. Like running and needing more air, your intake increases automatically.

Size loses its meaning even for the task when it is a faith-task. The bigness of a hill, a house and a molehill is all one to a bird flying over them. By faith *"we mount up on wings as eagles,"* and nothing is insurmountable. Active faith needs impossibilities. Religious faith, faith just in church, doesn't have enough impossibility. Robust faith grows in the outside weather, or it will be a sickly plant.

Perhaps you have never seen a mustard seed? You may need your glasses for one! But the people to whom Jesus spoke knew seeds. It was an agricultural world. Jesus spoke their farming language. Today we are a "high-tech" society, and our expressions are scientific. Jesus spoke the language of the people, and today our expressions come from technology. No doubt today, Jesus would use our common speech. Two thousand years ago, Jesus spoke about the *"mustard seed,"* a small thing with mighty potency. Maybe today He would talk about a microchip or fuse to illustrate His teaching: "If you have faith as small as an electric fuse, you could transplant trees from soil to sea." Like the mustard seed, the value of a fuse is not in breadth or length. The key is "conductivity." Your faith transfers the power of God to wherever it is needed.

"Righteous Anger" and right Priorities

In his intriguing story, God spoke to Jonah through a plant that grew up over him and then withered. Jonah was staying outside the city for awhile, waiting to see what would happen. The sun was very hot, and so Jonah had made himself a shelter. A plant provided by God grew up over Jonah to give him even more protection from the heat, but then it withered overnight. Its root had been destroyed by some kind of worm.

Jonah was furious. God said, *"Do you have a right to be angry about this plant?"* Well, Jonah thought he did. He claimed to be angry enough to die. So God stated His case – the last words of the Book of Jonah are the words of the Lord: *"You have been concerned about this vine, though you did not tend it or make it grow. It sprang up overnight and died overnight. But Nineveh has more than a hundred and twenty thousand people who cannot tell their right hand from their left, and many cattle as well. Should I not be concerned about that great city?"*

To Jonah, the plant seemed more important than the lives of people. This has a lesson to teach us about what is important to us. There are plenty of righteous causes around today. Europe is particularly known for its powerful lobbies affecting legislation on several great moral issues, such as concern for the environment. Some Christians may find themselves involved in such matters politically or professionally … and why not? The question is: "What are we choosing to be most angry about?"

"My sheep hear My voice, and I know them and they follow Me. And I give them eternal life, and they shall never perish, neither shall anyone snatch them out of My hand. My Father, Who has given them to Me, is greater than all, and no one is able to snatch them out of My Father's hand."

Jesus Himself exhibited anger when people were polluting His Father's House, but He was also quick to restore peace. Let that be your goal: to be a restorer of God's peace to the world.

Today's Scripture

But Jesus said, "Let her alone. Why do you trouble her? She has done a good work for Me. For you have the poor with you always, and whenever you wish you may do them good; but Me you do not have always."

(Mark 14:6-7)

Daily Power!

There are plenty of righteous causes around today, but I chose to make spreading the Gospel of Jesus Christ to all the world to be my priority.

Today's Bible Reading

*I Kings 8:1-66;
Acts 7:51-60
through 8:1-13;
Psalm 129:1-8;
Proverbs 17:1*

Mark my Word
(for further study)

*Jonah 4:1-11;
Mark 14:3-9;
John 10:27-29*

12

"By this we know love, because He laid down His life for us."

Christ's earthly life was very brief. He was crucified at thirty-three years of age, and was in the public eye for only three-and-a-half years. Jesus Christ was a **gift** to Mankind. His whole life was entirely **for us**. We were His exclusive concern. His life is a flawless example of dedication to Mankind. He was totally free of self-interest, and He had only one purpose for being here: we, the people.

He did not serve by being a humanitarian, political or social activist. He never gave anybody one penny, simply because He never had any money. Once, when He needed a penny for a sermon-illustration, someone had to lend Him one. But He gave people all He had – and that was Himself, His very heart. *"But if we walk in the light as He is in the light, we have fellowship with one another, and the Blood of Jesus Christ His Son cleanses us from all sin."*

Out of His hands flowed healing. When He had nothing left and He couldn't give anymore, yet He gave His own life's Blood – the Blood of Redemption … the price of our salvation. What He gave was far more than material things, or even healing. **He gave Himself.** In absolute abandon, He met the needs of Mankind with Himself: *"Who Himself bore our sins in His own body on the tree, that we, having died to sins, might live for righteousness – by Whose stripes you were healed."*

When they had no shepherd, He became the Good Shepherd. When they had no physician, He became the Great Physician. When they had no teacher, He became the Truth. When the crowds were hungry, He became the Bread of Life, and in the darkness, they found Him to be the Light of the world. This same Jesus Christ of two thousand years ago … He is the same One today, for you and for me!

Today's Scripture

I am the Good Shepherd. The Good Shepherd gives His life for the sheep.
(John 10:11)

Daily Power!

I know that Jesus Christ loves me unconditionally, completely, eternally.

Today's Bible Reading

I Kings 9:1-28 through 10:-129; Acts 8:14-40; Psalm 130:1-8; Proverbs 17:2-3

Mark my Word
(for further study)

John 10:7-18; I Peter 2:24; I John 1:7; 3:16

Overcoming Love

The Gospel is a message of love – and love is not presented by reason, but by loving. If you fell in love and wanted to ask a lovely girl to marry you, would you ask a lawyer to come and present your case to her? Imagine it! Would that win any woman? Marriage is either love ... or it is not marriage. The Gospel is both power and life ... or it is not the Gospel. Preaching is not a three-point homily. Preaching is a man burning in the pulpit for everybody to see. A preacher is an incandescent luminary. A sermon may be a neatly-turned and engineered presentation – like the casing of an armour-piercing shell – but it needs filling with explosive, or it will bounce off the case-hardened minds of unbelievers. Their prejudices are fortified with argument ... but the explosive power in a sermon filled with the Holy Spirit can demolish it.

When Peter stood up to preach that day in Jerusalem, he recounted instances from the ancient holy Scriptures which illustrated what was currently happening ... and he also sharply pointed out that the same Jews who had called for the death of Jesus – those on whose hands His Blood was guilty – were being offered an opportunity to repent of their great sin: *"'Therefore let all the house of Israel know assuredly that God has made this Jesus, Whom you crucified, both Lord and Christ.' Now when they heard this, they were cut to the heart ... Then Peter said to them, 'Repent, and let every one of you be baptized in the Name of Jesus Christ for the remission of sins; and you shall receive the gift of the Holy Spirit. For the promise is to you and to your children, and to all who are afar off, as many as the Lord our God will call.'"* The Gospel is always a surprise attack. It gets at people from a direction they never planned to defend. They are prepared for argument, but the Gospel doesn't argue. They are prepared for sentiment, but the Gospel is not sentimental. It comes with the melting waters of eternity flowing over their soul. On the Day of Pentecost, the Holy Spirit was outpoured, and that transformed the disciples totally. Manpower had been filled with God's power – and that is your secret for your life ... even today.

Today's Scripture

For the promise is to you and to your children, and to all who are afar off, as many as the Lord our God will call.
(Acts 2:39)

Daily Power!

I will always represent the Gospel of Jesus Christ with great compassion.

Today's Bible Reading

I Kings 11:1-43 through 12:1-19;
Acts 9:1-25;
Psalm 131:1-3;
Proverbs 17:4-5

Mark my Word
(for further study)

Acts 2:17-39

Today's Scripture

There are diversities of gifts, but the same Spirit. There are diversities of ministries, but the same Lord. And there are diversities of activities, but it is the same God Who works all in all.

(I Corinthians 12:4-6)

Daily Power!

Lord, show me today how best to use – to manifest – Your power through the gifts which You have already given to me.

Today's Bible Reading

I Kings 12:20-33 through 13:1-34; Acts 9:26-43; Psalm 132:1-18; Proverbs 17:6

Mark my Word
(for further study)

I Corinthians 12:1-31

Power demonstrated

The power of the Gospel is manifest power: *"The **manifestation** of the Spirit is given to each one for the profit of all."* This power is not simply our faith in power. It is not a matter of going through a routine service … and believing that the power of God is at work, invisibly. His power should be seen, be manifested. There should be effects – physical or personal – that can be attributed to the power of God – people's lives should be affected in some tangible way. The Holy Spirit is not a theory, a statement about what goes on in some distant world of which we are not aware, or a "soft-breathing influence." His power is power made manifest.

There are two forms of power, and the one most Christians speak of is "dunamis." We can identify with that word because we use it so much in English: dynamo, dynamite, dynamics. But actually those words express "power under wraps." Dynamite is simply a grey substance, which you can carry in your briefcase. Be careful though! It is a power pack. It is latent power, power stored up. Paul also uses another word, "energema" – energy. When the power of dynamite is released, it becomes energy. Energy is power let loose. In I Corinthians, the same word is translated "operations" (KJV) – power in operation. The "working of miracles" later used is a combination of both words – "power operating in energy."

Let's face it: Christianity is either supernatural … or nothing at all. We had – and still have – a supernatural Jesus, with a supernatural ministry, creating a supernatural Church, with a supernatural Gospel, and a supernatural Bible. Take the miraculous away … and you have taken Christianity's life away. The Church becomes an ethical society or a social club, when it is intended to be the grid system for transmitting the power of God into this powerless world. You and I are **conductors** of God's power to the world!

A World Vision

Among the Old Testament prophets, Jonah was the only one to leave Israel and actually preach the Word of the Lord openly in the streets of a foreign land. There was a kinship between Jonah and Jesus. Jonah was the only prophet with Whom Jesus personally associated Himself. He spoke of him as *"the sign to Israel."* Jonah had a God-given burden for a Gentile city. The next to carry such a burden was Jesus Christ Himself. His heart was big enough to hold the whole of Israel … and the whole Gentile world!

No other prophet of Israel ever carried the Word of the Lord to the outside world except when they themselves were carried away as captives of war. In Babylon, some maintained their witness to the Lord, the God of Israel. We read of these in the books of Daniel and Esther. But the northern tribes were absorbed in the Assyrian Empire and lost. In the Book of Psalms, we are told, *"Our captors asked us for songs … they said, 'Sing us one of the songs of Zion!' But their reply was, 'How can we sing the songs of the Lord while in a foreign land?'"* What a pity – those songs could have introduced the living God to the outside world.

The concern of God for His creatures extends to all equally, even to the most renegade and wicked. However, Jonah didn't feel the same way at all and was out of sympathy with his commission. He tried to get away from God. But God was determined he should go, and sent a storm at sea as Jonah tried to flee. It was God's storm of protest at Jonah's attitude, devoid of any pity.

God made Jonah a remarkable exception. He coerced him into doing what Israel was supposed to do but never did. God raised up Israel to make the Name of the Lord known throughout the whole earth! Even the original Church was entirely Jewish for maybe twenty years. Perhaps Jonah was, despite his shortcomings, one of the greatest of all the prophets! Today, allow God to speak to your heart about your own responsibility to a dying world.

Today's Scripture

Therefore He is also able to save to the uttermost those who come to God through Him, since He always lives to make intercession for them.
(Hebrews 7:25)

Daily Power!

Dear Lord, please remind me that – in every thing I say, everything I do – I am representing you to a sinful world.

Today's Bible Reading

*I Kings 14:1-31 through 15:1-24;
Acts 10:1-23a;
Psalm 133:1-3;
Proverbs 17:7-8*

Mark my Word
(for further study)

*Psalm 67, 96, 137:3-4;
Ezekiel 36:23;
Jonah 1:1-17; 2:1-10;
Matthew 12:39;
Hebrews 7:25*

16

Today's Scripture

No one can serve two masters; for either he will hate the one and love the other, or he will be loyal to the one and despise he other. You cannot serve God and mammon [money].

(Matthew 6:24)

Daily Power!

I want to be "rich in good works, ready to give, willing to share, storing up for myself good foundation for the time to come, that I may lay hold on eternal life."
(I Timothy 6:18-19; paraphrased)

Today's Bible Reading

I Kings 15:25-34 through 17:1-24; Acts 10:23b-48; Psalm 134:1-3; Proverbs 17:9-11

Mark my Word
(for further study)

*Jonah 1:1-17;
Matthew 6:24;
Luke 16:13;
Ephesians 4:11;
I Timothy 6:17-19;
II Peter 3:9*

Evangelism is God's Initiative

The initiative to save Nineveh came from God, not from Jonah. *"For God desires not the death of any man, but that all should repent."* The initiative for evangelism comes from God, and God both calls and equips us for this work. It was He Who gave some to be evangelists. At first, Jonah acted on his own initiative and went in the opposite direction – to Tarshish – instead of going East … and God responded by sending a ferocious storm. God has promised to bless and support His own divine plans. There is no Divine blessing upon our own plans, only upon His.

So where was Jonah going? Where is Tarshish? Various experts have studied this, trying to find out. The word "tarshish" is linked closely with the smelting of ore, silver, gold, and tin. The ships of Tarshish were treasure ships – famous for the expensive cargo they carried. They became symbols of wealth, power and pride. For Jonah, Nineveh represented only sacrifice. It was a stark choice: Nineveh, with its menace … or Tarshish, with its money.

"No servant can serve two masters, for either he will hate the one and love the other, or else he will be loyal to the one and despise the other. You cannot serve God and money." Are we "for hire" – where the biggest salary is offered? Is cash to be the deciding factor in our calling? Mammon and ministry don't mix too well. He profits most who serves best: *"Command those who are rich in this present age not to be haughty, nor to trust in uncertain riches but in the living God, Who gives us richly all things to enjoy. Let them do good, that they be rich in good works, ready to give, willing to share, storing up for themselves a good foundation for the time to come, that they may lay hold on eternal life."*

So make the decision today … to **serve God** … to **put Him first** … to **make Him your Number One Priority**. And then you'll see every other area of your life fit into place.

Low Resistance

A fuse is made of a metal, such as silver wire, which offers low resistance to current. Low resistance means high conductivity. Translated into the spiritual, the lower our resistance to the Word of God, the higher the power rating. The higher our resistance in obedience to the Word, the lower the operational power of God. A fuse with high resistance would either carry no power at all, or else soon blow. When we resist the Word by unbelief, the power of God can't come through. If we say we believe in the Word but disobey it, we negate our faith. It blows the fuse. **The power of God is little when the Word of God means little to us.**

Whatever else may be true, one thing is absolutely beyond contradiction – it is that Christianity is a power religion, or it is nothing. Liberals, teachers of rationalist doctrine, rely on logic. The apostles relied on the power of God: *"By wisdom the world knew not God. It has pleased God to save them that believe the foolishness of preaching."* Our head can be our doubt-box. Reasoning is too uncertain an instrument for vital personal relationships, especially with God. It is like using a shovel to read the night sky, instead of a telescope. When people turn to science with its algebraic equations, geology or philosophic deductions to approve religious faith, it is ridiculous. What can these things possibly have to do with spiritual experience? Science has no equipment to handle relationships with God. You may as well use a corkscrew to study music.

How do we believe or not believe in anybody? By mathematics? Have you ever felt you can't trust somebody but you couldn't put your finger on why? It is a gut feeling under your skin. A higher self, intuition, is at work and triggers off an alarm. But we believe in somebody else for the same reason … and what that is, we may not know. Instinct never warns us against Jesus. When we "get wise" to Him, we want to come closer. Knowing Him better, we heart-warm to Him. *"We love Him because He first loved us."* What unbelievers say means no more than what the barometer says. The proper way, the only possible way, is to trust Him. Remember: the effective center of true life … your life … is your heart, not your brain.

Today's Scripture

For with the heart one believes unto righteousness, and with the mouth confession is made unto salvation.
(Romans 10:10)

Daily Power!

The lower my resistance to the Word of God, the higher is my power rating!

Today's Bible Reading

I Kings 18:1-46;
Acts 11:1-30;
Psalm 135:1-21;
Proverbs 17:12-13

Mark my Word
(for further study)

Romans 10:10;
I Corinthians 1:21;
I John 4:19

18

Today's Scripture

I believe God that it will be just as it was told me.
(Acts 27:25)

Daily Power!

When I put my faith into action, God delivers!

Today's Bible Reading

*I Kings 19:1-21;
Acts 12:1-23;
Psalm 136:1-26;
Proverbs 17:14-15*

Mark my Word
(for further study)

Acts 27:25-26

Believing

Faith is not just "believing" with nothing special in mind – it is believing **unto** something and **for** something. The Word of God gives point, direction and purpose. Without the Bible, it is like "an arrow shot in the air that fell to Earth I know not where." In fact, it is the only Book that gives faith a positive goal. One wonders what some religions propose to do for folk who believe. They become a religious treadmill, believing for the sake of believing.

The apostle Paul was aboard a sinking ship, but he said, *"I have faith in God."* It wasn't a kind of defiant sentiment. It was specific:

"Now when neither sun nor stars appeared for many days, and no small tempest beat on us, all hope that we would be saved was finally given up … Then Paul stood in the midst of them and said … 'I urge you to take heart, for there will be no loss of life among you, but only of the ship. For there stood by me this night an angel of the God to Whom I belong and Whom I serve, saying, 'Do not be afraid, Paul … indeed God has granted you all of those who sail with you.' Therefore take heart, men, for I believe God that it will be just as it was told me. However, we must run aground on a certain island.'"

It was rather different for a man who was crossing the Atlantic Ocean in a storm. He asked the captain if they were safe, and the captain trying to reassure him, saying, "Sir, we are in the hands of God." The man replied, "Is it as bad as that?" Please hold this truth deep in your heart today – "when God gives you a promise, then you can stand securely upon it!"

One-Drink

19

Jesus said that when the Comforter has come, *"He will abide with you forever."* This is where the blessing of speaking with tongues is seen. We can't speak unless the Holy Spirit gives utterance – if He does, He is there. By that sign, we can go out and conquer, for He is with us. Our feelings are not a reliable indicator of the Holy Spirit's power within us. In the 19th century, before tongues were commonly heard, the problem was knowing when the Spirit had come. People would pray a great deal – "tarrying" – believing that power could be measured by the time spent in prayer … an idea quite foreign to the Bible. By the 20th century, it was taught for the first time that the sign of tongues (glossolalia) was the assurance of the baptism in the Spirit. This immediately triggered the greatest movement of the Holy Spirit of all time. My own faith was energized by the initial sign of tongues, which led me into this present ministry of evangelism.

Paul spoke about the importance of speaking in tongues, yet put it into perspective: *"Pursue love, and desire spiritual gifts, but especially that you may prophesy. For he who speaks in a tongue does not speak to men but to God, for no one understand him; however, in the spirit he speaks mysteries … He who speaks in a tongue edifies himself, but he who prophesies edifies the church. I wish you all spoke with tongues, but even more that you prophesied; for he who prophesies is greater than he who speaks with tongues, unless indeed he interprets, that the church may receive edification."*

When Jesus spoke to the woman at the well in Samaria, He referred to *"whoever drinks."* The Greek tense He used (aorist) means to drink once only, not to keep coming back with an empty water pot. That is the very thing the woman at the well of Sychar understood, for she said, *"that I need not come here to draw."* The one-drink results in *"a fountain of water springing up into everlasting life."* Water is frequently used as a symbol of the Holy Spirit in Scripture, just as it is here. Oh, come to that fountain again today … and every day … and drink of the well that will never run dry!

Today's Scripture

If you knew the generosity of God and Who I am, you would be asking Me for a drink, and I would give you fresh, living water.
(John 4:10; the Message)

Daily Power!

The gift of speaking in tongues enables me to speak to God what no one – including Satan – can understand.

Today's Bible Reading

*I Kings 20:1-43 through 21:1-29;
Acts 12:24-25 through 13:1-15;
Psalm 137:1-9;
Proverbs 17:16*

Mark my Word
(for further study)

*John 14:1-42;
I Corinthians 14:1-5*

20

Identified by Miracles

When I was in Brazzaville, the capital of the West African country of Congo, during a service God gave me a "word of knowledge" for a couple otherwise unknown to me, somewhere among the tens of thousands present. The wife had been in a coma for three days and had been carried into the meeting by her husband. By faith and obedience to God's prompting, I told the vast audience what the Spirit of the Lord had made known to me. As I spoke, the unconscious woman – though not hearing – came out of her coma and was healed. Mind over matter? Impossible … the patient knew nothing of what was going on until she revived. *"And these signs will follow those who believe: in My Name they will cast out demons; they will speak with new tongues; they will take up serpents; and if they drink anything deadly, it will by no means hurt them; they will lay hands on the sick, and they will recover."*

Another lady present needed urgent surgery. Her unborn baby had died in her womb, and the hospital had arranged for the baby to be removed the next day. When prayer was offered for the masses of needy ones in the service, the baby in her womb leaped. She rushed forward to the platform tearfully to testify … and just in time too – because straight afterward, she went into labor! She later gave birth to a bouncing baby boy. *"And as you go, preach, saying, 'The Kingdom of Heaven is at hand.' Heal the sick, cleanse the lepers, raise the dead, cast out demons. Freely you have received, freely give."*

These were not the only wonders that happened. They left me unable to sleep for excitement and joy. Most important of all, for six days the Holy Spirit swept through the crowd like a Heavenly dam-burst, carrying one hundred thousand precious Congolese on a wave of blessing into the Kingdom of God! That joy is yours today!

Today's Scripture

And as you go, preach, saying, "The Kingdom of Heaven is at hand." Heal the sick, cleanse the lepers, raise the dead, cast out demons. Freely you have received, freely give.

(Matthew 10:8)

Daily Power!

The Kingdom of God will be identified by miracles.

Today's Bible Reading

I Kings 22:1-53;
Acts 13:16-41;
Psalm 138:1-8;
Proverbs 17:17-18

Mark my Word
(for further study)

Matthew 10:8;
Mark 16:17-18

Acts Today

The Book of Acts reads better than any modern-day novel. It has clearly defined characters, with some in leading roles and others in support roles … it has action, adventure, triumphs, tragedies … the scenes change from Jerusalem to Damascus to Antioch to Rome, from prison cells to shipwrecks. Yet the marvellous thing about it – **it is completely true!** Seeing how the love of Jesus came into the life of Saul, the angry persecutor of Christians, and transformed him into the most powerful apostle of all – now that rings true! Reading about the arguments between the Jews-only faction and the Gentiles-too group – and that rings true too, for so many churches still squabble among themselves. The miracles of healing, the explosive growth of the Early Church, government leaders baffled and chagrined by the boldness of these ignorant peasants – these are all quite believable … and even applicable to our own day.

Sometimes people have suggested that **The Acts of the Apostles** ought to be re-named **The Acts of the Holy Spirit**. Perhaps. The Book describes the **acts of the apostles**, as its title indicates, but it certainly does not give an exhaustive account of **all the acts of the Holy Spirit** – He did not cease to operate at the end of chapter 28. The Day of Pentecost is already two-thousand-plus years long. The acts of the apostles carries on uninterrupted to the acts of the Early Church … and then to the acts of God's people today. The Book of Acts tells of the day of small things, which paved the way for the acts of today. It is a book that is still being written! I carry on with the work the apostles began – together with you. We are partners and co-workers with Christ on God's harvest fields. Together, let's make history for Christ!

Today's Scripture

Preaching the Kingdom of God and teaching the things which concern the Lord Jesus Christ with all confidence.

(Acts 28:31)

Daily Power!

Lord, make my chapter in the modern-day Book of Acts be one that completely honors You.

Today's Bible Reading

II Kings 1:1-18 through 2:1-25;
Acts 13:42-52 through 14:1-7;
Psalm 139:1-24;
Proverbs 17:19-21

Mark my Word
(for further study)

Acts 28:1-31

God raises the Dead

Today's Scripture

To open their eyes, in order to turn them from darkness to light, and from the power of Satan to God, that they may receive forgiveness of sins and an inheritance among those who are sanctified by faith in Me.

(Acts 26:18)

Daily Power!

Lord, give me the words to say that will indeed persuade others to become Christians.

Today's Bible Reading

II Kings 3:1-27 through 4:1-17; Acts 14:8-28; Psalm 140:1-13; Proverbs 17:22

Mark my Word
(for further study)

Acts 26:1-32

When preaching to King Agrippa, one of the most scholarly rulers of his day, Paul boldly proclaimed Jesus Christ crucified and resurrected – a fact hard to accept by the intellectual king. Paul asked, *"Why should it be thought incredible by you that God raises the dead?"* He continued with his testimony – how he had formerly persecuted his own people whom he considered to be blaspheming renegades, but was transformed by a divine appointment on the road to Damascus. He proclaimed: "[I am sent] *to open their eyes, in order to turn them from darkness to light, and from the power of Satan to God, that they may receive forgiveness of sins and an inheritance among those who are sanctified by faith in* [Christ]*."* Eventually, the king responded, *"You almost persuade me to become a Christian."*

Some people brush the resurrection aside. They say it is just another wonder from an unsuspicious and superstitious age. Fantastic marvels were commonly believed two thousand years ago. People were easily taken in – any whale of a tale would swallow them up. When Caesar was assassinated, it was whispered that the sheeted dead had walked the streets of Rome. Dragons, giants, omens in the sky, portents, oracles and magic were the order of the day. But they were all tales that were soon forgotten. One writer in those days, Aeschylus, said, "So gullible, their stories spread like wildfire, they fly fast and die faster." None of it changed history.

However, the news of the resurrection of Jesus did not fade and die. Hundreds testified – they had seen Him alive! Authorities were alarmed. Believers were threatened, beaten and imprisoned, but they could not be silenced. They convinced thousands. Then, as others believed, they also had glorious experiences. There was only one explanation for it: Jesus Christ was walking the Earth again … and as a result, history was changed! Today, these things still happen. Thousands discover that Jesus is alive; actually, one hundred fifty thousand people more today than yesterday. They stake their soul on it, build their lives on it, and they are never let down. So remember today to actively do your part in this on-going, end-time resurrection harvest of souls.

No Matter where we run

Aboard the ill-fated ship to Tarshish, the crew did not know Jonah was a prophet, nor did they know his God. The sailors were heathens, but they rebuked the prophet of God for sleeping on the job. *"'How can you sleep?' they said to him in the midst of the storm. 'Get up and call on your God! Maybe He will take notice of us, and we will not perish.'"*

The people of this world expect a prophet to speak up, whether they agree with what he says or not. Maybe they don't want to adopt Christian morals or the way of the Lord for themselves – yet they still believe morality is a good thing for other people to practice. If we don't preach what they know we believe, they feel cheated, let down. The Church must never fail to sound a clear note on what is right and wrong.

When backed into a corner, Jonah admitted who he was. This startled and even terrified the crew. These men were potential converts – they already recognized the power and authority of his God. Despite Jonah's poor testimony, they came to believe in Jonah's God: *"At this, the men greatly feared the Lord, and they offered a sacrifice to the Lord and made vows to Him."* Here was a man who knew the marvelous truth about God, and yet they had to ask him Who his God was. With Jonah aboard their ship, Who his God was should have been clear. Now ask yourself this hard question: "Do people know Who **my** God is?" Why not make sure that they do!

"There was a man sent from God, whose name was John. This man came for a witness, to bear witness of the Light, that all through him might believe" … *"The God of our fathers has chosen you that you should know His will, and see the Just One, and hear the voice of His mouth. For you will be His witness to all men of what you have seen and heard."*

Has God been good to you? Have you seen and heard His marvelous works? Then be a witness of that to all men … and they will know Who is your God!

Today's Scripture

For I am not ashamed of the Gospel of Christ, for it is the power of God to salvation for everyone who believes.
(Romans 1:16a)

Daily Power!

In every thought, action, word, and deed, dear Lord, let me be your representative to this world.

Today's Bible Reading

II Kings 4:18-44 through 5:1-27; Acts 15:1-35; Psalm 141:1-10; Proverbs 17:23

Mark my Word
(for further study)

Jonah 1:1-16; Romans 1:1-32

24

True Spirit of Evangelism

Jesus told His disciples that the Spirit of God is the Spirit of witness. Today we often talk about "power evangelism" – signs and wonders to confirm the Gospel. But Jesus said that even wicked people would work miracles although He never knew them. Paul also talked about the demonstration of the Spirit.

However, one cannot help but be impressed by the way the apostle manifested the reality of the Gospel in his daily life. He told the Corinthians that their lives were *"epistles ... known and read by everybody."* Looking at us, will people be able to say, "So, **that** is what your God is like"?

Evangelism means **to recommend Jesus**. The evangelistic method taught by Jesus was that we should recommend Him by our lives as well as by our words. We should be "Jesus people" ... or more precisely, "Jesus-of-the-Gospel people." We are *the light of the world"* – there should be no other options. *"And as you go, preach, saying, 'The Kingdom of Heaven is at hand.' Heal the sick, cleanse the lepers, raise the dead, cast out demons. Freely you have received, freely give ... You will be brought before governors and kings for My sake, as a testimony to them and to the Gentiles. But when they deliver you up, do not worry about how or what you should speak, for it will be given to you in that hour what you should speak; for it is not you who speak, but the Spirit of your Father Who speaks in you."*

Jonah fled from the presence of the Lord, but he carried a light in his soul that somehow shone through. He concealed his testimony from the captain and crew of the ship that he boarded at Joppa. But Jonah knew God – and that came across even when he tried to run away from God. The crew of a storm-tossed ship sensed it ... and caught the vision.

This is God's call to you and me today: to catch His vision for the world, and to be His tools to bring the lost to Christ.

Today's Scripture

You are the salt of the Earth, but if the salt loses its flavor, how shall it be seasoned? It is then good for nothing but to be thrown out and trampled underfoot by men. You are the light of the world.

(Matthew 5:13-14)

Daily Power!

Lord, let me be Your epistle written in the hearts of men, known and read by all men, and a clear signpost to You.

Today's Bible Reading

II Kings 6:1-33 through 7:1-20; Acts 15:36-41 through 16:1-15; Psalm 142:1-7; Proverbs 17:24-25

Mark my Word
(for further study)

Jonah 1:1-3; Matthew 5:13-14; 7:22-23; 10:16-26; John 15:26; I Corinthians 2:4; II Corinthians 3:2

Personal Presence

One thing has always amazed me: the disciples did not weep when Christ left them. They never showed any nostalgia for "the good old days." Luke tells us that after He ascended out of sight, they *"returned to Jerusalem with great joy, and were continually in the temple praising and blessing God."* Why did they display such a remarkable reaction to the departure of Jesus? The answer is the coming of the Spirit! When Christ was present, they were only eyewitnesses of His power. But when the Day of Pentecost came, they were more than eyewitnesses – they possessed power themselves and experienced the divine presence personally. It was different from when Christ was with them. That personal sense of the presence of God is nowhere said to be just for the disciples alone, as if they were some kind of elite band. Peter said, *"The promise is to you and to your children, and to all who are afar off, as many as the Lord our God will call."* He quoted the promise from the prophet Joel, where God said: *"I will pour out of My Spirit."* Wesley observed that this promise is not only for the Day of Pentecost – it described the **normal** Christian experience, as does the whole Book of Acts.

Another curious fact is that, although Jesus told the disciples to take bread and wine in memory of Him, they never used the language of "remembering." One does not "remember" a person with whom he or she lives. He is a living and abiding presence by the Spirit. *"From now on, we regard no one according to the flesh. Even though we have known Christ according to the flesh, yet now we know Him thus no longer."* To be filled with the Spirit brings us alive to Jesus … which is **even better** than being alive when Jesus was on Earth. Note too that the Spirit does not come to talk about Himself but to reveal Jesus. Paul said he preached Christ crucified in the power and demonstration of the Spirit. If we only preach the power of the Spirit without the Cross, we short-circuit the very power we preach about. The Spirit's primary interest is in the Cross. We don't preach power, but the Gospel of the Cross, which is the power of God by the Spirit.

Today's Scripture

And when they had prayed, the place where they were assembled together was shaken; and they were all filled with the Holy Spirit, and they spoke the Word of God with boldness.
(Acts 2:31)

Daily Power!

The Day of Pentecost described the normal Christian experience!

Today's Bible Reading

II Kings 8:1-29
through 9:1-13;
Acts 16:16-40;
Psalm 143:1-12;
Proverbs 17:26

Mark my Word
(for further study)

Joel 2:28;
Luke 24:52-53;
John 16:15;
Acts 2:17, 39;
II Corinthians 5:16

Pulling the Revival Trigger

Since my earliest attempts as a missionary in Africa, what we are seeing God do today is breathtaking. Following the footsteps of giants, we reap with joy where they had sown in tears. We came to Bukavu, first visited by missionary C.T. Studd, and still remote in the rain forests of Zaire. There we saw 70,000 people respond to the call of God's love. David Livingstone prophesied that where he hardly saw a convert, later there would be thousands – so it was. At Blantyre, Malawi – named after the town in Scotland where Livingstone was born – several hundred thousand responded to the call of salvation.

Today, witchcraft, occultism and evil make the Gospel as vital as a gun in a snake pit. Jesus sets the captives free wholesale. Cool and casual Christianity will do nothing. Nations urgently need the flaming message of the Cross now, not at our leisure. Sometime ago, our northerly thrust reached almost to the Sahara Desert at Ouagadougou, capital of Burkina Faso (formerly Upper Volta) … a country noted for its occultism. Gatherings totaled 800,000 people in six meetings, with almost a quarter-million people in the culminating service. Most of them professed Jesus Christ, including many Muslims and animists. Similarly later on, in the Nigerian city of Kaduna, 500,000 people gathered in a single service – a total of 1.67-million in six meetings. And then to top it all - our **Millennium Great Gospel Crusade** in Lagos, Nigeria where we preached the Gospel to over 6 million precious souls. 3.4 million had filled out decision cards. 1.6 million had gathered at the last day of this six-day crusade. The response to the power-Gospel is absolutely awesome!

For over 20 years I had a divine promise in my heart that we would see one million souls converted in a single meeting. We had acquired sound systems to reach crowds bigger than perhaps ever addressed before on Earth by one man face to face. Arrogant presumption? If the Crucified One is to *"see the labor of His soul, and be satisfied,"* dare we think in smaller terms? Would He be "satisfied" with anything less? Dare to have big faith! And … Yes we saw one million souls saved in a single service in Lagos. God's promise has been fulfilled and we are moving forward with God's Gospel-Combine bringing in the harvest en masse.

Today's Scripture

You have already won a big victory over those false teachers, for the Spirit in you is far stronger than anything in the world.
(I John 4:4; the Message)

Daily Power!

I will always endeavor to give my very best to Christ, and believe He will honor that faith.

Today's Bible Reading

II Kings 9:14-37 through 10:1-31; Acts 17:1-34; Psalm 144:1-15; Proverbs 17:27-28

Mark my Word
(for further study)

Isaiah 53:11; I John 4:4

The God who creates

Twice in the first chapter of Revelations, God called Himself, *"Him Who was."* *"The God that was"* is how half the world thinks of Him: the One Who created Heaven and Earth ... and has done very little ever since. Limited to that idea, people may as well have faith in Pharaoh Tutankhamun. Could a God of such creative imagination settle down to be a God of long ago, the past, sitting in Heaven with His hands folded in His lap? He filled the empty skies with unsurpassing beauty ... and then went to sleep? If we don't see further than that, we are not very perceptive. Could any of us build even a house and abandon it? Could God ignore His own universe?

"In the beginning God created the Heavens and the Earth." So what? Well, the question naturally is, "Why should God do any such thing?" He didn't do it to please anybody – there wasn't anybody else, only just Himself! He pleased Himself when He did it. He was not obliged to do so. He was not pressured. What anybody does because they want to do it shows what they are. If I sat down in my room, shut the door and played the organ, it would be for my own pleasure. It would tell anybody that's me, because I'm musical. I would do that. God brought the glittering stars and the planets into being. That's Him! *"The Heavens declare the glory of God; the skies proclaim the work of His hands."* So begins Psalm 19, and the writer is thrilled. But it is the aurora of God – not the splendor of the universe – that he is excited about ... he is distracted from Creation by the Creator!

Modern science takes everything apart, like taking a violin apart to see what makes the sound. It loses the Divine radiance. I imagine God standing by, pensive, watching us like children opening their Christmas stockings, while He is waiting to love us. But then, fathers are often forgotten for the sake of Christmas toys! God pulled a blank sheet of paper across His desk, thought ... and designed everything we see around us. Its substance was shaped out of His own grandeur – He Himself must be absolutely eternally breathtaking! And this is the God Who **loves you**!

Today's Scripture

The law of the Lord is perfect, converting the soul; the testimony of the Lord is sure, making wise the simple ... More to be desired are they than gold.

(Psalm 19:7-10)

Daily Power!

Oh Lord, You are beautiful; Your face is all I seek.

Today's Bible Reading

II Kings 10:32-36 through 12:1-21; Acts 18:1-22; Psalm 145:1-21; Proverbs 18:1

Mark my Word
(for further study)

Genesis 1:1; Psalm 19:1-14; Revelation 1:4, 8

Today's Scripture

For the Lord is good; His mercy is everlasting, and His truth endures to all generations.

(Psalm 100:5)

Daily Power!

My God is an awesome God Who reigns with wisdom, power and love.

Today's Bible Reading

II Kings 13:1-25 through 14:1-29; Acts 18:23-28 through 19:1-12; Psalm 146:1-10; Proverbs 18:2-3

Mark my Word
(for further study)

Genesis 1:31; Job 38:7; Psalm 100:3; John 3:16; Romans 8:28

The good God

God delights in activity, in color, beauty, wonder and life, and much more. He made US – why? Why do we long for children? As an opportunity for our instinct of love – God made us that way. He's like that Himself. What He is must come out as long as God exists, on and on. *"God saw all that He had made, and it was very good."* His idea of what was good was a material world, not just an abstract spiritual principle of goodness. God doesn't deal in abstractions. He is pragmatic, the God of earth and sea, animals, trees and birds, fishes … and people. *"We are His people."* He made it all, and made us and was happy about it. He loved it: *"God so loved the world."* He molded this beautiful globe, and said "Good! Good! Good!" seven times in Genesis chapter one. He clapped His hands with pleasure, and the morning stars sang together for joy. The whole process works towards good. Evil fights it, but it will never work out: *"All things work together for good."* God is good.

When things are wrong, we ask, "Why?" Of course we do. God put that in us. We hate evil because He does. God put that "Why?" in our souls. Even Jesus asked, "Why?" when He experienced the utmost agony on the Cross. A good God is the God of true faith. That is the God of the Bible. That is where the idea came from – the Bible. The pagans had not the remotest idea of a good God.

"God said let there be … and there was." Creation was the first and greatest of all miracles. If God could extrude the Himalayas and the Rockies through His cupped hands, and with His finger scoop out the hollows for the Pacific and the Atlantic, and cap the poles with miles-thick ice … what's the problem about God healing deaf ears or blind eyes? Are miracles possible? What a question! How dull can we be? But then, doubt does dull our thinking. It is absurd for anybody to say miracles can't happen. To know that, we would have to know everything about everything and about God. Nobody knows enough to declare it cannot be. It is the height of human arrogance to assume such omniscience. You can rest in the assurance of God's love for you.

Jonah's Problem

Jonah knew in his very bones what God was like: **He was gracious!** How could he – Jonah – preach judgment to Nineveh when he knew perfectly well that God was so kind and merciful? He would forgive their wickedness at the drop of a hat … or rather, at the first sign of repentance. So he fled from the presence of the Lord. To be where God was meant carrying the scent of grace in his clothes. The atmosphere was infected by compassion, and Jonah did not want to feel compassionate. He had no inclination for smiling kindly toward monsters like the lords of Nineveh.

Evangelism means **deliverance from judgment**. But Jonah strongly felt that Nineveh deserved judgment. His attitude was understandable, I suppose. Jonah's feelings are often echoed in the Book of Psalms.

When Jesus was traveling through Samaria with His disciples, He wanted to stay one night in a village. But the local inhabitants were hostile to the Jews and would not accommodate the party. The disciples had been enjoying the experience of using God's power to heal by the authority vested in them by Jesus. They knew Elijah had brought fire down from Heaven upon soldiers sent to arrest him, so they proposed doing the same to wipe out this unfriendly village – after all, God had done it to Sodom and Gomorrah! But Jesus said to them, *"You do not know what manner of spirit you are of. For the Son of Man did not come to destroy men's lives but to save them."*

Let compassion be your guiding word today, even as Jesus had compassion toward the most hardened sinner … you can have compassion on those He brings across your path.

"I will have mercy on whomever I will have mercy, and I will have compassion on whomever I will have compassion. So then it is not of him who wills, nor of him who runs, but of God Who shows mercy … For this very purpose I have raised you up, that I may show My power in you, and that My Name may be declared in all the Earth."

Today's Scripture

For the Son of Man did not come to destroy men's lives but to save them.
(Luke 9:56)

Daily Power!

It is my heart's desire, Lord, that I may be fit for Your Kingdom because I "… having put my hand to the plow, do not look back."
(Luke 9:62; paraphrased)

Today's Bible Reading

II Kings 15:1-38
through 16:1-20;
Acts 19:13-41;
Psalm 147:1-20;
Proverbs 18:4-5

Mark my Word
(for further study)

II Kings 1:8-14;
Psalm 18:37-45;
Jonah 1:1-3;
Luke 9:15-62;
Romans 9:15-17

Today's Scripture

It is not for you to know times or seasons which the Father has put in His own authority. But you shall receive power when the Holy Spirit has come upon you; and you shall be witnesses to Me in Jerusalem, and in all Judea and Samaria, and to the end of the earth.

(Acts 1:7-8)

Daily Power!

I choose to keep my focus on the Kingdom of God and how my witness can bring it alive in the hearts of the people of the Earth.

Today's Bible Reading

II Kings 17:1-41 through 18:1-12; Acts 20:1-38; Psalm 148:1-14; Proverbs 18:6-7

Mark my Word
(for further study)

Jonah 4:1-11; Acts 1:3-8

Our ultimate Objective

Social, environmental, moral issues are not trifles to be dismissed lightly. We ought to be angry about many of the abominations perpetrated by modern society. **But what about the issue of eternal salvation?** Pro-life people fight (rightly) for the lives of unborn babies … but what are we doing about the souls of the millions of people walking our city streets?

We cannot all be preachers or evangelists. There must be people who do all sorts of different jobs that keep society and our churches functioning. Yet, whatever our concern with the fabric of mortal life and the issues of society, **the call of Christ to preach the Gospel to all creatures must still be our ultimate objective.**

To put it another way, we can be like Jonah, whose most immediate problem was the loss of shade that had been provided by his now-dead plant …or so he thought. Are we more disturbed about endangered species in the North Atlantic than by the eternal danger in which Christ-rejecters stand?

When Jesus had risen from the dead and was about to ascend into Heaven, He gave them extensive teaching about the Kingdom of God. They asked Him, *"Are You at this time going to restore the Kingdom to Israel?"* That was not only their priority, but also their interpretation of "the Kingdom of God" – a nationalistic issue. They were interested in times and seasons. Jesus answered:

"It is not for you to know the times or dates the Father has set by His own authority. But you will receive power when the Holy Spirit comes on you; and you will be My witnesses in Jerusalem, and in all Judea and Samaria, and to the ends of the Earth."

Those were the last words of Jesus on Earth. True, not everybody can give up their fishing boats to fish for men. But the Great Commission must still remain the top priority for all believers … including you and me. Please accept the Great Commission as your opportunity to shine in this dark and dying world. Shine brightly today!

Sickness is not the ultimate evil,
therefore healing is not the ultimate good.
Sin is the ultimate evil and salvation is the ultimate good.
Yet salvation and healing go hand in hand.

The practice of the supernatural
without the message of Calvary is very dangerous!

John never called miracles miracles,
but called them signs,
because they were pointing at something.

Future Evangelism

The world can be evangelized sooner than most believe, even as we have begun the new millennium. There were only a few thousand believers when Jesus left this world – perhaps one Christian follower for every twenty thousand people. Yet within three hundred years, the entire Roman Empire became "officially Christian."

Today, it is estimated there are more than six hundred million born-again Christians on Earth. That is one in every ten people! If we are distracted by other issues and devote our time, money and energy to mere political and social concerns, the Gospel witness will decrease. **It must increase!** We need on final, all-out effort to reach the other nine-tenths of the world!

"Now to Him Who is able to establish you according to my Gospel and the preaching of Jesus Christ, according to the revelation of the mystery kept secret since the world began, but now made manifest, and by the prophetic Scriptures made known to all nations, according to the commandment of the everlasting God, for obedience to the faith."

When the Gospel has been preached in the entire world as a witness to all nations, the end will come at last.

Now we come to that part when you and I must ask ourselves: "What kind of an evangelist am I? Do I want to preach judgment – like Jonah or John the Baptist – and see God's wrath come against greedy, evil people? Am I more concerned about side-issues – even as Jonah was angry about the plant that withered and died – than I am about millions of lost and dying souls? Do I have the capacity to preach compassion and mercy – as Jesus did – and offer Good News to people? And what am I prepared to do about evangelism?"

These are important questions, and it is our responsibility to find the answers ... and then make them stick!

Today's Scripture

This Gospel of the Kingdom will be preached in all the world as a witness to all the nations, and then the end will come.
(Matthew 24:14)

Daily Power!

I have the capacity to preach compassion and mercy – as Jesus did – and offer Good News to people.

Today's Bible Reading

II Kings 18:13-25 through 19:1-37; Acts 21:1-16; Psalm 149:1-9; Proverbs 18:8

Mark my Word
(for further study)

Matthew 24:14; Romans 16:25-26

Today's Scripture

And be kind to one another, tender-hearted, forgiving one another, even as God in Christ forgave you.

(Ephesians 4:32)

Daily Power!

It shall be my privilege to stand alongside great heroes of the faith – and those most meek and lowly – and together praise God for His greatness.

Today's Bible Reading:

II Kings 20:1-21 through 22:1-2; Acts 21:17-38; Psalm 150:1-6; Proverbs 18:9-10

Mark my Word
(for further study)

Mark 16:15; Acts 10:34; Ephesians 4:1-32

A modern Man

The apostle Paul lived a modern man in his own times. His writings were filled with references and word-pictures that were clearly evident to his contemporaries. Therefore, in his letter to the Church at Ephesus – which was a city well-influenced by Rome's power – he taught principles with vivid images that would truly appeal to and be understood by the Ephesians. Yet, his imagery continues to inspire people throughout the centuries – and even today.

"I therefore, a prisoner of the Lord, beseech you to walk worthy of the calling with which you were called, with all lowliness and gentleness, with long-suffering, bearing with one another in love, endeavoring to keep the unity of the Spirit in the bond of peace. There is one body and one Spirit, just as you were called in one hope of your calling: one Lord, one faith, one baptism; one God and Father of all, Who is above all, and through all, and in you all. But to each one of us grace was given according to the measure of Christ's gift."

Here, Paul was writing to Christians who were slaves and free, lowborn and highborn, poverty-stricken and wealthy. Each person was treated exactly the same, as there are no favorites with God – *"In truth I perceive that God shows no partiality"* – and each person had the same responsibilities as a Christian to fulfill. What we learn today from Paul's ancient writings is that God expects the same of each of us – even as He expected of those Christians who were yet to be martyred for their faith, persecuted for their beliefs, stripped all of possessions for the sake of the Gospel. The number one assignment they were given: the same assignment given to the apostles as they watched the resurrected Lord and Savior Jesus Christ ascending into Heaven: to *"Go into all the world and preach the Gospel to every creature!"* That same assignment is yours and mine today!

Maxims of Faith

Here are some basics of faith:

- To be believers, we should know what we believe and Who we believe.
- The most basic lesson is we must take the Word of God at its face value.
- Without knowing God's will, faith is impossible.
- The Word is the eternal will of God.
- To question Scripture is to question the only guide we have … and to question God.
- The Word of God is an ultimatum, not an option for discussion.
- Democratic vote or consensus does not decide Bible truth. It is "settled in Heaven forever."
- The Bible is the Constitution of the Kingdom of God, and no two-thirds majority of any parliament on Earth can change it.

The Bible makes no bones about it and insists a thousand times on its own Divine authority. The prophets who spoke, for example, were not offering their private political opinions, but *"men spoke from God as they were carried along by the Holy Spirit."* They used the phrase: *"Thus says the Lord."* The Jewish conception was of a God of awful holiness, and they trembled before His awesome greatness.

Unless they had an overwhelming sense that God had sent them, no prophet of Israel would dare to claim to be the mouthpiece of this Almighty Being. Only absolute certainty would open their mouths. Moses reluctantly got into a lengthy argument with God when He commissioned him to return to Egypt for the liberation of His people. Jeremiah declared, *"If I say 'I will not mention Him or speak any more in His Name,' His word is in my heart like a fire, a fire shut up in my bones; I am weary of holding it in; indeed I cannot."* The Word of God is alive and real and powerful … in the lives of the prophets of old, and in your life today!

Today's Scripture

Then I said, "I will not make mention of Him, nor speak anymore in His Name." But His Word was in my heart like a burning fire, shut up in my bones; I was weary of holding it back.
(Jeremiah 20:9)

Daily Power!

The Word of God is alive and real and powerful in my heart and life today.

Today's Bible Reading

II Kings 22:3-20 through 23:1-30; Acts 21:37-40 through 22:1-16; Psalm 1:1-6; Proverbs 18:11-12

Mark my Word
(for further study)

Exodus 3:1-22; 4:1-17; Jeremiah 20:9; II Peter 1:21

4

Power anywhere

Great power-lines stretch across a whole country carrying perhaps 110,000 volts on a single cable. Day and night, the huge power turbines are feeding the vast system, harnessing the forces of coal, water, oil, or nuclear fussion, housed in towering buildings. All that! Then, at home a tiny sliver of wire fails ... and everything in your house stops, without power. The greatness of God ... the greatness of the work of Christ ... the greatness of the Word of God are all there – but without faith, as small as a fuse wire, none of that greatness avails. The circuit is broken ... the Power Bridge is down. If the faith-fuse fails, the dynamic of God is defused ... and will be refused by those to whom we preach ... indeed, they could be confused! Take the Word, put in the faith-fuse ... and the power of God comes through – there will be light, warmth, energy, salvation, healing, strength, and blessing.

I once went into a very smart hairdressing salon where two ladies worked, and one of them began to cut my hair. Typically of hairdressers, she talked while she worked and asked me whether I was a businessman. My reply was, "I am a man of God." It was perhaps a good hard knock – but it broke the ice, and we were launched. In a short time, I was leading both these ladies to Christ. They knelt in the shorn hair on the floor while they prayed the prayer of salvation. When I left the shop, I heard one with tears in her eyes saying to the other, "That man of God came in for a haircut – what a glorious day!" I went out very happy and moved. Then I met my colleague, Peter van den Berg. I said to him, "Peter, I see you need a haircut too. Go and get your hair cut in that salon. I've led two women to Christ in there. Go and do the follow up!"

"If you have faith as a mustard seed," Jesus said – so little! Our faith is no towering sensation that everybody sees and gasps. It is the hidden fuse. But by it, the energies of Heaven flow into the world. God uses main fuses and sub-fuses, but never subterfuge. Wherever we are, the hidden attitude of our hearts is God's missing link: *"Only believe and you shall see the glory of God."* Wherever you go in your life, take the power of God with you – and be a conduit of that power to change lives.

Today's Scripture

Rejoice because your names are written in Heaven.

(Luke 10:20)

Daily Power!

Father, give me opportunities to display Your power by the light that I shine.

Today's Bible Reading

II Kings 23:31-37 through 25:1-30; Acts 22:17-30 through 23:1-10; Psalm 2:1-12; Proverbs 18:13

Mark my Word
(for further study)

Matthew 17:20; Luke 10:20; John 11:40

In one Word – Compassion

Christ's gift to the world was not a new religion, or a new theory about life, or a new formula for Heaven. He gave Himself for us, *"the just for the unjust, that He might bring us to God."* Christianity is not a religion – it is Jesus! We can form doctrines around Him, but Jesus did not come to bring us theology. He came just to be here, available, never to leave or forsake us, personally.

One of the Old Testament names for God was "El Shaddai" – it means God All-Sufficient. That God came to Earth in the person of Jesus. He gave all of Himself ... and He is all we need! Another Old Testament title was "Jehovah Shammah" – it means the Lord is there. If He is there, that is all we want. Peter said, *"Unto us therefore who believe, He is precious."*

Jesus refused to live to benefit Himself. His motives could be summed up in the word **compassion**. He was driven by love – never by fear, gain or popularity.

"And Jesus, when He came out, saw a great multitude and was moved with compassion for them, because they were like sheep not having a Shepherd. So He began to teach them many things."

He lived absolutely **for us**. When He left the carpenter's bench in Nazareth, He first faced fierce temptations in the wilderness. In every instance, He was tempted to think about Himself. One test was to feed Himself by a miracle ... another to receive all the kingdoms on Earth as a gift ... the other to perform a wonderful sign that would have everybody acclaiming Him as Messiah. The Lord was repelled by the very suggestion. He went hungry ... He was crucified instead of crowned ... and He was charged with blasphemy instead of being deified. Jesus' love for you and for me is overwhelming at times, isn't it. . .but it's true! Let that love motivate you today. Let Christ's compassion drive you to action!

Today's Scripture

For Christ also suffered once for sins, the just for the unjust, that He might bring us to God, being put to death in the flesh but made alive in the Spirit.
(I Peter 3:18)

Daily Power!

I desire to be filled with the compassion that motivated Jesus Christ.

Today's Bible Reading

I Chronicles 1:1-54 through 2:1-17; Acts 23:11-35; Psalm 3:1-8; Proverbs 18:14-15

Mark my Word
(for further study)

Mark 6:34; I Thessalonians 5:10; I Peter 2:7; 3:18

6

Christ the Giver

When the people of Christ's day applauded Him, He wept for them. They tried to make Him King by force, but He chose the Cross. Going to His death, He told the women of Jerusalem to weep for themselves, not for Him – **they** were His last thought. Christ wasn't thinking of Himself at all … and even if it meant death, He would bear it **for us**. He was ready to save us from Hell by going through that Hell of torment Himself.

"Jesus answered and said to her, 'If you knew the gift of God, and Who it is Who says to you, Give Me a drink, you would have asked Him, and He would have given you Living Water.'"

He met a woman at a well, and asked her for a drink. In a couple of sentences, He became concerned **just about her**. Jesus was far more interested in **giving** her a drink at the Fountain of Eternal Life than quenching His own natural thirst. In fact, did she ever bring Him that drink? We never read that she did. That little episode lights up for us what Jesus **was**.

Christ lived for us to be one of us. A Christian is somebody related to God, in the Family of God. They are born-again by the Spirit of God. It is not a case of having a religious experience one day, or a vision, or feeling good or happy. It is a **relationship** – a closeness, a family tie. Christ lived for us to belong to us. If Christ belongs to me, then I am saved … if He belongs to you, then you are saved. Christ gave Himself **for** us, and gave Himself **to** us. Salvation means being united with Him. Jesus doesn't "send salvation" – He is salvation. He doesn't "send forgiveness" – He brings it. He forgives us and lives with us. Doesn't that thrill your soul to know that, today … you are living with Christ!

Today's Scripture

I have been crucified with Christ; it is no longer I who live, but Christ lives in me; and the life which I now live in the flesh I live by faith in the Son of God, Who loved me and gave Himself for me.
(Galatians 2:20)

Daily Power!

The relationship which I have in Christ Jesus is the one that gives me life.

Today's Bible Reading

*I Chronicles 2:18-54 through 4:1-4;
Acts 24:1-27;
Psalm 4:1-8;
Proverbs 18:16-18*

Mark my Word
(for further study)

*John 3:6; 4:3-26;
Galatians 2:20*

Resurrection – An impossible Hoax?

Some people think that resurrection is impossible. But how do they know that resurrection is impossible? Are they really that clever? Nobody knows enough to declare with absolute certainty that something is impossible. We would have to be God to know what God cannot do. The fact about us is that we are finite and limited. We can be awfully wrong.

Look at the past. Until this century, television seemed impossible. If anybody had said, two or three hundred years ago, that a person would be seen and heard all round the globe at the same moment, he would have been thought mad. The moon was considered unreachable … men could never fly … never travel faster than a horse … never live at the bottom of the ocean. All these were firmly believed to be impossible … but everybody was wrong. Television, aeroplanes and fast cars are now part of everyday life – we **know** that they are not figments of the imagination. Christ has risen also, so we know that it is possible. By definition, God is the Almighty. So if God is God, there is no problem with the resurrection.

"And with great power the apostles gave witness to the resurrection of the Lord Jesus. And great grace was upon them all."

The disciples were not the sort of characters who would be hoaxers. They did not treat Life as a huge joke. At first sight of the resurrected Jesus, they were frightened. Later, they were all persecuted – and some were killed – simply because they said Jesus was alive. Nobody dies to hoax people. Hoaxers do not lie to ruthless emperors. Hoaxers do not stand being tortured, being burned alive, or torn to pieces by wild beasts. The disciples simply could not deny the truth, no matter what. Let us be truth-tellers today as well.

Today's Scripture

I am the resurrection and the life. He who believes in Me, though he may die, he shall live. And whoever lives and believes in Me shall never die. Do you believe this?
(John 11:25-26)

Daily Power!

Lord Jesus, I believe in Your resurrection, therefore I too shall be resurrected!

Today's Bible Reading

I Chronicles 4:5-43 through 5:1-17; Acts 25:1-27; Psalm 5:1-12; Proverbs 18:19

Mark my Word
(for further study)

John 11:1-27; Acts 4:32

8

Today's Scripture

Let the weak say I am strong.

(Joel 3:10)

Daily Power!

Jesus Christ is alive in me – I am made strong in Him!

Today's Bible Reading

I Chronicles 5:18-26
through 6:1-81;
Acts 26:1-32;
Psalm 6:1-10;
Proverbs 18:20-21

Mark my Word
(for further study)

Joel 3:10;
John 1:12;
II Corinthians 5:17;
Galatians 6:14, 18
(the Message);
I Peter 3:18

Regeneration and Resurrection

We hear about evolution and revolution, but Christianity is regeneration and resurrection. The early Christians said they were a *"new creation."* The Creator has started work again, doing something even greater. *"Therefore, if anyone is in Christ, he is a new creation; old things have passed away; behold, all things have become new."* A higher order than the human biological order has come into existence – we are the children of God, born from above: *"For Christ also suffered once for sins, the just for the unjust, that He might bring us to God, being put to death in the flesh but made alive by the Spirit."* When God made Adam, He did not ask Adam's permission. Nobody is asked if they want to be born. But **it is up to us** whether we want to be born-again and belong to the new order! Now is the time to choose: *"As many as received Him, to them He gave the right to become children of God."* Resurrection life – eternal life – flows to those who do!

"For my part, I am going to boast about nothing but the Cross of our Master, Jesus Christ. Because of that Cross, I have been crucified in relation to the world, set free from the stifling atmosphere of pleasing others and fitting into the little patterns that they dictate … May what our Master Jesus Christ gives freely be deeply and personally yours, my friend." These new people astonished the Roman world. Rome tried to destroy them, but its policy of annihilation only served to multiply them. The Romans gloried in strength – the Christians gloried in their weakness. The Romans believed in hatred and revenge – the Christians believed in love and forgiveness. The Romans believed in imperial authority – the Christians said, "Jesus Christ is Lord." The Romans believed in the sword – the Christians said they would conquer the world with love. And praise God, they did … and still do! From where does that kind of strength come? From the most glorious fact of all: Jesus is alive! And He is alive in you and in me today!

Join the Orchestra!

9

"Why does God want us to do anything at all when He has all power?" Because He loves us, and He likes to share His pleasures and joys with us. You may feel you are a very small instrument, but each of us is vital in the full orchestra. The Lord of all the Earth has big things in mind, and they call for millions of helpers with varied gifts and capabilities. *"We have this treasure in earthen vessels, that the excellence of the power may be of God and not of us."* When I first began to move in the power of the Holy Spirit – even as a young boy – I have since learned that *"I can do all things through Christ Who strengthens me."* In Christ, we have the resources of God. To fulfill God's purpose, we should think of ourselves as humble conduits for His Word and Spirit to flow through. A copper pipe can't boast of the water that flows through it to the tap in our homes. We are to let living waters flow – and just stay unblocked. Whatever gifts or talents we lay at His feet, the Master can use them all. They become accessory parts, shaping the conduit through which God does what He wants.

This is a lesson we must take it deep into our hearts as the foundation for everything else we learn or do. God has given me my job. Many times I've been asked, "When did you begin to see miracles in your ministry?" or "Why do so many turn to Christ when you preach?" The answer is: **"God gives us the power to do what He commands."** That power comes through the baptism with the Holy Spirit. I experienced that wonderful baptism – and it has stayed with me, charging and surging within me. I spoke with tongues also, and it was such a marvelous thing to me that I've never doubted since that miracles are for today. Of course I had faith before. The Word itself has always stirred my faith. Then – when the promise of the Spirit was fulfilled for me, and became an ongoing constant filling – the whole experience boosted my faith like supercharging a car engine. And the Bible confirmed what was happening. Just remember today that what God has done for others (based upon His Word) He will do for you. If God has commanded you to do something … ask Him for the fullness of His power to help you do it!

Today's Scripture

For if I preach the Gospel, I have nothing to boast of, for necessity is laid upon me; yes, woe is me if I do not preach the Gospel!
(I Corinthians 9:16)

Daily Power!

I take my place in God's Grand Orchestra of Ministry, ready to play my part.

Today's Bible Reading

I Chronicles 7:1-40 through 8:1-40;
Acts 27:1-20;
Psalm 7:1-17;
Proverbs 18:22

Mark my Word
(for further study)

II Corinthians 4:7;
Philippians 4:13

Today's Scripture

And this is the real and eternal life: that they know You, the one and only true God, and Jesus Christ, Whom You sent.
(John 17:3; the Message)

Daily Power!

The fact is: nobody can understand what it is like to meet Jesus until they do.

Today's Bible Reading

I Chronicles 9:1-44 through 10:1-14; Acts 27:21-44; Psalm 8:1-9; Proverbs 18:23-24

Mark my Word
(for further study)

John 4:5-43; 17:3; Acts 9:1-22; Romans 1:28; Philippians 1:21; II Timothy 1:12

God isn't who some think He is

We can't get away with ignorance or unbelief – they both have effects. Faith in God brings obvious benefits, switching the light on. Unbelief releases the acid of cynicism. *"As they did not like to retain God in their knowledge, God gave them over to a reprobate mind."* We should do better to ignore creation than the Creator.

Paul the apostle said, *"I know in Whom I have believed."* It wasn't just anybody – Paul **hated** Christ … until he met Him. Multitudes have been like that, not even looking for somebody to believe in … and then meeting Jesus. They wouldn't believe very much in anything otherwise. But having met Him in some way, they have to believe in Him. It is easy not to believe in Jesus when you don't know Him. It takes no cleverness! But when Christ approaches or touches you, not believing is nearly impossible. No argument ever yet invented can nullify that experience.

The fact is that nobody can understand what it is like to meet Jesus until they do. Then they know why millions say as Paul: *"For me to live is Christ"* or, as John: *"This is eternal life: that they may know You, the only true God, and Jesus Christ."* It has happened like that, from the time, He first appeared. The sex-obsessed woman of Samaria described in John chapter 4 met Jesus for five minutes… and couldn't get over it. She roused the whole town in her excitement, and then when the men met Him, they felt the same. They didn't become "religious enthusiasts" – in fact, they **stopped** being that – they became followers of Jesus, the Savior of the world, as they called Him. Modern Christians are like that too – they have **found** Him: the One Who should come, Whose presence makes Heaven the wonderful place that it is! That's the Jesus Who lived and died for you!

A Mission for Africa

CfaN
CHRIST
FOR ALL NATIONS

Countries in which CfaN crusades have already been held

Countries in which a CfaN crusade has not yet been held

CfaN CfaN office   As of July 2001

Anni & Reinhard Bonnke and the CfaN international planning team

GOD'S LOGOS IN LAGOS, NIGERIA

1.6 million people in one single meeting!
3.4 million souls saved within five days.

Each delegate of the Fire Conference received a free copy of Reinhard Bonnke's 'Faith'- book.

God opened her ears!

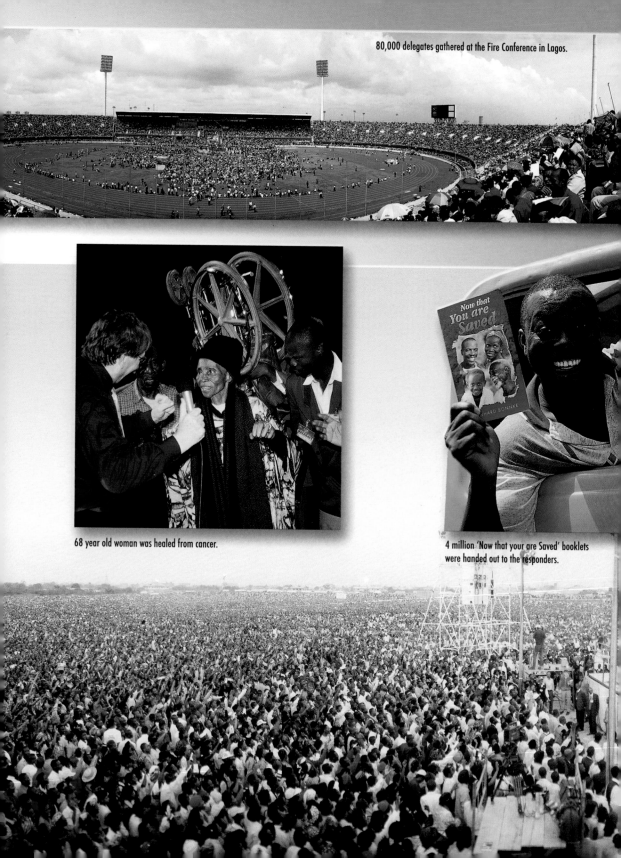

80,000 delegates gathered at the Fire Conference in Lagos.

68 year old woman was healed from cancer.

4 million 'Now that your are Saved' booklets were handed out to the responders.

300 hired busses brought people in from surrounding areas.

8,000 Fire Conference delegates heard the word of God.

Sudan

Up to 210,000 people attended the meetings at the Easter Celebration 2000 in Khartoum, Sudan.

All sorts of fetishes and even a human skull were burned in public.

This mans barren wife conceived after prayer in the 1987 crusade and this beautiful girl was born.

ABA Nigeria

600,000 people in one service.

She was paralysed for 10 months.
Now she can walk!

God touched this little girl
and healed her body.

Totally blind for the last six months, now he can see!

Freetown, Sierra Leone

CONCORD TIMES

NATION'S NO.1 NEWSPAPER — EXCELLENCE AND OBJECTIVITY

Don't you think you need a good newspaper on Sunday? You won't wait too long for it

THE PROPHESY OF REINHARD BONNKE

Sierra Leone is like Israel

Sierra Leone's President, Dr. Ahmed Tejan Kabba, visited the Gospel Campaign.

Suffering from polio, this lady could not walk. Now she will no longer need this crutch!

BENÍN CITY

500,000 people gathered in one single service.

Nigeria

Blind for many years, but now
"Jesus has opened his eyes"!

She can hear and
speak for the very first time!

Some 360,000 people attended one single meeting.

"Go into all the world and preach the gospel to every creature." (Mark 16:15)

Masses flock to the meetings.

Mbuji-Mayi,
Democratic Republic of the Congo

Hunger for the word of God was great.

Great rejoicing as witchcraft items are burned.

PORT HARCOURT

Nigeria

More than 1.1 million decisions for Christ in just 6 days of meetings.

This man demonstrates perfect healing of his eye.

Now he can walk without these crutches.

Lethsie III, King of Lesotho

Daniel T. arap Moi, President of Kenya

Yayah Jammeh, President of The Gambia

Frederick Chiluba, President of Zambia

*... you will be brought
before governors
and kings
as witnesses to them
and to the nations.*

Matthew 10,18

Bakili Muluzi, President of Malawi

Mathieu Kérékou, President of Benin

Captain Blaise Compaoré, President of Burkina Faso

Olusegun Obasanjo, President of Nigeria

Ammunition!

The Holy Spirit was God in earthly activity, just as Jesus had been. The baptism in the Spirit is not meant to be a single emotional event recorded in believers' diaries. It envelops believers permanently. The Spirit is their environment, the air they breathe moment by moment which provides the vitality of their Christian faith. When we bombard the world with the artillery of the Gospel, our ammunition is the explosive power of the Holy Spirit. The Spirit animates believers, their teachings, their preaching, their prayer, their service, and their very lives. The Spirit is the dynamic life force of the faith. Without the life of the Holy Spirit, Christianity is just another lifeless religious system that can only be kept going by human effort. But nothing can compete with the Holy Spirit! We can't replace the Holy Spirit with organization, magnificent churches, prestige, education, or anything else.

God Himself teaches us when we obey Him. We must understand that the Holy Spirit, God in action, leads us into action. We are not saved just to linger in fond contentment in the joy of salvation or to hold meetings to congratulate one another on our good fortune that we are redeemed. There are higher activities than church celebrations, Christian pop music concerts and a seemingly endless flow of new worship songs – Christian as they may be. Our Lord is worthy to be praised indeed, but worship choruses alone will never save the world. Songs that do not mention the Name of Jesus or have any Gospel content are especially powerless. Praise is not the power of God unto salvation – the Gospel is. We must not flatter ourselves into thinking that we can build a Throne for God with lots of new songbooks. Our contract with God contains the clause: *"Preach the Word."* *"It pleased by the foolishness of preaching to save them that believe."* We should do more than celebrate – we must **communicate**. As noted scholar, Richard John Neuhaus once observed, "It is not our securities and satisfactions we celebrate, but the perilous business of love, of that supreme love that did not and does not turn back from the Cross."

Today's Scripture

But we preach Christ crucified ... Christ the power of God and the wisdom of God; because the foolishness of God is wiser than men, and the weakness of God is stronger than men.
(I Corinthians 1:23-25)

Daily Power!

When we bombard the world with the artillery of the Gospel, our ammunition is the explosive power of the Holy Spirit.

Today's Bible Reading

I Chronicles 11:1-47 through 12:1-18;
Acts 28:1-31;
Psalm 9:1-12;
Proverbs 19:1-3

Mark my Word
(for further study)

I Corinthians 1:21-25

12

Today's Scripture

Delight yourself also in the Lord, and He shall give you the desires of your heart. Commit your way to the Lord, trust also in Him, and He shall bring it to pass.
(Psalm 37:4-5)

Daily Power!

The innermost desires, even the "wishes" of my heart, when expressed to God in the Name of Jesus through prayer, are of great concern to Him.

Today's Bible Reading

I Chronicles 12:19-40 through 14:1-17; Romans 1:1-17; Psalm 9:13-20; Proverbs 19:4-5

Mark my Word
(for further study)

Psalm 37:4-5; Acts 27:29; Romans 1:9; 5:2; James 5:16; III John 2

Reveling in Prayer

The New Testament has an astonishing array of references to prayer. The main word for "prayer" (Greek: *proseuche*) is used over 120 times. God gives many things without being asked – rain, sunshine, winter, summer – but He planned that we should receive other things by asking for them. The list is long: salvation … the Holy Spirit … guidance … equipment for spiritual battles … the Gifts of the Spirit … power to witness … strength … effectiveness … boldness … relief from anxieties … anti-devil weapons … our "daily bread" … the Kingdom to come … the will of God to be done … relief from trial and temptation … healing – and more. We are even to pray for our enemies.

Communicating with God is the Christian distinction. Jesus forbad *"vain repetition."* The disciples opened their hearts to God about everything, including their innermost feelings. They wrote letters in the style of those days, but changed the usual good wishes and pleasantries into prayers. Paul wrote to Christians in Rome: *"Without ceasing I make mention of you always in my prayers."* To believers in Corinth, Galatia, Ephesus, Philippi, Colossus, Thessolonika, and to Timothy, he wrote: *"Grace to you and peace from God our Father and the Lord Jesus Christ."* Some letters appear to be just extended prayers.

"If wishes were horses, beggars would ride," they say … but the first Christians addressed "wishes" to the Father in the Name of Jesus – and **did** receive! Praise God! The unbeliever wishes – the believer **prays.** In the Book of Acts, the soldiers and crew of a ship were in danger and *"kept wishing for daybreak to come."* Paul prayed – and they were saved! James "wished" in the Christian way: *"Pray [wish] for one another that you may be healed."* Like John writing to Gaius, *"I pray [wish] that you may prosper in all things and be in health."* Wishes become prayers – and answers are expected. The unbeliever sighs, "If only …" – the believer rejoices *"in the hope of the glory of God."* Today, be one whose wishes are prayerfully directed to God … and expect Him to hear and answer!

Blood that speaks

Having repeatedly seen a divine vision of a blood-washed Africa, I now desire nothing more than to see that glorious fulfillment. I vowed to God I would preach the message of the Blood of Jesus wherever He sends us. By the grace of God, we have made good progress over the years, have seen many nations in Africa shaken by the power of the Gospel, and millions of precious souls have received Jesus Christ as their Savior.

Hebrews 12 says that the Blood of Jesus Christ *"speaks a better word than the blood of Abel."* What better word? Abel was murdered by his brother, Cain. What did his blood say … and what does the Blood of Jesus Christ say? *"The voice of your brother's blood cries out to Me from the ground. So now you are cursed from the Earth, which has opened its mouth to receive your brother's blood from your hand."* Abel's blood cried out death and murder, and called for revenge.

The Blood of Christ also discolored the dust. But what better words does it say? It speaks **life**, not death! Abel's blood is death-blood, but the Blood of Jesus is Life-Blood. Abel's blood called for revenge, but the Blood of Jesus speaks **forgiveness.**

Cain was punished for Abel's death, but nobody suffered for Christ's death. Instead, Christ suffered death for us. The assassination of the Archduke Ferdinand started World War I, but Christ made *"peace through His Blood, shed on the Cross."* When soldiers used hammer and nails to spike Jesus Christ's living flesh to the timber gallows, His Blood splashed them. They literally had the Blood of Christ on their hands. Yet Jesus kept on praying, *"Father, forgive them, for they do not know what they do."* If God forgave the sin of those soldiers, it was only by the same Blood which they had caused to flow. *"Without the shedding of blood there is no forgiveness"* – and that only by the Blood of Jesus. You have received that forgiveness already – rejoice in that wonderful fact today!

Today's Scripture

To Jesus the Mediator of the New Covenant, and to the Blood of sprinkling that speaks better things than that of Abel.
(Hebrews 12:24)

Daily Power!

The Blood that Jesus shed for me will never lose its power.

Today's Bible Reading

I Chronicles 15:1-29 through 16:1-36;
Romans 1:18-32;
Psalm 10:1-15;
Proverbs 19:6-7

Mark my Word
(for further study)

Genesis 4:10-11;
Luke 23:34;
Colossians 1:20;
Hebrews 12:24

Close Encounters with God

When you take the steps to become a Christian, you can do so by praying to God in your own words, or by using this prayer. Take time to say these words … this is a once-in-a-lifetime moment! You are coming home! You are moving out of darkness and into God's wonderful light. Jesus said, *"Whoever comes to Me, I will never drive away."*

Dear Heavenly Father,

I respond to Your invitation and come to You in the Name of Your Son, Jesus Christ. I come with all my sins, heartaches and addictions. I turn away from evil and turn to You, Lord Jesus.

I put my faith in You alone. You are the Son of the Living God. I believe with my heart what I now confess with my mouth: You are my Savior, my Lord and my God.

Thank You for having accepted me as Your child. I open myself for Your Holy Spirit, and will follow You all the days of my life. I believe You and receive You. I ask it in the Name of Jesus – Amen!

If you have prayed this prayer (or a prayer in your own words), you are not alone. Millions of Christians around the world started to follow Jesus in just this way! You can be absolutely sure that God has heard and answered your prayer. Even if you do not "feel any different," you can be sure that you have entered into a new life! *"And this is the testimony: that God has given us eternal life, and this life is in His Son. He who has the Son has life; he who does not have the Son of God does not have life. These things I have written to you who believe in the Name of the Son of God, that you may know that you have eternal life and that you may continue to believe in the Name of the Son of God."*

Today's Scripture

Then Peter said to them, "Repent, and let every one of you be baptized in the Name of Jesus Christ for the remission of sins, and you shall receive the gift of the Holy Spirit. For the promise is to you and to your children, and to all who are afar off, as many as the Lord our God will call."

(Acts 2:38-39)

Daily Power!

My life has changed irrevocably because I have asked Jesus Christ into my heart. I will never be the same again.

Today's Bible Reading

I Chronicles 16:37-43 through 18:1-17; Romans 2:1-24; Psalm 10:16-18; Proverbs 19:8-9

Mark my Word
(for further study)

John 6:37; Acts 2:38-39; Romans 10:13-17; II Corinthians 5:17; I John 5:11-13

Fish in the Sea of Nations

The disciples were not anglers sitting on a serene riverbank, trying this bait or that fly. They were sea fishers, using nets. Galilee was their sea – and a treacherous one it was. Winds swept down the hills and almost scooped the waters out of their bed. A storm on the Sea of Galilee was frightening even for experienced sailors. In their minds, the sea was always a foreign element – an abyss where monsters and devils lurked, where winds shrieked and wailed like lost souls. The sea awoke every superstition. The sea is mentioned nearly five hundred times in Scripture, usually as a fearsome place, an enemy to be reckoned with. The Psalms talked about those that go down to the sea in ships, and men calling upon God to save them as they are tossed high on the waves and brought low into the depths. The sea represented uncontrolled forces, raging, wild, and threatening. It was the haunt of primeval elements, ghosts and demons, the place of the dead. The fishermen-apostles braved the Sea of Galilee, but always with trepidation and anxiety. It was a battle with the waves to wrest a living from the deep.

In Scripture, the sea represents **the nations**. Jesus refers to the sea and the waves roaring, the people in uproar, in war, and in distress. The sea symbolizes the masses of the godless. *"The wicked are like the troubled sea ... whose waters cast up mire and dirt."* The sea was terrifying and menacing. Putting that all together: the apostles were sent to fish in the raging nations, the tumultuous waters of mankind, in foreign fishing grounds, amidst enormous dangers in uncharted waters. They had caught fish from the angry Sea of Galilee – but now they would be fishers of men from the angry seas of the nations. It would be dangerous. There would be storms and casualties. The winds would always be contrary to them. They would launch out against the currents of the world. Sometimes mountainous waves would lash them and threaten to swallow them up. They could get off course and be driven up and down. All that ... but they would be still fishers of men! And you and I are so commissioned by Him today.

Today's Scripture

Then [Jesus] said to them, "Follow Me, and I will make you fishers of men."
(Matthew 4:19)

Daily Power!

Thank You, Lord, that You have called me to be a fisher of men.

Today's Bible Reading

I Chronicles 19:1-19 through 21:1-30; Romans 2:25-29 through 3:1-8; Psalm 11:1-7; Proverbs 19:10-12

Mark my Word
(for further study)

Isaiah 57:20; Matthew 4:18-19; Luke 21:25

16

The Lord of the Seas of Nations

Jesus demonstrated to His disciples that they could have a miracle-catch from the Sea of Galilee. He was teaching them that they could have a miracle-catch in the Sea of Nations as well. It would bring them a great haul of fish if they put their nets down at Christ's command. When Jesus said, *"Let down your nets,"* somehow half the fish in Galilee felt disposed to jump in. When Jesus said, *"I will make you fishers of men"* – half the world could be netted!

The nations were a troubled sea, but Jesus could handle the raging elements. He literally **walked on** the waters. The sea may have been a monster, but Jesus trod it underfoot. When the elements frothed and foamed against Him – whipped into a frenzy, howling like dogs of Hell, opening wide their dribbling mouths to engulf Him – He rebuked them. Like whimpering hounds, they cowered at their Master's heels. Make no mistake about it – **Jesus Christ is Lord.**

"Why do the nations rage, and the people plot a vain thing? The kings of the Earth set themselves, and the rulers take counsel together, against the Lord and against His Anointed, saying, 'Let us break their bonds in pieces and cast away their cords from us.' He Who sits in the Heavens shall laugh; the Lord shall hold them in derision. 'Ask of Me, and I will give you the nations for your inheritance, and the ends of the Earth for your possession.'"

Jesus Himself used similar language in Acts: *"You shall be witnesses to me … to the end of the Earth."* He is the Lord of Heaven and Earth, of the sea and the sky. He makes the very seas His own, and scoops from them their wealth. Go and teach all nations. You and I are part of God's equation. So, please, as one of His laborers, continue to trawl the Sea of Nations for Jesus Christ today!

Today's Scripture

Then [Jesus] called His twelve disciples together and gave them power and authority over all demons, and to cure diseases. He sent them to preach the Kingdom of God and to heal the sick.
(Luke 9:1-2)

Daily Power!

Make me Your fisher of men, Your harvester of souls!

Today's Bible Reading

I Chronicles 22:1-19 through 23:1-32; Romans 3:9-31; Psalm 12:1-8; Proverbs 19:13-14

Mark my Word
(for further study)

Psalm 2:1-4, 8; Luke 5:4, 9:1-2; Acts 1:8

Compelling Evidence

With the compelling and dramatic evidence of the gift of salvation freely provided by Jesus Christ, it is a strange thing then that even some church members seem unsure.about their fate and do not expect to learn until the great Day of Judgment! They use the words "perhaps" and "hope." God says: *"He who believes in the Son of God has the witness in himself; he who does not believe God, has made Him a liar, because he has not believed the testimony that God has given of His Son. And this is the testimony: that God has given us eternal life, and this life is in His Son. He who has the Son has life; he who does not have the Son of God does not have life. These things I have written to you who believe in the Name of the Son of God, that you may know that you have eternal life, and that you may continue to believe in the Name of the Son of God."*

Note that these reassuring Scriptures do not say that you **will** have eternal life, but they say you **already have** it – **now!** These are powerful promises which the apostle John received from the Holy Spirit. They contain the key elements about the assurance of salvation: written ... believe ... Son of God ... know ... have ... eternal life. These keys are given in the Word of God, which means you must read what is written in the Word.

The Biblical principle is that every matter must be established by the testimony of two or three witnesses: *"One witness shall not rise against a man concerning any iniquity or any sin that he commits; by the mouth of two or three witnesses the matter shall be established."* This was well-known in Bible days, but in our world today, "hearsay" or "circumstantial" evidence is not admissable – only "corroborative" evidence: two or three witnesses stating the same fact independantly. However, assurance is so important that God has given it a double anchorage in the rock of two faultless witnesses, both divine: the **Word of God** and the **Spirit of God**. That is God's Word to you today!

Today's Scripture

And this is the testimony: that God has given us eternal life, and this life is in His Son.
(I John 5:11)

Daily Power!

I know, by the Word and the Spirit, that I am the recipient of eternal life through Jesus Christ.

Today's Bible Reading

I Chronicles 24:1-19 through 26:1-11;
Romans 4:1-12;
Psalm 13:1-6;
Proverbs 19:15-16

Mark my Word
(for further study)

Deuteronomy 19:15;
Matthew 18:16;
II Corinthians 13:1;
I John 5:10-13

18

Today's Scripture

Be sober, be vigilant; because your adversary the devil walks about like roaring lion, seeking whom he may devour. Resist him, steadfast in the faith, knowing that the same sufferings are experienced by your brotherhood in the world.
(I Peter 5:8-9)

Daily Power!

As a member of the Royal House of God, I am marked internally, externally and eternally by the Blood-mark of Jesus Christ.

Today's Bible Reading

I Chronicles 26:12-32 through 27:1-34; Romans 4:13-25 through 5:1-5; Psalm 14:1-7; Proverbs 19:17

Mark my Word
(for further study)

Genesis 3:15; Matthew 10:1; 16:23; I Peter 5:8

The eternal Mark

The Blood-mark of Jesus is eternal. The Blood-mark stays there. It does not rub off. It outlasts Time. We need to appreciate our salvation, though, and keep on following Jesus. The Blood of Jesus is no license to sin. But God has given us everlasting salvation, and we are His forever, not just when we feel well. Hallelujah! All Heaven will be filled with the Blood-marked saints, and not one will be in Hell – not even by accident.

Somebody said that the Blood of Jesus has "reduced the devil." The Bible says that Satan is *"like a roaring lion."* He comes in the darkness and tries to frighten the children of God with his mighty roar. But when you switch on the light of the Word of God, you discover that there is no lion – there is only a mouse with a microphone!

John Bunyan said the lion at the side of the path has neither fangs nor claws. Christ pulled them out at Calvary: *"He shall bruise your head, and you shall bruise his heel."* And at Calvary, it happened: That nailed-scarred foot of Jesus nevertheless came down on Satan's head – and crushed it. Since that moment, the devil has suffered some kind of "brain-damage." He can no more think the things of God. In the Garden of Eden, God already knew that the Blood of His mighty Son would destroy the works of the devil.

It was no empty promise that Jesus gave His disciples, which includes you and me: *"He … gave them authority to drive out evil spirits and to heal every disease and sickness."* He could do that because Jesus has power over the devil. Jesus' power leaves nothing untouched body, soul, mind, spirit, heart. It reaches right to the depths of our being. His Blood is the secret of victory. Let Jesus mark you, **internally, externally, eternally,** and you will be a child of God, a member of the Royal House of the Lord!

From Faith to Faith

They say the great Greek writer, Homer, wandered from town to town begging his bread and telling his stories of the siege of Troy. Storytellers did make a living that way. There were no theatres, dramas, books, or television … and everybody loves a good story. Scripture uses that method to teach us. It is not a book of academic theology. But with a Divine Author, there is all the subtle character drawing that creates faith in God. Let's look at some Gospel incidents.

There was the "royal official" mentioned in John chapter 4. He showed faith in Christ's powers by coming all the way from Capernaum to Cana – a day's journey to ask Christ to go to his house and heal his son who was dying. Jesus said a strange thing to the poor man: *"Unless you people see miraculous signs and wonders, you will never believe."* It was strange because he had believed enough to come to see Christ … but Jesus had another kind of faith in mind. The man was not put off by this apparently "cold" reception – he still believed and said, *"Sir, come down, before my son dies!"*

Jesus simply responded to the man, *"You may go. Your son will live."* This meant extra faith. He had believed that Jesus could heal his son if He came – and it would involve a journey to do it – but now he had to believe Jesus was bigger than that. The official departed and we read: *"The man believed the word that Jesus had spoken to him."* It was the next day before he arrived. All that way, all the man had was this brief word from Jesus, every step and every minute. But when he discovered a miracle had taken place, then John records that real faith came: *"He and all his household believed!"* It was not the miracle they believed – that was there to **see**, not just to be **believed** – for they believed in the way John always talks about believing: commitment to Christ.

You may have only a single word of Jesus to cling to – but that one word contains all the explosive resurrection power you will ever need!

Today's Scripture

For assuredly I say to you, whoever says to this mountain, "Be removed and be cast into the sea," and does not doubt in his heart but believes that those things he says will be done, he will have whatever he says.
(Mark 11:23)

Daily Power!

Thank You for miracles that cause me to believe unto commitment to Christ.

Today's Bible Reading

I Chronicles 28:1-21 through 29:1-30; Romans 5:6-21; Psalm 15:1-5; Proverbs 19:18-19

Mark my Word
(for further study)

Mark 11:23; John 4:46-54

20

Completing Faith

Today's Scripture

Now we know that God does not hear sinners; but if anyone is a worshipper of God and does His will, He hears him.

(John 9:31)

Daily Power!

Let this be my daily motto: "Lord, I believe!"

Today's Bible Reading

II Chronicles 1:1-17 through 3:1-17; Romans 6:1-23; Psalm 16:1-11; Proverbs 19:20-21

Mark my Word
(for further study)

John 9:1-34

John chapter 9 tells a story that demonstrated developing faith. Without even asking, Jesus healed a blind man. He plastered mud across his eyes and sent him to wash – the man came back with good sight. When questioned, the formerly blind man replied, *"A Man called Jesus made clay, anointed my eyes and said to me, 'Go to the pool of Siloam and wash.' So I went and washed, and I received sight."* The people, unfamiliar with Christ's identity, asked, *"Where is this Man?"* The once-blind man didn't know where Jesus had gone. Dissatisfied, the authorities decided, *"This Man is not from God."*

However, faith began to arise. They queried, *"How can a sinner do such miraculous signs?"* Who was Jesus? The man who was healed replied, *"He is a prophet."* But the authorities had already agreed to excommunicate from the Temple anybody who said Jesus was the Christ … and faced with such a fact as a man born blind man now seeing, they tried to prompt him to state that Jesus was a sinner. But he would not – instead declaring, *"God listens to the Godly Man Who does His will … If this Man were not from God, He could do nothing."*

His faith was developing. For this, he suffered persecution, and was blamed as a disciple of Jesus. Jesus then found the man. He had been thrown out of the Temple – typical of a world which rejects those who testify to the goodness of God. He had one important question to ask the man – not whether he felt grateful, or if he had started to work – but: *"Do you believe in the Son of Man?"* The man was puzzled: *"Who is He, Sir? Tell me, so that I may believe in Him."* He had enough faith in Jesus to feel his way to the pool of Siloam when blind because Jesus told him to go – that brought him physical sight – but another kind of faith could bring him far greater illumination … and his faith had not yet reached that point. Then Jesus replied, *"You have now seen Him; in fact, He is the One speaking with you."* The man looked at Christ, and his faith exploded – he had no problem accepting Christ's declaration. He answered, *"Lord, I believe!"* Then *"he worshipped Him"* – faith was complete.

Christ is our Home

Christ *"dwelt among us."* He made His home with us – or rather, He made a home, and when we believe, we cross the doorstep and walk in. **God is our true home. Away from Him, we are away from home.** That is why Christ lived for us. He wants to be with us, and us with Him – at home.

"And the Word became flesh and dwelt among us, and we beheld His glory, the glory as of the only Begotten of the Father, full of grace and truth."

The Bible is full of references to "home." The Prodigal Son came home. Jesus went into many homes. He talked about the Eternal Home: *"In My Father's House are many mansions. I go to prepare a place for you, that where I am, you may be also."*

Christ lived for us to show us how to live. The Bible speaks of Christ as being without sin, the spotless Lamb of God. He lived **for us** the perfect life, leaving us an example to follow in His footsteps. What was His perfection? It was very simple: **obedience to God**. He did not live by a set of rules to govern every action of His life. He wasn't a walking encyclopedia of the Law, which He consulted every second from getting up in the morning to going to sleep again at night. He simply did what He knew would please the Father.

That is how we should live. He lived for us to show us how to live. To please God is all that is wanted. We may have great moral problems, and we don't know which is the right thing to do. Well, there is only one reason why we should be good at all … and that is to be like Jesus, and to please God! Let us choose to live pleasing unto God today.

Today's Scripture

In Him was life, and the life was the light of men.
(John 1:4)

Daily Power!

Christ showed me how to live. I want to be like Jesus, and to please God.

Today's Bible Reading

II Chronicles 4:1-22 through 6:1-11; Romans 7:1-13; Psalm 17:1-15; Proverbs 19:22-23

Mark my Word
(for further study)

John 1:4, 14; 14:2

22

The Glory of the Lamb

The "glory of princes" is flashing jewels, uniformed splendor, public adulation, and military display. The glory of Man is conquest, the honor of a world, which has false gods and false desires. The glory of Christ is not triumph over slaughtered armies and pitiless bloodshed. We read in the account of Jesus' first miracle at Cana in Galilee, that Jesus *"manifested His glory"* in simple red wine! This speaks to us through Christ's words at the Last Supper: *"This is My Blood of the New Covenant, which is shed for many."*

In the first chapter of his Gospel, John wrote, *"We beheld His glory,"* and made sure that we appreciate what that glory really was in chapters 12 and 13. It had nothing to do with the heroic ring by which the world recognizes its kind of glory, but rather pointed to the horror of an ugly – but necessary! – death. *"The hour has come that the Son of Man should be glorified ... Unless a grain of wheat falls into the ground and dies, it remains alone."*

We read on in the account of the Last Supper to the point when Judas Iscariot went out to betray Jesus: *"So, when he had gone out, Jesus said, 'Now the Son of Man is glorified, and God is glorified in Him. If God is glorified in Him, God will also glorify Him in Himself, and glorify Him immediately.'"*

The glory of Jesus broke forth at Calvary, the true glory. The glory of Heaven was revealed in those streams of abounding mercy – water and blood from His heart – twin rivers of cleansing and love. They sing about it in Heaven: *"The Lamb, the Lamb! Glory and power be unto Him!"* ... *"By that will we have been sanctified through the offering of the body of Jesus Christ once for all! ... Worthy is the Lamb Who was slain to receive power and riches and wisdom, and strength and honor and glory and blessing!"* Honor the Lamb of God today, and you **will** see His glory!

Today's Scripture

He who loves his life will lose it, and he who hates his life in this world will keep it for eternal life. If anyone serves Me, let him follow Me; and where I am, there My servant will be also. If anyone serves Me, him My Father will honor.
(John 12:25-26)

Daily Power!

It is my desire to always glorify My Father.

Today's Bible Reading

II Chronicles 6:12-42
through 8:1-10;
Romans 7:14-25
through 8:1-8;
Psalm 18:1-15;
Proverbs 19:24-25

Mark my Word
(for further study)

Mark 14:24;
John 1:14; 2:1-11;
12:23-24; 13:31-32;
Hebrews 10:10;
Revelation 5:12

Rivers!

When speaking about the Holy Spirit, the Scriptures repeatedly use the word rivers. This "ideal" for believers – rivers of the Holy Spirit – was anticipated by Isaiah: *"You shall be like a spring of water, whose waters do not fail."* For many people in our reserved Western culture, exuberance is foreign, unnatural and embarrassing. For those who stand within the Kingdom of God, however, the culture of the world matters little – they shout for joy!

The Septuagint (Greek version of the Old Testament) uses a surprising word about the Spirit of God acting in the lives of Samson and Saul: it says the Spirit "leapt" upon them. This rare word "allomai" is used twice in Acts 3: leaping up (exallomenos) and leaping (allomenos). "Leaping life" and "dancing waters" are Biblical descriptions of the activity of the Holy Spirit. It is not surprising when people who have not been in the Upper Room of Pentecost deride Spirit-filled people as "enthusiasts" or "fanatics." Even the apostles had critics. The onlookers in Jerusalem – completely ignorant of the facts – thought the apostles were drunk. *"When the Feast of Pentecost came, they were all together in one place. Without warning there was a sound like a strong wind, gale force – no one could tell where it came from … Then, like a wildfire, the Holy Spirit spread through their ranks, and they started speaking in a number of different languages as the Spirit prompted them. There were many Jews staying in Jerusalem just then, devout pilgrims from all over the world … When they heard, one after another, their mother tongues being spoken, they were thunderstruck … 'They're speaking our languages, describing God's mighty works!' …They couldn't make head or tail of any of it. They talked back and forth: 'What's going on here?' Others joked, 'They're drunk on cheap wine.'"*

How mistaken the world is when they only stand on the banks of the **river** to describe the genuine flow of the Holy Spirit in your life. Remember, it's a **river** flowing through you. Go with the current. Let it lift you up and carry your load. The world may describe it differently … but they'll soon stand amazed when they see what that **river** can do in your life.

Today's Scripture

They're speaking our languages, describing God's mighty works!
(Acts 2:11)

Daily Power!

I shout for joy because I stand within the Kingdom of God!

Today's Bible Reading

II Chronicles 8:11-18 through 10:1-19; Romans 8:9-21; Psalm 18:16-36; Proverbs 19:26

Mark my Word
(for further study)

Isaiah 58:11; Acts 2:1-13 (the Message); 3:8; Ephesians 3:16

The Cross and Kingdom Miracles

Today's Scripture

The message of the Cross ... is the power of God.
(I Corinthians 1:18)

Daily Power!

Believers are the light of the world, but they need the Holy Spirit to switch them on.

Today's Bible Reading

*II Chronicles 11:1-23 through 13:1-22;
Romans 8:22-39;
Psalm 18:37-50;
Proverbs 19:26-29*

Mark my Word
(for further study)

John 17:4-5

The power of the Kingdom, the Holy Spirit and the Gospel of the Cross are welded together. It was the work of Christ, especially in His death, which tore down the wall between this world and the other world of God's Kingdom. Since then, the Holy Spirit has invested everything in the crucified Christ. He works His wonders solely on redemption ground. The Spirit supports the Gospel only, always and everywhere. What more do we need? One man filled with the Spirit is better than a hundred committees which "keep minutes but lose hours." When God so loved the world, He didn't form a committee – He sent His Son. When His redemptive work was done, the Son sent the Spirit. Christ said believers are the light of the world, but they need the Holy Spirit to switch them on.

No doubt many people are eager for miracles ... but it will save many from disillusionment if they know that miracles belong only to the Gospel – nothing else. No marvels for the sake of marvels. God is not in the business of supplying marvels to bring fame to any strutting egotist. The Holy Spirit – in league with the crucified Christ – has one goal: to defeat the devil through the Gospel. The Gospel is totally comprehensive, leaving nothing untouched – Earth, Hell or Heaven. Theologian George Lindberg, in The Nature of Doctrine, says, "A scriptural world is able to absorb the universe."

As a Christian, I knew that the Cross had a spiritual effect in my life ... but when I spoke with tongues, it reached me as an earthly person. The Father in Heaven and the Son on Earth are both concerned with redemption, each in His own sphere, as Jesus expressed: *"I have brought You glory on Earth by completing the work You gave Me to do. And now, Father, glorify Me in Your presence with the glory I had with You before the world began."* Christ's work on Earth affected Earth, and the Father's work affected glory. Jesus came here – for here. If it was only to get us an entrance into Heaven, He might have arranged it in Heaven – but salvation had to be produced on Earth for earthly purposes. My baptism in the Spirit touched both my spirit and my body, typical of the true nature of the Christian faith. Open your heart to the Spirit today!

Fear not the Future

25

What the future holds for anybody depends very much on themselves. When Dumah asked the prophet Isaiah, *"Watchman, what of the night?"* the prophet replied, *"The morning comes, and also the night."* This was not ambiguous – it simply pointed out that the answer was contingent on Edom's response to God. If Edom turned to God, it would be day – if not, it would be night. Similarly Jesus spoke of the latter days, when *"men's hearts would fail them for fear,"* adding, *"when these things begin to happen, then look up and lift up your heads."* For those whose hands are not in the hand of Jesus, the landscape of tomorrow is full of fearful specters. For those who have come to Him, the future is the province of a victorious Christ.

The scythe of Father Time will cut short the days of many people, bringing their lives to an end. The way some people talk, the new millennium is the only point of change. Many are concerned about the future after that date … but what about the future in the hereafter that may begin before the next millennium? Again for those who know the Lord, *"Neither death nor life … nor things present nor things to come … shall be able to separate us from the love of God that is in Christ Jesus our Lord."* No born-again Christian fears the future. Several times Jesus said, *"Fear not"* … and because He said so, we certainly *"fear not"* – otherwise, where is our faith? We look for the coming of Christ – it identifies believers. His coming is not doomsday, except for those who reject Him. We read that when He comes, the godless will try to hide *"from the face of the Lamb."* Frightened of a lamb – the Lamb of God! How badly they must have treated Him to fear Him! For those who know Jesus, the future is full of His glory. It lights the dawn of every day for those with eyes to see. And you have those believer's eyes!

Today's Scripture

For I know that my Redeemer lives, and He shall stand at last on the Earth.
(Job 19:25)

Daily Power!

No born-again Christian fears the future.

Today's Bible Reading

I Chronicles 14:1-15 through 16:1-14; Romans 9:1-21; Psalm 19:1-14; Proverbs 20:1

Mark my Word
(for further study)

Isaiah 21:11-12; Luke 21:26, 28; Romans 8:38-38

26

"Get it straight, Boys!"

Today's Scripture

*What you'll get is the
Holy Spirit!*
(Acts 1:8; the Message)

Daily Power!

*God's power is not given
for personal glory or
gain, but to enable me to
be His witness.*

Today's Bible Reading

*II Chronicles 17:1-19
through 18:1-34;
Romans 9:22-33
through 10:1-13;
Psalm 20:1-9;
Proverbs 20:2-3*

Mark my Word
(for further study)

*Acts 1:1-14
(the Message)*

When we read the opening verses of the Book of Acts, we see why Jesus twice stressed the coming of the power of the Holy Spirit in His last conversation on Earth: *"In the first volume of this book, I wrote on everything that Jesus began to do and teach, until the day He said good-bye to the apostles – the ones He had chosen through the Holy Spirit – and was taken up to Heaven. After His death, He presented Himself alive to them in many different settings over a period of forty days. In face-to-face meetings, He talked to them about things concerning the Kingdom of God. As they met and ate meals together, He told them that they were on no account to leave Jerusalem, but 'must wait for what the Father promised: the promise you heard from Me. John baptized you in water; you will be baptized in the Holy Spirit. And soon.' When they were together for the last time, they asked, 'Master, are You going to restore the Kingdom to Israel now? Is this the time?' He told them, 'You don't get to know the time. Timing is the Father's business. What you'll get is the Holy Spirit. And when the Holy Spirit comes on you, you will be able to be My witnesses in Jerusalem, all over Judea and Samaria, even to the ends of the world.' Those were His last words. As they watched, He was taken up and disappeared in a cloud."*

Jesus had given His final instructions to the apostles after His resurrection, and told them to wait for the Promise of the Holy Spirit. That seemed fine – surely they had got the point and knew what was going to happen. But no! In verse 6, they were floundering again in the old notion that Jesus had spent three years trying to get out of their system: that of political triumph for Israel led by Jesus as the Warrior-Lord. Jesus had to correct them, and insist that their interests were not to lie in the direction of restored political power for Israel – they were to go beyond Israel and preach the Gospel to all nations! The power He would give would not be for political or military victory, but to achieve a far more significant result: the moral and spiritual victory of the Kingdom of God. You and I have the responsibility to continue to preach and proclaim in your own way … the Gospel to the nations today.

Jesus corrects us

After being with Him for three years of miracle-ministry, what the disciples wanted to know from Jesus at the last was this: *"Will You at this time restore the Kingdom to Israel?"* In other words, they were asking, "What are You going to do, Lord?" Jesus, in effect, replied, "Me? What am I going to do? You've missed the point! It's you! You shall be My witnesses!"

We are all praying for worldwide revival. The more we see it taking place, the more we are encouraged to keep praying for it. But are we simply saying to God, "Lord, **You** do it. **You** send revival. Lord, **You** must enter the field. Lord, **You** take over. Lord, bring in the Kingdom"? Jesus corrects all that. He says, "I give **you** the power, **you** must get on with the job. Evangelize! Preach! Labor! Work! Go! Preach! Heal! Get going with **your** part." Once you and I go through the gate, we will get the tools, the power equipment. God never does our job for us … and He knows what we need to enable us to do it.

It is the same all the way through the New Testament: *"And when they had prayed, the place where they were assembled together was shaken; and they were all filled with the Holy Spirit, and they spoke the Word of God with boldness … And with great power the apostles gave witness to the resurrection of the Lord Jesus. And great grace was upon them all"* … *"For I am not ashamed of the Gospel of Christ, for it is the **power** of God to salvation for everyone who believes, for the Jew first and also for the Greek."*

Preaching releases the **power** of God. You can't pray for power … and then keep it in the deep freeze. Preach it … and it is manifested! Receive God's power today in your life.

Today's Scripture

But when the Helper comes, Whom I shall send to you from the Father, the Spirit of Truth Who proceeds from the Father, He will testify of Me. And you also will bear witness.
(John 15:26-37)

Daily Power!

God has given me an assignment: to preach His Word with the power of the Holy Spirit.

Today's Bible Reading

II Chronicles 19:1-11 through 20:1-37;
Romans 10:14-21 through 11:1-12;
Psalm 21:1-13;
Proverbs 20:4-6

Mark my Word
(for further study)

John 5:39;
Acts 1:6; 4:31, 33;
Romans 1:16;
I Corinthians 2:1-4

We can't escape

Our rebellion and wickedness in no way changes God's mind about His love for us, for *"while we were yet sinners, Christ died for us."* The object was that *"in Christ Jesus you who once were far off have been brought near by the Blood of Christ."* The Son of God – our Lord, Jesus Christ – could bear our sins and die for us simply because of the live link between Creator and creature. We are *"bound in the bundle of life with God."* We can't escape what happens to God – and God cannot escape what happens to us.

Job asked why God had to do with him in his sin – that was answered at the Cross, where the curtains are drawn aside and what sin had been doing to him was exposed. Jesus became Man and walked this very Earth to restore the God-and-Man Family relationship. He didn't come to us as aliens, a race of unknown parentage, to adopt us. He had fathered us. We were prodigals, *"sons of disobedience."* The opening chapters of the Bible present the shock of Cain murdering his brother Abel. God's reaction showed it as the antithesis and disruption of God's fundamental purpose. It broke the life-bond of Family.

This throws open the tremendous truth that this very day the Spirit of son-ship is at work, constantly working *"to bring many sons into glory."* He is creating again – not another Adam – but new creatures, endued with eternity-lasting life. We don't know God's final purposes. We don't know that anything will be final with God … but one thing is clear and certain: the mark of Heaven will be His Eternal Fatherly embrace for His children. His plan *"for the fullness of the times He might gather together in one all things in Christ, both which are in Heaven and which are on Earth – in Him … Now we are children of God; and it has not yet been revealed what we shall be."* Rejoice in that today!

Today's Scripture

For He Himself has said, "I will never leave you nor forsake you."
(Hebrews 13:5)

Daily Power!

I am linked to God my Father through the Blood of Jesus Christ, His Son.

Today's Bible Reading

II Chronicles 21:1-20 through 23:1-21;
Romans 11:13-36;
Psalm 22:1-18;
Proverbs 20:7

Mark my Word
(for further study)

I Samuel 25:29;
Romans 5:8;
Ephesians 1:10; 2:2, 13;
I John 3:2

"Bondage is Truth corrupted"

People have talked about those who "bury themselves in religion" – but Christianity is Christ … and you can't call Christ a religion! He is the Resurrection and the Life. Christ said, *"If you hold to My teaching … then you will know the truth, and the truth will set you free."* He is no deceiver. Millions have found themselves gloriously free through the Gospel. His words do not stifle us with rules and commandments. His yoke is easy and His burden is light. The Sermon on the Mount describes what Christians are naturally, what they want to do, not what people should be like.

There is a warning Christ gave us over and over which is particularly important to those just beginning the Christian life – or anybody else for that matter: **"There would be false prophets."** They are not all in the cults either, though there are over five thousand sects in the United States. Many are a threat to the concept of liberty. By definition, a cult means **control**. *"By their fruits you will know them."* Once they get hold of you, they keep you under their thumb, control your money, what you do, where you go, what you think, and who your friends are. Their evil effect is to destroy self-reliance, and breed dependency. Their leaders are not shepherds – they are wardens, religious policemen.

"Beware of false prophets, who come to you in sheep's clothing, but inwardly they are ravenous wolves. You will know them by their fruits. Do men gather grapes from thorn bushes or figs from thistles? Even so, every good tree bears good fruit, but a bad tree bears bad fruit. A good tree cannot bear bad fruit, nor can a bad tree bear good fruit. Every tree that does not bear good fruit is cut down and thrown into the fire. Therefore by their fruits you will know them." Some teach the Scriptures … but turn Bibles into chains, standing truth on its head, like the Scribes and Pharisees. They use the Gospel of deliverance to bind their converts, falsifying the very spirit and purpose of the message. There are sad souls who lack true faith and accept handcuffs to gain a sense of security … please guard your heart and don't become one of them.

JULY

29

Today's Scripture

Enter by the narrow gate; for wide is the gate and broad is the way that leads to destruction, and there are many who go in by it. Because narrow is the gate and difficult is the way which leads to Life, and there are few who find it.
(Matthew 7:13-14)

Daily Power!

Lord, help me always stay true to Your Word and to bear good fruit.

Today's Bible Reading

*II Chronicles 24:1-27 through 25:1-28;
Romans 12:1-21;
Psalm 22:19-31;
Proverbs 20:8-10*

Mark my Word
(for further study)

*Matthew 7:13-20;
John 8:32-32*

Today's Scripture

But the hour is coming, and now is, when the true worshipers will worship the Father in spirit and truth; for the Father is seeking such to worship Him.

(John 4:23)

Daily Power!

Lord, I believe.

Today's Bible Reading

II Chronicles 26:1-23 through 28:1-27; Romans 13:1-14; Psalm 23:1-6; Proverbs 20:11

Mark my Word
(for further study)

John 4:1-42

Leaps of Faith

The woman of Samaria in John chapter 4 teaches a powerful lesson on faith, an illustration of a sinner taking a profound leap of faith into the supernatural heights. An unnamed woman came to draw water from a well when Jesus was resting there from a long, hot walk. He asked her for a drink of water, and this astonished her – she thought He was an odd Jew to be so free, breaking all the rules by speaking to a Samaritan … even more so when He said He could give her a drink of water that would be *"a spring of water welling up to eternal life."* At that point, she decided to humor Him, thinking Him slightly irrational; she joked, *"You just give me a drink like that so I won't get thirsty and keep coming back to this well!"* – she certainly expected nothing of the kind. Jesus simply answered, *"Go and bring your husband."* With an air of innocence, she replied that she had no husband. Jesus then shattered her with a recitation of her sullied life, and her Hollywood-like record of husbands. The woman stared at Him, shocked, *"I can see You are a prophet."* She had advanced in perception and faith.

Next Jesus shook her ideas about worship. She retorted a four hundred-year old argument – but Christ's reply was totally new: worship had nothing to do with place or time … worship was anywhere, everywhere and always. The people God wanted were those whose worship was not confined to a local spot or fixed schedule. She felt lost in such theological depth, so she tried to edge around it, saying such matters would be settled when the Messiah came. The woman was getting closer – then Jesus revealed, *"I, Who speak to you, am He."* Her faith soared! She looked at this Man Who saw her past like a filmed record and swept her out of her depth with His profound teaching. Excited, she rushed into the town telling everybody about Jesus: *"Could this be the Messiah?"* Many went to see this Man Who had so affected her. They too fell under His divine magnetism, inviting Him to stay – for two days, He was among them, with the result that they declared, *"This Man really is the Savior of the world!"* The woman had believed, sinful as she was … and that is all Christ asks of you and of me – *"believe."*

Faith embrace

In the Bible stories of the blind man healed by Christ ... the Samaritan woman who met Him at the well ... the nobleman who traveled a great distance to receive healing for his dying son – each of these incidents showed that the development of faith was swift and always ended by a commitment, a relationship, and taking hold of Jesus personally. Being a mere believer in God has a long way to go, but it is a gap that can be leaped, as fast as light – one minute far from God ... and the next minute bound to Him eternally through faith, *"one with Christ."* We become, in a moment, as He said about the disciples to the Father, *"They are Yours ... and Yours are Mine, and I am glorified in them ... and none of them is lost."*

The Greek expression used for faith **in** Christ means moving close to Him in trustful love. It is an embrace. This kind of loving embrace between Man and his Maker comes only through Christ. Jesus is the great beloved One. The dry, loveless religious world of the Jews had no spiritual experience that corresponded to this love relationship – any passionate embrace between Heaven and Earth was unknown ... until Jesus came. He is the Divine Lover ... and we are those He came to love.

A woman emptied a flask of priceless ointment upon the head of Christ in holy adoration. A street-girl washed His feet with the water of her eyes and toweled them with her hair. A hard-hearted tax collector went wild with joy and wanted to give his money away. Jerusalem had never seen anything like that. They had seen fanatical fury burning murderously in men's eyes, but not this adoring wonder. But then, He began it Himself, for we read, *"Having loved His own who were in the world, He loved them unto the end ... knowing ... that He had come from God and was going to God, rose from supper and began to wash the disciples' feet."* Jesus was the Lord God Whom everyone could fling his or her arms around. His mother Mary did ... so did Mary Magdalene ... and so can you and I ... by faith!

Today's Scripture

And this is eternal life, that they may know You, the only true God, and Jesus Christ Whom You have sent.

(John 17:3)

Daily Power!

Jesus Christ is my Divine Lover – He came to Earth to love me.

Today's Bible Reading

II Chronicles 29:1-36; 14:1-23; Psalm 24:1-10; Proverbs 20:12

Mark my Word
(for further study)

John 13:1-5; 17:3; 9-12

God brings changes,
but He never changes Himself.

When Jesus said, "I am with you always"
He didn't make a promise, but He stated a fact!

Peter didn't walk on the water.
He walked on the word "come!"

"This same Jesus"

The glory of Christ will be revealed again when He comes again. It will not be the glory of overpowering might, but of the all-conquering Cross. He comes with the honor of the Father encircling His thorn-torn brow. When He comes again, it will be *"this same Jesus"* Who went away to Heaven with pierced hands and feet, wounds received *"in the house of His friends."* That Christ is the Christ Who will return – not a "healed Christ" Whose death for sinners has been forgotten … but a Christ Who bears the still-active marks of indelible grace. Heaven and Earth know Him forever as the Crucified One: *"The Lamb slain from the foundation of the world."* **The Lamb on the Throne will be King.**

Who else bore our sins in agony and blood? What other Savior could there be but He Who carried our transgressions and suffered the penalty for our sin? At last, that which was foolishness to the Greeks and a stumbling-block to the Jews – which people could never grasp – is revealed. What glory!

If Christ's glory had been that of mere dazzling splendor, it would have been overwhelmed in the darkness of Calvary. If it had been fame, success, wealth, or achievement, it all would have ended in that awful catastrophe of Crucifixion. But the glory of Christ can never die. Put Him in a manger in a limestone cave among cattle … and kings fall down before Him. Send Him out as a wandering preacher walking the dusty village roads of a barren land … and His glory breaks upon all who come near. Herod is troubled, the rulers take counsel together against Him … but the masses of common people hear Him gladly and want to make Him King. They have seen glory in this Carpenter-Preacher. Take the time … open your heart … and look for His glory today!

Today's Scripture

Blessing and honor and glory and power be to Him Who sits on the Throne, and to the Lamb, forever and ever!
(Revelation 5:13)

Daily Power!

I find my glory in the power of the Cross.

Today's Bible Reading

*II Chronicles 30:1-27 · through 31:1-21;
Romans 15:1-22;
Psalm 25:1-15;
Proverbs 20:13-15*

Mark my Word
(for further study)

*Zechariah 13:6;
Acts 1:11;
Revelation 13:8*

Time to grow up!

Jesus was not a spiritual policeman. He did not discipline the disciples. That is not what "disciple" means. He never ordered them about, interfered or dictated in daily affairs. They came and went as and when they wished. It was all left to their wisdom and discretion. That is how Christ deals with us. Give Jesus our lives … and He makes them our own. If we blindly obey a church leader, we are still responsible before God for what we do. No man should appropriate to himself authority over others. Scripture forbids leaders to *"rule as lords over God's heritage."* Jesus said, *"One is your Master, even Christ."* Truth comes from the Word of God, which sets us free. God is a Deliverer. Laws, like the Sabbath, were made for us, not us for the laws.

The disciples came in every shape and size, with every personality difference and outlook on life. There was Peter – impetuous, courageous, foolish … Matthew – thoughtful, detail-oriented, faithful … James and John – competitive, affectionate, tenacious. Each had faults and strengths. Each had to learn to understand and accept the Messiah coming to them in their day … and then learn how to communicate the wonder of the Son of God and the Son of Man in one Person – the ultimate Sacrifice. We have hindsight to our advantage, so we automatically think, "Yes, of course I would have recognized that Jesus was the Son of God, and I would have been faithful to the end without hesitation." But put today's average Christian in a hostile environment – such as the early Christians experienced in Jerusalem or Rome – and we quickly discover that our character is tested and tried! Too often we fall back on "the letter of the Law" to hide our own deficiencies, rather than open ourselves to the discipline of the Holy Spirit and grow in Him. Or we are lazy and abdicate our responsibility for our own spiritual growth onto church leadership, even as we too readily turn over Christian education of our children to Sunday School teachers. It is time that Christians grew up and accepted their duties to be bright shining lights in a darkened world! **Let your light shine today!**

Today's Scripture

And I, brethren, could not speak to you as to spiritual people but as to carnal, as to babes in Christ. I fed you with milk and not with solid food; for until now you were not able to receive it, and even now you are still not able.

(I Corinthians 3:1-2)

Daily Power!

Lord, help me to accept my responsibilities as a mature Christian.

Today's Bible Reading

II Chronicles 32:1-33 through 33:1-13; 15:23-33 through 16:1-7; Psalm 25:16-22; Proverbs 20:16-18

Mark my Word
(for further study)

Acts 20:8; I Corinthians 3:1-2; Ephesians 5:8; Philippians 2:15

Dynamic Power Points

*"I did not come with excellence of speech or of wisdom declaring to you the testimony of God ... My speech and my preaching were not with persuasive words of human wisdom, but in demonstration of the Spirit and of **power**, that your faith should not be in the wisdom of men but in the **power** of God."*

The Holy Spirit and the Gospel of Christ's redeeming love are inseparable, tied together in the bundle of Life. If you want to see the power of God – never mind all the techniques, manipulation and psycho-suggestion – just preach the Word! That is where the power of God is secreted: right in the Gospel. Separate the power from the Word ... and you get a counterfeit thrill only. I don't take only one thing out of God's treasure chest. I proclaim the whole Gospel, which contains everything we human beings need, all in the same box – salvation, healing, peace, hope and deliverance.

*"The Gentiles should be fellow heirs, of the same body, and partakers of His promise in Christ through the Gospel, of which I became a minister according to the gift of grace of God give to me by the effective working of His **power** ... Now to Him Who is able to do exceedingly abundantly above all that we ask or think, according to the **power** that works in us."*

These are only a handful of texts. They use the word **power** ... but in fact, the entire New Testament could illustrate that power, which is the essence of Christian witness. It is not "a Gospel accessory." It is not the bell on a bicycle – it's the whole "machine"! There is never the slightest hint that some disciples would be powerless. If you are a believer, then power is available. Paul spent three and half years preaching the whole counsel of God to the Ephesians, yet he had to write to them later: *"I pray ... that the eyes of your understanding being enlightened; that you may know ... what is the exceeding greatness of His **power** to those who believe."* God empowers those He sends – you and me.

Today's Scripture

And He said to them, "Assuredly I say to you that there are some standing here who will not taste death till they see the Kingdom of God present with power."
(Mark 9:1)

Daily Power!

I cannot live without a daily infusion of Your power, Lord!

Today's Bible Reading

*II Chronicles 33:14-25 through 34:1-33;
Romans 16:8-27;
Psalm 26:1-12;
Proverbs 20:19*

Mark my Word
(for further study)

*I Corinthians 2:1-5;
Ephesians 1:18-19;
3:6-7, 20*

Today's Scripture

Nor is there salvation in any other, for there is no other name under Heaven given among men by which we must be saved.

(Romans 4:12)

Daily Power!

As the old hymn goes, "I'm saved, and I know that I am!"

Today's Bible Reading

II Chronicles 35:1-27 through 36:1-23; I Corinthians 1:1-17; Psalm 27:1-6; Proverbs 20:20-21

Mark my Word
(for further study)

John 5:24; Romans 3:24, 4:10-12, 8:16; Revelation 12:10-11

"Proving" Salvation

The subject of salvation is important to me – and it occupies the entire Bible! "Liberal people" today like to rationalize that it is impossible to know you possess salvation, and we'll have to wait until the "after-life" ("if there is such a thing," they like to say) to discover if salvation had indeed provided eternal life. But Jesus made it very clear that we **can know** that we are saved, and that confidence can inspire us to share our salvation with others: *"Let it be known to you all, and to all the people of Israel, that by the Name of Jesus Christ of Nazareth, Whom you crucified, Whom God raised from the dead, by Him this man stands here before you whole. There is the Stone Which was rejected by you builders, Which has become the Chief Cornerstone. Nor is there salvation in any other, for there is no other name under Heaven given among men by which we must be saved."*

However, Satan still tries to undermine that confidence in the gift of salvation provided by Christ Jesus on the Cross, so we must continually be on guard against his lies and accusations, which he won't stop doing until the end of time: *"Now salvation, and strength, and the Kingdom of our God, and the power of His Christ have come, for the accuser of our brethren, who accused them before our God day and night, has been cast down. And they overcame him by the Blood of the Lamb, and by the word of their testimony, and they did not love their lives to the death."*

Being saved is not a casual experience, something you would hardly notice. When you repent and believe and come to the Lord and Savior Jesus Christ, He receives you, and you are cleansed in His precious Blood! Salvation is absolute and complete. How ridiculous to think that Jesus would find you and receive you, but would not want you to know this! In fact, He would not keep it from you: *"The Spirit Himself testifies with our spirit that we are God's children."* There is something greater still: you are *"justified freely by His grace."* What a Divine promise for you to hold onto today!

Critics don't get it

5

As we learn more about the activities of the Holy Spirit, we should never be worried by critics. No doctrine, teaching or great work of God has ever remained unchallenged by those who thought they knew better. Theologian Ronald A. Knox showed contempt for John Wesley by describing him as a mere "enthusiast" – an overwrought or unbalanced person. Father Knox may be an example of cool scholarship, but from his book, Enthusiasm, it is clear that he would not have been with the one hundred and twenty on the Day of Pentecost … or stood shoeless at the burning bush with Moses … or been with Joshua before the Man with the drawn sword. The intellectual bishop of Bristol, Joseph Butler, told Wesley that he considered charismatic experiences to be quite "horrid." O.T. Dobbin came to Wesley's defense in 1848: "We admit that Wesley was an enthusiast, but only to the degree in which a man more than ordinarily filled with the Holy Ghost would be an enthusiast." Wesley's first rule for stewards of the Methodist Society, quoting Ephesians 3:16, was, *"You are to be men full of the Holy Ghost."* George Whitefield, the great evangelist, was another man full of the Holy Spirit.

The question we must ask is this: if Christ did exactly what He promised and baptized people in the Holy Spirit and fire, what would they be like? Cool, self-contained? With glorious currents of divine radiance flowing through them, would they sit – as Shakespeare said – like their "grandsire cut in alabaster"? The emblem of God is fire, not stone. What is more ridiculous – people dancing for joy with the vision of God … or people as immovable as the Sphinx (which remained unmoved even when Napoleon fired a cannon at it)? We cannot experience the Spirit and show no sign of it. What we have in earthen vessels is "treasure" which reveals that this all-surpassing power is from God. This power will seem totally strange to minds alienated from God. As Festus said to Paul, *"You are beside yourself! Much learning is driving you mad!"* Why should it be any different today when people experience the original brand of Christianity, instead of some diluted, gutted, tranquilized, sentimentalized version of it? *"You hath He quickened,"* we read in Ephesians – not *"You hath He stiffened."*

Today's Scripture

And you He made alive, who were dead in trespasses and sin.
(Ephesians 2:1)

Daily Power!

We cannot experience the Holy Spirit, and show no sign of it.

Today's Bible Reading

Ezra 1:1-11 through 2:1-70; I Corinthians 1:18-25; Psalm 27:7-14; Proverbs 20:22-23

Mark my Word
(for further study)

Acts 26:24; II Corinthians 4:7; Ephesians 2:1

The Spirit's Difference

The prophets struggled in vain to bring Israel back to God. But when Spirit-filled Peter preached, three thousand people surrendered to God. Without the Holy Spirit, Christianity is reduced to religion, which is no more effective than the Old Testament system which existed before the Age of the Spirit. Jesus said, *"You will receive power when the Holy Spirit comes on you."* Without that vitality, we have a secularized, nominalized, rationalized, harmless religion. Mystical contemplation bears no resemblance to New Testament dynamism. Quietism is for Buddhists, not Christians.

Before the Charismatics arrived, there were those who were fired up and Spirit-filled, or "pneumatized." Whatever chill may have frozen the Church, however much "enthusiasm" was disapproved of, and even when Christianity was only "churchianity," there were always some lively Spirit-filled people around. The springs of spiritual waters in this century came from rains which fell centuries before. Some trace them to Wesley and his teaching, which he called "perfect love." But whatever it was called, the vision and experience Wesley had came from earlier men and women of God.

Many different terms are used for the same experiences in Scripture. All the terms, such as "coming upon," "being filled," "drinking," and "anointing" describe the same divine gift of the Spirit. Christ said we should *"Ask! Seek! Knock!"* This applies to receiving the baptism of the Spirit also. Those who receive the Spirit in New Testament style surely have a right to call their experience by a New Testament name. The *"baptism in the Holy Spirit"* is a New Testament expression used by both John the Baptist and Jesus. The personal experience of millions conforms to the New Testament promise whether it is called baptism or anything else. If it looks like such a baptism, sounds like it, feels like it and operates like it, then what else is it? It cannot be argued out of existence by debates about what to call it. If you do what the apostles did and you get what the apostles got, its name doesn't matter any more.

Today's Scripture

As His divine power has given to us all things that pertain to life and Godliness, through the knowledge of Him Who called us by glory and virtue.

(II Peter 1:3)

Daily Power!

Without the Holy Spirit, I am just a "religious Christian" – but with Him, I am on fire!

Today's Bible Reading

Ezra 3:1-13 through 4:1-24; I Corinthians 2:6-16 through 3:1-4; Psalm 28:1-9; Proverbs 20:24-25

Mark my Word
(for further study)

Matthew 7:7; Acts 1:9; II Peter 1:3

Ghostly Terrors

Unbelief populates the future with giant fears. The "millennium bug" created widespread panic. It didn't cause anything but minor inconveniences when compared to the real hazards of Life – but many were getting ready for a world disaster, preparing safe retreats in forests and underground shelters defended by armed guards, going down into their burrows like frightened rabbits. To gain admission, applicants at one shelter were required to have a gun, a thousand rounds of ammunition and enough food for a year. Such terror inspired by a ghost!

"The wicked flee when no one pursues," but God whispers secret assurance to those who love Him. He has the future in hand for us. Unbelievers exist in the permanent shadow of uncertainty and anxiety. In times gone by, the heathen were terrified by stellar events, but Jeremiah said: *"Do not be terrified by signs in the sky, though the nations are terrified by them. He is the Maker of all things ... the Lord Almighty is His Name."* The phrase *"fear not"* is a special Biblical feature, occurring sixty-six times ... but the Bible deals positively with fear over five hundred times!

The one certainty about the future is Christ's Second Advent. I am aware that expectations of Jesus' return to Earth reached fever pitch at various different times in the past. The 17th century Puritans who founded settlements in America were filled with anticipation that Christ would soon appear ... and great men like Milton and Newton shared these expectations. The same belief powerfully affected everyone a thousand years before, in the 8th century ... and again, of course, in AD 1000. Indeed, it was the sustaining hope of the earliest Christians. Fine men of God in the 19th and 20th centuries have given dates for the return of Christ ... but have gotten it wrong. However, mistakes and questions do not in the slightest diminish the truth that He is coming again. The signs are all in place. That melody keeps ringing in my soul: "It is the last time!" Watch for Him!

Today's Scripture

It is not for you to know times or seasons which the Father has put in His own authority. But you shall receive power when the Holy Spirit has come upon you, and you shall be witnesses to Me ... to the ends of the Earth.
(Acts 1:7-8)

Daily Power!

Mistakes and questions do not diminish the truth that Christ is coming again.

Today's Bible Reading

Ezra 5:1-17 through 6:1-22 ; I Corinthians 3:5-23; Psalm 29:1-11; Proverbs 20:26-27

Mark my Word
(for further study)

Proverbs 28:1; Jeremiah 10:2, 16; Acts 1:7-8

Today's Scripture

If we confess our sins, He is faithful and just to forgive us our sins and to cleanse us from all unrighteousness.

(I John 1:9)

Daily Power!

Because God's Word says it, I know that I have already crossed over from death to life.

Today's Bible Reading

Ezra 7:1-27 through 8:1-20; I Corinthians 4:1-21; Psalm 30:1-12; Proverbs 20:28-30

Mark my Word
(for further study)

John 5:24; Hebrews 10:23; I John 1:9; 3:2

Sure of Salvation

To be sure of salvation, you do not need to be sure of everything, but only of God, Who *"is faithful and just to forgive us our sins, and to cleanse us from all unrighteousness"* and Who *"is faithful Who promised."*

Let me use a simple illustration. I am Reinhard Bonnke ... whether I feel like it or not. If I am asleep, I do not think about it ... but I am still Reinhard Bonnke. Even if I should suffer from a loss of memory, my identity remains the same, I am still me. My birth certificate states that I am who I am, and that settles it.

So it is with the Word of God. If you have received the Lord Jesus Christ as your personal Savior, you have been born into the farnily of God – **"born–again."** The Bible is your birth certificate. If you cannot believe that, then you will not know who you are ... it is that simple!

"Most assuredly I say to you, unless one is born again, he cannot see the Kingdom of God ... Unless one is born of water and the Spirit, he cannot enter the Kingdom of God. That which is born of the flesh is flesh, and that which is born of the Spirit is spirit."

John said: *"**Now** we are the sons of God, and it has not been revealed what we shall be."* **What** we shall be we do not yet perceive, but we know **who** we are: we are children of God. Jesus said: *"Most assuredly I say to you, he who hears My Word and believes in Him Who sent Me has everlasting life, and shall not come into judgement, but has passed from death into life."*

That is powerful! It says that if you **have** repented and **have** received Jesus as your own Savior, then you **have** everlasting life and **have** crossed over from death to life. Praise the Lord!

Switch on the Light!

When the apostle Paul preached in Corinth, he did not feel physically robust and full of vigor. He was weak and trembling. In fact, he even talked about despairing of life sometimes. His preaching was simple and direct. He did not go storming in, relying on brilliant speech to overwhelm his hearers, yet he preached in *"the demonstration of the Spirit and of power."* The effects were mighty, and many repented and received salvation. How could that be? What did he preach to have such effects? The secret is this: he said, *"For I determined not to know any thing among you, save Jesus Christ, and Him crucified."* The Gospel is the Word of God, Peter said, and that Gospel is the Word of the Cross. Salvation is not a theory. It does not rest in mere words, not even in stirred emotions ... but on what happened, on a fact, a deed: *"Christ died for our sins according to the Scriptures."*

If you want assurance that **today** God smiles upon you and is on your side, and that one day you will be welcomed in Heaven, this is how it happens. First, you hear or read the Gospel that Christ died for your sins. Next, you believe the Gospel and repent, and the power of God applies the benefits of Christ's redeeming death to your heart. Then, something wonderful happens: the Word of God quickens your dead spirit, and you become alive in God, cleansed and made whole. **What Jesus did for you on the Cross, the Holy Spirit transfer into your life.**

Let me illustrate this: you may have electricity in your home. The house is wired and connected to the power plant. If you go home on a dark night, there is no light or heat there, but you know what to do: you press the switch, and power comes through. You have instant light and warmth. Believing Christ died for you is like turning the switch on. Everything else is ready. The Gospel message is like the wires and cables that are connected to the power station, Calvary's Cross. Lines of truth have already been laid. The power is there waiting. Then you believe ... which turns the spiritual switch on ... and the saving power flows to you, giving you light. **You are saved.**

Today's Scripture

Christ died for our sins according to the Scriptures.
(I Corinthians 15:3)

Daily Power!

I have the Light of Christ Jesus alive in me, illuminating my world.

Today's Bible Reading

Ezra 8:21-36 through 9:1-15; I Corinthians 5:1-13; Psalm 31:1-8; Proverbs 21:1-2

Mark my Word
(for further study)

I Corinthians 1:8; 2:2-4; 15:3

Life Blood

The Blood of Jesus brings life. He said so Himself: *"Whoever eats My flesh and drinks My blood has eternal life, and I will raise him up at the last day."* "Drinking" is, of course, a figure of speech, not literal, for Jesus was still alive when He spoke these words. It means taking God's forgiveness through the Blood of Jesus by faith, and spiritually applying His Blood to our need. Now the true heights of Calvary's mountain soar before us. When the spear opened the heart of Jesus, and blood and water came forth, the heart of God was opened too. When life-streams flowed on the Cross, an eternal fountain of life and mercy began *"still it flows as fresh as ever, from my Savior's wounded side."*

After Abel's murder defiled the ground, another killing, by Lamech, is recorded. The weapon forged by Tubal-Cain and the wicked deed – glorified in music by Jubal – prompted more and more bloodshed. Abel's blood that had cried in solo from the Earth swelled to a mighty choir of voices – and God heard. We read that finally: *"The Earth also was corrupt before God, and the Earth was filled with violence."* So God declared, *"And behold, I Myself am bringing floodwaters on the Earth."* God called Noah into the Ark, and *"all the fountains of the great deep were broken up, and the windows of Heaven were opened."* Swirling waters covered the Earth to the mountain tops. Was the Earth washed clean? Indeed not. Immediately after the Flood, God told Noah that only blood can cleanse sin. God had much to teach Mankind: *"Whoever sheds man's blood, by man his blood shall be shed."* There was only one way: *"Behold! The Lamb of God Who takes away the sin of the world!"* and *"The Blood of Jesus Christ His Son cleanses us from all sin."* His Blood removes it all. Some people think that the waters of baptism can cleanse their souls. As they pass through the waters, they imagine that the religious ceremony has taken their sin away. But it simply cannot do that. If the waters of baptism could remove our sin, Jesus Christ would never have needed to die such a cruel death – but there was no alternative. Be free in Christ – your sins are forgiven and you have His new life!

Today's Scripture

Behold! The Lamb of God Who takes away the sin of the world!

(John 1:29)

Daily Power!

I take God's forgiveness through the Blood of Jesus by faith, spiritually applying His Blood to my need.

Today's Bible Reading

*Ezra 10:1-44;
I Corinthians 6:1-20;
Psalm 31:9-18;
Proverbs 21:3*

Mark my Word
(for further study)

*Genesis 4:11, 21-24;
6:11, 17; 7:11; 9:6;
John 1:29; 6:54;
I John 1:7*

The precious Oil

The Bible uses a very striking explanation and illustration for the principle of unity: **oil!** We should first understand that oil in Scripture always represents the Holy Spirit. When Scripture talks about oil in lamps, anointing oil, cosmetic oil or perfumed oil, it is pictorial language for the work of the Spirit. The idea originates from Psalms: *"How good and pleasant it is when brothers live together in unity! It is like precious oil poured on the head."* This was referring to the ceremony of pouring special perfumed oil upon the head of the High Priest of Israel.

Why is unity like oil? Because the Holy Spirit is oil … and He brings unity. That is the link. *"Make every effort to keep the unity of the Spirit through the bond of peace."* Unity through the oil of the Spirit poured upon us is like the oil poured on the head in Psalm 133: *"It is like the precious oil upon the head, running down into the beard … of Aaron, running down to the edge of his garments. It is like the dew of Hermon, descending upon the mountains of Zion; for there the Lord commanded the blessing – life forevermore!"* Notice this oil was not poured out skimpily, but lavishly, running all the way down to the hem of Aaron's robe … enough oil was poured out to cover even an entire mountain! Unity has wide-reaching effects. The purpose of this outpouring of Holy Spirit oil is to *"prepare God's people for works of service … until we all reach unity in the faith."* So faith also comes into it – faith, the Holy Spirit, and in unity, all play their parts.

Now Scripture doesn't say: "Become united, be one" – it says: *"Keep the unity!"* You can't keep what doesn't exist … but unity **does** exist – you only have to maintain it. That unity is the presence of the Holy Spirit in every believer. This fact should be demonstrated: you are one in Him from the moment you believe.

Today's Scripture

Til we all come to the unity of the faith and of the knowledge of the Son of God, to a perfect man, to the measure of the stature of the fullness of Christ.
(Ephesians 4:13)

Daily Power!

The oil of the Holy Spirit flowing in my life enables me to walk in unity with my brothers and sisters in Christ.

Today's Bible Reading

Nehemiah 1:1-11 through 3:1-14; I Corinthians 7:1-24; Psalm 31:19-24; Proverbs 21:4

Mark my Word
(for further study)

Psalm 133:1-2; Ephesians 4:3, 13; 4:12-13

12

Today's Scripture

If we live in the Spirit, let us also walk in the Spirit.
(Galatians 5:25)

Daily Power!

The Holy Spirit is the bonding Element that unifies my life with fellow-believers.

Today's Bible Reading

Nehemiah 3:15-32 through 5:1-13;
I Corinthians 7:25-40;
Psalm 32:1-11;
Proverbs 21:5-7

Mark my Word
(for further study)

John 10:30;
Galatians 5:25; 6:2;
Ephesians 4:4; 6:11

Commitment

Nobody can have unity by himself. You can't be married by yourself. There's no such thing as an independent believer. You can't have unity by belonging nowhere. Some say that they belong to the universal church, but are committed nowhere particularly. Well, that means nobody can rely upon these people. Churches can't be built on floaters.

Every born-again believer is "in Christ" together with all others. *"There is one body and one Spirit"* – a great body of believers in Heaven and on Earth. Everything in the New Testament points to unity. We are to bear one another's burdens, for example: *"Bear one another's burdens, and so fulfill the law of Christ."* How can we do that if we have nothing to do with other Christians?

The New Testament **always** assumes that all believers are attached to one another locally. The epistle to the Ephesians is all about the Church … and everything said is to the whole Church, not to isolated individuals. It is the whole Church, for example, which must have *"the whole armor of God,"* for it is a fighting force, an army. Certainly there are people who like to imagine themselves as one-man armies – a whirlwind of energy and enthusiasm, single-handedly combating the enemy, ripping through communities and nations … usually leaving a path of destruction behind. Even as Christ Jesus Himself was accountable to His Heavenly Father – *"I and My Father are One"* – so are we, the Church today, accountable to each other for our actions … that is why we **must** live in the community of churches.

The Holy Spirit is the Spirit of unity. He is the bonding Element. This bonding is a wonderful effect of faith in Christ. It is creative. It brings about a new kind of oneness not even known in the closest of Earthly families.

Only God can reveal God

Unless God allowed it, we could never know Him. Only God can reveal God. Many great thinkers have spun God out of their rational thoughts, but their projections are about as heart-warming as an iceberg. Scholars have veiled the face of Jesus with their unbelief, calling Him "the Man nobody knows." They deny His miracles and resurrection, reducing Jesus to their own eye-level. He is too big for their logic, so they present Him as a miniature Jesus. But Christians know the Jesus Whose face is the glory of God! Human imagination is very limited and cannot reach God. We can only imagine something as good as we know, not better. False gods are made in the image of men or women: *"Eye has not seen, nor ear heard, neither has entered into the heart of man the things which God has prepared for them that love Him."* The experience of Christ is beyond those who are strangers to it.

Isaiah mocked those who tried to make images of their gods. Images are like gargoyles. A block of wood cannot become like the Creator of Heaven and Earth. Their character is usually as distorted as their appearance. The gods of the Greeks and Romans were lustful and treacherous. The early American tribes worshipped deities who demanded human sacrifices until the temple walls were coated inches thick with dried blood. Science fiction writers have ideas of other forms of life that are usually ghastly nightmare figures, and their other-world scenes make New York or London look like Paradise in comparison. Every attempt to portray God comes up against the depravity of the human mind. In the same vein are the curious ideas circulating about Heaven and how to get there. Our only ideas come from the Bible, and only the Bible has the right to tell us how to get there or who will get there. The Bible itself describes it as a place where only those cleansed in the Blood of Jesus dare enter. If we turn elsewhere to know God, we feel depressed. The sacred writings of India, China, or Islam bring fear but little cheer. Open the Bible … and a thousand rainbows of wonderful light stream out! The more you understand that Book, the more your mind opens to its revelations, as flowers to the rising sun – the power that inspired it, designed your soul to receive it.

Today's Scripture

No one's ever seen or heard anything like this, never so much as imagined anything quite like it – what God has arranged for those who love Him.
(I Corinthians 2:9; the Message)

Daily Power!

The experience of Christ is beyond those who are strangers to it.

Today's Bible Reading

Nehemiah 5:14-19 through 7:1-60;
I Corinthians 8:1-13;
Psalm 33:1-11;
Proverbs 21:8-10

Mark my Word
(for further study)

I Corinthians 2:9

14

Divine Promises

It is human nature to depend on people's promises until we are disillusioned. Tricksters and con men trade on it. We trust people when they give us their word. We should be able to trust God as He has given us His Word. A hundred generations have proved Him, and He has given us the same reason for relying upon Him, express declarations of what He will undertake to do for us. Somebody went through the whole Bible and counted – finding 7,874 promises that God made to us! That glittering array covers our understanding of God and what we can expect of Him.

Outside these promises is possibly outside the Word of God. Nevertheless, there is no hard boundary to the kindness of God. He is gracious. Experience shows He may allow beyond the fringe of His precise Word. When that happens, it is not to be taken as setting a precedent for others to demand the same of Him. But the scope of 7,874 promises should be wide enough for all circumstances needing God's help. Many of the promises come in the form of a covenant.

God does a lot for us without our asking Him: *"Your Father in Heaven ... causes His sun to rise on the evil and the good, and sends rain on the righteous and the unrighteous."* God is good, and good to all. Millions give Him no credit, although they are quick to blame Him when things which are not good hit them. The processes of nature seem unchangeable and regular. To this day, nobody has shown that God has no part in this. He keeps His promises to *"the birds, the livestock and all the wild animals, every living creature on Earth"* ... *"As long as Earth endures, seedtime and harvest, cold and heat, summer and winter, day and night will never cease."* Jesus took it further and included the flowers, saying, *"Consider the lilies of the field, how they grow; they toil not, neither do they spin, and yet ... even Solomon in all his glory was not arrayed like one of these."* Rejoice in God's loving kindness and caring faithfulness ... even His creation declares His miraculous provisions for you.

Today's Scripture

[God] gives His best – the sun to warm and the rain to nourish – to everyone, regardless: the good and bad, the nice and nasty.
(Matthew 5:45; the Message)

Daily Power!

The scope of 7,874 promises should be wide enough for all circumstances needing God's help!

Today's Bible Reading

Nehemiah 7:61-73
through 9:1-21;
I Corinthians 9:1-18;
Psalm 33:12-22 ;
Proverbs 21:11-12

Mark my Word
(for further study)

Genesis 8:22; 9:10;
Matthew 5:45;
6:28-29; 7:7-11

The golden Gift of Faith

One minute, we do not believe ... the next moment, faith is suddenly there! Perhaps in a less than dramatic fashion, we step over a border, and we believe. We just know Who Jesus is. It doesn't always come framed in all the right words, or it may not conform to a classic conversion experience ... but within our souls, there is intuition. We see it, we know He is the One Who should come if this world has any meaning. He is the key, the answer to the riddle of existence, the focus. Jesus Christ crystallizes people's ideas about God.

In the Old Testament, revelation came to people about God, but it seemed to be only to rare individuals, such as Abraham, Jacob, and the prophets. The mass of people moved very slowly – and often moved backwards. God used various circumstances and methods to help them to have faith. But the coming of Jesus has swept the world. Somehow, Calvary does what the awesome manifestations of Sinai couldn't do. Jesus is the great Faith-Creator. Looking back over the long, cheerless world history of uncertainty and doubt, we can see when it changed. It came with the Gospel. It awakened sleeping trust. The dawn had come. *"I am the way, the truth and the life. No one comes to the Father except through Me ... The words that I speak to you I do not speak on My own authority, but the Father Who dwells in Me does the works. Believe in Me that I am in the Father and the Father in Me."*

Jesus said, *"No one comes to the Father except through Me."* It was a pragmatic, simple fact. Nobody ever had found God – and nobody ever has to this day – except through Christ. There are religions enough, pointing a thousand different ways, but Christ **is** the way ... He doesn't point to a way. He **is** the door ... and flings Heaven wide open: *"Come unto Me ... and I will give you rest"* ... *"Fear not."* These are His promises to all Mankind ... and for you and for me.

Today's Scripture

Come unto me, all you who labor and are heavy laden, and I will give you rest. Take My yoke upon you and learn from Me, for I am gentle and lowly in heart, and you will find rest for your souls. For My yoke is easy and My burden is light.
(Matthew 11:28-30)

Daily Power!

Living with Jesus Christ in my heart gives meaning and hope to my life.

Today's Bible Reading

Nehemiah 9:22-37 through 10:1-39; 9:19-27 through 10:1-13; Psalm 34:1-10; Proverbs 21:13

Mark my Word
(for further study)

Matthew 11:28; Luke 12:32; John 14:5-11

Faith in three Tenses

Today's Scripture

He Who has begun a good work in you will complete it.
(Philippians 1:6)

Daily Power!

I purpose in my heart to learn what the will of God is ... and then to do it.

Today's Bible Reading

Nehemiah 11:1-36 through 12:1-26; I Corinthians 10:14-33 through 11:1-2; Psalm 34:11-22; Proverbs 21:14-16

Mark my Word
(for further study)

Psalm 27:3; Philippians 1:6; I Timothy 4:8; I John 2:17

Today, "Yesterday" knocks on our door, telling us about "Tomorrow." What we believe will be, comes from what was. Like the weather, Life is a matter of probabilities – except one thing: the will of God. God is not affected by changes. God's will is the key to bring order from chaos. This business of faith is needed for the whole business of Life. We have to take it on trust that the water from our taps is not toxic. Making money or making a living are the same. But my concern is living itself: we can make a mess of it, or a good job. We can fail in living while succeed in making a living – a good living but a poor life – and *"Godliness is profitable for all things, having promise of the life that now is and of that which is to come."*

Faith can snap us out of our snug little burrows and get us going for God. God gave me a world-sized job – to publish and distribute a first-class Gospel booklet for every home in many nations. I had no money for such a fantastic scheme … but I had faith. Now I have "seen" God meet the need in the British Isles, Germany, Austria, Switzerland, Norway, Sweden, Denmark, Finland, Greenland, Iceland and the Faroe Islands, Hong Kong and 12 millions Gospel books were distributed to homes in the U.S. and Canada as well. At present, a total of over 103 million books have been translated into 123 languages and dialects, and are being printed in 42 different countries.

What God has done before indicates to me what will happen next. No matter with whom we deal, we don't know what they will be like soon … but we just take it on trust if they have been trustworthy. Even circumstances change and we have to take a chance. There is no other way. Faith is a fact of life, like the need to breathe. I trust God because He has a "proven track record," as they say. He has always handled things well, ten thousand times in my work.

There are three tenses of faith: *"Being confident of this, that He Who began a good work … will carry it on to completion."* The Christian confidence is that what God was, He is and will be. *"Though war break out against me, even then will I be confident."* His will cannot be challenged or changed – it shapes the future. In His will, you are secure. *"The man who does the will of God lives forever."*

The Source of Oil

The great National Temple in Jerusalem had a famous golden lamp-stand, the seven-branched "menorah" described in Exodus chapters 25, 35, 37, 39. The Romans carried it off when they plundered Jerusalem in AD 70, and it is depicted on the Arch of Titus seen daily by tourists in Rome. The **menorah** is the badge of modern Israel. This lamp-stand – or lamp standard – had neither joint nor weld, being made out a single piece of gold. Each arm had a lamp, a mere wick, and the oil came from a single source in the central stem. The seven lights shone as one light and had no shadow of itself. Jesus talked about oil in lamps, a symbol of the Holy Spirit.

In the Book of Revelation, the apostle John described Christ standing among seven golden lamp-stands, each lamp standard representing a church: *"I was in the Spirit on the Lord's Day, and I heard behind me a loud voice, as of a trumpet, saying, 'I am the Alpha and the Omega, the First and the Last,' and 'What you see, write in a book and send it to the seven churches which are in Asia' … Then I turned to see the voice that spoke with me. And having turned I saw seven golden lamp-stands, and in the midst of the seven lamp-stands stood One like the Son of Man."* Also, he said that before the Throne, seven lamps were blazing. These are the seven Spirits of God. The seven flames of each candelabrum had a single fuel source: the Spirit of God, casting a single light. There is one Spirit as we read, although manifested in many gifts, ministries and operations.

If believers shine and bring a little brightness into our drab world, it is by the Holy Spirit – otherwise they are dead wicks. A wick can't shine without fuel, no matter how hard it tries. Christ sets hearts aglow, and we can blaze for God. Nobody just believes – if you believe, you shine!

Today's Scripture

But the manifestation of the Spirit is given to each one for the profit of all.
(I Corinthians 12:7)

Daily Power!

The Source of oil in my lamp is the Holy Spirit of God.

Today's Bible Reading

Nehemiah 12:27-47 through 13:1-31;
I Corinthians 11:3-16;
Psalm 35:1-16;
Proverbs 21:17-18

Mark my Word
(for further study)

Exodus 25:1-40; 35:1-35; 37:1-29; 39:1-43;
I Corinthians 12:4-11;
Revelation 1:10-13; 4:5

Today's Scripture

For where two or three are gathered together in My Name, I am there in the midst of them.

(Matthew 18:20)

Daily Power!

I shall strive to "unlearn the business of questioning God" so that I may be a more effective believer.

Today's Bible Reading

Esther 1:1-22 through 3:1-15; I Corinthians 11:17-34; Psalm 35:17-28; Proverbs 21:19-20

Mark my Word
(for further study)

Mark 16:17-18; John 14:23

Getting somewhere

Wisdom itself loses its way without revelation. For instance, a modern poet, Philip Larkin, tried it. He was an atheist. Journalist Martyn Harris wrote about Larkin just before he died in 1996, saying his godlessness left him "drunk, suicidal, self-obsessed and paralyzed by misery." Larkin himself described his desolation facing a bleak eternity in his poem, Aubade. He waited for the "the total emptiness forever. The sure extinction that we travel to, and shall be lost in always."

Faith in God seems a vague sentiment, but it solidifies into reality. We can "cast ourselves upon the ocean of the unknown" with wonderful assurance. Jesus said, *"Those who love Me will keep My Word, and my Father will love them."* The major lesson I personally had to learn when arriving in Africa from Germany was to **unlearn the business of questioning God**. We question politicians ... but believe God! For example, Christ said: *"These signs shall follow those who believe ... they shall lay hands on the sick and they shall recover."* It is not for me to consult intellectuals for their approval, but simply to obey the Word. I do what God says, and then He does what He said. God changed the polarity of my heart and spirit ... and then began to use me to shake whole nations! God used the rod of Moses ... and so He uses us when we follow His orders. I see His power at work time after time. My faith-fuse has held, and the currents of blessing have flowed through my life to millions of precious people to redeem their souls by the Blood of the Lamb.

You can't generate power by anything you do – music, worship, atmosphere. As soon as two or three gather in His name, Christ is there! Immediately, the Throne is built ... and you don't need to take an hour of worship to build it or pull power down from Heaven. It is impossible for Christians even to meet in His Name without Christ being there in power! Every day, **plug into** the power that is yours in Christ Jesus!

Flash Flood!

God says, *"For the Earth will be filled with the knowledge of the glory of the Lord, as the waters cover the sea."* How do the waters cover the sea? So thoroughly that there is not a single dry spot on the bottom of the sea! This clearly illustrates God's plan: the knowledge of His glory, power and salvation will be spread across the world like a flash flood. There won't be a single dry spot, no ignorant country, city, town, village, family, or individual. *"The whole Earth is full of His glory!"* cried the seraphim to the prophet Isaiah.

This knowledge of God comes through His own Son, Jesus Christ: *"There shall come forth a Rod from the stem of Jesse, and a Branch shall grow out of his roots. The Spirit of the Lord shall rest upon Him, the Spirit of wisdom and understanding, the Spirit of counsel and might, the Spirit of knowledge and the fear of the Lord ... For the Earth shall be full of the knowledge of the Lord as the waters cover the sea."*

We must see the culmination of a century of global evangelism and revival, the consummation of the toils and tears of former generations of God's anointed. The Church is a life-boat, not a pleasure-boat. Entertainers are not needed or wanted. From the captain to the cook, all hands are needed on deck for soul-saving. The Church that does not seek the lost is "lost" itself. Some excuse themselves saying that in today's pluralistic societies, the Christian half can never penetrate the other half. But was not our situation anticipated by God? People ask, "What is God saying to the Church today?" Why is that a problem? Does God speak so inaudibly? He says nothing today that is not in His Word already. I know one thing that God is saying – and if our prophets are true, they will be voicing the same urgency as Jesus Christ, and echoing the same Great Commission: *"Go into all the world and preach the Gospel to every creature."* That's God's **command** to you today.

Today's Scripture

And in that day there shall be a Root of Jesse Who shall stand as a Banner to the people; for the Gentiles shall seek Him, and His resting place shall be glorious.
(Isaiah 11:10)

Daily Power!

The Church is a life-boat, not a pleasure-boat ... all hands on deck for soul-saving.

Today's Bible Reading

Esther 4:1-17 through 7:1-10;
I Corinthians 12:1-26;
Psalm 36:1-12;
Proverbs 21:21-22

Mark my Word
(for further study)

Isaiah 6:3; 11:1-2, 9-10;
Habakkuk 2:14;
Mark 16:15

20

Miracles characterize the Kingdom

Miracles are normal for the Kingdom. Christ sent His disciples out and said, *"When you enter a town and are welcomed, heal the sick who are there and tell them, 'The Kingdom of God is near you.'"* Before Christ, in Old Testament times, miracles were rare, being special, historic visitations of God that were divinely brought about by His sovereign will. There were no gifts of healings for the blind, crippled or deaf. Outstanding people – such as David, Ezra, Nehemiah, Jeremiah, and Esther – never once witnessed a physical wonder, and some never experienced anything they could call supernatural. Ezra never felt the moving of the Spirit – he never had a vision, a call, a voice or even an appointment as a prophet. He could trust the Word alone. Generally, the few signs and wonders that were seen were demonstrations to reprove rulers, such as the despotic lords of Egypt, Babylon and Israel. These wonders were aimed at humbling them, as they did with Nebuchadnezzar. He was forced to admit that God's *"dominion is an eternal dominion, His Kingdom endures from generation to generation … glorify the King of Heaven!"*

Usually such events were judgments, like the plagues of Egypt. But the higher qualities of Kingdom power were kindness and mercy. John the Baptist, the last of the Old Testament prophets, expected harsh judgment when the Messiah came. He spoke of the fire cleansing and burning up the chaff. But when Jesus baptized with fire rather than destruction and judgment, the blaze of love came. Jesus healed the sick. Jesus sent John the Baptist a message to show that His fire was His rage against the evils men suffered. He was the One who should come. The gifts of the Spirit are benevolent and kind. One of the chiefest of the Spirit-gifts is **love**: *"And now abide faith, hope, love – these three; but the greatest of these is love."* Walk joyfully in God's love today.

Today's Scripture

God also bearing witness both with signs and wonders, with various miracles, and gifts of the Holy Spirit, according to His own will.
(Hebrews 2:4)

Daily Power!

The higher qualities of Kingdom power are kindness and mercy.

Today's Bible Reading

*Esther 8:1-17
through 10:1-3;
I Corinthians 12:27-31
through 13:1-13;
Psalm 37:1-11;
Proverbs 21:23-24*

Mark my Word
(for further study)

*Daniel 4:34, 37;
Luke 8:9-10;
I Corinthians 13:13;
Hebrews 2:4*

His greatest Work

Salvation is the Holy Spirit's greatest work. It does not bring about only minor results, like patching you up, making you religious or tuning you in to nature. The creation of Heaven and Earth took God just six days … but He spent centuries preparing for Mankind's salvation. He was working in different locations – Egypt … Israel … Babylon … Rome – through good men and bad, throughout history … until in *"the fullness of the time,"* Jesus came. It affected everything and everyone, even God. God's Son, torn from His side, depriving angels of their joy, faced life from a humble stable in Bethlehem. Then He faced death on Calvary, making war on Satan. In that struggle, the Earth was shaken, the rocks rent, the sun blackened out of the sky.

"Now from the sixth hour until the ninth hour there was darkness over all the land … And Jesus cried out again with a loud voice, and yielded up His Spirit. Then, behold, the veil of the temple was torn in two from top to bottom; and the earth quaked, and the rocks were split, and the graves were opened; and many bodies of the saints who had fallen asleep were raised … So when the centurion and those with him, who were guarding Jesus, saw the earthquake and the things that had happened, they feared greatly, saying, 'Truly this was the Son of God!'"

Cowed by such awesome scenes, His enemies – who had howled like wolves for His Blood – crept away in fear. Hell felt the impact. Jesus Christ broke out of the granite of the sealed tomb, unhinging the gates of death, leading out captives and ascending far above all authorities to present His wounds to the Father. Wounded for you and me! These are the mighty events which made your salvation and mine possible. It is too big a thing for you not to know you are saved! It is not just being hopeful or optimistic – the Word says it. Have confidence in Christ, that you have indeed received His greatest gift. Thank Him for that Gift … walk in it … share it … enjoy it … and apply it to your challenges today.

Today's Scripture

For this reason I also suffer these things; nevertheless I am not ashamed, for I know Whom I have believed and am persuaded that He is able to keep what I have committed to Him until that Day.
(II Timothy 1:12)

Daily Power!

Thank God I have the assurance of His Word and His Spirit that salvation is mine.

Today's Bible Reading

*Job 1:1-22
through 3:1-26;
I Corinthians 14:1-17;
Psalm 37:12-29;
Proverbs 21:25-26*

Mark my Word
(for further study)

*Matthew 27:45-56;
Galatians 4:4;
II Timothy 1:12*

Today's Scripture

You have known Him from the beginning ... because you are strong, and the Word of God abides in you, and you have overcome the wicked one.

(I John 3:14)

Daily Power!

I will accept no imitations, no substitutes for real, vibrant Christian living.

Today's Bible Reading

*Job 4:1-21
through 7:1-21;
I Corinthians 14:18-40;
Psalm 37:30-40;
Proverbs 21:27*

Mark my Word
(for further study)

*Matthew 7:16;
II Timothy 1:12; 2:19;
II Peter 1:4;
I John 3:14*

No Imitations

"The solid foundation of God stands, having this seal: 'The Lord knows those who are His' and 'Let everyone who names the Name of Christ depart from iniquity.'" There is a false confidence which shows in arrogance, boasting of an experience of salvation which never shows in a person's character, behavior and life style – *"you will know them by their fruits"* – such people are phony Christians. *"We know that we have passed from death to life, because we love our brothers. Anyone who does not love remains in death."* There is a subtle danger. People can be imitators and live **like** Christians, but not be saved.

Some people have pet parrots. Parrots are born mimics. A friend of mine has a fine African gray named Polly, who can repeat what people say, seemingly in their own voices. Sometimes it is hard to tell who is speaking. The bird talks as if it were one of the family and uses a human-sounding voice. It tries to join in the conversation quite often. But alas, poor Polly ... though it talks like a human being and maybe even thinks it is one, it is still only a parrot. Plenty of people live like Christians by imitation. They do what Christians are supposed to do. They parrot all the words ... but not the music – none of that glorious song of the redeemed responding to Heaven. Their lives are all works and effort. They might be pretty good mimics too, doing better than real Christians sometimes. But are they Christians? Christians have the "Divine nature," being born-again from above, their true spiritual Father being in Heaven. They sing, "The Spirit answers to the Blood and tells me I am born of God." When you are truly His, you should know it.

Now we all may fail, but salvation goes on working in us to overcome our weaknesses. Our desires to please the Lord must be true at least until the day when our redemption is completed and we see His wonderful face. Until then, whatever comes, we can say as Paul said: *"I ... am persuaded that He is able to keep that which I have committed unto him against that day."* Agree with that today!

Boast only in Christ

Nobody can take away Christ's glory, and age cannot dim it. It is there in Himself, and is not produced by artificial pomp or outward circumstance. He needs no triumphalism, no trumpets, no brilliant display. His glory shines through His peasant's garment. Put Him on a Cross, and it can destroy nothing of Him. He triumphs over it, transforms it and turns this thing of shame and scandal into the greatest symbol of glory on Earth.

Jesus Christ was crucified on a rough wooden cross – the cruelest form of execution yet known to Man. He was stripped naked (unlike the "dressed-up" pictures we're most accustomed to seeing), the ultimate humility, and hung for hours without any protection from the elements … or from shame. The cross was planted in the ground in such a way that the remnants of sunlight pierced directly into His eyes for as long as He lingered in agonizing death-throes. When finally the death-squad came to ensure His death, they thrust in their spears … and water came out, because Jesus permitted **all** of His Blood to be poured out for Mankind: *"So [Thomas] said to them, 'Unless I see in His hands the print of the nails, and put my finger into the print of the nails and put my hand into His side, I will not believe' … Then [Jesus] said to Thomas, 'Reach your finger here and look at My hands, and reach your hand here and put it into My side. Do not be unbelieving, but believing' … Blessed are those who have not seen and yet have believed.'"*

The ugliest instrument of human torture and hate – sticky with blood and guts – is so transfigured until a former enemy had to call out, "Forbid it, Lord, that I should boast, save in the death of Christ my God." There is no way to destroy His glory. The more you attack Him, the more His mercy, His compassion and His patience appear. The one who is His enemy only gives Him an opportunity to forgive, to seek, to save, and to display the eternal glory of His indestructible love. Out loud, let us exclaim, "Hallelujah, what a Savior!"

Today's Scripture

But God forbid that I should boast except in the Cross of our Lord Jesus Christ, by Whom the world has been crucified to me and I to the world.
(Galatians 6:14)

Daily Power!

Jesus forgives, saves, and displays the eternal glory of His indestructible love for me!

Today's Bible Reading

Job 8:1-22 through 11:1-20; I Corinthians 15:1-28; Psalm 38:1-22; Proverbs 21:28-29

Mark my Word
(for further study)

Isaiah 22:23; John 19:1-42; 20:24-39; Galatians 6:14

Today's Scripture

Wash me, and I shall be whiter than snow. Make me hear joy and gladness, that the bones You have broken may rejoice. Hide Your face from my sins, and blot out all my iniquities. Create in me a clean heart, O God, and renew a steadfast spirit within me.

(Psalm 51:7-10)

Daily Power!

My Jesus, my Savior, has washed me completely from my sins; now I wear His righteousness.

Today's Bible Reading

Job 12:1-25 through 15:1-35; I Corinthians 15:29-58; Psalm 39:1-13; Proverbs 21:30-31

Mark my Word
(for further study)

*Isaiah 53:1
John 13:1-17; 19:37*

What a Servant!

Who is the greatest in the Kingdom of God? Maybe the unknown … but certainly, the one who serves without an ulterior motive. Undoubtedly, the greatest of all is the One Who took a towel and washed the disciples' feet … and then – when water would not do – He poured out His life's Blood for humanity's cleansing. Jesus Christ, what a Servant, Who came to wash the hearts and feet of all Mankind! *"Jesus, knowing that the Father had given all things into His hand, and that He had come from God and was going to God, rose from supper and laid aside His garments, took a towel and girded Himself. After that, He poured water into a basin and began to wash the disciples' feet, add to wipe them with the towel with which He was girded … So when He had washed their feet, taken His garments, and sat down again, He said to them, 'Do you know what I have done to you? You call Me Teacher and Lord, and you say well, for so I am. If I then, your Lord and Teacher, have washed your feet, you also ought to wash one another's feet.'"*

He is the One we shall see: *"They shall look on Him Whom they pierced."* That is His special identity – He is "the pierced One." And *"He shall see the labor of His soul, and be satisfied."* His coming in glory will be with His saints, the Blood-washed ones. Not the sycophants, the pushy, the social climbers, the name-droppers, the collectors of wealth and awards, cups and medals – but the redeemed ones. He redeemed them, sought them, found them, and glorified them!

What glory! He has perfumed the odious with grace. The polluted are now clothed in righteousness. The unclean have been washed with His tears, prayed for under the olive trees of Gethsemane, where Jesus sweat drops of blood, and captured by the Captive on the Tree. Determine today (afresh and anew) that you'll **never** forget to honor and value Jesus Christ, the Lamb of God.

Power Conductors

If it were **our** work to produce the power of God, **we** would be the power generators. But **Christ gave us power**. We are not called to go into the entire world with our own little power plant so folk will think how wonderful we are. We could parade our own charisma and make the sparks fly for an hour ... but soon our power-plant would run out of fuel, and begin coughing and dying. We are not generators – but conductors. *"Out of His fullness we have all received"* ... He is *"the fullness Who fills all in all."* We are channels, not the source. *"As the branch cannot bear fruit of itself, unless it abides in the vine, neither can you, unless you abide in Me."*

God does not need any of our energy dynamos. He has His own – two of them – right here on Earth: the Cross, and the Empty Tomb. Power flows forever from those sources, day and night, without power cuts or breakdowns. The voltage is unfailing and reliable. There is no fluctuating flow *"from the Father of lights, with Whom is no variableness."*

"That I may know Him and the power of His resurrection, and the fellowship of His sufferings, being conformed to His death, if, by any means, I may attain to the resurrection from the dead."

Here is our full equipment: the spiritual energies of the Cross and the Resurrection ... the power-lines of the Word of God ... the fuse of our faith, the vital link. They give us: power for every need ... power to change lives ... power to break vicious habits ... power to heal the sick ... power to light the storm-darkened Highway of Life. No power known on Earth created in test-tubes or in industry, can do any of those things. The power of God is the great force on Earth to deal with the intractable problems of living! Tap into that power today!

Today's Scripture

That I may know Him and the power of His resurrection.
(Philippians 4:10)

Daily Power!

Because of Christ Jesus, I have unlimited access to God's unlimited power.

Today's Bible Reading

*Job 16:1-22
through 19:1-29;
I Corinthians 16:1-24;
Psalm 40:1-10;
Proverbs 22:1*

Mark my Word
(for further study)

*John 1:16; 15:4;
Ephesians 1:23;
Philippians 3:10-11;
James 1:17*

26

Today's Scripture

Behold, God is my salvation, I will trust and not be afraid; for Yah, the Lord, is my strength and song; He also has become my salvation.
(Isaiah 12:2)

Daily Power!

Dynamic life in Jesus Christ fills me with joy.

Today's Bible Reading

Job 20:1-29 through 22:1-30; II Corinthians 1:1-11; Psalm 40:11-17; Proverbs 22:2-4

Mark my Word
(for further study)

Nehemiah 8:10; Isaiah 12:2

Plugged in

At a conference, I overheard some young people say, "We must be switched on for Jesus. All it takes is to be switched for Him." I turned to them, "Yes, it is good to be switched on for Jesus – but it is more important to be **plugged in**. Switching on for Jesus will be useless unless we are plugged in. We must be connected first." Being switched on to ourselves produces no current.

The power of God coming through the Word reaches the faith-fuse first – and that could be the preacher. That tiny bridge of power can become very warm. A preacher of the Word is the first to feel that warmth. He burns with the charge. He is likely to show it, and should. He is a communicator, not of his own thoughts, but of the power of God. He should be a live wire.

A preacher is a man having an experience with God in public. If he represses his exuberance and puts polish, elegance and propriety first, he should remember those are not fruits of the Spirit – but joy is. *"The joy of the Lord shall be your strength,"* not your weakness.

If an experienced electrician touches a bare wire and gets a shock, he may just say, "Ouch!" But anybody having an electric shock for the first time is likely to react in more dramatic fashion: "Wow!" God's power is not a fiction but a fact. It is the greatest reality we know.

If God does manifest Himself, what would anybody expect? A graveyard … or a resurrection? Dynamic life may seem unseemly at first … but when people experience the flowing current of Divine blessing, they will appreciate why. Nobody knows what it is like to meet Jesus Christ until they do. One exuberant preacher was told, "Please restrain yourself!" He replied, "I **am** restraining myself!" Don't let the cares of this world, nor appearances or pride, let you be anything less than joyful about your life in Christ!

The secret Side of Faith

Often afflicted people are thought to be less intelligent. The Bible isn't like that. An example is the leper mentioned in Matthew 8. He was outstanding in acumen and saw what few others ever expressed. He met Jesus and said, *"If You will, You can make me clean."* Many put the cart before the horse, saying "If You·**can**, You **will**." That is human thinking, not revelation … and not Bible talk. God always can, but will He?

For the leper, it was a revelation. He saw that everything depended on Christ's will. The leper's faith was reasonable: *"If You will, You can."* The Bible was not written to tell us what God **can do** – we all know that. God is Almighty or we wouldn't call Him God. The Bible is here to tell us what He **will do** – that is what we want to know. So, what is He willing to do? The answer is, "His Word is His will" – a short answer, but it comes in a long book: sixty-six Bible books, in fact. Each book gives us special help – it builds our understanding of God and His character. Then we know what He will do.

Christ taught us to pray, *"Thy Kingdom come. Thy will be done on Earth as in Heaven."* The will of God is certainly not done always on Earth now. God's goodness continues, but a bad devil is permitted freedom for the time being and complicates every issue. If this were a perfect world, faith would not be needed. When we get to Glory, faith will not apply. Everything in Heaven will be secure – faith becomes sight, and evil is excluded. But this world is imperfect. Sin and the devil produce uncertainties. Logically, logic can't produce hope. Logic can't predict the next five minutes. It has to be faith in God.

The key words are **"I will."** God is the God of goodwill. When we come to Him, we find His arms open with a willing welcome: *"All day long have I held out my hands."* His face shines upon you!

Today's Scripture

Behold, I stand at the door and knock. If anyone hears My voice and opens the door, I will come in to him and dine with him, and he with Me.

(Revelation 3:20)

Daily Power!

By faith, I hear God knocking on the door of my heart, and I willingly open my heart to Him.

Today's Bible Reading

Job 23:1-17 through 27:1-23; II Corinthians 1:12-24 through 2:1-11; Psalm 41:1-13; Proverbs 22:5-6

Mark my Word
(for further study)

Matthew 6:10; 8:2; 12:18; Romans 10:21

Purely from the Word

The Book of Judges tells us about Gideon, who had heard the great things God had done when He brought His people out of bondage of Egypt, and wanted to see the same God at work. He believed the mighty arm of two centuries before had not lost its strength. Gideon rightly asked, *"Where are all His miracles which our fathers told us about?"* God showed him! The story of Gideon tells how a great triumph came about without human prowess and power. God delivered little Israel again as He delivered them before from Egypt, defeating the largest army of desert people ever mustered in those days so soundly that they never recovered to invade Israel again. Gideon only knew God from the past until then.

Some years later, Ezra – who belonged to the Jewish priestly caste, was brought up in Babylon, a palace officer highly thought of by the emperor of Medo-Persia – brought nearly six thousand of his exiled people back home, traveling through countryside infested with lawless tribesmen who ruthlessly preyed on travelers. The Emperor wanted Ezra and his people to travel under military protection during their five months' journey … but Ezra boasted that God – Who had looked after Israel for forty years in the wilderness and brought them out of Egypt – could well take care of them for five months. That sounds very religious … but the truth is that neither Ezra, nor anybody else then, had ever seen a vision, ever heard God's voice, witnessed a healing, or miracle, or had any sign from God whatever. Ezra was not a prophet … Ezra had nothing but the Scriptures. But He believed God, resting purely upon the written Scriptures. He put the whole project into operation under the wings of the Lord. This kind of "raw faith" based purely on the Word of God is available to you today!

Today's Scripture

The hand of our God is upon all those for good who seek Him; but His power and wrath are against all those who forsake Him.

(Ezra 8:22)

Daily Power!

Your Word I have hidden in my heart that I might not sin against You.

(Psalm 119:11)

Today's Bible Reading

Job 28:1-28
through 30:1-31;
II Corinthians 2:12-17;
Psalm 42:1-11;
Proverbs 22:7

Mark my Word
(for further study)

Judges 6:1-40;
7:1-25; 8:1-35;
Ezra 1:1-11
through 10:1-44;
Psalm 119:11

Quickened by the Spirit

Being filled with the Spirit is shown to have a dynamic and energizing effect or "power" (dunamis) in the New Testament and in the lives of millions. There is little Scripture to suggest that the Spirit comes upon men like a quiet breath, unobtrusive and unnoticed. It is usually very noticeable – manifestations of the Spirit include fire, wind, noise, wonders, outward signs, powers, and visible effects. God does not give His gifts to the unconverted nor His Holy Spirit to the world … but when we are born-again, we are encouraged to be filled, just as Paul admonished the churches.

I must emphasize again that we are seeing what Scripture says about these things. Some turn to Church history, trying to prove that apostolic power died out with the apostles. Church history, not the Bible, settles their doctrine. They could have wondered why it died down at the end of the apostolic age (although, in fact, it did not completely vanish). But there is not a single scrap of Bible evidence to indicate that it should have done this. A true scholar would want to know why. If we have learned anything from Church history, we know that unbelief and spiritual decline set in, and the power of the Spirit was therefore unlikely to be manifested widely.

Christianity was never intended to be anything but an outpouring of the Spirit. It is a reviving, quickening, renewing energy. Revival is not an extraordinary work above and beyond normal Christianity. Christianity is revival. There are not two Spirits – the Spirit received at new birth … and the Spirit of revival, which "sometimes comes down from Heaven and takes the field." The Spirit of God took the field long ago, and has never withdrawn from the battle! He does not "visit" now and then – He came to stay permanently. Having put His hand to the plow, He did not look back. Revival is always there when the Word is preached and the Spirit is present. Always be on the lookout for the impact of those components in your own life!

Today's Scripture

But if the Spirit of Him Who raised Jesus from the dead dwells in you, He Who raised Christ from the dead will also give life to your mortal bodies through His Spirit Who dwells in you.
(Romans 8:11)

Daily Power!

The Word and the Spirit are present and active in my life.

Today's Bible Reading

Job 31:1-40 through 33:1-33; II Corinthians 3:1-18; Psalm 43:1-5; Proverbs 22:8-9

Mark my Word
(for further study)

Ephesians 5:18

Intercession

Intercession is a special form of prayer for believers. But what exactly does it involve? First, it is a special assignment for believers. We are called to a special work, not just to ask for things for ourselves, but to stand before God for others. This is a vital feature of the superstructure of world redemption. Christ is the great Intercessor, and we are called to a similar role. Christ's intercessory work is on a different level from ours, but He is still our Role Model: *"So now we have a High Priest who perfectly fits our needs: completely holy, uncompromised by sin, with authority extending as high as God's presence in Heaven itself. Unlike the other high priests, He doesn't have to offer sacrifices for His own sins every day before He can get around to us and our sins. He's done it, once and for all: offered up Himself as the sacrifice. The law appoints as high priests men who are never able to get the job done right. But this intervening command of God, which came later, appoints the Son, Who is absolutely, eternally perfect."*

Intercession needs knowledge of those for whom we intercede, and of the One to Whom we address our prayers – this is a dual knowledge. Jesus took our nature on Himself, and also carried the nature of God in perfection – He was fully human, and fully divine. He identified Himself with us, and with God. We are human but have received "the Divine nature." We have kinship with both God and Man. And so we are fitted for the work to which God has appointed us: *"God's Spirit is right alongside helping us along. If we don't know how or what to pray, it doesn't matter. He does our praying in and for us, making prayer out of our wordless sighs, out aching groans. He knows us far better than we know ourselves, knows our pregnant condition, and keeps us present before God. That's why you can be so sure that every detail in our lives of love for God is working into something good."* What a powerful promise for you today! Think of it: because you love God, every detail in your life is being worked out for your **ultimate good**!

Today's Scripture

Take heed to the ministry which you have received in the Lord that you may fulfill it.

(Colossians 4:17)

Daily Power!

With Christ as my Role Model for intercession, I gladly will "stand in the gap" on behalf of my brothers and sisters in the world.

Today's Bible Reading

*Job 34:1-37
through 36:1-33;
II Corinthians 4:1-12;
Psalm 44:1-8;
Proverbs 22:10-12*

Mark my Word
(for further study)

*Ezekiel 22:30;
Romans 8:26-28
(the Message);
Colossians 4:17;
Hebrews 7:22-28;
II Peter 1:4*

Christ-like Compassion

We need more than just determination to enter into true intercession. Our Role Model, Jesus, poured out a flood of compassion. This was His sole motivating force. The effective power of intercession derives from a spontaneous outflow of concern and love. Generally speaking, it is naturally for our own family and friends – now it must embrace all the world. Although the Christian basis of prayer is not in the Old Testament, it is there that we find some great examples of intercession. Abraham interceded for Abimelech, and for the doomed cities of Sodom and Gomorrah. Moses, Solomon, Elijah, Hezekiah, Daniel, Ezra, Esther, Jeremiah, and the prophets all interceded for the nation of Israel. There are even intercessory Psalms!

As an evangelist, I am called to stand before very big crowds – but I dare not preach unless I know that intercessory prayer has ascended for those very people. Workers go out to the crusade area in advance and spend several weeks there, specifically to "prepare the ground" through intercession. Christians are recruited locally and instructed to "storm Heaven" with pleadings for the souls of men and women. Indeed, when these teams of intercessors knock on the Door of Glory, it adds weight to the prayers of tens of thousands of people around the whole world that the souls of those in the crowd may be delivered and saved!

During our evangelistic crusades, a spirit of prayer and intercession soaks my soul, often making me jump out of bed at three o'clock in the morning. Hundreds – sometimes thousands – of intercessors uphold me in prayer while I am ministering on the platform. This provides my spirit with "lift" like a powerful thermal for an eagle. I glance across a sea of faces … and rejoice that the devil's hand has been struck off their shoulders. **This is the most important thing that you can ever do for me – prayerfully intercede! Thank you for being my prayer partner!!!**

Today's Scripture

Likewise the Spirit also helps in our weaknesses. For we do not know what we should pray for as we ought, but the Spirit Himself makes intercession for us with groanings which cannot be uttered.
(Romans 8:26)

Daily Power!

I am committed to daily prayer and intercession for Evangelist Reinhard Bonnke and his worldwide ministry because I want to be a partner in this vast harvest of souls!

Today's Bible Reading

Job 37:1-24 through 39:1-30; II Corinthians 4:13-18 through 5:1-10; Psalm 44:9-26; Proverbs 22:13

Mark my Word
(for further study)

Romans 8:26-28

The rich must foot the bill
for the poor to hear the Gospel.
That's divine social justice.

I don't want to be a dollar millionaire,
but a souls millionaire.

I can't purr like a cat
when millions are perishing every day.
I want to roar like a lion!

Endurance

The Spirit-filled life is not an experience to be cultivated in special conditions, like indoor crocuses. Christians are not flowers, and they don't believe in "flower power." During the early expansion of the industrial cities of England, some clergymen could not be persuaded to take a parish among the hordes of unwashed workers because they said it might spoil their "spirituality." The Holy Spirit makes believers tough specimens for all conditions. They carry perpetual springtime in their souls and are "winterized," just as homes are prepared for the cold weather.

The apostles discovered a new resilience, a new strength within them, power that operated in their weakness and sent them out into a brutal pagan world to demolish its idol establishment and change history. That is a true mark of the Spirit-filled life. *"We are bound to thank God always for you, brethren, as it is fitting, because your faith grows exceedingly, and the love of every one of you abounds toward each other, so that we ourselves boast of you among the churches of God for your patience and faith in all your persecutions and tribulations that you endure, which is manifest evidence of the righteous judgment of God, that you may be counted worthy of the Kingdom of God, for which you also suffer."*

Things like that are happening today. A new age of persecution is testing the Church throughout the world. We may have to lay down our physical lives, but we are proving that the baptism in the Spirit makes people undefeatable. *"Who shall separate us from the love of Christ? Shall tribulation, or distress, or persecution, or famine, or nakedness, or peril, or sword? As it is written: 'For Your sake we are killed all day long; we are accounted as sheep for the slaughter.' Yet in all these things we are more than conquerors through Him Who loved us."*

Today's Scripture

Staying with it – that's what God requires. Stay with it to the end. You won't be sorry, and you'll be saved. All during this time, the Good News – the Message of the Kingdom – will be preached all over the world, a witness staked out in every country. And then the end will come.
(Matthew 24:13-14; the Message)

Daily Power!

Nothing shall separate me from the love of God which is in Christ Jesus.
(Romans 8:39)

Today's Bible Reading

Job 40:1-24
through 42:1-17;
II Corinthians 5:11-21;
Psalm 45:1-17;
Proverbs 22:14

Mark my Word
(for further study)

Matthew 24:13-14;
Romans 8:35-39;
II Thessalonians 1:3-5

2

When Arson is not a Crime

Today's Scripture

I'm baptizing you here in the river, turning your old life in for a Kingdom Life. The real action comes next: the main Character in this drama – compared to Him, I'm a mere stagehand – will ignite the Kingdom Life within you, a fire within you, the Holy Spirit within you, changing you from the inside out.

(Matthew 3:11-12; the Message)

Daily Power!

Let me burn on for Thee, dear Lord.

Today's Bible Reading

*Ecclesiastes 1:1-18
through 3:1-22;
II Corinthians 6:1-13;
Psalm 46:1-11;
Proverbs 22:15*

Mark my Word
(for further study)

*Exodus 3:2;
Matthew 3:11-12*

God sets driftwood on fire. Dry old sticks can burn for God, just like Moses' bush did: *"And the Angel of the Lord appeared to [Moses] in a flame of fire from the midst of a bush; so he looked, and behold, the bush was burning with fire, but the bush was not consumed."* Hallelujah! I don't pray, "Let me burn out for Thee, dear Lord." I don't want to be an ash heap. The amazing feature of the bush was that it didn't burn out. Too many of the Lord's servants are burning out. The cause of that is some other kind of fire. I say instead, "Let me burn **on** for Thee, dear Lord." The altar flame should never go out.

Without fire, there is no Gospel. The New Testament begins with fire. The first thing said about Christ by His first witness concerned fire. John the Baptist – himself a *"burning and shining light"* – declared: *"He will baptize you with the Holy Spirit and with **fire**. His winnowing fan is in His hand, and He will thoroughly clean out His threshing floor, and gather His wheat into the barn; but He will burn up the chaff with unquenchable **fire**."*

John the Baptizer introduced Jesus the Baptizer, the Baptizer with a vast difference. John used water – a physical element – but Christ was to use a spiritual element – holy fire. Water and fire … what a contrast! Not that John the Baptist had a "watery" religion (although there is plenty of that around, often combined with ice!). John the Baptist stood in the cold waters of Jordan baptizing – but Jesus the Baptizer stands in a river of liquid Fire!

The notable work of John was baptism. He announced the notable work of Jesus as baptism also. Baptism is the Lord's present great work. **Jesus, the Baptizer in the Holy Spirit.** This is Christ's major experience for you after you become a born-again believer.

The Sinner's Prayer

For those who have been Christians for a long time, hearing the Sinner's Prayer sometimes seems automatic, simply by rote. But when you and I are privileged to lead a single sinner (or a large number of sinners!) into a new relationship with Jesus Christ, that famous Prayer becomes fresh, new, exciting, powerful, life-changing. Never let us take this Prayer for granted … I often remember the wonderful transaction which took place in my own life, one that I shall never forget or underestimate. Jesus said: *"Whoever comes to Me, I will never drive away."* This includes you, wherever and whoever you are. When you repeat the following Prayer from the bottom of your heart, God will hear and answer, and save you on the spot:

Dear Heavenly Father,
I come to You in the Name of Jesus Christ.
I come with all my sins, burdens and addictions.
Wash me now with the precious Blood of Jesus shed on Calvary.
Break the chains of sin and Satan in my life and family.
Mark me with Your precious Blood externally, internally and eternally.
I want to be Your spirit, soul and body, for my time on Earth and in eternity.
I put my faith in You alone, Lord Jesus Christ.
You are the Son of the living God.
I believe with my heart what I now confess with my mouth:
You are my Savior, Lord and God.
Now I am born-again – a child of God!
I believe it and receive it in the Name of Jesus.
Amen.

Let the life-changing beauty of this prayer be one you choose to share with others.

Today's Scripture

And Jesus said to them, "I am the Bread of Life. He who comes to Me shall never hunger, and he who believes in Me shall never thirst."
(John 6:35)

Daily Power!

The most precious gift I possess is salvation through Jesus Christ my Lord.

Today's Bible Reading

Ecclesiastes 4:1-16 through 6:1-12;
II Corinthians 6:14-18 through 7:1-7;
Psalm 47:1-9;
Proverbs 22:16

Mark my Word
(for further study)

John 6:35-37

4

Household Salvation

*"Yet a man has risen to pursue you and seek your life, but the life of my lord shall be **bound in the bundle of the living** with the Lord your God; and the lives your enemies He shall sling out, as from the pocket of a sling."* If you want your family to keep together and know the Lord, you are on a winning ticket, everything going for you. The whys of it show you are wise. Look at this famous Bible incident:

"But at midnight Paul and Silas were praying and singing hymns to God, and the prisoners were listening to them. Suddenly there was a great earthquake, so that the foundations of the prison were shaken; and immediately all the doors were opened and everyone's chains were loosed. And the keeper of the prison, awaking from sleep and seeing the prison doors open, supposing the prisoners had fled, drew his sword and was about to kill himself."

The apostles Paul and Silas were in jail at Philippi when a midnight earthquake sprang the prison doors open and the jailer expected he had lost his prisoners. The discipline consequences were so terrifying to him that he was about to commit suicide. However, Paul, with typical presence of mind, shouted to reassure the poor man they were all still there. The reply of that jailer became classical: *"Sirs, what must I do to be saved?"*

Now the jailer had called them, "Sirs" – and Paul saw a chance for a witty play on words. Sirs in their language is the same word as Lord (Greek: "kurioi" and "kurion"). When the jailer asked, *"Sirs, what must I do to be saved?"* – Paul's answer was, *"Believe in the Lord Jesus, and you will be saved."* The jailer had called on Paul and Silas as kurioi, (which can mean lords), but they could not save him. The only one was *"The Lord Jesus."* Remember today: salvation is not in a host of lords, but in the Lord of Hosts!

Today's Scripture

Blessed be the Lord Who daily loads us with benefits, the God of our salvation! Our God is the God of salvation; and to God the Lord belong escapes from death.
(Psalm 68:19-20)

Daily Power!

The Lordship of Jesus is part of the salvation-package.

Today's Bible Reading

Ecclesiastes 7:1-29 through 9:1-18;
II Corinthians 7:8-16;
Psalm 48:1-14;
Proverbs 22:17-19

Mark my Word
(for further study)

I Samuel 25:29;
Acts 16:16-34

Working out His Will

We are privileged to learn from the experience of those who first ventured on the faith road, the pioneers: *"These things ... were written for our admonition upon whom the ends of the age have come."* Bible people struggled with God's goodness and the problems of evil. Their stories help us in the good fight of faith. We should remember that they had the same human nature, lived in the same world, and had the same God. James reminds us, *"Elijah was a man of the same feelings as ourselves."* In fact, the world was a far more frightening and mysterious place for them than for us with our advanced knowledge – but they learned to lean on God! Israel was the most harried and persecuted race on Earth, yet it was Israel who gave us the most glorious recommendation to trust in God: *"When you pass through the waters, I will be with you; and the rivers ... will not sweep over you. When you walk through the fire, you will not be burned ... for I am the Lord your God, the Holy One of Israel, your Savior."* After three thousand years, Israel is still present!

The story of the three Hebrews who were cast into a furnace alive and came out alive – is a picture of their race. For twenty-five hundred years, the Chosen People have gone through the furnace of affliction but emerged ... and occupy newspaper columns every day! No wonder the Psalmist wrote: *"If the Lord had not been on our side* [let Israel say] *... the raging waters would have swept us away."* The Bible message of faith comes to us out of the crucible of suffering, and yet it is the happiest Book ever written. It contains six hundred fifty-three references to joy and gladness! Some people can believe anything, even if it took place a long time ago, or will take place a long time ahead. They can accept a promise like: *"All things work together for good to them that love the Lord"* – which might mean eternity ... but they find it harder to believe: *"I am the Lord Who heals thee."* They believe in the God of Moses and Elijah, that Jesus did work miracles, that the Holy Spirit empowered the disciples ... but that is hollow believing unless it transfers to **today**, believing that He will carry on the good work! Be a present-tense believer!

Today's Scripture

Our help is in the Name of the Lord, Who made Heaven and Earth.
(Psalm 124:8)

Daily Power!

My time on Earth is finite, but my life with You, God, is eternal.

Today's Bible Reading

*Ecclesiastes 10:1-20 through 12:1-14;
II Corinthians 8:1-15;
Psalm 49:1-20;
Proverbs 22:20-21*

Mark my Word
(for further study)

*Exodus 15:26;
Isaiah 43:2-3;
Psalm 124:1, 5;
Romans 8:28;
I Corinthians 10:11;
James 5:17*

6

Action Words

Today's Scripture

Blessed be the God and Father of our Lord Jesus Christ, Who has blessed us with every spiritual blessing in the Heavenly places in Christ.
(Ephesians 1:3)

Daily Power!

My God is an active God, One intimately concerned with the details of my life.

Today's Bible Reading

Song Of Songs 1:1-17 through 4:1-16; II Corinthians 8:16-24; Psalm 50:1-23; Proverbs 22:22-23

Mark my Word
(for further study)

Exodus 3:1-22; 4:1-31; 6:5; Ephesians 1:3

About eight centuries after Abraham, God said He had not forgotten His covenant with Abraham – the father of all who believe – and so He spoke to Moses, telling him what He was doing. Look at these action words: *"The Lord **said**, see what I will **do** ... I **appeared** ... I have **established** My Covenant ... I have **heard** ... I have **seen** ... I am **come down** ... I **know** ... I **will send** thee ... I will **be with** thee ... I will **stretch out** My hand ... I have **remembered** ... I will **rid** you out of their bondage ... I will **redeem** you with a stretched out arm ... I will **take** you to Me for a people ... I will **be** to you a God ... I did **swear** to give, and I will **give**."*

That is a swift pen-sketch of the God of the past. One could build on that picture through the Scriptures when God became the God of Israel ... Samuel ... David ... Isaiah ... and then *"the God and Father of our Lord Jesus Christ."* That's the God that used to be. However, for some people, God stays as a used-to-be God. Millions get no further, and God for them is perhaps around "somewhere," but He generally seems to have gone into retirement. Or they say, "Jesus did wonderful things, was crucified, raised and taken to Heaven, end of the episode." Full stop. Their God is firmly anchored in history, Christ beyond the blue, never to be active again.

There is a book that claims God withdrew from the Bible. But since Jesus came, God becomes more and more vivid in the Bible, and in the world to this very day. It took three hundred forty-eight pages for this writer to put his theory together ... but just one miracle demolishes the idea! If anybody thinks God has dwindled away or done the vanishing trick, let them come to Africa. I've seen Him there, manifested in greater power than anywhere in the Old Testament, expelling demons, restoring the sick, healing the blind, the cripples and the deaf. God is shaking cities and nations. Perhaps that's where God "disappeared" – among people who believe Him! This is a fact of your Christian faith: your God is alive and real today, as much as He ever was, or ever will be!

The Proof of Jesus

The Church of Pentecost demonstrated that Jesus is alive. The proof that Jesus is alive should be in the Church itself – demonstrated by its energy, love and vitality. I am alive. I don't know any book being written, any lectures being delivered, or anybody who is trying to prove that I am alive – it isn't necessary. Living people tend to show up! **All Jesus wants is a chance to show that He is alive** – in the Church. When the Church spends its time trying to prove that Jesus was resurrected, people naturally think, "If Jesus is alive, why do they have to devote so much effort and reason to proving it? It should be obvious." **Compassion for the suffering and that matchless quality of Christ-like goodness that only He can impart must be there, clearly in evidence.**

"So Jesus answered and said, 'Assuredly I say to you, there is no one who has left house or brothers or sisters or father or mother or wife or children or lands, for My sake and the Gospel's, who shall not receive a hundredfold now in this time – houses and brothers and sisters and mothers and children and lands, with persecutions – and in the age to come, eternal life.'" When Jesus gave the Great Commission, He was talking to twelve men only – twelve ordinary men. It must have sounded an outrageous assignment! No king, no tyrant ever expected so much of so few. But Jesus did. **You can know the true Jesus because He demands the impossible.** That's how you can identify Him. That's Jesus every time – telling you to do what is beyond your natural abilities. "Kill Goliath! … Be a giant, not a grasshopper! … Move mountains! … Be perfect! … Walk on the waves! … Cleanse the lepers! … Raise the dead! … Teach all nations! … Preach the Gospel to **every** creature!" The idea of being saddled with the task of the Great Commission without Pentecostal power is (in my opinion) ridiculous. Whenever Jesus demands the impossible, He is there – the living Christ – to make it possible. That is the principle of a life with Jesus – all the glory goes to God! Hallelujah!

Today's Scripture

But Jesus looked at them and said, "With men it is impossible, but not with God; for with God all things are possible."
(Mark 10:27)

Daily Power!

When God asks me to do the impossible, I know He will equip me with His power and ability to fulfill the task.

Today's Bible Reading

Song of Songs 5:1-16 through 8:1-14;
II Corinthians 9:1-15;
Psalm 51:1-19;
Proverbs 22:24-25

Mark my Word
(for further study)

Mark 10:23-31

8

A Conquest of Christ

"When He ascended on high, He led captivity captive, and gave gifts to men." In his letter to the Ephesians, Paul used a word-picture that was all-too-familiar to the Ephesians, long accustomed to Roman domination. When Roman armies subdued some new part of the world, they brought back prisoners-of-war and paraded them through the streets of Rome in triumphal processions. The conquering general was celebrated and exalted on high. Prisoners were his booty, and he proudly gave captives as gifts to eminent Romans citizens. They became captive slaves of Romans – "captivity was led captive" – or the captives had new masters. Paul thought of himself as one of Christ's conquests, once a slave of sin. He called himself *"the prisoner of Christ,"* and added, *"Surely you have heard about the administration of God's grace that was given to me for you ... I became a servant of this Gospel by the gift of God's grace given me through the working of His power."* Notice that he says, *"God's grace ... was given to me for you"* – he was **given** the gift in order to **be** a gift.

Everyone whom Christ conquers is given a gift in order that they may **be** a gift. **No man is saved for himself alone.** Paul mentions five gifts: apostles, prophets, teachers, evangelists, and pastor-teachers. But I think we should be very clear about this: they are not the only gifted ones – others are needed too. That becomes more obvious when we know what the aim is. Paul describes it: *"So that the body of Christ may be built up until we all reach unity in the faith and in the knowledge of the Son of God, and become mature, attaining to the whole measure of the fullness of Christ."* That is the aim.

If you have believed that accepting Christ's gift of salvation is the same as buying a Heavenly insurance policy and that's it – then you've been deceived by the enemy, who wants to keep you powerless and ineffective in God's Kingdom. Being a Christian entails a responsibility to share your faith in Jesus Christ, to reach others with His loving, life-changing power, to grow in your faith, using the gifts which God has placed **within you** for His glory! Amen!

Today's Scripture

I, therefore, the prisoner of the Lord, beseech you to walk worthy of the calling with which you were called, with all lowliness and gentleness, with long-suffering, bearing with one another in love, endeavoring to keep the unity of the Spirit in the bond of peace.

(Ephesians 4:1-3)

Daily Power!

I choose to grow in my faith in Christ, and to share my faith with others.

Today's Bible Reading

Isaiah 1:1-31
through 2:1-22;
II Corinthians 10:1-18;
Psalm 52:1-9;
Proverbs 22:26-27

Mark my Word
(for further study)

Ephesians 3:1-21; 4:1-32

Miracle challenge to Faith

The supreme miracle in the New Testament was the raising of Lazarus from the dead. This story from John chapter 11 provides some classic lessons in faith. When Christ arrived, Martha met Him, saying, *"If You had been here, my brother would not have died."* In other words, Martha displayed a **marvelous faith for yesterday**: "If You had been here five days ago, I believe there would have been a miracle." **If** was Martha's word – a favorite word for believers believing for the past. Anything could have happened yesterday "if." Old faith is like the old manna from yesterday described in the books of Exodus and Numbers. If they kept yesterday's manna, it would breed worms and stink. Faith has to be today's faith. Jesus assured Martha, *"Your brother will rise again,"* and Martha replied, *"I know he will rise again, in the resurrection at the last day."* Martha had **faith for tomorrow** – the last day. It is so often like that: "There will be a miracle sometime … in God's good time … when revival comes … when things are different."

"Then many Jews who had come to Mary and had seen the things Jesus did, believed in Him. But some of them went away to the Pharisees and told them the things Jesus did. Then the chief priests… gathered a council and said, 'What shall we do? For this Man works many signs. If we let Him alone like this, everyone will believe Him, and the Romans will come and take away both our place and nation.'" When Christ worked miracles in the common streets of villages and cities … but according to the scholars of His day, it was the wrong time. It was only to happen when the apocalyptic world dawned. They believed one day the lame would leap like the heart and the blind would see – but not now, with Roman soldiers occupying the holy city! The miracles they saw in Jerusalem or Galilee couldn't be genuine – "It must be the devil at work," those old rabbis thought. Today, we are still inundated with skeptics … but we have a firm, unshakable faith in Christ Jesus our Lord! So give Him praise from your heart today!

Today's Scripture

Didn't I tell you that if you believed, you would see the glory of God?
(John 11:40; the Message)

Daily Power!

I have the benefits of both the treasury of the Word and the witness of the Holy Spirit in my heart, which enables me to believe.

Today's Bible Reading

Isaiah 3:1-26
through 5:1-30;
II Corinthians 11:1-15;
Psalm 53:1-6;
Proverbs 22:28-29

Mark my Word
(for further study)

John 11:1-57

Faith Breakthough

God plans for nothing to be ordinary. Jesus pointed to the lilies as examples of superb beauty – they were probably hyacinths, every petal and leaf of utter perfection: *"Consider the lilies, how they grow; they neither toil nor spin, and yet I say to you, even Solomon in all his glory was not arrayed like one of these."*

In the Kingdom of God, the extraordinary is so common it is ordinary. There is a story told about a rich man who somehow managed to persuade God to allow him to bring a suitcase filled with gold bars when he died and went to Heaven. Proud of his Earthly accomplishments of wealth and riches, this man opened the suitcase up when he arrived at the Pearly Gates. St. Peter scratched his head and asked, "Why are you bringing pavement?" Even the streets of Heaven are paved with gold!

More importantly, each person is special. The Shepherd with a hundred sheep searches for one gone astray. The boy David – the young outsider in Jesse's warrior family – was chosen to be anointed as the future king. Christianity is the religion of the unwanted. Faith is fertile ground in which God grows His plants and trees. He plants qualities in the man or woman of faith, which presently become admired anywhere. Little people take on stature by faith in Christ. They have zest, a grip on life, and tackle difficulties with determination and confidence. It is common for believers to perform beyond their natural capacity. Jesus said to the unlearned fisher lads on Galilee, *"I will make you!"* They switched direction … and also elevation.

That is very good, but some say, "I'm not a faith person." Well, here's bad news and good news. The bad is that: *"Without faith it is impossible to please God."* The good is that we can all be "faith persons!" Faith is so vital that God intends nobody to be faithless. The road to faith is wide open. You have faith today!

Today's Scripture

But without faith it is impossible to please Him, for he who comes to God must believe that He is, and that He is a Rewarder of those who diligently seek Him.
(Hebrews 11:6)

Daily Power!

The faith which God has given to me is vital to my every-day life.

Today's Bible Reading

Isaiah 6:1-13
through 7:1-25;
II Corinthians 11:16-33;
Psalm 54:1-7;
Proverbs 23:1-3

Mark my Word
(for further study)

Matthew 6:33;
Luke 8:14; 12:27;
Hebrews 11:6;
James 4:3

Laser Beams

In Western churches, comparatively few unbelievers venture to expose themselves to evangelism. Usually they are brought to a meeting by somebody who has sought God on their behalf – perhaps for years – and the ground is watered with tears and prepared. What about the teeming populations of Africa, Asia, China, India, Japan, and Indonesia? How many are ever named personally before the Lord? These great unprayed-for masses are struggling human beings like ourselves, however remotely acquainted we are with them. If we do not intercede for them, who will?

Everyone who calls, "Help, God!" gets help. But how can people call for help if they don't know Who to trust? And how can they know Who to trust if they haven't heard of the One Who can be trusted? And how can they hear if nobody tells them? And how is anyone going to tell them, unless someone is sent to do it? That's why Scripture exclaims, *"A sight to take your breath away! Grand processions of people telling all the good things of God!"*

In the darkness of a bedeviled world, our prayers cut the darkness like lasers, becoming channels through which God's blessing may reach Earth, and transmitting the power-currents of Calvary and the Resurrection: "Believing-prayer will heal you, and Jesus will put you on your feet … The prayer of a person living right with God is something powerful to be reckoned with." Intercession jams the wavelengths of the devil: *"Resist the devil and he will flee from you."* Certainly the devil will resist – and the world will howl in protest – too long undisturbed. The works of Satan are many, but they **must go**: *"For this purpose was the Son of Man manifested, that He might destroy the works of the devil."* Remember: the prayers that you pray today will not help and bless you … they will be used by God to help dismantle the works of the devil … in ways you may never see with your eyes. Keep Praying!

Today's Scripture

Let your light so shine before men, that they may see your good works and glorify your Father in Heaven.
(Matthew 5:16)

Daily Power!

Father, give the eyes of my heart a wider vision, to see all the peoples of the world as Yours.

Today's Bible Reading

Isaiah 8:1-22 through 9:1-21; II Corinthians 12:1-10; Psalm 55:1-23; Proverbs 23:4-5

Mark my Word
(for further study)

Matthew 5:13-16; Romans 10:13-18 (the Message); James 4:7; 5:18 (the Message); I John 3:8

The Distinction of Intercession

Intercession honors those for whom we pray ... better than recommending them for "the Honors List." In II Kings, we read about a woman who was called *"great"* – but she was not famous, nor did she want to be. She gave quiet hospitality to Elisha the prophet ... and to thank her, he asked, *"Do you want me to speak on your behalf to the king or to the commander of the army?"* *"No!"* she said – high circles did not attract her – but she **did** want Elisha to name her to God. He did so, and this began the thrilling miracle story of the birth of her long-awaited son, his tragic death, and eventually his being raised to life again! Elisha named her to the Lord ... and it brought her immortal fame.

Praying brings distinction to ourselves, and to those for whom we pray. It highlights them, makes "nobodies" into "somebodies" before God. He turns His attention to them – just think of that! *"I looked for a man among them who would build up the wall and stand before Me in the gap on behalf of the land so I would not have to destroy it, but I found none."* Politicians, talkers, musicians ... but not one intercessor. If He had found a man, his name would be in The Book, immortalized. To intercede means we join an elite company notable in Heaven.

It may be the only practical thing we can do for some people. Elisha could only pray for his hostess. To omit prayer from our activities is loveless, grieving to the Spirit of God. Samuel looked at wayward Israel and said, *"You have done all this evil. As for me, far be it for me that I should sin against the Lord by failing to pray for you."*

It is not difficult for us to think of individuals who need our prayers ... but we should never forget the awesome power of interceding for nations. **Your prayers make a difference.**

Today's Scripture

Therefore I exhort first of all that supplications, prayers, intercessions, and giving of thanks be made for all men.
(I Timothy 2:1)

Daily Power!

Prayerful intercession is a practical, powerful weapon ... and I will use it every day.

Today's Bible Reading

Isaiah 10:1-34
through 11:1-16;
II Corinthians 12:11-21;
Psalm 56:1-13;
Proverbs 23:6-8

Mark my Word
(for further study)

II Kings 4;
II Samuel 12:20, 23;
Ezekiel 22:30;
I Timothy 2:1

God and His Children

God has many good things in store for His children. The promise is: *"Seek and you shall find,"* for they are obtainable only by direct application. Actually, they are promised and most of them are listed in Scripture: *"No good thing does He withhold from those whose walk is blameless."* When we come to the end of natural provision, Jesus said, *"Ask and you shall receive"* ... *"Everyone who asks receives ... If you then ... know how to give good gifts to your children, how much more will your Father in Heaven give good gifts to those who ask Him?"* If we ask for good, He will not send evil, never! *"All **good** gifts come down from the Father of lights."*

The exercise of faith in prayer is a healthy activity. The bird in the nest must learn to fly and gather what is available. Having to ask is an excellent reminder to us of our dependency on God, and is arranged to bring us to seek Him. It gives birth to a spirit of childlikeness, looking to our Heavenly Father at all times. It is fellowship – **family fellowship with our Father**. Jesus described this family relationship clearly – after all, He lived in a human family Himself! The parallels between human and Heavenly families are obvious: the nurturing Father, the kids just learning to get along: *"Father, reveal Who You are. Set the world right. Keep us alive with three square meals. Keep us forgiven with You, and forgiving others. Keep us safe from ourselves, and the Devil ... Don't bargain with God. Be direct ... If your little boy asks for a serving of fish, do you scare him with a live snake on his plate? If your little girl asks for an egg, do you trick her with a spider? ... Don't you think the Father Who conceived you in love will give the Holy Spirit when you ask Him?"* It is our Father's desire that you have a healthy relationship with Him, and with the others in His great family.

Today's Scripture

Don't bargain with God. Be direct. Ask for what you need. This isn't a cat-and-mouse, hide-and-seek game we're in. If your child asks for bread, do you trick him with sawdust? If he asks for fish, do you scare him with a live snake on his plate? As bad as you are, you wouldn't think of such a thing. You're at least decent to your own children. So don't you think the God Who conceived you in love will be even better?
(Matthew 7:7-11; the Message)

Daily Power!

Having to ask (in prayer) is an excellent reminder of our dependency on God, and is arranged to bring us to seek Him.

Mark my Word
(for further study)

Psalm 84:11;
Matthew 7:7-11;
Luke 11:2-4, 11-13
(the Message);
John 16:24;
James 1:17

Today's Bible Reading

Isaiah 12:1-22
through 14:1-32;
II Corinthians 13:1-14;
Psalm 57:1-11;
Proverbs 23:9-11

Today's Scripture

If you ask anything in My Name, I will do it.
(John 14:14)

Daily Power!

If we want God to work, we must work in prayer, with right motivation.

Today's Bible Reading

Isaiah 15:1-9 through 18:1-7; Galatians 1:1-24; Psalm 58:1-11; Proverbs 23:12

Mark my Word
(for further study)

Genesis 2:15; John 14:13-14; James 4:2-3 (the Message)

Interdependency

God could have arranged to do everything for us ... but the object is to lead a child to stand on his own two feet. God's ultimate purpose is that we will not be just helpless dependants – like babes at the breast – but His co-workers. At present, prayer is our sole access if we wish to be useful to Him. It is so often forgotten that He actually created the kind of world in which prayer would be necessary. Prayer was not an afterthought when the devil upset things. Even Jesus prayed.

To help the ongoing affairs of the Kingdom of God, prayer is essential. A lot goes on that God does not want, but we should pray that His will shall be done. We ask, **then** He performs – He planned we should cooperate in that way, just as He put Adam *"into the Garden of Eden to dress it and keep it."* That is how to read the promise: *"I will do whatever you ask in My Name."* We ask for whatever is necessary for the will of God on Earth to be fulfilled. *"I will do whatever you ask in My Name"* – we are His collaborators. The world and the people in it need care, and the promise that Christ will do whatever we ask is for the fulfillment of that purpose, not to get the moon or half a dozen Rolls Royce cars.

It is obvious that the apostle James (the half-brother of Jesus) grew up in an all-too-human family, with all the tugs and pulls of siblings. His description of human family life – and how God wants us to learn to view Him as our Father – rings so true: *"Where do you think all these appalling wars and quarrels come from? Do you think they just happen? Think again. They come about because you want your own way, and fight for it deep inside yourselves. You lust for what you don't have and are willing to kill to get it. You want what isn't yours and will risk violence to get your hands on it. You wouldn't think of just asking God for it, would you? And why not? Because you know you'd be asking for what you have no right to. You're spoiled children, each wanting your own way."* God is not going to wet-nurse us. He feeds the sparrows ... but does not throw food into their nests. If you want God to work, you must work in prayer, with right motivation.

Fire-Starters

The Gospel is a fire lighter. The Holy Spirit is not given just to help you preach eloquent sermons – He is to put a flame into human hearts. Unless Christ sets you alight, you can bring no fire to Earth: *"Without Me, you can do nothing."* Jesus instructed the disciples not to do anything until they were to receive *"power from on high."* When that power came, the Spirit revealed Himself as tongues of flame sitting upon each one of them.

Jesus previously had sent the disciples out in pairs. It reminds me of Samson sending foxes out two-by-two, as the animals carried torches for an arson raid on the enemy's corn shocks and vineyards. The disciples also were sent out two by two, carriers of the divine torch, fire-starters for God, scorching the devil's territories with the fire Gospel. They were new Elijahs bringing fire from Heaven.

Until the fire falls, evangelism and church activities can be very routine and unexciting. Pulpit essays, homilies, moralizing, or preaching about how you think the economy of the country should be run – all that is glacial work. No divine spark brings combustion to ice. No one goes home ignited. In contrast, the two who listened to Jesus on the Emmaus road went home with warmed hearts. I am sure He didn't talk politics to them, nor offer suggestions and advice. That wouldn't make their hearts burn. Jesus came *"to send fire on the Earth."* The mission of Jesus is not a holiday picnic – Satan is determined it will not be. He is a destroyer. The Lord sends out His servants with a warning of physical dangers: *"And do not fear those who kill the body but are not able to kill the soul. But rather fear Him Who is able to destroy both soul and body in Hell."* What is mere physical hurt, compared to a life ablaze with the joy and zest of Jesus? What is bodily danger compared to the Crown of Life or to the wonderful work He gives us to do? *"Heal the sick, cleanse the lepers, raise the dead, cast out demons. Freely you have received, freely give."* Allow the Holy Spirit to set your heart alight today!

Today's Scripture

Whatever I tell you in the dark, speak in the light; and what you hear in the ear, preach on the housetops. And do not fear those who kill the body but cannot kill the soul; but rather fear Him Who is able to destroy both soul and body in Hell.
(Matthew. 10:27-28)

Daily Power!

What is mere physical hurt, compared to a life ablaze with the joy and zest of Jesus?

Today's Bible Reading

Isaiah 19:1-25
through 21:1-17;
Galatians 2:1-16;
Psalm 59:1-17;
Proverbs 23:13-14

Mark my Word
(for further study)

Judges 15:1-8;
Matthew 10:8, 28;
Luke 10:1; 12:49; 24:49;
John 15:5

Two Courtroom Dramas

What a relief to know that Jesus Christ acts as our own Advocate in the Court of Heaven, bringing our case before the Most High and Mighty Judge: God the Father. Imagine it: the Courtroom of Heaven, with serious-looking officials, uniformed police, the prosecutor (Satan himself), and the Judge. Having reviewed the evidence – we were all born in sin, none were righteous – the prosecutor makes his summation and rests his case. After a brief interval, the jury returns with a verdict: "Guilty as charged." The defendant stands in the dock condemned. He must suffer the penalty, pay the price. If he asked to be justified, the solemn Court would burst into disbelieving laughter.

Now picture a different scene: a sinner stands before the highest Judge of all. The accuser, Satan, is there, and dazzling ranks of sinless angels look on. The sinner knows he is guilty. The Judge of all the Earth must act justly. The sinner's Advocate, Jesus, appears and challenges the accuser, "Where is your evidence?" That causes quite a stir! The accuser is embarrassed. He cannot produce any evidence, no damning exhibit, no deposition, no record. Not a single scrap of proof. No sign of this man's wrongdoing can be discovered in all the Universe. What has happened to it?

I will tell you: our sinful evidence has been destroyed! Christ Jesus gathered it all unto Himself and carried it into the fires of divine judgment which swept across Calvary. During those awful hours, the record was consumed, leaving no trace. Colossians 2 describes it: *"He forgave us all our sins, having blotted out the written code, with its regulations, that was against us and that stood opposed to us; he took it away, nailing it to the Cross."* "Blotted out" means not just crossed out, but wiped out. Those sins are **yours** and **mine** – gone because of the Blood of Jesus!

Today's Scripture

My little children, these things I write to you so that you may not sin. And if anyone sins, we have an Advocate with the Father, Jesus Christ the righteous. And He Himself is the propitiation for our sins, and not for ours only but also for the whole world.

(I John 3:1-2)

Daily Power!

My Attorney, Jesus Christ, offers His services free-of-charge, paid for with His own Blood.

Today's Bible Reading

Isaiah 22:1-25 through 24:1-23; Galatians 2:17-21 through 3:1-9; Psalm 60:1-12; Proverbs 23:15-16

Mark my Word
(for further study)

Colossians 2:13-14

"Made innocent!"

In the Court of Heaven, Jesus the Advocate makes His sensational claim: "There is no evidence against this man." Then the Throne of Justice becomes the Throne of Grace. Satan the accuser retires in baffled rage. The Judge beckons the accused and hands him a document called "The New Covenant." He opens it. There he sees that it carries the red seals of the sprinkled Blood of Jesus. It is a royal exoneration declaring, "This court finds no evidence and therefore no case against you." *"There is therefore now no condemnation to them which are in Christ Jesus."* The Judge has signed it saying: *"I will remember their sins and their misdeeds no more."*

The prisoner is free, justified by grace. Then the whole Court rises and applauds, for there is joy in Heaven over one sinner who repents. When you are justified by grace, God the Judge wants you to know it. Those who wait for the Day of Judgment to discover whether they are saved or damned, do not understand salvation at all. Knowing the promise of Jesus – *"Most assuredly I say to you: he who hears My Words and believes in Him Who sent Me has everlasting life, and shall not come into judgement, but has passed from death into life"* – is part of salvation. He lifts that fear from you when you get saved.

"Therefore let it be known to you, brethren, that through this Man is preached to you the forgiveness of sins; and by Him everyone who believes is justified from all things from which you could not be justified." The word "judgment" in that Scripture is the Greek word "krisis", from which the word "crisis" is derived. So you can say that a born-again believer will never know such a "crisis" hour, standing in the judgment, waiting to find out whether he is saved or lost. The matter is already settled. Because of Christ, you have already passed judgment – Hallelujah!

Today's Scripture

There is therefore now no condemnation to those who are in Christ Jesus, who do not walk according to the flesh, but according to the Spirit.
(Romans 8:1)

Daily Power!

I once was lost, but now I'm found; was blind, but now I see.

Today's Bible Reading

Isaiah 25:1-12 through 28:1-13; Galatians 3:10-22; Psalm 61:1-8; Proverbs 23:17-18

Mark my Word
(for further study)

Luke 15:7; John 5:24; Acts 13:38-39; Romans 8:1; Hebrews 10:17

Family Salvation

When we pray and plan for the salvation of our own families, we are moving in the stream of Divine activity. God especially wants to be in our families. The Bible anticipates the *"the whole family in Heaven and Earth."* The family is not just a human ideal to help strengthen society, its value is more than just social. It is the way God planned the world should be run! It is part of His eternal objective.

The secular world talks about the families being the "building blocks" of society. They are – but building blocks need building together, not left lying around. Families can structure society only when cemented together. There is one element on Earth to do this – not patriotism, but the Gospel. It explains the Church, the Family of God: *"Since He gives to all life, breath, and all things; and He has made from one blood every nation of men to dwell on all the face of the Earth, and has determined their pre-appointed times and the boundaries of their dwellings."* With Bible truths like this behind us, we can plan for the salvation of our household. Blood is thicker than water. If we pray especially for our loved ones, it is natural – the way God meant it – and we have everything going for us. In Acts 16, Paul showed that if the jailer was saved, the whole family was on the way to salvation.

One of the wonderful possibilities and blessings of Godly parents is that children will not break their hearts and wreck their own lives. Churches are so often composed of family generations – a wonderful stabilizing and assuring thing, children honoring Godly parents. *"Blessed is every one who fears the Lord, who walks in His ways … You shall be happy and it shall be well with you. Your wife shall be like a fruitful vine in the very heart of your house, your children like olive plants all around your table … Behold, children are a heritage from the Lord."* It doesn't take long to show. It may seem a youthful blip when a teenage girl becomes interested in a boy … but if he is a born-again child of God, it can mean the start of another new Godly dynasty to last for generations.

Today's Scripture

So that they should seek the Lord, in the hope that they might grope for Him and find Him, though He is not far from each one of us.

(Acts 17:27)

Daily Power!

The importance of families in God's grand design is never to be underestimated.

Today's Bible Reading

Isaiah 28:14-29 through 30:1-11; Galatians 3:23-29 through 4:1-31; Psalm 62:1-12; Proverbs 23:19-21

Mark my Word
(for further study)

Psalm 127:3; 128:1-4; Acts 17:25-26

No Alternative

Scripture stresses the importance of children brought up in the fear of God, not yoked with unbelievers. This is more than a social category – such as training children to become faithful Baptists, or staunch Pentecostals, or good Methodists – but a matter of children learning the critical necessity of following Christ, putting God before prestige, living by a spiritual code and for the Gospel of Christ. Nothing in the world is important except that which ties in with the Gospel. The rest will vanish.

There is no alternative. Children either have a spiritual basis or no basis, either a guiding light or no light. The world – the great illusion – will compete for their hearts … and it has a magnetic and immediate appeal. Secular pressures bear down powerfully upon everyone, and inexperienced children should be shown the other side: eternal and spiritual realities. Time and place should be given to the counter-measure of the things of the Spirit, and their minds protected with the Word of God. It forms a watertight bulkhead against however great the ocean.

One text from the devil's credo: "Don't push religion down our throats!" This is a cynical, breathtaking remark … and downright hypocritical! Godlessness is pushed down our throats without apology. People openly sneer at Christians with no other intention but godlessness. Another Satanic maxim: "Don't foist upon children your own religious prejudices. Let them feel free to believe with an unprejudiced mind." Free? The world leaves nobody free and unprejudiced: *"He made you alive, who were dead in sins, in which you once walked according to the course of this world, according to the spirit who now woks in the sons of disobedience, among whom also we all once conducted ourselves in the lusts of our flesh, fulfilling the desires of the flesh and of the mind."* How much Godly influence really touches us day by day? In our secular cities, the day is likely to be completely devoid of any spiritual influence … but the pressures will be an environment of godlessness, blasphemy, corruption, unbelief and cynicism. Make Godly living your daily bread!

Today's Scripture

Do not be unequally yoked together with unbelievers. For what fellowship has righteousness with lawlessness? And what communion has light with darkness?
(II Corinthians 6:14)

Daily Power!

Nothing in the world is important except that which ties in with the Gospel.

Today's Bible Reading

Isaiah 30:12-33 through 33:1-12; Galatians 5:1-12; Psalm 63:1-11; Proverbs 23:22

Mark my Word
(for further study)

II Corinthians 6:14-18; Ephesians 2:1-3

20

A Warning about Faith

For all the wonderful things we know about faith, it is also important to know: faith is not for the gold-digger. God – Who made all the wealth there is – is not against wealth … but those whose god is gold can expect no help from Heaven!

There has been an epidemic of people who have deliberately misused the message of faith to disguise their pursuit of wealth – shame on them! These people are idol-worshippers – placing false doctrines and other "things" ahead of their relationship with God – and their lives are bound to fall into ruin: *"The idols of the nations are silver and gold, the work of men's hands. They have mouths, but the do not speak; eyes they have, but they do not see; they have ears, but they do not hear; nor is there any breath in their mouths. Those who make them are like them; **so is everyone who trusts in them**."* Stay away from these people who hide their unrighteousness behind a façade of "teaching true faith"!

Jesus' Parable of the Sower uses a word which has passed into the English language: "hedonism" (Greek: "hedonon"), the pursuit of pleasure. *"That which fell among thorns are they, which, when they have heard, go forth, and are choked with cares and riches and **pleasures** of this life, and bring no fruit to perfection."* The same plain words address us in James: *"When you ask, you do not receive, because you ask with wrong motives, that you may spend what you get on your pleasures."* A life-aim of riches is stupid, because at the end, we can't take it with us. But it is eternal profit to follow Christ's directions: *"Seek first the Kingdom of God and His righteousness, and all these things shall be added to you."* You line your faith up with the pure Word of God – and it cannot fail!

Today's Scripture

Give your entire attention to what God is doing right now, and don't get worked up about what may or may not happen tomorrow. God will help you deal with whatever hard things come up when the time comes.
(Matthew 6:33; the Message)

Daily Power!

I know that faith is a powerful weapon in my hand, and I will always use it for God's glory.

Today's Bible Reading

Isaiah 33:13-24 through 36:1-22; Galatians 5:13-26; Psalm 64:1-10; Proverbs 23:23

Mark my Word
(for further study)

Psalm 135:15-18; Matthew 6:33; Luke 8:14

Divine Principle of Action

The absolute ABC of faith is that as we act, God acts. We respond to Him by faith, and He responds to us for faith. Paul found that it operated like the blood flowing through his veins. *"I live; yet not I, but Christ lives in me: and the life, which I now live in the flesh, I live by the faith of the Son of God."*

Here are some examples from Scripture: *"They were all filled with the Holy Ghost and began to speak with other tongues as the Spirit gave them utterance"* – **They** spoke and the **Spirit** gave them language … *"Work out your own salvation with fear and trembling. For it is God Who works in you both to will and to do of His good pleasure"* – this has a play on words: *"God is in you to do His goodwill"* or He puts the desire in us to do His desire. That is what being "led of the Spirit" means … *"Holy men spoke as they were moved by the Holy Ghost"* – Jesus said, *"When they shall deliver you up, take no thought how or what ye shall speak: for it shall be given you in that same hour what ye shall speak. For it is not ye that speak, but the Spirit … in you"* … *"The steps of a good man are ordered by the Lord"* – we walk and God steers us … *"O Lord, I know that the way of man is not in himself: it is not in man who walks to direct his own steps"* … Three times we read, *"He makes my feet like hinds feet"* – which is what Isaiah meant: *"They shall run and not be weary; they shall walk and not faint."*

God doesn't want you to be like a pair of gloves, uselessly waiting to be picked up off the shelf, lifeless. People pray, "Use me, oh Lord" – but do nothing. There's the idea that being used of God means being another Luther, Wesley or Livingston. But you are alive to get on with the task at your elbow! That is all-important for you. Today, purpose to be used by God!

Today's Scripture

Those who wait on the Lord shall renew their strength; they shall mount up with wings like eagles, they shall run and not be weary, they shall walk and not faint.
(Isaiah 40:31)

Daily Power!

Being used by God is the only way to live successfully.

Today's Bible Reading

Isaiah 37:1-38 through 38:1-22; Galatians 6:1-18; Psalm 65:1-13; Proverbs 23:24-25

Mark my Word
(for further study)

II Samuel 22:34; Psalm 18:33; 37:23; Isaiah 40:31; Jeremiah 10:23; Habakkuk 3:19; Acts 2:4; Philippians 2:12-13; Galatians 2:20; II Peter 1:21

Today's Scripture

Men always ought to pray and not lose heart.
(Luke 18:1)

Daily Power!

God speaks to us anytime He wants ... He doesn't wait until we pray."

Today's Bible Reading

Isaiah 39:1-31
through 41:1-16;
Ephesians 1:1-23;
Psalm 66:1-20;
Proverbs 23:26-28

Mark my Word
(for further study)

Habakkuk 2:1;
Luke 18:1-8

God doesn't pray

Prayer is the act of speaking to God, not God speaking to us. God speaks to us anytime He wants ... He doesn't wait until we pray. In fact, nobody in the Bible seemed to be praying when God spoke to them. God is close to us and can speak at all times. It may be that we can't hear Him sometimes because we are clamoring for Him to say something different. Prayer is basically a time to pour out our hearts to Him. Listening is another thing. We should constantly be ready, for He speaks at any time. It is no use rising from our knees and saying He hasn't spoken. We can't demand that He should speak at that precise time, like switching on the radio. **We should never be switched off.** He may interrupt our own program with specific personal instructions at any time.

It may seem strange to Christians today that there is nothing whatever in Scripture about praying to hear from God, for guidance or anything else. There is plenty about hearing His voice, but almost nothing about waiting to hear – except when Habakkuk stood at his watch to hear from God. If we pray and wait to hear, we may hear ... but whatever voice speaks, we need to know who it is. The dangers are obvious. It is a fact of our nature – a psychological fact – that our own desires can be so loud that they sound like Divine commands. Shout long enough about what we already want to do, and the echo will come back sooner or later ... but it is our own voice, not the voice of God.

People talk of how they wrestled with God over a decision. Looked at honestly, that is an invidious procedure. Is God like that? In fact, they are wrestling with their own will, not God. They want Him to agree. Do we really imagine we must wrestle with God to pry the secret out of Him about what He wants us to do? Surely He would just tell us without an all-out wrestling match with the Almighty! It is ridiculous to approach God that way, as if He were unwilling to tell us His will. The business of asking God for directions suggests He has neglected to guide us as He said He would. God **never** shuts His children out – that means He **always** hears you!

Three Pillars of Wisdom

God uses Manpower … Man needs God's power … God works when people work. These are three pillars of wisdom. To unfold these principles, I shall begin with the basics. Millions of sermons are preached and heard by hundreds of millions of people, but the effect is not so great. Preachers complain, "The people don't do what I say." That is it, of course. Of all those who listen, how many feel like exerting themselves, putting themselves out to serve the Lord? Are the rest content only to sing, worship and enjoy a good sermon? God wants us to be *"doers, and not hearers only."* I am not passing on mere knowledge, but trying to lead everybody into the dynamic power and blessing of God.

Let me encourage you first. You can be absolutely sure that God has something for you to do now, and a special privileged place in which to put you. You are perhaps already there … but just haven't realized it. Many think that God has some great thing for them to do – one day. Perhaps He has, but what you are doing **now** is important too, if you are obeying Him. There's a job to suit you, and a job for which you are being prepared. If you think you are not in on these things, it isn't true. Don't deprive yourself of your right and proper place in the glorious scheme of God.

Once you realize that first point – that **God uses Manpower** – you can move on. If God wants you to do something, He will give you the ability to do it. Very likely it may stretch you beyond what you have done before. He wants you to grow. Whatever lies before you, God put it there. You can move mountains. Say this to yourself: "God means me to be more than I thought I was." Don't measure what you should do by your gift – measure the gift by what you should do. It will match. God specializes in the impossible. He thinks only in terms of the impossible. He wants this fact to show in the lives of those who belong to Him. He commands the impossible – and then makes it possible – to His glory. My purpose is to reveal to you the ways to His power.

Today's Scripture

I'm so grateful to Christ Jesus for making me adequate to do this work. He went out on a limb, you know, in trusting me with this ministry.
  (I Timothy 1:12; the Message)

Daily Power!

I am in partnership with my Heavenly Father to fulfill His work on Earth.

Today's Bible Reading

Isaiah 41:17-29 through 43:1-13; Ephesians 2:1-22; Psalm 67:1-7; Proverbs 23:29-35

Mark my Word
(for further study)

I Timothy 1:12; James 1:22

24

Powers of a new Order

I have seen countless mighty wonders and unclean spirits cast out by the finger of God. Christ explained it: *"If I cast out demons with the finger of God, surely the Kingdom of God has come upon you."* We must look carefully at that explanation. *"The Kingdom"* – what is it? If we are to catch the real secret of the faith, we must understand the Kingdom. Jesus talked about it all the time. (And He knew what He was talking about: the Pharisees tried to accuse Him of representing the kingdom of Satan!) We only need to consider it from one angle at this point.

We have had different historical ages – the Stone Age, the Bronze Age, the Dark Ages, and so on. These time periods were given special names to show their main features. We also have the Christian Age. We even register our calendars and clocks by designating Anno Domini – "in the year of our Lord." Is this just another division of history? No. This Age is unique. During the Christian Age, another age also broke in: "the Kingdom of God." Jesus began to preach: *"Repent, for the Kingdom of God is at hand."*

The Kingdom is the realm of God in which God's power is supreme. When Christ came, He introduced the activity of God – the Holy Spirit – into our mundane affairs. It was a new resource … not physical power like water, wind or nuclear energy, for these are all part of the natural world. This was the power of a world with laws far above the laws of nature.

Read this sentence carefully: **"In the beginning, God made this world by the power of another world."** In Christ Jesus, He re-introduced the powers of that creative world into the earthly scene. That is the Kingdom of God. And that is where you and I live today!

Today's Scripture

There are some standing here who will not taste death till they see the Kingdom of God with power.

(Mark 9:1)

Daily Power!

The Kingdom of God was brought in this world by a word.

Today's Bible Reading

Isaiah 43:14-28
through 45:1-10;
Ephesians 3:1-21;
Psalm 68:1-18;
Proverbs 24:1-2

Mark my Word
(for further study)

Matthew 4:17;
Mark 9:1;
Luke 11:20

A million-candlepower Light

When Paul the apostle was preaching in an upstairs room in Troas, *"there were many lights"* there. The Bible writers had a way of saying that kind of thing with conveying a spiritual truth. There were two kinds of lights there – the oil lamps ... and the room full of Christians who were the true *"many lights."* This is what believers are. *"You were once darkness, but now you are light in the Lord."* Believers are stars – unbelievers are black holes from which light never escapes. Faith makes us *"children of God without fault in a crooked and depraved generation, in which* [we] *shine like stars in the universe."*

A Christian believer needs a church – just as a candle needs a candlestick, a tree needs soil, an electric bulb needs a socket. Without a candlestick, a candle cannot stand ... without soil, a tree cannot grow ... without a socket, an electric bulb cannot shine. Neither can you. Without fellowship, a Christian can neither stand nor grow nor shine.

Jesus doesn't put you on the shelf. He has a special niche especially for each of us in His edifice. He said, *"You are the light of the world"* – single lamps, and also many lights together. It was a single lamp when He said it should be *"put on its stand, and it gives light to everyone in the house."* One-candlepower for one house. But He also said, *"You are the light of **the world**. A city set on a hill cannot be hidden."* A city is not one-candlepower but a million-candlepower. When Christ said, *"**You** are the light of the world,"* it was a plural *"you."* He brings *"many lights"* together, people combining, mingling flame with flame. The *"city set on a hill"* is a **church**. In Troas, there were *"many lights"* together because it was a big room. The world is a big place and many lights are needed. The children's hymn said: "You in your small corner and I in mine" ... but there's more than dark corners – there's an entire dark planet. There is no light where there is no faith in God. If you have a living faith in God, always remember the whole globe needs your light. Let others see your light wherever you go!

Today's Scripture

On this rock I will build My church, and the gates of Hades shall not prevail against it.
(Matthew 16:18)

Daily Power!

It is my heart's desire to shine as brightly as I can for Christ, for as long as I can, to as many people as I can.

Today's Bible Reading

Isaiah 45:11-25 through 48:1-11; Ephesians 4:1-16; Psalm 68:19-35; Proverbs 24:3-4

Mark my Word
(for further study)

Matthew 5:14-15

Business in great Waters

Spiritually, the world today is like it was at the very beginning: *"darkness was upon the face of the deep."* **but** *"God said, 'Let there be light,' and there was light."* Today, God is saying, *"Let there be light!"* … *"God, Who commanded the light to shine out of darkness, has shined in our hearts, to give the light of the knowledge of the glory of God in the face of Jesus Christ."*

After Christ rose from the dead, the disciples began brightening up the world with the light of the Gospel. We should do the same. The establishment complained that they had *"filled Jerusalem with* [their] *doctrine,"* and a little later it was said, *"Those who have turned the world upside down have come here also."* That is exactly what God said He would do: *"The way of the wicked he turns upside down."* The way of unbelief is upside down, but God turns it the right way up. That is my job and your job. We are God's agents for putting a topsy-turvy world upright.

When Christ beckoned to His first followers, they were unknown, quietly getting on with their own business, fishing on a lake. But He sent them out *"to do business in great waters,"* and *"to the uttermost parts of the Earth."* In Scripture, the sea represents nations – the waves roaring and turbulent. Christ once stilled the storm on the waters. He sends us to fish in every nation, though the waters of the world *"roar and be troubled."* The Lord speaks peace to the nations.

Jesus does not call us just to sit in church and vegetate as if in a rest home. We have a job to do – not a hobby – and the biggest job of all is to change the world! It is a joint-effort, together and with Christ. He said, *"I **will** build My Church."* So today … whatever He asks you to do … even if it seems to be something simple and small … do your best to do your part in building His Church today.

Today's Scripture

Oh that men would give thanks to the Lord for His goodness, and for His wonderful works to the children of men! Let them sacrifice the sacrifices of thanksgiving, and declare His works with rejoicing. Those who go down to the sea in ships, who do business on great waters, they see the works of the Lord and His wonders in the deep.

(Psalm 107:21-24)

Daily Power!

Lord, take me out in the deep waters of the nations and help me pull in a bountiful harvest of souls.

Today's Bible Reading

Isaiah 48:12-22 through 50:1-11; Ephesians 4:17-32; Psalm 69:1-18; Proverbs 24:5-6

Mark my Word
(for further study)

Genesis 1:1-31; Psalm 46:3; 107:23; 146:9; Matthew 16:18; Acts 1:8; 5:28; 17:6; II Corinthians 4:6

Before-and-after Heroes

Here are certain before-and-after attributes of Bible "heroes of faith":

Abraham – This pioneer is notable because *"Abraham believed God, and God counted it to him as righteousness and he became the friend of God."* Abram in Ur was in terrible shape, possibly idolatrous. Faith came to him quite late in life, but it made him the most dominant character the Middle East has ever known, except Christ.

Jacob – The grandson of Abraham; at first, Jacob didn't even claim he belonged to God. Then came a night when God wrestled with him, and Jacob experienced a breakthrough. It changed him so much that God changed his name to **Isra-el**.

Gideon – A young, frustrated son of the local chief who rose literally overnight to be a national leader. He began with very shaky faith, even complaining about God. God nurtured Gideon's faith. He faced an invading army five hundred times bigger than his, unarmed, and *"put to flight the armies of aliens"* – a classic operation of faith.

Jehoshaphat – He was a nervous king, not always pleasing to God. When he and the nation were in danger, God's Spirit fell upon a man in prophecy, bringing a breakthrough. Jehoshaphat's expectations soared, leading to a victorious episode in the annals of Israel.

Thomas the Twin (better known as "Doubting Thomas") – He said, *"I will not believe."* He was a practical-minded type, of the kind who needs hard evidence … but even he experienced a faith breakthrough when He saw Jesus!

Dare to do the impossible through God and for His glory!

Today's Scripture

Now faith is the substance of things hoped for, the evidence of things not see.
(Hebrews 11:1)

Daily Power!

Because I have faith, I dare to do the impossible through God and for His glory.

Today's Bible Reading

*Isaiah 51:1-23 through 53:1-12;
Ephesians 5:1-33;
Psalm 69:19-36;
Proverbs 24:7*

Mark my Word
(for further study)

*Genesis 32:28;
Judges 7:1-25;
II Chronicles 20:1-37;
John 20:25; 21:1-25;
Romans 4:11;
Hebrews 11:34;
James 2:23*

28

I ask the God of our Master, Jesus Christ, the God of glory – to make you intelligent and discerning in knowing Him personally, your eyes focused and clear, so that you can see exactly what it is He is calling you to do, grasp the immensity of this glorious way of life He has for Christians, oh, the utter extravagance of His work in us who trust Him – endless energy, boundless strength!
(Ephesians 1:17-19; the Message)

Daily Power!

Even as a small child trusts his parents, so do I trust my Heavenly Father.

Today's Bible Reading

Isaiah 54:1-17 through 57:1-13; Ephesians 6:1-24; Psalm 70:1-5; Proverbs 24:8

Mark my Word
(for further study)

Ephesians 1:17-19

Eye-opening Prayer

I wish people would be more exact when searching Scripture. Take Ephesians 1:17–19, where Paul prays for believers to experience a breakthrough: *"That the God of our Lord Jesus Christ, the Father of glory, may give to you the spirit of wisdom and revelation in the knowledge of Him, the eyes of your understanding being enlightened; that you may know what is the hope of His calling, what are the riches of the glory of His inheritance in the saints, and what is the exceeding greatness of His power towards us who believe, according to the working of His mighty power."*

In the matter of power, Paul – neither here nor anywhere else – ever prays for power. The New Testament never talks about a new infilling or another Pentecost ... even if the convention speakers do. He prayed only that *"the eyes of* [their] *understanding* [be] *enlightened"* – that is, to see what resources lay at their very finger tips! We pray for power ... when Christ has all power – and that's all that matters. It follows that as we obey His command, He will back us without our having to spend half our time begging Him to do so. The power breakthrough for the Ephesians was a faith breakthrough in realization of what was theirs already in Christ. We take it by faith, not through merit by the labors of prayer.

We talk of "big believers" with "great faith" – but some event encouraged them. They took their opportunity, changed their attitude and believed. God honors such a holy resolve. Jesus commended one or two for their "great faith," but not one of them arrived at that happy position by a long and arduous process. They met Jesus. That was all and enough. Faith is just that – faith in Him. What Jesus commended was the **quality** of their faith, not its scope. Ever-increasing faith is not some kind of trapeze act. It is as a little child who trusts his parents more as he grows older. Be child-like in faith!

The Fire Age

Why was Jesus exalted to the right hand of God? Christ's ascension seems to be a neglected study. Is it of such little importance? Jesus declared His ascension to be expedient. He told us that unless He went to the Father, a most essential experience would never be ours. Without the Lord's ascension, we could never be baptized into the Spirit. Look back upon all that Jesus did. John writes that His works were so many that, if they were all written, the whole world could not contain the books. So what could there be that He did not do when He was on Earth? There was one thing, the very thing which John the Baptist said He would do: baptize in fire and in the Holy Spirit! He didn't do that when He was on Earth. Jesus came from Heaven and had to return there – via the Cross and the tomb – before the final part of His mission could begin.

Nothing Jesus did on Earth could be described as baptizing with the Holy Spirit and with fire. In none of His mighty works – His preaching, His teaching, His healing, or in His death and resurrection – did He baptize with the Holy Spirit. Jesus did much for His disciples – He gave them authority to carry out healing missions – but He went away without baptizing them into the Holy Spirit. Such a baptism could not have happened until He went to the Father. Indeed, the Lord not only said it, but He emphasized it. He entered Glory to take up this brand new office, the office of the Baptizer into the Holy Spirit. **This** is the reason He ascended to the Father! The Old Testament knows nothing of such a baptism. It is God's "new thing." Jesus brings us many other blessings now, of course. He is our High Priest, our Advocate, our Representative. But He Himself did not name these works. He only described the sending forth of the Spirit. After He ascended – and not before – the Spirit came and *"divided tongues, as of fire, and one sat upon each of them."* Years before, the altars of the Tabernacle of Moses and the Temple of Solomon had been set ablaze by the pure fire from Heaven. The flames in the Upper Room of Pentecost came from the same Heavenly source. Jesus has all power at His command. He is in the control room … and **you** are in the palm of His hand.

Today's Scripture

It is to your advantage that I go away; for if I do not go away the Helper will not come to you; but if I depart, I will send Him to you.

(John 16:7)

Daily Power!

The Holy Spirit is given to me to continue the work that Jesus began.

Today's Bible Reading

Isaiah 57:14-21 through 59:1-21; Philippians 1:1-26; Psalm 71:1-24; Proverbs 24:9-10

Mark my Word
(for further study)

John 16:7; 21:25; Acts 2:3

Reunited

Christ is coming back to bring Heaven and Earth together. Jesus said, *"I will come again … that where I am, there you may be also."* It is not wishful thinking taken from a few Scripture verses, not a minor event – but the culmination of all time and the purpose of Creation itself! God's purposes revolve around this planet. His Son came here, not to some other world. Earth is the battlefield where evil and Satan will be overthrown in the sight of all those whom he has deceived. Our calling is not only Heavenly but also Earthly. God loves this world. He never said He loved Heaven as He loves the world, although He made both Heaven and Earth. Jesus was born on Earth, and became a Man Who breathed, lived and died … He was raised again as Man, and now appears in glory as the First Man, the Son of Man. To come back to this world as Man is what it is all about. Jesus loves **people** – not just souls – and has a future for this old world … when His presence will be sensed on every square yard. What we sometimes enjoy now will be experienced vividly by all. His coming is His "parousia" – that is, His presence. Ezekiel said that in the Temple, the Lord's Name is "Shammah" – "the Lord is there" – but when Jesus comes again, this will be said of the whole Earth.

John's actual Greek says, *"It is the last hour"* – which is God's viewpoint. With the Lord, one day is like a thousand years … and represents His patience as He waits for the world to turn back to Him. John and Peter both spoke as if they were in the last days, and they were – just as we are. Now two thousand years have moved along, we can only speak of the last **hours**. If anybody thinks delay means it was all a mistake about Jesus coming back – and he or she can just live it up – they are living in a fool's paradise. No generation lives forever – for every generation there is a last hour. As God's servants, we can only save one generation. We do not have the third millennium to save the world. Most people alive today will be gone soon after it begins. *"The last hour"* is an expression for the swift shuttle of mortal existence. **Live** in each minute – each second – of this last hour, this last day!

Today's Scripture

Don't let this throw you. You trust God, don't you?
(John 14:1; the Message)

Daily Power!

As God's servants, we can only save one generation.

Today's Bible Reading

Isaiah 60:1-22 through 62:1-5; Philippians 1:27-29 through 2:1-18; Psalm 72:1-20; Proverbs 24:11-12

Mark my Word
(for further study)

Ezekiel 48:35; John 14:1, 3

When you seek the saved, you produce conferences,
When you seek the lost, you produce crusades.

Evangelism must lead into the local church.
An evangelist brings his nets and
borrows the pastor's boats and together
they go out and bring in a catch of souls.
Then the evangelist shakes out every fish
into the church and moves on
to the next potential harvest.

I want one thing, "Hell empty and Heaven full!"

Consumed by Fire

Baptism in the Holy Spirit means that everything to do with Him and with the Gospel should be characterized by fire! It should burn. There should be fire in those who witness and work … fire in those who preach … fire in the Truth we preach – *"Is not My Word like a fire?"*… fire in the Lord we preach – *"For our God is a consuming fire"* … fire in the power to preach – *"tongues as of fire"* … fire in the Spirit by which we preach – *"the Holy Spirit and fire"*!

There were two sacrifices on Mount Carmel: one was performed by the priests of Baal … the other by Elijah. The sacrifice to Baal never burned – it was fireless. The sacrifice was there, the sacrificers were intensely earnest – they prayed to Baal all day, and they lanced themselves with knives to show how desperate their sincerity was. They put everything they had into it … and yet their sacrifice brought no fire. If the devil could have brought up a spark or two from Hell to make a blaze, Satan would have … but the altar just stayed cold.

Fire did not fall just because Elijah set up a sacrifice either – it came when Elijah **prayed and believed!** Elijah followed the instructions of Moses to the letter … but no fire resulted purely from his obedience. **Faith brought the blaze.** God sent the fire on the sacrifice only. There would be no point in sending the fire without the sacrifice. Armchair Christians receive no fire. There is no such thing as an "anointed couch-potato." Sometimes people pray for fire when they are not yielded to God at all … and subsequently do little for Him. They give up little time or money, and render no effort. If they had God's fire, what would they do with it? Sit at home and just enjoy it? The fire is not to save us trouble in winning the world – **it is to empower us to preach the Gospel** in spite of trouble. Tap into that fire today!

Today's Scripture

Since we are receiving a Kingdom that cannot be shaken, let us have grace by which we may serve God acceptably with reverence and Godly fear; for our God is a consuming fire.
(Hebrews 12:28-29)

Daily Power!

Holy Spirit fire is to empower us to preach the Gospel.

Today's Bible Reading

Isaiah 62:6-12 through 65:1-25;
Philippians 2:19-29 through 3:1-4a;
Psalm 73:1-28;
Proverbs 24:13-14

Mark my Word
(for further study)

I Kings 18:1-46;
Jeremiah 23:29;
Matthew 3:11;
Acts 2:3;
Hebrews 12:29

2

Today's Scripture

And the power of the Lord was present to heal them.

(Luke 5:17)

Daily Power!

When faith breaks through, you glorify God, have power, boldness, are empowered.

Today's Bible Reading

Isaiah 66:1-24;
Philippians 4:3b-21;
Psalm 74:1-23;
Proverbs 24:15-19

Mark my Word
(for further study)

Luke 5:17-26

Faith Breakthrough

Four men had a literal breakthrough of faith: *"As [Jesus] was teaching, there were Pharisees and teachers of the Law sitting by, out of every town of Galilee, Judea and Jerusalem.* **And the power of the Lord was present to heal them.** *Then men brought on a bed a man who was paralyzed, whom they sought to bring in and lay before Him. When they could not find how they might bring him in, because of the crowd, they went up on the housetop and let him down with his bed through the tiling into the midst before Jesus. When He saw* **their** *faith, He said to him, 'Man, your sins are forgiven you.' The scribes and the Pharisees began to reason, 'Who is this Who speaks blasphemies? Who can forgive sins but God alone?' When Jesus perceived their thoughts, He answered, 'Why are you reasoning in your hearts? Which is easier to say – your sins are forgiven – or – rise up and walk? That you may know that the Son of Man has power on Earth to forgive sins' – He said to the man who was paralyzed, 'Arise, take up your bed, and go to your house.' Immediately he rose up before them, took up what he had been lying on, and departed to his own house, glorifying God. They were all amazed, and they glorified God and were filled with fear, saying, 'We have seen strange things today!'"* (emphasis mine).

Christ was in a house crowded with people, believers and unbelievers alike. Many had physical troubles, and *"the power of the Lord was present for Him to heal the sick"* – but none of these religious people were healed. Then four men brought a paralyzed man on a stretcher, and – because they could not get through the crowd – they went up the outside stairs of the flat-roofed house, pulled apart the coverings and lowered the man down right in front of Jesus. Seeing **their** faith, He restored this man to health. It was a double breakthrough. They (physically) broke through the roof … and they (spiritually) broke through the unbelief of the crowd, which had kept them back from Christ. *"They were all amazed … and [some] were filled with fear."* Fear is one of Satan's favorite tricks to try to undermine miracles. It is also possible to lose your healing if you allow unbelief to undermine what God has done. But when faith breaks through, it causes **you** to glorify God, it brings a power, a certainty, a boldness that enables **you** to withstand fear and unbelief, and empowers **you** to be a stronger witness than ever before!

Faith Giants

3

Every time somebody is healed, it breaks through the unbelief of the world. It has to, or we will never get near Jesus at all. Believe God! It will please some people … and amaze everybody else. Jesus dealt with people's varying degrees of faith. Some tried to keep theirs hidden – like the sick woman who crept through the crowd to touch them hem of His garment but who didn't want others to know … He healed her anyway. Some had "risky" faith – like the four friends who wanted healing for their paralytic friend (whose faith was it anyway, that brought healing to the sick man – that sick man's or his friends'?) … that miracle caused rejoicing in believers, but fear in the hearts of the unbelievers. Or there was faith based on authority – such as the centurion (probably a pagan) who yet believed that Jesus was more than capable of healing by His word … and who received Jesus' commendation: *"I have not found such great faith, not even in Israel!"* as well as healing for his servant.

We are surrounded every day by doubters. Godlessness is the order of the day. Newspapers, radio, television, all of them push irreligion and godlessness down our throats for breakfast, dinner, tea, and supper. If we want faith, we should try a different diet than all this rationalistic chaff. Feed on the Bible, prayer, Christian encouragement, and faith-building reading. Come hopefully, exercising faith (however nervously) … and you will get more faith! The believer is destined to be a giant, walking tall, riding high above the spiritual poverty of the world, the representative of a greater order of creation, a strength and a pillar: "The loss of wealth is much, the loss of health is more; the loss of faith is such, that nothing can restore." Be one who is known as having "great faith"!

Today's Scripture

Then Jesus answered and said to her, "O woman, great is your faith! Let it be to you as you desire." And her daughter was healed from that very hour.
(Matthew 15:28)

Daily Power!

I intend to be a giant among pygmies, riding high above the spiritual poverty of the world.

Today's Bible Reading

Jeremiah 1:1-19 through 2:1-30; Philippians 4:1-23; Psalm 75:1-10; Proverbs 24:17-20

Mark my Word
(for further study)

Matthew 8:5-13; 9:19-26; 15:28; Mark 2:1-12

4

"Born again"

When Christ Jesus bridged the gulf between the natural world and the spiritual, one of the possibilities He opened up for us was to be *"born again."* This Greek expression can also be translated *"born from above."* Men and women can be made new – new creatures, the Bible says – by the power of Heaven, the Kingdom power of God. Obviously, people "born from above" would never be satisfied with a world which was only material. They need spiritual links as well as physical ones. The present world, with its limited scientific laws, is not big enough for a converted Christian anymore than a cage is for an eagle. It needs extending, and that extension goes beyond our three-dimensional world into the fourth dimension of the Spirit. We *"walk in the Spirit,"* we are *"seated with* [Christ] *in the Heavenly realms."*

The Book of Acts shows the disciples drawing upon new resources as they moved through the world blessing the people with salvation and healing. The first new people in Christ, these new creatures of the Kingdom, were sent out to bring others into the same Kingdom order with new instincts, new powers and new laws written on their hearts.

After I was baptized in the Spirit and spoke with tongues, it didn't take me long to realize that this gift opened up new possibilities. If I spoke with tongues through the Spirit, then there could be other wonders through the Spirit. I have learned to live in the Spirit. I am on new ground where signs and wonders happen. Praise God! If it weren't for that, nothing could happen as it does. Vast multitudes come to my meetings. They represent an intimidating accumulation of needs. But I am baptized in the Holy Spirit. I know the powers of the coming age and how to tap those resources. A great conviction grips me that God has something for them. That is not only my secret, but it is also the conviction of hundreds of millions today. If I have any other "secret," it is the message itself. I am confident of its effectiveness. It is *"the power of God to salvation."* You too can be confident in this.

Today's Scripture

Most assuredly I say to you, unless one is born again, he cannot see the Kingdom of God.
(John 3:3)

Daily Power!

There are limitless wonders through the Holy Spirit to be learned and experienced.

Today's Bible Reading

Jeremiah 2:31-37 through 4:1-18; Colossians 1:1-20; Psalm 76:1-12; Proverbs 24:21-22

Mark my Word
(for further study)

John 3:3; Romans 1:16; Galatians 5:16; Ephesians 2:6; Hebrew 8:1-13

My first missionary Efforts

As a young missionary in Africa, I sometimes preached to five people. Beyond our mission there were 450-million souls in Africa, most ignorant of salvation through Jesus Christ. Yes, they could all be evangelized by the way we were tackling it ... but only if they stayed alive for about 5,000 years! However, small audiences did not dismay us – after all, revival could come and save us a lot of trouble! This hope kept us patient and starry-eyed, for had not our spiritual great-grandfathers banked upon this with unquestioning faith? Later it struck me that **the Gospel is not Good News to people who don't hear it – that an unpreached Gospel is no Gospel at all.** Another small ray of illumination penetrated my heart: in the New Testament, we never read about God going forth on His own, but that, *"They went out and preached everywhere, the Lord working with them."* God acted when they acted. So, He was waiting for us and – I couldn't get away from it ... that included me!

I set up a Bible correspondence course, and 50,000 people enrolled. So many! Like a periscope from a submarine, it revealed that I was submerged in an ocean of salvation-hungry humanity. Additionally, a vision followed me: night after night, I saw the entire African continent washed in the Blood of Jesus, country after country. We had waited for revival, thoroughly and patiently, through a hundred long years of earnest prayer. Surely God must answer now? Seemingly on a wild impulse (which proved to be of God), I booked a 10,000-seat stadium for a campaign with a church of forty members ... and **ten thousand people came!** The first ripe wheat! For the first time, I witnessed thousands running forward to respond to the call of salvation. God opened my eyes and I actually saw an invisible, mighty wave of Holy Spirit-power arrive in the stadium. A mass baptism in the Holy Spirit, accompanied by many healing miracles, took place. I wept like a boy and vowed to the Lord that in obedience, I would move across all of Africa to bring the vision to pass. I reasoned that if God can do that to 10,000 people, He could do it to 450-million. That's the kind of aggressive evangelistic faith I hope to impart to you today.

Today's Scripture

And they went out and preached everywhere, the Lord working with them, and confirming the Word through the accompanying signs. Amen.

(Mark 16:20)

Daily Power!

The Gospel is not Good News to people who don't hear it – an unpreached Gospel is no Gospel at all.

Today's Bible Reading

Jeremiah 4:19-31 through 6:1-14; Colossians 1:21-29 through 2:1-7; Psalm 77:1-20; Proverbs 24:23-25

Mark my Word
(for further study)

Mark 16:20

Invasion!

Our world has been invaded ... and the authority of the Kingdom of God has drawn near to us. It is a superior, miracle order that over-arches natural or scientific order. Just as higher laws can overrule physical laws – the spiritual can overrule the material. That happens in the baptism of the Holy Spirit, and when His gifts operate.

John's Gospel says that all things were made by the Word – that is, by the Son of God, *"the Word became flesh."* He Who is the Source of everything we see – He Himself came into His own creation, the One **Who *"came down from Heaven."*** That very important statement means that He became the Bridge reaching from the higher, invisible world to the visible. Jesus later portrays Himself as a Jacob's Ladder set up between Heaven and Earth. There are two orders, with their own forces or powers. Jesus is the link between them, the Heavenly and the Earthly order. The power of Heaven is the creative power of God, by which the Earth was made. Through Christ – the link with Heaven – things are possible on Earth which were not possible before He came. He is called *"the new and living way."* Through Jesus Christ, by the Holy Spirit, commerce has begun between Earth and Heaven. The angels of God are coming and going.

Because of Christ in our world, God can exercise His will here – through our prayers. It is a case of God wanting manpower ... and our needing God's power, for Jesus taught us to pray, *"Your will be done on Earth as it is in Heaven."* He has not shut Himself out of any part of His universe. He is Lord. He applies greater forces, and the natural laws obey the Spirit of God. We call that a miracle. God is dealing with us in a new way. There is, of course, a grand purpose behind it. The object is not to pull off a few sensational wonders, like stage tricks, but the redemption of the world. You can tap into that power today!

Today's Scripture

In the beginning was the Word, and the Word was with God, and the Word was God. He was in the beginning with God. All things were made through Him, and without Him nothing was made that was made.
(John 1:1-3)

Daily Power!

God's ultimate object is the redemption of the world.

Today's Bible Reading

Jeremiah 6:15-30
through 8:1-7;
Colossians 2:8-23;
Psalm 78:1-31;
Proverbs 24:26

Mark my Word
(for further study)

Matthew 6:10;
John 1:1-3, 14, 51; 6:38;
Hebrews 10:20

Natural and spiritual Laws

Every time you move, you bring natural laws under your authority. Left to nature, rocks would not fly, but we human beings introduce a **higher** law – that of our will. We can throw rocks and make them fly. We are not the slaves of the laws of nature – they are our slaves. We can use scientific laws to leave this planet altogether. We can move into a state of weightlessness or even fly to the moon. Better still – we can move, and act, and minister in the Word of God!

When people say that miracles are contrary to the laws of nature, they completely ignore the fact that where there is a superior will and superior power – with Man, as well as omnipotent God – all the laws of nature can be overridden. The difficulty arises when people don't believe in God. Bring God into it … and nothing is impossible. And that is what has happened: the Kingdom of God is among us – therefore, devils are cast out, the sick are healed, and we speak with tongues.

Human beings are both flesh and spirit. God linked us to two worlds, the earthly and the spiritual. By our five senses, we are aware of this world … and by our spirits, we sense the nonphysical world – and, on occasion, fear it. But something has gone wrong. A great calamity has befallen us – sin has almost destroyed the link between body and spirit! After the fall of Adam, only occasional flashes of the supernatural were seen … until Jesus came. Only a breakthrough now and then is recorded in the Old Testament. Sometimes God exercised His sovereignty and initiated a spate of wonders, as He did with Moses and the Elijah/Elisha ministries. God's power and His authority were rarely seen directly.

Then a radical change came about: Christ's marvelous coming – God in the flesh – opened up the resources of creative power. He was, and is, Lord of all things. He announced it Himself, saying, *"The Kingdom of God is at hand."* That's the Kingdom you and I live in!

Today's Scripture

When you see these things happening, know that the Kingdom of God is near.
(Luke 21:31)

Daily Power!

The God-ordained link between Heaven and Earth is through His Son, Jesus Christ.

Today's Bible Reading

Jeremiah 8:8-22 through 9:1-26;
Colossians 3:1-17;
Psalm 78:32-55;
Proverbs 24:24

Mark my Word
(for further study)

Mark 1:14;
Luke 21:31

What God is saying

If God has anything to say to the Church as a whole, it is what Christ said when He left this world: *"Go into all the world and preach the Gospel."* Until that Commission is completed, God has no after-thoughts or overriding concerns to get us busy about side issues, such as church structures and organizations.

Even as a young boy, Jesus had a burning in His heart to fulfill His mission on Earth as the Messiah. He came to win the lost, even willing to suffer a brutal death for our sakes. But in the years prior to that, He "itched" to be busy with His Father's work: *"Now so it was that after three days, they found Him in the Temple, sitting in the midst of the teachers, both listening to them and asking them questions. And all who heard Him were astonished at His understanding and answers. So when they saw Him, they were amazed, and His mother said to Him, 'Son, why have You done this to us? Look, Your father and I have sought You anxiously.' And He said to them, 'Why did you seek Me? Did you not know that I must be about My Father's business?'"* From the beginning, Jesus intended to preach the Gospel of the Kingdom to the world! He did not get sidetracked, not even once.

God has a revealed will, so, *"If we ask anything according to His will, He hears us."* That is why Christ gave us the petition, *"Thy will be done on Earth as it is in Heaven."* Jesus said again, *"If ... My words remain in you, ask whatever you wish and it will be given you."* The primary aim of prayer is not for our will to be done, but to bring about the revealed will of God ... not to persuade God to our way of thinking or to force His hand. His expressed will is that God desires all men to come to repentance. Everything in the New Testament spells that out clearly. If we ask according to that will, God hastens to answer. It is expressed in the prayer, *"Thy Kingdom come, Thy will be done on Earth as it is in Heaven."* It is the Gospel that will achieve it. **You** have a part to play in that Kingdom today!

Today's Scripture

If you abide in Me, and My words abide in you, you will ask what you desire, and it shall be done for you. By this My Father is glorified, that you bear much fruit; so you will be My disciples.
(John 15:7-8)

Daily Power!

The primary aim of prayer is to bring about the revealed will of God.

Today's Bible Reading

Jeremiah 10:1-25
through 11:1-23;
Colossians 3:18-25
through 4:1-18;
Psalm 78:56-72;
Proverbs 24:28-29

Mark my Word
(for further study)

Matthew 6:10;
Mark 16:15;
Luke 2:45-49;
John 15:7;
I John 5:14

Evoking Thoughts of God

Anointing was like a perfume. Paul quoted David: *"Your Throne, O God, is forever and ever; a Scepter of righteousness is the scepter of Your Kingdom. You love righteousness and hate wickedness; therefore God, your God, has anointed You with the oil of gladness more than your companions. All Your garments are scented with myrrh and aloes and cassia"* in referring to Christ. Cassia came from the distant Far East. Israel probably obtained it from passing traders. It provided a distinctive fragrance associated only with the dwelling place of God and its priests – it evoked thoughts of God.

Scripture calls Jesus the Anointed One: *"Peter answered and said, 'You are the Christ* [the Anointed One], *the Son of the Living God."* He was the Christ. Jesus is as exclusively anointed as He was exclusively the Son of God. "Christ" is from the Greek christos, which translates as the Hebrew "Messiah." Everything denoted by the anointing of the Tabernacle and priests and kings is fulfilled in Jesus. Christ is our priest-king: *"Your garments are scented."* He carried the purity and odor of Heaven, that evocative and subtle beauty of spirit which makes Him the Anointed One, distinguished from all others. He drew people – not merely by power or "charisma" in the popular sense – but by love, moving in the atmosphere of His own holiness which people had never breathed before. If we can put it this way: Jesus was God's "Alabaster Box," broken for us on the Cross … and now filling the world with His fragrance!

We have opportunity to "participate" in Christ's anointing, even as Mary did: *"Then Mary took a pound of very costly oil of spikenard, anointed the feet of Jesus, and wiped His feet with her hair. And the house was filled with the fragrance of the oil."* Our most intimate acts of worship – where we humble ourselves at His feet and give our best to Him – causes His anointing to "spill over" into our lives. We carry the fragrance of Jesus upon us … our "odor" is associated with the dwelling place of God. It's true: that Christ-like fragrance extends beyond you … into the whole world!

Today's Scripture

They recognized them as companions of Jesus.
(Acts 4:13; the Message)

Daily Power!

We carry the fragrance of Jesus upon us.

Today's Bible Reading

Jeremiah 12:1-17 through 14:1-10;
I Thessalonians 1:1-10 through 2:1-9;
Psalm 79:1-13;
Proverbs 24:30-34

Mark my Word
(for further study)

Psalm 45:6-8;
Matthew 16:16;
John 12:3;
Acts 4:13;
Hebrews 1:8-9

Nobody is a "Nobody"

Today's Scripture

Brethren, my heart's desire and prayer to God for Israel is that they may be saved.

(Romans 10:1)

Daily Power!

The ultimate aim of intercession is evangelism. Even on my knees in prayer, I am reaching the world for Christ.

Today's Bible Reading

Jeremiah 14:11-22 through 16:1-15; I Thessalonians 2:10-20 through 3:1-13; Psalm 80:1-19; Proverbs 25:1-5

Mark my Word
(for further study)

Genesis 37:30; Luke 22:44; 23:34; John 8:39-44; I Timothy 2:1-4

To God, nobody is a "nobody." Each individual has a value beyond computation. Our prayers should be in direct proportion to the desperate wickedness from which people need saving. The worse the wickedness, the more the intercession. Nobody should have to go through life without somebody praying for him (or her).

Read from the New International Version of I Timothy 2: *"I urge, then, first of all, that requests, prayers, intercessions, and thanksgiving be made for everyone – for kings and all those in authority, that we may live peaceful lives in all Godliness and holiness. This is good, and pleases God our Savior, Who wants all men to be saved and to come to a knowledge of the truth."* So the ultimate aim of intercession is evangelism: God *"wants all men to be saved."* Intercession is not a say-so, but a heart-cry. Not "Lord, bless me and everybody everywhere, Amen!" Our Lord Jesus prayed for us until He sweat drops of blood! He even prayed for the soldiers hammering nails through His quivering flesh.

Pray for all men, for Christ-lessness is terrible. There in only one Savior – and if He is rejected, what can people do? Their cry is like Reuben's when he found Joseph had gone: *"And I, where shall I go?"* There is nowhere to go. So people just drift along, perhaps together, perhaps alone, unknowingly heading for a "Sargasso Sea" called Hell. Christ-less religion is Hell on Earth! Religious leaders killed Christ. We see it today in unbridled hate, terrorism, murder, and oppression in the Name of God. Jesus said, *"If you were Abraham's children, then you would do the same things Abraham did. As it is, you were determined to kill Me ... Abraham did not do such things ... You belong to your father, the devil ... He was a murderer from the beginning."* Intercession is urgent. Intercession brings divine intervention. We have one generation in which to save a generation – not a century! That's God's challenge to you and to me! Do your part **today** ... and you'll help pave the way for others who will soon follow.

See and believe!

Some people seem to know all about the Cross. They wear a cross or carry a crucifix. But it is merely a superstition which does nothing for them. Knowing all about a power station can still leave you in the cold and dark. You can touch the very walls of a nuclear power plant, but still be freezing. Yet you can plug in to the power of God because the wiring system is completed by the preaching of the Gospel, the truth! When you hear it and believe it, you are tapping in to the resources of God, which are inexhaustible. Then you **know** that you are saved.

There were people actually at the foot of the Cross while Jesus hung there, but they were not saved. The Bible describes some who *"sitting down, they watched Him there."* That is all they did, so they were not saved. Today, thousands of people do the same thing. They are just onlookers, curious perhaps, or even pitying, feeling sorry about Christ's death … but never receiving what He died to give them: an assurance of God's forgiveness and His acceptance of them.

When faith comes, assurance comes. You cannot separate them, and sometimes in Scripture the two words are exactly the same. I want to show you how this can be. We read in Mark 15 that *"those who passed by hurled insults at him, shaking their heads and saying … 'Let this Christ, this King of Israel come down now from the cross, that we may see and believe.'"* They actually saw Jesus dying for them, but they did not believe and were not saved. See and believe! Mark had his answer to that. He wrote that one man, a Roman captain, was different. *"And when the centurion, who stood there in front of Jesus, heard His cry and saw how He died, he said, 'Surely this man was the Son of God!'"* This soldier had seen the whole thing – and with a more perceiving eye, saw the truth. He did not need to see a wonder, a miracle, a display of magic, like Christ detaching Himself from the nails and walking around, or Elijah coming to release Jesus, as some had hoped. He was seeing the true wonder, the love of God, the greatness of Christ. He saw the glory of God in the face of Jesus Christ. **See and believe!**

Today's Scripture

Truly this Man was the Son of God!
(Mark 15:39)

Daily Power!

My faith in Jesus Christ has given me rock-solid assurance of salvation.

Today's Bible Reading

Jeremiah 16:16-21 through 18:1-23; I Thessalonians 4:1-18 through 5:1-3; Psalm 81:1-16; Proverbs 25:6-7

Mark my Word
(for further study)

Matthew 27:36; Mark 15:29-39

The Axe and the Orchestra

The Church is Christ's battle-axe. Every axe has a handle, a head and a cutting edge: a handle for the handler … a head for weight … and a sharp edge to do the work. Whether we make God's work possible by the thousand jobs that must be done … give weight to the work by our support … are on the attacking-and-cutting-edge of evangelism – we are **all** vitally needed! I, Reinhard Bonnke, have no churches … but I depend on churches. They give the weight to what I do, and my team looks after the endless matters that must be organized – yet we are one tool in the hand of the Master.

The Church is also Christ's orchestra. I never attempt anything alone. A soloist needs accompaniment, perhaps a whole orchestra. All of our work has to be arranged, whether campaigns, literature, TV, films, books, or whatever. There are hundreds and even tens of thousands of back-up players in tune with my aims, with special gifts, abilities, or with their prayers and gifts – and I work along with their same aims and purposes. Every melody needs harmonizing, and is perfected and enriched by the qualities of other instruments, musical talents and choreography. I never go to any country except when groups of churches ask me to go. We must all work together.

No man seemed stronger in faith than the apostle Paul did. When he heard that Christians had appeared in Rome, he wrote to them: *"I long to see you so that I may impart to you some spiritual gift to make you strong, that is that you and I may be mutually encouraged by one another's faith"* – mutual faith. Each of us is like one sheet of paper that can't stand up on its own edge alone. But a ream of paper is a block of five hundred sheets – all able to stand on edge comfortably together, supporting one another. Every believer needs support. The world won't help. The world is no friend to the friends of Jesus. So wherever you are … whatever you do … stay in fellowship with other believers, and stand up for Jesus!

Today's Scripture

Two are better than one, because they have a good reward for their labor. For if they fall, one will lift up his companion … Again, if two lie down together, they will keep warm, but how can one be warm alone? Though one may be overpowered by another, two can withstand him, and a threefold cord is not quickly broken.
(Ecclesiastes 4:9-12)

Daily Power!

Team work! That will bring about the Kingdom of God faster than solo-play.

Today's Bible Reading

Jeremiah 19:1-15 through 21:1-14;
I Thessalonians 5:4-28;
Psalm 82:1-8;
Proverbs 25:8-10

Mark my Word
(for further study)

*Ecclesiastes 4:9-12;
Romans 1:11*

Evangelists sought!

There are thousands of evangelists in church jobs to which God never called them. It is time for the Body of Christ to boldly reaffirm the Office of Evangelist! Some pastors become angry if you ask why God has given evangelists. The fact remains forever that God's concern today, as at Calvary, is the salvation of souls. And when Jesus Christ ascended into Heaven, He established the work of evangelists within the Church to help accomplish this great work.

The past holds tragedies. When doors opened, some Christian workers were found jealously guarding their monopoly, as gold miners did their claims. Sometimes rivalries ruined revivals. The harvest must not go unreaped while reapers merely defend their "own" flock. Christ did not die to give people a career, but to save the lost. I do not preach "means and methods," but spiritual principles. God will give you resourcefulness. There are as many methods as He directs. We need more imaginative approaches, rather than people doing things by "tried and proved" methods – including methods I have tried and proved. Methods which have made little impact in the past are not likely to produce an impact now. Plodding along mechanically might be called faithfulness … but our primary concern in evangelism is effectiveness, not a twisted type of faithfulness.

During my years as an evangelist and missionary, I have discovered a number of limiting factors hindering the Gospel. I know from experience that many of the "traditional and accepted" methods of evangelism have remained unchanged for generations. Others are doctrines and sentiments which tell us to "leave it all to God." Some insist God's way is revival, but they fail to carry out the Great Commission in the meantime. Some think that if people are to be saved, they will be saved anyway. I know this is **not** true … and I trust you will come to understand that too.

Today's Scripture

Do you not say, "There are still four months and then comes the harvest"? Behold, I say to you, lift up your eyes and look at the fields, for they are already white for harvest!

(John 4:35)

Daily Power!

Christ did not die to give people a career, but to save the lost.

Today's Bible Reading

Jeremiah 22:1-30 through 23:1-20; II Thessalonians 1:1-12; Psalm 83:1-18; Proverbs 25:11-14

Mark my Word
(for further study)

Ephesians 4:8-16

Singleness of Heart

It is an awful risk to rest the eternal destiny of souls upon a controversial interpretation of Scripture or turn of a Greek verb. One can be "dead right" … but dead nonetheless! We dare not neglect the task of evangelism. I would rather use a method despised by man but approved by God, than a method approved by Man which gets no results. I make no apology for this – I desire to share God's anointing on all those who are ready to step out in faith. My perspective runs hot – very hot. Its flames can scorch. Some who read these pages would do well to take out fire insurance, for I guarantee many old concepts will be set to the torch!

My message is not one-sided, but it does come from a singleness of heart. I hammer away at the Great Commission, for I know it cannot be overemphasized. I cry to God day and night for greater effectiveness in winning our generation for Him. **Evangelism by Fire** is the only feasible solution. I constantly scan the horizons for other anointed men and women who may take up this challenge of the Word of God for Holy Spirit evangelism. I believe the best is yet to be. The time is coming soon when the whole world will resound with the praises of our God and Savior. In all nations and in every language, the day is almost here when every tongue will confess that *"Jesus Christ is Lord, to the glory of God the Father."* God has taught me many things, has allowed me to experience much over the years. I am sharing this with you today for one reason alone: to inspire **you** to *"Do the work of an evangelist."* I have laid out the principles necessary for any Holy Spirit ministry. Read this – not to discover how **I** operate in my evangelistic crusades – but to discover how God operates through **Anyone** willing to follow His plan … and that means **you**!

Today's Scripture

Therefore God also has highly exalted Him and given Him the Name which is above every name, that at the Name of Jesus every knee should bow, of those in Heaven, and of those on Earth, and of those under the Earth, and that every tongue should confess that Jesus Christ is Lord, to the glory of God the Father.

(Philippians 2:9-11)

Daily Power!

We dare not neglect the task of evangelism.

Today's Bible Reading

Jeremiah 23:21-40 through 25:1-38; II Thessalonians 2:1-17; Psalm 84:1-12; Proverbs 25:15

Mark my Word
(for further study)

Philippians 2:9-11; II Timothy 4:5

A Gospel that isn't

The Gospel has been reinterpreted in ways that take the heart out of it – and out of us. Liberal and rationalistic thought is based on the shifting sands of biblical criticism, speculation and philosophy. No assured grounds for the frightened millions have ever been offered by this new thought. It is a theology of chaff, a diet of starvation for those hungry for God. Too many scholars have made truth depend on questions that can never have any certain answers, never reach finality – guesswork that is doomed to do absolutely nothing for lost nations and devil-stricken masses. If God is the only Savior, He cannot save by a message of "perhaps" or "if" or "it is my opinion." The world needs people with a live link to Heaven!

For all classes of people, no matter how cultured or how primitive, there is one word of truth – the Cross – to the wise, the barbarian, the Greek, the Jew, everyone. The Gospel is the power of God. The Gospel preacher is an ambassador demanding surrender to the Kingdom of Heaven. It is God's ultimatum. He shows us the way things are. The Gospel is neither a theory nor an abstraction, but the reality behind everything. We either recognize it … or perish.

When you grasp what I am are saying here, then you join the Army with the battering ram of the Word and of the Cross. It will pulverize the strongholds of the devil. It is the thundering drumroll of God's invincible Army on the march. When God filled me with His Spirit and opened my lips to speak with tongues, He opened my ears to hear the triumphant blast of the trumpet announcing that Jesus has all power in Heaven and on Earth. What a gift! Be certain that the Gospel you follow is one of life and power.

Today's Scripture

Listen to the Message. It was preached to those believers who are now dead, and yet even though they died (just as all people must), they will still get in on the life that God has given in Jesus.
(I Peter 4:6; the Message)

Daily Power!

The Gospel which I believe is linked to the power of God through the Holy Spirit of Christ Jesus.

Today's Bible Reading

Jeremiah 26:1-24 through 27:1-22; II Thessalonians 3:1-18; Psalm 85:1-13; Proverbs 25:16

Mark my Word
(for further study)

I Peter 4:6

16

Today's Scripture

I will pray with the Spirit, and I will also pray with the understanding. I will sing with the Spirit, and I will also sing with the understanding.

(I Corinthians 14:15)

Daily Power!

My "life in the Spirit" is filled with His fruit – love, joy, peace.

Today's Bible Reading

Jeremiah 28:1-17
through 29:1-32;
I Timothy 1:1-20;
Psalm 86:1-17;
Proverbs 25:17

Mark my Word
(for further study)

Psalm 144:5;
Isaiah 64:1

Marching Orders

Both David and Isaiah prayed, *"Lord, rend the Heavens and come down."* It happened when Jesus came … therefore, New Testament believers need never pray it again. Christ tore the Heavens and came down to us. He then returned through the Heavens, ensuring that they remain open. The rent Heavens have been opened forever and have never been sewn up again, either by a needle-wielding Satan or any other hand. Through that open Heaven, the Holy Spirit then began to descend: the *"latter rain."* Hell cannot impose sanctions and blockade the Kingdom of God, nor deprive its citizens. The new and living way is established beyond enemy control.

In his book, "Joy Unspeakable", the great teacher D. Martyn Lloyd-Jones concluded that revival is the baptism in the Holy Spirit. He laid down firm proof that there is a Scriptural reception of power after conversion, that it is the baptism with the Spirit, and that it is revival. Since 1901, when that truth was recovered, the restoration of Bible signs and wonders has brought hundreds of millions into the Kingdom of God.

No New Testament Christian confined himself to religious meditation. Mystics usually ended up with erroneous teachings. The apostles were activists. Smith Wigglesworth was right: *"The Acts of the Apostles was written because the apostles acted."* They did not visit shrines or keep the relics of holy men. They were in vital contact with God themselves through the Spirit. They went directly to Him, not through saints and their bones.

The entire Christian life is *"in the Spirit."* By the Spirit, the Son of God was the Anointed One. This set the pattern. Just as He went about doing good because He was anointed with the Spirit, so must you. Like Jesus, you and I are told to walk in the Spirit … pray in the Spirit … love in the Spirit … live in the Spirit … be filled with the Spirit … sing in the Spirit … and have the fruit of the Spirit.

The Authority of Christ

God spoke … and Heaven and Earth materialized: *"He spoke, and it was done. He uttered His voice, and it stood fast."* Then John's Gospel makes the tremendous assertion that *"the Word became flesh."* The same Voice that created all things now spoke to us. What He said comes with absolute authority. It is the Word of the Lord.

When Christ spoke, He said Heaven and Earth would pass away, but not His words. He was not like the prophets – they spoke FOR the Lord, but Christ spoke AS the Lord. The prophets said, *"Thus saith the Lord,"* but Christ said, *"Truly, truly I say to you."* The Jews listened to Moses, but Jesus went beyond Moses: *"Moses said … but I say."* There was something else different. The prophets were sent **with** a message, but Jesus **was** the message. The prophets spoke **about** the Lord, but Jesus spoke about **Himself**. He not only brought the Word of God, but He **was** the Word of God. He didn't point to the way – He **was** the way. Jesus was not one of the roads that led to God – He was where the road led!

That is why we have no right to doubt the Word of God or bend God's exclamation mark into a question mark. If we do so, *"To whom else shall we go? You alone have the words of life,"* as the apostle Peter recognized. We either obey or die. Using our technology language, we blow the fuse and suffer a lifelong power failure. The heating fails, the lights go out, communications cease, the systems break down, and cold eternal night settles in. Liberal teachers scorn people like us. They say we have an "authoritarian religion". But do they teach without any authority? All learning is based on authority, either Divine or human. Some trust in the authority of scholarship, but nothing is less trustworthy. Their arguments are steps in sand. Scholars never agree with one another. Remember: the Word of God has been a light to a hundred generations, and that lamp has never flickered.

Today's Scripture

By the Word of the Lord the Heavens were made, and all the host of them by the breath of His mouth … Let all the Earth fear the Lord; let all the inhabitants of the world stand in awe of Him. For He spoke, and it was done; He commanded, and it stood fast.
(Psalm 33:6-9)

Daily Power!

Gladly I place myself under the authority of Jesus Christ, the Son of God.

Today's Bible Reading

Jeremiah 30:1-24 through 31:1-26; I Timothy 2:1-15; Psalm 87:1-7; Proverbs 25:18-19

Mark my Word
(for further study)

Psalm 33:9; Matthew 19:8-9; 24:35; John 1:14; 6:68

Fire comes by Faith

Today's Scripture

*Jesus said,
"I am the Road,
also the Truth,
also the Life."*
(John 14:6; the Message)

Daily Power!

*To preach the Gospel is
to be on Fire!*

Today's Bible Reading

*Jeremiah 31:27-40
through to 32:1-44;
I Timothy 3:1-16;
Psalm 88:1-18;
Proverbs 25:20-22*

Mark my Word
(for further study)

*Isaiah 4:5;
John 5:35; 14:6;
Acts 7:38*

It is Holy Spirit fire that matters. Laying out and setting up a sacrifice is not enough. God won't save souls and heal the sick until we lay our all on the altar for Him – that is true. But our sacrifice is not **why** He does it – He performs His wonders of salvation and healing because of His mercy and grace. Elijah's Godliness did not generate the awesome lightning that burned up everything on the altar. The fire did not come from his holiness. Your tithes and offerings cannot buy a tiny candle flame of the celestial flame. The fire of God comes – not because of our sacrifice – but because of Christ's sacrifice. Therefore, thank God, the fire is for all! Revival fire is not a reward for good people. It is God's gift. Why struggle for it? People talk about "paying the price." But is it a case of "you pay much too much for what's given freely"? Fire comes by faith.

We can be dead right … but dead nonetheless. We can insist on the "body of truth," but it may be a cold corpse. Jesus did not merely say: *"I am the way and the truth"* – He said: *"I am the way, the truth and the life."* God said He would put in Zion *"the shining of a flaming fire."* Jesus testified that John the Baptist was *"the burning and shining lamp."* These are images of light and heat. The Gospel is a hot Gospel, no matter how much the silly world smiles at it. I do not know how to preach the *"living oracles"* of God without being lively. The Gospel is to be on fire. To preach the Gospel coolly and casually would be ridiculous.

One day a lady told me that there was a "demon" sitting on her, although she was a born-again Christian. I said to her, "Flies can only sit on a cold stove, and on a cold stove they can sit very long! Get the fire of the Holy Spirit into your life, and that dirty demon will not dare to touch you, lest he burn his filthy fingers." The Gospel provides its own fiery power. It is natural, therefore, for a preacher to be fired-up. And it should be natural for **you** to walk in that fire too!

Origins of the Anointing

"Anointing" is sometimes taken as one of the latest "in" things for those seeking a higher stratum of spirituality, but it is not new. In the Old Testament, **all** who served God had to be anointed – in the New Testament, this was replaced by the Holy Spirit for all believers. There was actually an Old Testament practice of oiling the head of sheep for their protection … but the anointing of the Spirit, or the baptism with the Spirit, is much more than a protective measure – it refers to the anointing of the Spirit, or the baptism with the Spirit.

In the house of Simon the Pharisee, Jesus used similar language to that in Psalm 23, saying, *"You did not anoint My head with oil."* It was the social welcome for guests to anoint them with fragrant oils and greet them with the double kiss on the cheeks, as is still the practice in the East. Jesus compared Simon with an unknown woman, who had poured perfumed oil upon His feet and continued kissing His feet, while Simon had done nothing. Simon had been too casual, showing Jesus no such respect. The social anointing of guests was meant to impart a pleasant smell to the guests and to help their appearance by making their faces shine, which was considered admirable in those days. Jesus accepted the anointing from this woman who lavished Him with the best ointment that money could buy.

Mary Magdalene also anointed Jesus. Her ointment was spikenard, a very rare and precious preparation of nard brought from northern India at great expense and prepared with the secretive art of the perfumer. Sold in long, slender alabaster containers, it kept for years, and would even improve in quality and value. When filled with ointment, they were kept as an investment, a household treasure. The fragrance of Mary's oil was so rich we are told it pervaded the whole house. It was a tremendous sacrifice, an act of love's bountiful extravagance. It speaks of the love of God through Jesus Christ, which brings us the priceless gift of the anointing of the Holy Spirit. It is no cheap experience. It is God's best. Holy Spirit anointing is God's gift for **you**!

Today's Scripture

The Earth is satisfied with the fruit of Your works … Wine that makes glad the heart of Man, oil to make his face shine, and bread which strengthens Man's heart.

(Psalm 104:13-15)

Daily Power!

I accept God's best blessing, His Holy Spirit, as His gift to me today.

Today's Bible Reading

Jeremiah 33:1-26
through 34:1-22;
I Timothy 4:1-16;
Psalm 89:1-13;
Proverbs 25:23-24

Mark my Word
(for further study)

Psalm 23:5; 104:15;
Luke 7:36-50

True Anointing

Today's Scripture

It shall come to pass in that day that his burden will be taken away from your shoulder, and his yoke from your neck, and the yoke will be destroyed because of the anointing oil.

(Isaiah 10:27)

Daily Power!

An ancient tradition of anointing oil has been given new life through the baptism of the Holy Spirit.

Today's Bible Reading

Jeremiah 35:1-19 . through 36:1-32; I Timothy 5:1-25; Psalm 89:14-37; Proverbs 25:25-27

Mark my Word
(for further study)

Exodus 30:1-38; Esther 2:12; Song of Solomon 3:6; Matthew 1:17

The most common ingredient of cosmetic ointment was **myrrh**, which was refined from a perfumed, resinous substance from the small commiphora myrrha nees tree. The girl loved by Solomon had fingers dripping with sweet-smelling myrrh … Solomon himself came from the dusty wilderness *"perfumed with myrrh and frankincense"* … part of Esther's beauty treatment for presentation to King Xerxes was six months with oil of myrrh … value was shown when the Magi brought myrrh to the baby Jesus as a special gift … taken medically, myrrh was used as an opiate – Jesus refused it on the Cross.

The special anointing oil described in Exodus 30 was used only for the Lord's tabernacle and priests, to ordain them for service. Kings were also anointed. Most commentaries also say prophets were anointed … but from what I can see in Scripture, not one of them ever was: they were independent men of God, not socially appointed. God chose and gave them the real anointing with the Spirit. Nobody made prophets – they were God's men. By divine command, Elijah should have anointed Elisha, but failed to do so. God Himself anointed Elisha with the Spirit.

It was the habit to call the Spirit of God by the name of a prophet – *"the spirit of Moses"* or *"the spirit of Elijah"* – as a personal and rare distinction. The spirit of Moses was to be put upon the elders of Israel, and Elisha wanted a double portion of the spirit of Elijah. When God anoints believers today, it is with *"the spirit of the prophets."* The true anointing is always by the Lord. Oils, unguents and ointments were poured upon priests and kings as mere symbols that God's Spirit had chosen to rest upon them. God was the Originator, and such men were therefore called *"the anointed of the Lord"* – especially Christ (from "Messiah" or "anointed"), Who is *"the Anointed of God."* Today among believers, the anointing is a sovereign act of God … an act which He desires to lavish upon **you**.

How big is Hell?

21

The angel who appeared to Cornelius in Acts chapter 10 was not allowed to mention the Name of Jesus, or to speak about salvation to the man. That high and holy privilege was – and is – reserved for men … people like you and me. All the angel was allowed to say was, *"Now send men to Joppa, and send for Simon whose surname is Peter."* This mighty seraphim from deep Heaven had to bow to Peter's higher privilege. It pleases God to call and to send people like you and me. It has always been this way. God used four evangelists – Matthew, Mark, Luke, and John – to write down the story of the Gospel of Jesus Christ. Such a pattern is linked, in my mind, to the four men in Old Testament times who carried the Ark of the Covenant. Carriers of the Gospel change from generation to generation … but the Gospel remains the same. **Now we are here … and today it is our turn!** God has called you and me. The Gospel needs to be taken to the ends of the Earth. This is the Great Commission of the Lord to us – and the King's business requires haste.

I do not believe that God's plans call for Hell to be bigger than Heaven. Although Scripture speaks about *"many"* who are on their way to eternal destruction, these same people must be intercepted by men and women preaching the original Gospel. Provision has been made to bring *"many sons to Glory,"* and – praise God! – the Book of Revelation speaks of a successful conclusion! Jesus instructed, *"Go … and make disciples of all the nations."* There is no alternate plan in case the Gospel fails **because it won't!** More people are being saved, healed and baptized into the Holy Spirit today than ever before in Man's history. The tempo is increasing, leading to but one conclusion: **Jesus is coming soon!** That is your greatest hope!

Today's Scripture

But in every nation whoever fears Him and work righteousness is accepted by Him.
(Acts 10:35)

Daily Power!

It pleases God to call and to send people like you and me.

Today's Bible Reading

Jeremiah 37:1-21 through 38:1-28;
I Timothy 6:1-21;
Psalm 89:38-52;
Proverbs 25:28

Mark my Word
(for further study)

Matthew 7:13; 28:19;
Acts 10:1-48;
Hebrews 2:10;
Revelation 7:9

Dummy Ammunition

Fire is the ensign of the Gospel, the sign of the Son of Man. When we see fire, that is evidence that Jesus – and nobody else – is at work. It is the identifying hallmark of His activity, the true outburst of Christian faith. Elijah made the same point: *"The God Who answers by fire, He is God!"* What does your spiritual thermometer read? Does it even register? There are theologies and teachings as fire-proof as asbestos, religious books that provide heat only if put in a bonfire. Such faith-chilling items have nothing to do with the Christ of Pentecost. Whatever He touches catches fire. Church efforts to whip up enthusiasm are, spiritually, as pitiful as rubbing two sticks together.

Only the fire of God was allowed on the altar of Moses, not fire produced by human means. Nadab and Abihu made fire themselves and lit their incense with it – it was labeled "profane fire" … then Divine fire gushed from the tabernacle, swallowing up the false fire and bringing death to the rebel priests. Today, we have profane fire being offered: strange gospels which are not Gospel at all, theologies of unbelief, the thoughts of men and their philosophies, criticisms and theories. They bear no trace of the glory-heat from Heaven. Nothing in them produces any combustion except controversy. What lies behind all this is what Jesus said to Satan: *"Get behind Me, Satan! You are an offense to Me, for you are not mindful of the things of God, but the things of men."*

There are the thoughts of God and those of Man. Satan thinks as men think. The fact is: Satan simply cannot grasp God's outlook at all. That is strange when you remember that he was originally Lucifer, a throne angel of God. Jesus bruised the serpent's head, and I think He inflicted some kind of brain damage upon the devil! Once Satan was full of wisdom, but today that *"prince of the power of the air"* is baffled by what God is doing … and especially by what the Lord did at the Cross! This type of confusion is brought on by sin. **You** have been "enlightened" by the entrance of the pure Word of God!

Today's Scripture

For whoever desires to save his life will lose it; but whoever loses his life for My sake will find it.
(Matthew 16:25)

Daily Power!

Jesus bruised the serpent's head, and I think He inflicted some kind of brain damage on the devil!

Today's Bible Reading

Jeremiah 39:1-18 through 41:1-18; II Timothy 1:1-18; Psalm 90:1-17 through 91:1-16; Proverbs 26:1-2

Mark my Word
(for further study)

Leviticus 10:1-2; I Kings 18:24; Isaiah 55:8-9; Matthew 16:23

"Crazy Joy"

The disciples were crazy with joy when they cast out devils, but Jesus said that was nothing: *"Then the seventy returned with joy, saying, 'Lord, even the demons are subject to us in Your Name.' And He said to them, 'I saw Satan fall like lightning from Heaven. Behold, I give you the authority to trample on serpents and scorpions, and over all the power of the enemy, and nothing shall by any means hurt you. Nevertheless do not rejoice in this, that the spirits are subject to you, but rather rejoice because your names are written in Heaven.' In that hour Jesus rejoiced in the Spirit and said, 'I thank You, Father, Lord of Heaven and Earth, that You have hidden these things from the wise and prudent and revealed them to babes. Even so, Father, for so it seemed good in Your sight. All things have been delivered to Me by My Father, and no one knows Who the Son is except the Father, and Who the Father is except the Son, and the one to whom the Son wills to reveal Him.' Then He turned to His disciples and said privately, 'Blessed are the eyes which see the things you see; for I tell you that many prophets and kings have desired to see what you see and have not seen it, and to hear what you hear and have not heard it.'"* **We** are so privileged to see and hear what the Lord Jesus Christ does **today!**

Peter heard Christ say those words, and he took in that lesson; later he wrote this about believers: *"Whom having not seen you love. Though now you do not see Him, yet believing, you rejoice with joy inexpressible and full of glory, receiving the end of your faith – the salvation of your souls."* Rejoice in undertones? Worship in whispers? Participate in silent celebrations? That is not what the word "rejoice" means in this Scripture. It means "to exult, shout, be rapturous" – **Crazy Joy!** Try doing that without emotion, without fire! The fire of the Holy Spirit is for real. It must flow through the Church of Jesus Christ like blood through the veins. God's people on fire, and the Church as a whole on fire, will win our lost generation for Him. Let your inhibitions go – let the fire of God run through you!

Today's Scripture

That the genuineness of your faith, being much more precious than gold that perishes though it is tested by fire, may be found to praise, honor and glory at the revelation of Jesus Christ.
(I Peter 1:7)

Daily Power!

The fire of the Holy Spirit must flow through the Church like blood through the veins.

Today's Bible Reading

Jeremiah 42:1-22 through 44:1-23; II Timothy 2:1-21; Psalm 92:1-15 through 93:1-5; Proverbs 26:3-5

Mark my Word
(for further study)

Luke 10:17-24; I Peter 1:7-9

24

Today's Scripture

Jesus Christ, the faithful Witness, the Firstborn from the dead, and the Ruler over the kings of the Earth. To Him Who loved us and washed us from our sins in His own Blood.

(Revelation 1:5)

Daily Power!

Truth-telling was a key attribute of Jesus Christ – His faithfulness is trustworthy.

Today's Bible Reading

Jeremiah 44:24-30 through 47:1-7; II Timothy 2:22-26 through 3:1-17; Psalm 94:1-23; Proverbs 26:6-8

Mark my Word
(for further study)

John 8:13-14, 18; 14:1; Revelation 1:1-29

Revelation in Revelation

One man entrusted with the message of a past, present and future faith was John the apostle. When he was up against the whole Roman Empire, he wrote a marvelous and triumphant book. He wrote: *"I, John, both your brother and companion in the tribulation and kingdom and patience of Jesus Christ, was on the island that is called Patmos for the Word of God and for the testimony of Jesus Christ."* John was close to Jesus. It was a unique friendship. He also suffered for Christ. John was the man who saw what things meant. He read the signs with prophetic insight. What he saw was difficult to explain. It was new on Earth. Nobody had thought of it, especially in one sentence. So let's look at what he said: *"Grace to you and peace from Him Who is and Who was and Who is to come, and from the seven Spirits Who are before His Throne, and from Jesus Christ, the faithful Witness, the Firstborn from the dead, and the Ruler over the kings of the Earth."*

How can Jesus be a "faithful witness"? We are witnesses to Christ, but to what does Christ witness? This Scripture refers back to another passage, where the Pharisees were arguing: *"Here You are, appearing as Your own witness; Your testimony is not valid."* Jesus answered, *"Even if I testify on my own behalf, My testimony is valid for I know where I came from and where I am going … I am One Who testifies for Myself; My other Witness is the Father, Who sent Me."* Jesus witnessed to Himself. He said, *"Believe in God; believe also in Me."* By His life and mighty deeds, He has shown us what He is – faithful to what He told us He is.

He doesn't disappoint us. If He were different now, He would not be a faithful witness – He is consistent with what He said and did. The life of Jesus spells hope for sinners and the sick, and concern for everybody. He writes, "Yours faithfully, Jesus Christ." Our Lord Jesus is **always** faithful to you and to me, praise His Name!

Read carefully

25

Punctuation is important! In John 7:37-38, Jesus cried, *"If any man thirst, let him come unto Me, and drink. He that believeth on Me, as the Scripture hath said 'out of his belly shall flow rivers of living water.'"* This is quoted from the King James Version … but not exactly. I left out a comma, **which makes a difference**. No comma is there in the Greek original. So we should read it like this: *"He that believeth on Me as the Scripture hath said."* That is, rivers of living water will flow from those who *"believe on Me as the Scripture has said."* It is not living waters that Jesus says the Scripture talks about – but Himself and those who believe on Him. People have not found which Scripture Jesus had in mind when He spoke of waters, although we have suggested Isaiah 58:11. The promise of living water originates with Jesus Himself, and as Peter preached, *"The promise is to you and to your children, and to all who are afar off, as many as the Lord our God will call."*

It is even more important to look at John 3:34 again. The King James Version reads, *"He Whom God hath sent speaketh the words of God: for God giveth not the Spirit by measure **unto Him**."* Now the words shown in boldface – ***"unto Him"*** – are not in the original text. The New International Version translates it correctly: *"God gives the Spirit without limit"* – that is, to us all, as John 1:16 tells us, *"Of His fullness we have all received."* Literally *"because of His fullness,"* we are filled without measure.

Fullness lies in Christ Jesus and flows out of Him to fill us. He is the Source. So long as Christ is full, we shall *"be being filled."* He is *"full of grace and truth,"* and out of Him we receive *"grace for grace,"* or grace constantly being renewed.

Today's Scripture

To know the love of Christ which passes knowledge, that you may filled with all the fullness of God.
(Ephesians 3:19)

Daily Power!

I shall never lack the dynamic of the Holy Spirit – the fullness of joy, peace, love – because I have been limitlessly filled with Him and by Him.

Today's Bible Reading

Jeremiah 48:1-33 through 49:1-22; II Timothy 4:1-22; Psalm 95:1-11 through 96:1-13; Proverbs 26:9-12

Mark my Word
(for further study)

Isaiah 58:11; John 1:14-16; 3:34; 7:37-38; Acts 2:39

26

True Faith

We pray for Christian revival – why? To see the church full, pay the bills, ease the labors of evangelism, as a religious duty? Look at the pitiful attempts of Christ-less people to save themselves, making their own impotent gods. Let us weep for them. Let us cry out to God: *"Gird yourselves and lament, you priests; wail, you who minister before the altar; come, lie all night in sackcloth, you who minister to my God. For the grain offering and the drink offering are withheld from the House of your God. Consecrate a fast, call a sacred assembly, gather the elders and all the inhabitants of the land into the House of the Lord your God, and cry out to the Lord … 'Now, therefore,' says the Lord, 'turn to Me with all your heart, with fasting, with weeping, and with mourning.' So rend your heart, and not your garments; return to the Lord your God, for He is gracious and merciful, slow to anger, and of great kindness; and He relents from doing harm."* God is moved when our hearts – not just our mouths – are moved.

A true intercessor has faith. All the great prayers of intercession in Scripture were triggered Heavenward from the launch-pad of faith. Faith is assurance of the changeless character of God's goodness, believing He is faithful to what He says He is. If prayer is controversial, then everything is. If all answers to prayer were printed, they would fill the Atlantic depths.

Faith is **faith in God**, not just in some "miracle happening." The great Bible intercessors did not always see what they asked for. God heard Abraham, but in the end, the cities of Sodom and Gomorrah were destroyed. **Pray on** … and leave matters in God's hands to do whatever He knows is good.

Today's Scripture

Seek the Lord while He may be found, call upon Him while He is near. Let the wicked forsake his way, and the unrighteous man his thoughts; let him return to the Lord, and He will have mercy on him, and to our God, for He will abundantly pardon.
(Isaiah 55:6-7)

Daily Power!

Faith is assurance of the changeless character of God's goodness, believing He is faithful to what He says He is.

Today's Bible Reading

Jeremiah 49:23-39 through 50:1-46; Titus 1:1-16; Psalm 97:1-12 through 98:1-9; Proverbs 26:13-16

Mark my Word
(for further study)

Isaiah 55:6-7; Joel 1:13-14; 2:12-13

The real Anointing

Disciples and apostles were never anointed with oil. In the New Testament, Christians received the Spirit for their work of service. Oil was never poured upon Jesus – except by a woman for His burial, as He said. Before the Day of Pentecost, priests were anointed and carried the fragrance with them … but **since the Day of Pentecost, believers have carried the aura of Jesus:** *"They realized that they had been with Jesus"* – the real anointing had come!

Anointing with oil was retained only for the healing of the sick in the New Testament. Our anointing flows out of Christ's anointing, and we receive it only from Him: *"Of His fullness we have all received."* To John the Baptist, it was revealed that *"the Man on Whom you see the Spirit come down and remain is He Who will baptize with the Holy Spirit."* He identified the Source: Jesus Christ, the Giver and the Authority of the giving.

"God anointed Jesus of Nazareth with the Holy Spirit and with power, Who went about doing good and healing all who were oppressed by the devil, for God was with Him."

We may pray and lay hands on people to be baptized in the Spirit, as the apostles did … but we must realize that a man cannot and need not give his anointing to someone else. It is out of Christ's fullness, not somebody else's fullness. I want my own anointing from God, not a second-hand anointing. To bestow an anointing, even as a temporary effect, is foreign to Bible thought. God alone is the Baptizer. The blessings of God may flow in many ways through our lives as rivers of living water from Christ, but that is very different from doing what only Jesus can do: impart the Spirit. The virgins refused to share their oil and were counted wise. Value the anointing that God gives you … treasure it and allow it to empower you to be a blessing to others.

Today's Scripture

Then Jesus arrived from Nazareth, anointed by God with the Holy Spirit, ready for action. He went through the country helping people and healing everyone who was beaten down by the devil. He was able to do all this because God was with Him.
(Acts 10:38; the Message)

Daily Power!

I want my own anointing from God, not a second-hand anointing.

Today's Bible Reading;

*Jeremiah 51:1-53;
Titus 2:1-15;
Psalm 99:1-19;
Proverbs 26:17*

Mark my Word
(for further study)

*Matthew 25:7-10;
John 1:16, 33;
Acts 4:13; 8:17; 10:38;
James 5:14*

28

George Jeffreys and me

"Anointing" has acquired a broader meaning among believers today: "general blessing." When people offer to bring anointing by laying their hands upon us, we need not object. Scripturally, there is no such thing as "an anointing" – only "**the** anointing." But we need not be pedantic about the use of a word – providing, of course, that it does not convey bad theology or that the exclusive sense of giving the Holy Spirit is not intended but only a prayer for help, strength or any other need.

Once, by divine leading, I found myself far from where I should have been, staring at a house in Clapham, London. A board outside referred to George Jeffreys, whom many consider to have been the greatest British revivalist since John Wesley. He filled the greatest halls, pioneered in the face of universal opposition and proclaimed the glorious message of Jesus Christ, Savior, Healer, Baptizer, and coming King. I could hardly believe it – I had just read one of this great man's books! Was he really there? I dared to go and ask … he heard my voice and invited me in. There he prayed with me, and it was as if his mantle had come upon me (to use a Scriptural expression). God heard that man's prayer for me. I was already baptized in the Spirit – anointed – but sometimes we lack language to describe all that God does. I know that making contact with George Jeffreys and hearing his prayer for me had been a special experience which brought me a sense of equipping and readiness for service. Earlier that day, I had left the Bible college at Swansea to begin my full-time service for God. God had already called me to His work … and now this special experience seemed to cover me.

David was anointed by Samuel as king, which David took to mean that he was *"the Lord's anointed."* Later, the elders of Israel also anointed him as their assurance of his call to them as king. Anointings are not to be expected every time we meet a special evangelist or teacher. For me it was only once, after my call, when I met a man who had done the same work as God wanted me to do. It was like Elisha following Elijah. Seek God's anointing for your own life!

Satan's Chess Game

Satan thinks as men think – this means men think as the devil thinks. They too find the Cross foolishness and cannot grasp the things of God, as the Apostle Paul remarked. Paul also could not "see" it at first. Cold fury against the believers ate away in his heart. He was a "dragon man," breathing out threats and slaughter. Full of zeal, his brain was full of clever unbelief. Scales fell from his eyes when he believed.

I wonder if Hell would like to send espionage agents into the Kingdom of God, just to see what secrets are there? The demons wouldn't understand these secrets anyway. Hell is completely baffled. To Satan, Christ's sacrifice is a deep-rooted plot devised by God for His own advantage. The devil devours people – that is his evil nature. If we were to fight the devil on the level of human thought, we must remember that he thinks as men think. Satan invented a human chess game and has played this game for thousands of years. The devil anticipates our every move, and he will checkmate us ten moves ahead. Satan has experience from the time of Adam onward, and he knows every trick of human ingenuity on the board. You cannot produce faith by the wisdom of words. The devil always has a counterstatement for whatever you say.

The Gospel didn't come out of somebody's head. A university professor didn't give it to us. We have to move into the divine dimension, as there the enemy cannot follow us. The devil is no match for the mind of the Holy Spirit. If we plan, preach, witness and evangelize as men, Satan will foil us. He can handle psychology and propaganda. The answer is: move in the Spirit and preach the Gospel as it is. Then the arch-confuser becomes confused, and he can't follow the game at all. The devil doesn't even know the Holy Spirit's alphabet! It is so good to know that **you** are on God's team!

Today's Scripture

Keep a cool head. Stay alert. The devil is poised to pounce, and would like nothing better than to catch you napping.
(I Peter 5:8; the Message)

Daily Power!

The devil is no match for the mind of the Holy Spirit.

Today's Bible Reading

*Lamentations 1:1-22 through 2:1-19;
Philemon 1:1-25;
Psalm 101:1-8;
Proverbs 26:20*

Mark my Word
(for further study)

I Peter 5:8

30

God's Fire in Jesus

In human experience, God's fire translates into passion – the type of passion we saw in Jesus. Perhaps He wasn't only passionate in His words ... when Jesus was going to Jerusalem for the last time, we read that He was walking ahead of His disciples, and they saw how He urged Himself onward: *"Now they were on the road, going up to Jerusalem, and Jesus was going before them; and they were amazed. And as they followed, they were afraid."* Why? **Somehow the fires in His soul were evident in the way He walked.**

When they arrived, Jesus saw the desecration of the Temple. The disciples then had further evidence of His passionate feeling – His reaction turned Him into an awesome figure! The disciples were reminded of the Psalm: *"Because zeal for Your House has eaten Me up."* But it's a love-anger, not a cold fury. Jesus wasn't a frenzied fanatic ... He loved His Father's House, that's all. It was His desire to see people in the Temple, worshipping with freedom and happiness. But commercialism in the Temple had spoiled all that ... and His heart overflowed like a volcano – the fire in His soul made Him cleanse the Temple. His actions were frightening, and many fled from the scene because of them.

The children, the blind and the lame stayed, however, and He healed them. That was what He had wanted to do anyway, and that was the reason His anger achieved furnace heat. His indignation aimed for joy. Jesus got the children singing, *"Hosanna!"* This was the only occasion in Scripture where excitement about God was rebuked, the only time a hush was demanded in the Courts of the Lord. The silence was demanded by the Pharisees – the praise of the Lord was drowning the tinkling of their commercial tills. "Money music" was muted! This was all part of the picture of the fire of the Lord. Purpose to have that fire alive in your heart today.

Today's Scripture

Have you never read, "Out of the mouths of babes and nursing infants You have perfected praise."
(Matthew 21:16)

Daily Power!

In human experience, God's Fire translates into human passion.

Today's Bible Reading

Lamentations 2:20-22 through 3:1-66;
Hebrews 1:1-14;
Psalm 102:1-28;
Proverbs 26:21-22

Mark my Word
(for further study)

Psalm 69:9;
Matthew 21:1-17;
Mark 10:32

Parakletos

Before Christ, nobody had been "baptized in the Spirit." This term means something different from the "attachment of the Spirit" to Old Testament men and women. Samuel took the horn of oil and anointed David, and the Spirit of the Lord *"came upon David from that day forward."* But such experiences are never described as a baptism, for the Holy Spirit's relationship with blood-washed, born-again believers is new. *"The Spirit of truth … dwells with you and will be in you."* That is why a new expression is used – it describes a new kind of experience. To deny Christians the right to use the phrase "baptized in the Spirit" leaves them limited to the same kind of experience as in the Old Testament dispensation.

The Old Covenant people knew nothing of speaking with tongues, casting out demons or healing by the laying on of hands. These signs were reserved for the "age of the Spirit." A new Kingdom, a New Covenant with new features, a new Gospel for spirit and body describe the Christian age. Jesus used a new word for the Holy Spirit – "parakletos" – used five times in John's Gospel. It is translated "Comforter" and "Counselor." It belongs to the Greek word parakaleo – "to call for somebody, to enlist their sympathy," and is translated "comfort, consolation." To understand this promise, we need only emphasize the word **Comforter**. He Himself had been the parakletos to His disciples. Jesus said, *"I will not leave you comfortless"* – in this case, the Greek word is "orphanous" ("orphans"), or as James wrote, "fatherless." Jesus constantly used only one word for God – "the Father" – and that is the relationship He has established for all who receive Him, the Son of God. So when He gave His last assurances to His disciples, He said, *"Wait for the gift My Father promised – you will be baptized with the Holy Spirit."* He also related the gift of the Spirit to the Father: *"How much more will your Heavenly Father give the Holy Spirit to those who ask Him!"* If we were orphans, we would not receive the Spirit: *"Those who are led by the Spirit of God are sons of God."* **You** are a child of God!

Today's Scripture

I will talk to the Father, and He'll provide you another Friend so that you will always have Someone with you. This Friend is the Spirit of truth … You know Him already because He has been staying with you, and will even be in you!
     (John 14:16-17; the Message)

Daily Power!

A new expression – "the baptism in the Holy Spirit" – is used to describe a new kind of experience … a New Testament experience!

Today's Bible Reading

Lamentations 4:1-22 through 5:1-22; Hebrews 2:1-18; Psalm 103:1-22; Proverbs 26:23

Mark my Word
(for further study)

I Samuel 16:13; Mark 16:17; Luke 11:13; John 14:16-18; Acts 1:4-5; Romans 8:14; James 1:27

Christians shouldn't run from the devil,
the devil should run from them.

Many are called but few make a choice.

Those eternally seeking the will of God
are overrun by those who do the will of God.

Dead, boring Christians

A burning message – and nothing but that – was supposed to be presented to the world. There doesn't have to be fireworks. Firebrands don't need to be hotheads. Everything about the Church, however, should reflect the warm light of God, to the very highest steeple: *"And in His Temple everyone says, 'Glory.'"* We read that God makes His ministers *"a flame of fire."* His people should be torches. Not only evangelists … but witnesses, ministers, church officials, leaders, workers, teachers, and administrators should all glow with the Holy Spirit, like torches in a cold street. The business meeting should see Holy Spirit fire just as much as the revival meeting (perhaps even more so).

A fish has the same temperature as the water in which it swims. Too many Christians are like fish – they have no more warmth of spirit than the cold, unbelieving world around them. Men are warm-blooded creatures – that's the way the Lord made us. That is also the way He chose us to take the Good News: **with warmth!** The Lord does not send us out because we have cool heads and dignity. Nor does He choose us because of our self-composure. He sends us out with live coals from the altar, as witnesses to the Resurrection, to testify that we have met the God of Pentecost. I've heard sermons that were like lectures on embalming the dead. Would such a talk remind anyone of the Living Jesus? Neither Jesus, Peter nor Paul left congregations sitting like marble statues in a museum.

Logic can be set alight and still be logic, like the logic of Isaiah or Paul, for example. Logic need not belong to the glacial period. Fire implies fervor, not ignorance. Learn, by all means … but not if it puts your fire out. Remember: radiance before cleverness: *"And you shall love the Lord your God with all your heart, with all your soul, and with all your mind, and with all your strength."* The Lord wants you to have an "on fire" heart, and to radiate joy, compassion and love. Set your heart on fire today!

Today's Scripture

And you shall love the Lord your God with all your heart, with all your soul, with all your mind, and with all your strength. This is the first commandment.
(Mark 12:30)

Daily Power!

God made me a warm-blooded creature, alive with His Holy Fire.

Today's Bible Reading

Ezekiel 1:1-28 through 3:1-15;
Hebrews 3:1-19;
Psalm 104:1-23;
Proverbs 26:24-26

Mark my Word
(for further study)

Psalm 29:9;
Mark 12:30;
Hebrews 1:7

2

Today's Scripture

I say to you that likewise there will be more joy in Heaven over one sinner who repents than over ninety-nine just persons who need no repentance.

(Luke 15:7)

Daily Power!

I believe an evangelist's job is to light a fire in the human spirit.

Today's Bible Reading

Ezekiel 3:16-27
through 6:1-14;
Hebrews 4:1-16;
Psalm 104:24-35;
Proverbs 26:27

Mark my Word
(for further study)

Luke 19:40

Human dignity takes on a new meaning when people are rapt in praise to God. Have you ever seen fifty thousand people weeping, waving, jumping, and shouting in gladness to God? What else would you expect to happen when a mother stands on our platform, testifying that her child has just been healed of congenital blindness … or deafness … or perhaps of twisted limbs? I have seen these miracle testimonies so often. It is a glorious scene – the height of human experience. It is not to our credit when we keep perfectly cool as the lame walk and the blind see. Such reserve isn't clever … it is foolish. Dance – now that's more in keeping with such moments! We should take joy in the presence of the Lord! Jesus said that, at such times, even the stones would cry out.

I look at the precious men and women – black or white, many who were so sad earlier – standing in a meeting, hands pressed together in emotion or lifted in worship, eyes glistening with glad tears, faces turned up to God, lips moving in wondering thankfulness. I say to myself, "How beautiful they are!" In such moments, I wish I was an artist. When dignity comes before our delight in God, that is a catastrophe! If God does not touch our feelings, the devil will. How can God convict sinners and help them come to repentance unless they feel moved? How can He grant them the joy of sins forgiven, without giving them any sensation in their souls? **I believe an evangelist's job is to light a fire in the human spirit.** Getting folks saved is more than getting their names on a dotted line. Christianity isn't a club they are joining. Salvation is spiritual surgery. What is the forgiveness which we proclaim? What sort of forgiveness did Jesus give? It was the real kind of mercy. This forgiveness made a cripple walk again … it melted a street woman's hardness, causing her to wash His feet with tears. It was the sort of forgiveness which made people love much. It was the kind which made them do something extravagant, like throw a party, as Levi did. This forgiveness caused Mary to break open a box of spikenard worth a small fortune … and Zacchaeus to give away lots of money. When you remember what God has done for you, you **will** rejoice lavishly!

Live Ammunition

When we open up our evangelistic meetings to the Holy Spirit completely, the results are thrilling. Whole nations are challenged by the mighty power of Christ! Where false religion and doctrines of demons previously have prevailed, they are shaken and broken! No preacher could do this, no matter how popular or clever. Such success happens only when God does it His way. When He enters the field, there is a mighty victory. He can, will and **does** succeed – every time we allow Him to take over. These breakthroughs are part of the End Time blessings the Lord promised. The Day of Pentecost continued – it did not stop at Jerusalem, but is for *"the end of the Earth."* I offer this challenge: let anybody begin to work on the level of the Holy Spirit … and see if he experiences anything less than the Lord's own rescue and deliverance. This kind of evangelism will break Satan's back worldwide, and he will be routed. It is this Holy Fire which cannot be imitated.

When a gun is loaded with blanks, the bang and recoil are the same as they would be with live ammunition. A difference can be observed in the use of live ammunition and blanks, but not in the noise. The dummy ammunition makes no mark on the target, because it never reaches it. The real bullet can hit its mark. We are not interested in mere bang and recoil, excitement and spectacular Gospel displays, even if those draw hundreds of thousands of people. We want to see something live hitting the bull's-eye! The crowds may come, but we must, by faith, let loose a true broadside of Holy Spirit fire-power in order for something to be accomplished. Multitudes are born again, lives are completely changed, churches are filled, Hell is plundered and Heaven is populated. Hallelujah!

Today's Scripture

"And He commanded us to preach to the people, and to testify that it is He Who was ordained by God to be Judge of the living and the dead. To Him all the prophets witness that, through His Name, whoever believes in Him will receive remission of sins." While Peter was still speaking these words, the Holy Spirit fell on all those who heard the Word.
(Acts 10:43-44)

Daily Power!

Let anybody begin to work on the level of the Holy Spirit, and see if he experiences anything less than the Lord's own rescue and deliverance.

Today's Bible Reading

Ezekiel 7:1-27 through 9:1-11;
Hebrews 5:1-14;
Psalm 105:1-15;
Proverbs 26:28

Mark my Word
(for further study)

Acts 1:8; 10:43-44

4

Today's Scripture

Stay alert. You have no idea when [Jesus] might arrive.
  (Matthew 25:13; the Message)

Daily Power!

Jesus is saving you – don't you worry! – now start helping Him to save others!

Today's Bible Reading

Ezekiel 10:1-12 through 11:1-25; Hebrews 6:1-20; Psalm 105:16-36; Proverbs 27:1-2

Mark my Word
(for further study)

Mark 16:15 I Corinthians 9:16

Eternal Purposes

The fire of God is not sent just for the enjoyment of a few emotional experiences ... however, it **does** have that glorious side effect: Holy Spirit power produces lively meetings! But just being happy does not satisfy God's design – the Holy Spirit works for eternal purposes. I think of this when I see the now almost-extinct old steam engines puffing away. These "iron horses" are like living creatures, breathing steam with fire in their bellies. The fireman's job is to stoke the fire and get a full head of steam going. When the steam pressure is up, the driver can do one of two things: he either can pull the whistle lever ... or he can turn the lever that directs power onto the pistons. The whistle will blow off steam until there's none left, making itself heard for miles around. However, if power is directed onto the pistons, the steam can turn the wheels with far less fuss, drawing no attention to itself. The train then rolls away, carrying its load across the land. Thank God for the train whistle! It is important. But if blowing a whistle was all that steam could do, making a fire under the boiler and stoking it up wouldn't be worthwhile.

The fire of the Holy Spirit brings power. Never mind the noise – let us apply this power to get on the move! Thunder is justified after lightning has struck. The proper purpose of Pentecost is to get the wheels rolling for God in every church, thereby transporting the Gospel across the face of the whole Earth: *"Go into all the world and preach the Gospel to every creature."* The Church is a "Go" church, not a "Sit" church. Look outward to where our Lord is moving across the continents. Some are looking inward, everlastingly examining their own souls, incapacitated by introspection. Jesus is saving you – don't you worry! – now start helping Him to save others! If the Holy Spirit has come, then be up and going. He does the work, not you or me. *"Woe is me if I do not preach the Gospel!"* And woe to them to whom we fail to preach it. Let's be busy for Christ, not lazy.

Worship and Praise

A true intercessor delights in worship and praise. Throughout the intercessory Psalms, there is not a single instance of honor to God being omitted in some shape or form – the single psalm of unrelieved gloom, Psalm 88, makes no petition and offers no praise. But intercession rises to God on the wings of worship. Requests and praise are two sides of the same coin. *"Do not be anxious about anything, but in everything, by prayer and petition, with thanksgiving, present your requests to God"* … *"So then, just as you received Christ Jesus as Lord, continue to live in Him … overflowing with thankfulness. Devote yourselves to prayer, being watchful and thankful"* … *"Rejoice always, pray without ceasing, in everything give thanks"* … *"Let the heart of those rejoice who seek the Lord!"*

Intercessors do not come to God being offended about what He has not done. Moaning is not praying. Our burden for the world's needs is lifted as we pray in remembrance and thanks for what He can – and will – do. Often, our prayers of intercession are based on knowing that what God has done for ourselves, He will do for others too: *"I give You all the credit, God – You got me out of that mess, You didn't let my foes gloat. God, my God, I yelled for help and You put me together. God, You pulled me out of the grave, gave me another chance at life when I was down and out. All you saints, sing your hearts out to God! Thank Him to His face! … You did it: You changed wild lament into whirling dance; You ripped off my black mourning band and decked me with wildflowers. I'm about to burst with song; I can't keep quiet about You. God, my God, I can't thank You enough."*

The Lord's Prayer begins: *"Our Father, hallowed be Your Name."* That is the beginning of all true intercession … and the end is: *"For Yours is the Kingdom and the power and the glory for ever and ever. Amen."* Make that the beginning and the end of your prayers today … and you just might see your prayer life rise up to a new level of effectiveness.

Today's Scripture

Rejoice always, pray without ceasing, in everything give thanks, for this is the will of God in Christ Jesus for you.
(I Thessalonians 5:16-18)

Daily Power!

My prayers will always rise to God on wings of worship and praise.

Today's Bible Reading

Ezekiel 12:1-28 through 14:1-11; Hebrews 7:1-17; Psalm 105:37-45; Proverbs 27:3

Mark my Word
(for further study)

Psalm 30:1-12 (the Message); 105:3; Matthew 6:9-13; Philippians 4:6; Colossians 2:6-7; 4:2; I Thessalonians 5:16-18

Faith and Knowing

Today's Scripture

But now the righteousness of God apart from the Law is revealed ... through faith in Jesus Christ, to all and on all who believe ... Being justified freely by His grace through the redemption that is in Christ Jesus ... that He might be just and the Justifier of the one who has faith in Jesus.
(Romans 3:21-26)

Daily Power!

True faith means to place confidence in something trustworthy.

Today's Bible Reading

Ezekiel 14:12-23 through 16:1-42; Hebrews 7:18-28; Psalm 106:1-12; Proverbs 27:4-6

Mark my Word
(for further study)

Romans 3:21-26

True faith means to place confidence in something. That does not mean that anything at all will do – whatever we trust must be **trustworthy**. Christian faith is faith in Christ – this is not irrational. "Blind faith" is careless and irresponsible, like putting your money into the hands of somebody you know nothing about. A Christian brother felt sorry for people who had been in jail, so he employed men who had been in prison in order to give them a new start. He showed his confidence in one man by making him his general manager. Secretly, the man robbed him, and his thefts almost ruined the business. Later, he learned that the reason for this trusted employee's previous sentence was embezzlement! Blind faith!

All over the world, people are putting faith in an endless variety of religions, systems, gods, theories, sects, cults, and self-proclaimed messiahs. Only a fool would trust an unknown deity ... but fools do when techniques and strong emotional pressures are applied. They have, in recent times, committed mass suicide in their deluded hopes. The vast majority of "faiths" (or religions) – old as well as new – promise nothing this side of eternity, but "pie in the sky when you die." The late Ayatollah Khomeini sent very young teenagers into mined battlefields with the promise that, if they died killing infidels, they would go straight to Paradise. How can killing people make anybody fit for Heaven? Who would believe it? But it is an example of the deceitfulness of satanic influence. The Spanish Emperor at the time of the Inquisition was stricken with anxiety about his own salvation because he thought he had not burned enough Jews and others who were not Catholics! Few "faiths" are like the common experience of Christian believers – in fact, no real experience of God at all, no miracle, no forgiveness, no victory over sin, no strength in adversity, no peace with God, no joy. Some of them promote resignation to fate as a great virtue. But Christian believers overcome fate. They don't bow to the inevitable. **Know** what **your** faith in Christ means to **you**!

False Faiths

Most religions impose rules, prayers to pray, practices to observe, and offer (as a reward) some kind of future hope. This is a day of suicidal fanaticism, violent assertion, screaming threats, and murder, but Abraham – the father of three present-day religions – indulged in no raving demonstrations. In Christ's day, there were those claiming to be children of Abraham who fumed with hate and wanted to kill Jesus. He said, *"If you were Abraham's children ... then you would do the things Abraham did. As it is, you are determined to kill Me ... Abraham did no such things. You are doing the things your own father* [the devil] *does ... he was a murderer from the beginning."* People who know the truth don't get into a demented rage. When critics arise, they let the truth prove itself. The very method for spreading Christian truth shows what kind of Gospel it is: no threats, no swords, nor intimidation. *"It has pleased God by the foolishness of preaching to save them that believe."* The first Christians said, "We will conquer the world by love" ... and they did.

We are commonly told, "Keep an open mind about religion. Never be dogmatic." That is the liberal view: "You can never be sure." If we keep an open mind about it, we brush aside all Christ's wonderful promises and enjoy nothing that He promises. Christians do **not** keep an "open mind" – they embrace the positive blessings of Christ! Their minds are settled, not "open." How many would board an aircraft if the pilot kept "an open mind" about flying, the destination and how to get there? Passengers want **a very** dogmatic pilot! He must be dead-sure they will not end up dead, for sure! Keeping an open mind about our journey through life is equally perilous. The Bible does not encourage anybody to be "dogmatic" – but its language is always that of a sure and certain hope. "We know" is a typical New Testament expression. The simple attitude of Christians is to be sure of tomorrow and of God – what He has done, He will do ... what He is, He will be. *"I know Whom I have believed, and am persuaded that He is able to guard what I have entrusted to Him for that day."* That kind of certainty is no more than we would expect from any God worth calling God. **You** can have that assurance today.

Today's Scripture

But I have no regrets. I couldn't be more sure of my ground – the One I've trusted in can take care of what He's trusted me to do right to the end.
   (II Timothy 1:12; the Message)

Daily Power!

Christians are sure of tomorrow and of God – what He has done, He will do ... what He is, He will be.

Today's Bible Reading

Ezekiel 16:43-63 through 17:1-24; Hebrews 8:1-13; Psalm 106:13-31; Proverbs 27:7-9

Mark my Word
(for further study)

John 8:39-41, 44; I Corinthians 1:21; II Timothy 1:12

Anointing and Appointing

Today's Scripture

You are a chosen generation, a royal priesthood, a holy nation; His own special people, that you may proclaim the praises of Him Who called you out of darkness into His marvelous light.
(I Peter 2:9)

Daily Power!

The anointing is given to me for service in the Master's Kingdom.

Today's Bible Reading

Ezekiel 18:1-32 through 19:1-14; Hebrews 9:1-10; Psalm 106:32-48; Proverbs 27:10

Mark my Word
(for further study)

Judges 14:6; I Corinthians 12:23-24; I Peter 2:9

Some experiences which we may call "anointings" (for lack of a better expression) may come as the assurance of God to a particular call, like that of the elders of Israel, David and Elisha. To some they have come when listening to some other man of God, when they knew God was thrusting them forward as what Paul calls *"the more honorable"* members of the body of Christ. My colleague, George Canty, had been put off by the methods of some healing evangelists and was critical of such activity. God had been pressuring him for some time, asking him, *"Where are all your mighty miracles?"* One day, he sat listening as a healing evangelist spoke. As soon as the man quoted his text, George felt a sudden spiritual elevation to a new plane. He knew he would do what the preacher had done and heal sick people. The impression was so vivid he had to look around to assure himself that the building was real, because it seemed such a visionary and transcendent moment. He knew he was different from that moment on.

Anointing and appointing go together. The only people anointed were those selected for a particular task, especially that of priest or king. It was not an experience for mere emotional enjoyment. Anointing did not signify that a special level of holiness had been attained. The anointing was given solely to equip and condition ordinary people to serve the Lord. The anointing was not available apart from service. Today, the anointing is for all believers, for all are to serve – we are *"a royal priesthood."* Note carefully that anointing is not a kind of emotional pleasure, but it comes into activity when we serve. David did not feel anointed in any particular sense … but when he faced Goliath, his anointing became apparent. Samson became strong only when he went into action for God … then the Spirit of God came upon him. A strong man does not feel his strength when he's sitting down – only when he exerts himself. Look for every opportunity to "serve" the Lord today … and watch the anointing from God rise up big within you!

Warfare Gifts

The gifts of the Spirit are given to us freely: *"Now we have received, not the spirit of the world, but the Spirit Who is from God, that we might know the things that have been freely given to us by God."* There are cheap imitations on the market: religious novelties, vibrations, spirit-powers, healing sunbeams, and sweetness and light from nowhere in particular: *"But know this, that in the last days perilous times will come ... having a form of godliness but denying its power; and from such people turn away! ... always learning and never able to come to the knowledge of the truth."* In many countries, our work disturbs those who have their own claims to power, protection and healing. I recall an especially powerful witch being brought over from America to cast a spell and destroy what I was preaching. She stood at the back of the crowd and went through her performance. I wore the whole armor of God as she attempted to launch a spiritual attack against me: *"Put on the whole armor of God, that you may be able to stand against the wiles of the devil. For we do not wrestle against flesh and blood, but against principalities, against powers, against the rulers of the darkness of this age, against spiritual hosts of wickedness in heavenly places. Therefore take up the whole armor of God, that you may be able to withstand in the evil day, and having done all, to stand."* Her attempt was futile against a Blood-bought child of God.

The Holy Spirit waits at the Cross, and those who kneel at that altar – and there alone – receive His limitless blessings. At Calvary, there are benefits far beyond the labored results of mantras, New Age processes and occultism. These are *"the weak and beggarly elements"* that Paul described. *"Let no one deceive you with empty words, for because of these things the wrath of God comes upon the sons of disobedience. Therefore do not be partakers with them. For you were once in darkness, but now you are light in the Lord. Walk as children of light* [for the fruit of the Spirit is in all goodness, righteousness, and truth], *finding out what is acceptable to the Lord. And have no fellowship with the unfruitful works of darkness, but rather expose them."* Walk as God's child in His light.

Today's Scripture

For you were once darkness, but now you are light in the Lord. Walk as children of light.
(Ephesians 5:8)

Daily Power!

Satanic attempts are futile against a Blood-bought child of God.

Today's Bible Reading

Ezekiel 20:1-49;
Hebrews 9:11-28;
Psalm 107:1-43;
Proverbs 27:11

Mark my Word
(for further study)

I Corinthians 2:12;
Galatians 4:8-11;
Ephesians 5:6-11;
6:11-14;
II Timothy 3:3,5,7

Young and Old in the last Hour

I am eternally grateful that I was a young man when Christ Jesus entered my heart and called me into His service. I knew He called me to be His servant … and I have never regretted a single moment, a single day of my life of service to Him. The response to His gift of salvation and then the response to His call for service – these are important milestones in the lives of all believers, young or old. The awareness that we are living in *"the last hour"* is also pressing on our hearts, motivating us to be *"doers of His Word, not hearers only."*

Young people have a slightly different status in the same last hour, however. When an old person gets saved, a soul gets saved. When a young person gets saved, both a soul **and** a lifetime are saved. The young person has an hour which could be a lifetime, and what a glorious hour that can be! An hour full of love, joy, peace, purpose, and security, even if the last hour lasted an entire lifetime. The only way to live tomorrow is to live in faith and activity for Jesus today.

I once prayed for an old and dying man. Suddenly, a strange thought challenged me: "What would you pray if you were in his place?" A famous politician who expressed his last wish asked for, "One delicious pork pie!" It didn't take long before I knew the answer for myself: I would ask the Lord to give me the strength and help to conduct one more Gospel Crusade! I would like to hit the bull's-eye once more, to once more lead one hundred thousand souls to the foot of the Cross of Christ. There is nothing grander than that – nor is there a more glorious way to die, than fighting on that victorious battleground. I **strongly encourage you** to make that **your** goal!

Today's Scripture

I am well on my way, reaching out for Christ, Who has so wondrously reached out for me. Friends, don't get me wrong: by no means do I count myself an expert in all of this, but I've got my eye on the goal, where God is beckoning us onward – to Jesus. I'm off and running, and I'm not turning back.
(Philippians 3:12-14; the Message)

Daily Power!

There is nothing grander, nor is there a more glorious way to die, than fighting on that victorious battleground for lost souls!

Today's Bible Reading

Ezekiel 21:1-32 through 22:1-31; Hebrews 10:1-17; Psalm 108:1-13; Proverbs 27:12

Mark my Word
(for further study)

James 1:22

Whirlwinds

In our great African Gospel crusades, there are mighty victories over satanic powers and over sorcery. Gigantic piles of witchcraft materials are brought and burned. Their owners have been delivered from satanic fears and oppressions when they received Jesus as their Lord and Savior. I often have pointed to the flames, saying: "That is like where the final home of the devil will be ... in the Lake of Fire!" Satan is not in control of Hell's fire – those flames are his judgment. When those *"works of the devil"* are reduced to ashes, we see the true Fire of the Lord fall on crowds "en masse."

The anti-anointing is a strange fire of destruction and death. But the flame from the presence of the Lord will devour it, just as it devoured the profane fire of Nadab and Abihu. After that, a sweet anointing of peace will flow over the Church, all the way down to its feet and robe hems. Let us forget old fights among God's people over issues which do not lead to the salvation of men and women. Our enemy is not another denomination, or even denominationalism. Our enemy is the devil, and the many lies by which he deceives the world – the lie that God is dead ... the lie that God is indifferent ... the lie that we can do without Jesus. *"They overcame him by the Blood of the Lamb."* Note that "him" is singular! We have one enemy: the devil. There is one power to oppose him: the anointing of the Holy Spirit. *"And the yoke will be destroyed because of the anointing."* When we walk in God's anointing – yielded vessels, ready for service, filled with holy fire – then we are whirlwinds of destruction upon the enemy's stolen territory ... we are unstoppable weapons of purpose and zeal, taking back what the enemy has stolen: the lives of men and women all around the world! Let that be **your** purpose today!

Today's Scripture

The thief does not come except to steal, and to kill, and to destroy. I have come that they may have life, and that they may have it more abundantly.
(John 10:10)

Daily Power!

When we walk in God's anointing ... we are whirlwinds of destruction upon the enemy's stolen territory.

Today's Bible Reading

Ezekiel 23:1-49;
Hebrews 10:18-39;
Psalm 109:1-31;
Proverbs 27:13

Mark my Word
(for further study)

Leviticus 10:1-2;
Isaiah 10:27;
John 10:10;
Revelation 12:11

The Word brings Faith

The Creator Who cares enough to let this Human Race continue obviously does not want to leave us in the dark about Himself. He reveals Himself – that is the only way we could know Him. Our hard reasoning is like flint that only makes sparks, not light. *"Behold, all you that kindle a fire, that compass yourselves about with sparks: walk in the light of your fire … [but] you shall lie down in sorrow."* Sparks, flashes of thought, don't illumine Life's path very much. The philosophers are as lost as anybody, and yet they seek to guide us – the blind leading the blind. God says, *"Let there be light!"* He brought light to Abraham, Moses, David, the prophets, and finally through Jesus Christ.

"I've banked Your promises in the vault of my heart so I won't sin myself bankrupt … Oh, how I love all You've revealed; I reverently ponder it all the day long. Your commands give me an edge on my enemies; they never become obsolete … By Your words I can see where I'm going; they throw a beam of light on my dark path." Too many toss the Bible out of the window without realizing what damage they do. The Bible is dynamite. Scripture is unexplored territory to many, although "the gold of that land is good." To unfasten the clasps of the Bible and turn these healing leaves needs the fingers of faith. Yet *"faith comes by the Word of God."* God gives us faith to read it so we can gather faith – if we want it.

To get faith to read the Word, just read it. It is self-proving. Its chemistry explodes and brings us confidence about itself. *"Faith comes by hearing, and hearing by the Word of God"* and *"Hearing, you shall hear."* Abraham believed God when God spoke. The Creator fitted us with the power to recognize His voice, just as Abraham did. That is what we will do now: let the Bible speak for itself to bring **you** faith!

Today's Scripture

Now to Him Who is able to establish you according to my Gospel and the preaching of Jesus Christ, according to the revelation of the mystery kept secret since the world began but now made manifest – to God, alone wise, be glory through Jesus Christ forever. Amen.
(Romans 16:25-27)

Daily Power!

To open the Bible and turn these healing leaves needs the fingers of faith.

Today's Bible Reading

Ezekiel 24:1-27 through 26:1-21; Hebrews 11:1-16; Psalm 110:1-7; Proverbs 27:14

Mark my Word
(for further study)

Genesis 1:3; 2:12; Psalm 119:11, 97-98, 105; Isaiah 50:11; Matthew 13:14; Romans 10:17; 16:25-27

Faith and the Promises

13

What is faith? It is not a thing, a lump of something, an extra brain lobe or a piece stuck on our soul. We choose to believe. Faith is an attitude. Faith is the only basis possible for any workable relationship. It seems to me that faith in God is not only good, but it is the only decent thing to do. It is ridiculous to expect dealings with God on any other terms – how else can an invisible God relate to us ... and for the unknown future? If we can't go that far, what are we worth? If we can't trust the Almighty of all beings, who do we think we are? It is the least God can expect: *"Without faith it is impossible to please God."* If anybody says, "I'm not a great believer" – that's too bad, because God is not pleased with them! Would they – or anybody else – be pleased if somebody didn't trust **them**?

Faith is not certainty ... it is a personal issue. Somebody may have proved himself up to now ... but the future holds only personal assurances. We trust them because we **know** them. It is bound to be a matter of trust. If we thought they would change, we would not trust them. We read in the Bible Who God is. We may have proved Him for ourselves up to this moment ... but for the future we can do no other but trust. No faith is needed to believe two plus two make four, but life is a degree more complicated. Circumstances change like the ocean. The vastness of things affects the future. Obviously, what God **might** do is affected – He doesn't cut across events as if they didn't occur. He may work no magic, turn no pumpkins into golden coaches. But He is all wise and all powerful, so much so that we have to leave things to Him to sort out, for we may understand no more of what He is doing than we would understand the chaos of a shipyard building a fifty thousand-ton luxury liner. We look to Him ... and that is something God takes into account. He made the world that way. Prayer and faith will enable Him to do what He could not otherwise do. No doubt it is true that God can do anything ... but He doesn't – without those who believe. That is His planned providence, His promise to **you**.

Today's Scripture

It's impossible to please God apart from faith.
(Hebrews 11:6; the Message)

Daily Power!

God can do anything, but He doesn't – without those who believe.

Today's Bible Reading

Ezekiel 27:1-36 through 28:1-26;
Hebrews 11:17-31;
Psalm 111:1-10;
Proverbs 27:15-16

Mark my Word
(for further study)

Hebrews 11:6

14

Today's Scripture

So teach us to number our days that we may gain a heart of wisdom.
(Psalm 90:12)

Daily Power!

Little children, this is the last second of the last hour!

Today's Bible Reading

Ezekiel 29:1-21 through 30:1-26; Hebrews 11:32-40 through 12:1-13; Psalm 112:1-10; Proverbs 27:17

Mark my Word
(for further study)

Psalm 90:12; Matthew 24:36; Romans 13:11; I John 2:18

Your last Hour

Suppose this was your last hour – what would you be doing? What a flurry of anxious preparations there would be! But let me tell you, it **is** "the last hour": *"Little children, it is the last hour."* I know that it seems that "this last hour" has lasted very long – as John wrote those words two thousand years ago – but don't let that "fact" confuse you. Of one thing we can be certain: if it was the last hour then, it most certainly is now! If John were writing today, he probably would write, "Little children, it is the last second of the last hour." When John wrote this verse, he was watching God's clock, not ours. Its hands have not stood still. How long will God's hour last, measured by Earthly time-keeping methods? The one thing we know is that we **don't** know how near we are to the end: *"But of that day and hour no one knows,"* Jesus said. It is obvious, however, that we are much closer to the end every day. Paul saw it that way too: *"Knowing the time, that now it is high time to awake out of sleep; for now our salvation is nearer than when we first believed."*

If anybody thought they had only sixty minutes left, they would certainly not spend the time on trivialities. With the microseconds running out like fine sand in an hourglass, they would see what was really important to them. They would not go shopping for the latest fashionable hat, or run an eye down the financial columns to see how their shares were doing. Focusing on the end would put all of life into its proper perspective. Somebody once said that most people live as if this life were a permanent arrangement. The Bible's message is that our days are *"numbered"* – not numberless. There is actually **only** time for the important things. I am thinking about the Church of Jesus Christ in particular. People often point out that Life consists of a thousand details, but the minor must not outweigh the major. The Church is to concern itself with one aim: the war with Satan and the campaign for souls. The great quality of Jesus is that He came when the Father sent Him. And the great quality about us should be that we go when Jesus sends us. *"As the Father has sent Me, I also send you."* The Church should plan to neglect anything which interferes with going. Be mindful of the number of your days.

Last Hour Logic

When the Bible proclaims, *"It is the last hour,"* it truly is. For the message of the Gospel, it is **always** the last hour. If you want to know how a single individual like Paul did so much, read his disclosure in Corinthians ... he lived as if the end of all things was at hand: *"But this I say, brethren, the time is short, so that from now on even those who have wives should be as though they had none, those who weep as though they did not weep, those who rejoice as though they did not rejoice, those who buy as though they did not possess, and those who use this world as not misusing it. For the form of this world is passing away."* The Gospel is eternal – but we haven't eternity to preach it. One would think we had forever when we view the often-leisurely operations of the Church. We have only as long as we live to reach those who live as long as we live. Today, over five billion souls are alive ... alive in our present world, not in an indefinite future age which needs to be evangelized. **It is the last hour.**

To make sure the Prodigal Son was welcomed home properly, the father **ran**! I have wanted to run too since the Holy Spirit charged me with this: *"It is the last hour."* The world's airlines have found me to be a good customer! One of Paul's favorite Greek words was "spoude" – meaning "to stretch out the neck as a man running to get to the finish line." It is translated: *"study, be diligent, be earnest, hasten, be zealous, be forward."* Many churches are very active ... doing what? To bring the Gospel to a dying world is the true relevance! Giving all our thoughts to our personal spirituality when the fires of Hell have broken out is like members of the fire brigade having a shave before answering a fire call. The command to evangelize is all that matters, snatching men from the flames of an eternal Hell. That divine command was not given in a passing mood of the Lord. God Himself is driven by the peril in which human beings stand without Christ. Calvary was His imperative! *"Other sheep I have which are not of this fold; them also I must bring, and they will hear My voice; and there will be one flock and one Shepherd."* **Run** to be a soul-winner!

Today's Scripture

Let us lay aside every weight and the sin which so easily ensnares us, and let us run with endurance the race that is set before us.
(Hebrews 12:1)

Daily Power!

The Gospel is eternal – but we don't have eternity to preach it.

Today's Bible Reading

Ezekiel 31:1-18 through 32:1-32; Hebrews 12:14-29; Psalm 113:1-9 through 114:1-8; Proverbs 27:18-20

Mark my Word
(for further study)

Luke 15:11-31; John 4:35; 10:16; I Corinthians 7:29-31; I John 2:18

The Beauty of God

Personal beauty is never condemned in Scripture. Pride, lack of modesty, provocative dress, and brazen flirting certainly are. God makes people beautiful, and does not expect us to belong to the cult of ugliness and make the worst of ourselves. I don't believe God took pleasure in the "saints" of the early centuries who boasted of the population of lice in their hair and beards. Nor was He pleased with the nuns who boasted that water never touched their feet except when they crossed a river.

God does not give special honor to those who dress out-of-fashion, dowdy or drab to win His favor. He creates beautiful things – from the glory of the dawn and majesty of the sunset ... to the star-spangled velvet of the night sky. His dwelling is the light of the setting sun, multi-colored and glorious. Our very means and ability to create beauty come from Him. *"He makes everything beautiful in its time"* ... *"Let the beauty of the Lord our God be upon us."* That is what the anointing is.

"The beauty of holiness" forbids pride. Pride is the *"dead flies [that] putrefy the perfumer's ointment, and cause it to give off a foul odor."* Our proud efforts at holiness are described as smelly and unclean: *"All our righteous acts are like filthy rags."* That is because they produce a judgmental and condemnatory attitude toward those who we suppose have lower standards. We put on spiritual airs with an unattractive, narrow and negative correctness. A legalistic life has about as much chance of producing true fruit of the Spirit as arctic ice has of producing orchids. But when we *"Give to the Lord the glory due His Name; bring an offering and come before Him; oh, worship the Lord in the beauty of holiness"* – then we invite the fragrance of God to permeate our lives. It may sound strange to hear this ... but now you know how I mean it when I say: "Smell like Christ today!"

Today's Scripture

Let the beauty of the Lord our God be upon us, and establish the work of our hands for us.
(Psalm 90:17)

Daily Power!

God makes everything – and everyone! – beautiful in its time.

Today's Bible Reading

Ezekiel 33:1-33 through 34:1-31; Hebrews 13:1-25; Psalm 115:1-18; Proverbs 27:21-22

Mark my Word
(for further study)

I Chronicles 16:29; Psalm 90:17; Ecclesiastes 3:11; 10:1; Isaiah 64:6

Paid by the Hour

Years ago in northern Germany, I had the privilege of leading an elderly lady to the Lord. For most of her life, she had been a church organist ... but yet had never known Jesus as her own Savior. When she heard the Gospel and opened her heart to the Lord, she was overwhelmed with the joy of the Holy Spirit. Three days later I met her again, but this time she was completely broken. Puzzled, I asked her why this was. With tears in her eyes, she told me, "I am already seventy years of age and have only just received Jesus as my Savior. I may live perhaps another five or ten years ... but I have totally wasted seventy."

Of course, this touched me deeply. Then I said, "Yes, but I know what is going to happen. One day we shall stand before the Judgment Seat of Christ. But He will not be as concerned as much about how **long** we cut the furrow of our life for Him, as how **deep**. Five or ten years, all-out for Jesus, are much more than having been a lukewarm Christian for fifty years."

Do you remember the laborers in the parable of Jesus? By the clock, some had worked only a single hour, but the farmer generously rewarded them, paying them the same as those who had labored throughout the day. Why? Because they had worked as long as they had the chance to work. This is the principle of God. If anybody is worried about not having been at Jesus' side in the harvest when they could have been, the answer is to leave that with the Lord of the Harvest. Don't waste time on tears. Give God, from this moment on, wholeheartedly what is His due! The Apostle Paul's advice is this: *"Brethren, I do not count myself to have apprehended; but one thing I do, forgetting those things which are behind and reaching forward to those things which are ahead, I press toward the goal for the prize of the upward call of God in Christ Jesus."* As long as you have breath within you, you are in time to be in on the last hour, the last day, the last month or the last year. **You** are not too late for that.

Today's Scripture

Forgetting those things which are behind and reaching forward to those things which are ahead, I press toward the goal for the prize of the upward call of God in Christ Jesus.
(Philippians 3:13-14)

Daily Power!

I shall purpose to work for the Master as long as I have the opportunity to work.

Today's Bible Reading

*Ezekiel 35:1-15 through 36:1-38;
James 1:1-18;
Psalm 116:1-19;
Proverbs 27:23-27*

Mark my Word
(for further study)

*Matthew 20:1-16;
Philippians 3:13-14*

Faith Objectives

James was the half-brother of Jesus, and his Epistle carries us back to the typical teaching of Jesus as no other book. *"You do not have because you do not ask God. When you ask, you do not receive, because you ask with wrong motives, that you may spend what you get on your pleasures ... Friendship with the world is hatred toward God. Anyone who chooses to be a friend of the world, becomes an enemy of God."* This discussion concerns prayer for material goods. But if we pray as materialists of the world, we shall get no answer. To set our affection on possessions, affluence, and prestige is materialism and worldliness, and pushes God and His purposes aside. *"Do not lay up for yourselves treasures on Earth, where moth and rust destroy and where thieves break in and steal; but lay up for yourselves treasures in Heaven, whether neither moth nor rust destroys and where thieves do not break in and steal. For where your treasure is, there your heart will be also."*

The number one prayer of many people is about number one: themselves. But when the Kingdom of God is Number One, there is no wrong in asking God for His good things: *"Every good and perfect gift is from above, coming down from the Father of heavenly lights, Who does not change like shifting shadows."* The material gifts around us are from God as gifts to His creatures. *"He satisfies the longing soul[s],"* whatever their instincts or tastes. God gives us the power to get wealth, but nothing whatever was made only for materialists. Riches are not the primary object of faith. Faith has been given to lay hold of possessions. God didn't display His vast wealth in our wonderful world just as a temptation to test Christians. Believers have as much claim on the good things of this life as anyone else does. To concentrate our desires and prayers on them is a different thing, however. The motive for getting is giving – to relieve the hungry and distressed, and to make known the Name of the Lord. Faith and prayer are a single subject, depending on one another. Keep them both active in your life, and watch them flow from you as **one** powerful force of blessing.

Today's Scripture

Every desirable and beneficial gift comes out of Heaven. The gifts are rivers of light cascading down from the Father of Light.
(James 1:17; the Message)

Daily Power!

To set our affection on possessions ... is worldliness, and pushes God aside.

Today's Bible Reading

Ezekiel 37:1-28 through 38:1-23; James 1:19-27 through 2:1-17; Psalm 117:1-2; Proverbs 28:1

Mark my Word
(for further study)

Deuteronomy 8:18; Psalm 107:9; Matthew 6:19-21; James 1:17; 4:2-4

Swelling Power

Marine scientists say ocean waves travel thousands of miles, under the surface, across apparently calm stretches. Approaching land, they develop a majestic crescendo, hunch their mighty shoulders, and build up in rapid momentum and volume, to burst finally and magnificently upon the shore. A glorious swell of Holy Spirit power is gathering to a spontaneous crescendo today, world wide, as if hurrying to the shore. The lifting of the waves proves that the shore cannot be far. Jesus is coming soon! **It is the last hour!** The latter day Pentecostal outpouring of the Spirit began in 1901, and the truth of *"the baptism in the Holy Spirit, with signs following"* was recovered. The mightiest revival of all swept onward like a wave from Heaven, the same tidal wave that started in Jerusalem nineteen hundred years before. A divine deluge of power – *"floods on the dry ground"* – had blessed the world for two or three hundred years ... **then** – through unbelief and worldliness – it seemed to ebb. The Church even taught that such power was only for the apostles and the early disciples. The Holy Spirit became a mere Third Article of the Creed, locked up and relegated to the past.

With the outpouring of His Spirit, the Lord gave believers power to do the job: to evangelize and send out missionaries. John wrote: *"As you have heard that the antichrist is coming, even now many antichrists have come, by which we know it is the last hour ... But the anointing which you have received from* [Christ] *abides in you."* The Church is being anointed for the last hour. The spirit of the age would be antichrist or anti-anointed. John's warnings concerning the last times have come home to us today, striking with an almost frightening truth about our times. The spirit of antichrist permeates human thinking and society, causing moral collapse. Hostile elements are raging worse and worse, like early moments of a gathering storm. God's answer: His anointing for an anti-anointed latter day. He will never allow the devil to get the upper hand. The outpouring of the Spirit is His special provision for the last hour: *"And it shall come to pass afterward that I will pour out My Spirit on all flesh ... before the coming of the great and awesome day of the Lord."* Christ's whole Body on Earth will be mobilized and armed for the last onslaught of the enemy. **Remember:** Satan, the eternal loser, will lose again.

Today's Scripture

But you have an anointing from the Holy One.
(I John 2:20)

Daily Power!

God's answer to the antichrist: His anointing.

Today's Bible Reading

Ezekiel 39:1-29 through 40:1-27;
James 2:18-26 through 3:1-18;
Psalm 118:1-18;
Proverbs 28:2

Mark my Word
(for further study)

Isaiah 44:3;
Joel 2:28, 31;
I John 2:18-27

20

Daily Power!

Each of us are led of God if we are His children.

Today's Bible Reading

Ezekiel 40:28-49 through 41:1-26; James 4:1-17; Psalm 118:19-29; Proverbs 28:3-5

Mark my Word
(for further study)

Isaiah 8:20; John 14:14-15; Romans 8:14

God's true Voice

After Jerusalem fell, many of the people wanted Jeremiah to inquire if they should leave the land. In their hearts, they wanted to go to Egypt and meant to do so – they only wanted Jeremiah to persuade God to approve their plans. Jeremiah inquired … and God did not approve at all. They went anyway, saying Jeremiah had lied about what God said … and they ran into great trouble as a result! God had not said anything about them leaving in the first place because He had no new plan.

There is a safeguard for all "voices" and impulses – and that is the Word: *"If they speak not according to this Word, there is no light in them."* It claims for itself the unique privilege of being the means through which God speaks. He has nothing to say except according to its precepts. His Word may come to us through ministry or prophecy – which often we need – but personal directives never come through a third party. He tells nobody else what you should do. There may be comfort, edification, and exhortation … but each of us is led of God if we are His children: *"For as many as are led by the Spirit of God, these are sons of God."*

None of the great men and women in Scripture who heard God's voice for themselves were asking and waiting for it. God wanted to speak and did so. People ask, "What is God saying to the Church?" Why should God always be saying something to the Church? Has He left us all in the dark about what He wants? There are spiritually superior persons who profess to know what nobody else knows, as if they were Divine favorites who really stood before Him as nobody else. The Spirit of the prophets is now the Spirit given to all believers. God reveals His secrets to His prophets, and we are all in that category today in Christ. When God speaks, it is a broadcast message, not a telephone call. **You** can hear His voice speaking clearly.

Many Callings

Evangelism happens to be my calling. There are other callings which will grip men and women: apostles, pastors, teachers, prophets, elders, musicians, organizers, intercessors, workers in a thousand different capacities. When God puts His Hand upon us, He does two things: first He gives us a ministry ... then He opens a door to service. Each one of us has a unique and vital place in His Kingdom. Every believer is individually chiseled, *"skillfully wrought in the lowest parts of the Earth."* Some are far from being run-of-the-mill ... yet they are hardly likely to be welcomed with a great cheer.

A new vision can be disturbing – not only to those who receive it, but to those who don't ... especially if it puts a man in the limelight. There can be resentment, criticism, even jealousy. Sometimes a man's close friends and colleagues can't believe God has put a call into his soul. But there is no accounting for God's choice, as Paul pointed out about Jacob. A call is entirely God's counsel, not man's. If God calls, the best proof is our patience when we are misjudged and criticized. The man who knows God has sent him will rest in God, and leave those who disapprove or misunderstand for the Lord to handle: *"Therefore humble yourselves under the mighty hand of God, that He may exalt you in due time."* We must be careful not to mishandle criticisms. Sometimes through the eyes of others, you see the back of your own head! What others say about us is important – be they foe or friend. I praise the Lord for those choice men and women to whom He has guided me, for their perception and insight. I would be a fool not to listen to them. Just like any other minister, evangelists need advice. The evangelist cannot be a law to himself. He is a member of the Body of Christ. Find out where **you** fit in the Body and allow yourself to be useful there!

Today's Scripture

May [all] grow up in all things into Him Who is the Head – Christ – from Whom the whole body, joined and knit together by what every joint supplies, according to the effective working by which every part does its share, causes growth of the Body for the edifying of itself in love.
(Ephesians 4:15-16)

Daily Power!

The man who knows God has sent him will rest in God, and leave those who disapprove or misunderstand for the Lord to handle.

Today's Bible Reading

Ezekiel 42:1-20 through 43:1-27; James 5:1-20; Psalm 119:1-16; Proverbs 28:6-7

Mark my Word
(for further study)

Psalm 139:15; Ephesians 4:15-16; I Peter 5:6

22

Dan and his Ship Shops

Israel had many troubles, often oppressed by invaders. God raised up charismatic leaders to unite and help them to defend themselves. One of these judges was Deborah, a prophetess. A Canaanite king, Jabin, sent in his men under Sisera to plunder and kill Israel. The Spirit of God stirred Deborah to resist, using her persuasive powers to inspire Israel to rally under the leadership of Barak. Each tribe received Deborah's call to unite and do what they could not do alone: stand against Sisera. It is interesting to see how the various tribes reacted – in fact, this old story is like a mirror held up to the face of the Church today. After their victory, Deborah asked one penetrating question about the tribe of Dan: *"And why did Dan remain on ships?"* (The Danites ran a mercantile marine service for Israel, bringing goods from far corners. Then, moored in a harbor, their ships became shops, selling directly to the public.) So here was Dan himself at the till of his shop, totaling receipts with satisfaction. Suddenly, a messenger arrives with a dispatch for Dan: "Dear Dan: Sisera is ravaging Israel. We are fighting with everything at our disposal, but the tribes must all unite to repel the enemy. Come and help – **Now.** Your fellow Israelites are bleeding and dying. Please respond. Deborah (Judge of Israel)."

Dan, the businessman, was deeply moved. He looked inland where hostilities were in progress, possibly hearing the clash of arms and cries of his dying brothers. Just as suddenly came other thoughts: "If I go and fight, won't I be risking my flourishing enterprise? The Canaanites are my customers – I mustn't upset them! Shouldn't I remain neutral?" He hurriedly stuffed a bundle of money into the messenger's pockets, saying, "Regretfully I can't come myself, but here's my contribution. Tell Deborah I'm with her in spirit." So Dan went on counting his cash while his brethren rallied round the standard of Deborah and Barak. Let others die for Israel, but Dan had a business to attend to. There was Dan in his ship of Self-Interest, Self-Love, and Greed. That sounds like our world today! Whatever you do, don't get on board that same kind self-serving vessel or lifestyle. But rather, set a higher standard based on God's Word and His will … and stay standing there next to that standard of righteousness.

Today's Scripture

Thus let all Your enemies perish, O Lord! But let those who love Him be like the sun when it comes out in full strength.

(Judges 5:31)

Daily Power!

I do not want to be a self-interested, self-loving, greedy Christian!

Today's Bible Reading

Ezekiel 44:1-31 through 45:1-12; I Peter 1:1-12; Psalm 119:17-32; Proverbs 28:8-10

Mark my Word
(for further study)

Judges 4:1-24; 5:1-31

Immortal Work for Mortals

To be called by God costs nothing, as God does the calling ... but to birth the call is another matter entirely! I was a hard-working missionary in Lesotho ... but the vivid vision of a Blood-washed Africa haunted me. Divine pressure always accompanies vision. An all-consuming desire drove me to make my first ventures towards mass-evangelism. Still I was hesitant – the members of my mission board disapproved. They were good, spiritual men, but they lacked vision. "Normal missionary work is the fruitful approach to the salvation of Africa, not mass evangelism. If this is God's way, why are other men not doing it?" While missionaries were content with the mission tradition – I was in turmoil. Divine pressure on my spirit grew stronger. Fellow evangelists shared a common experience of official discouragement. They had the burning fire of the Spirit within, the challenge of vast possibilities around ... but criticism from without. I spent hours in prayer to keep my poise and peace. "How long would it take to bring about a Blood-washed Africa without aggressive evangelistic crusades? We have only one generation to save a generation." I reached a crisis point ... and locked myself in a hotel room, determined not to let go of God until I had a clear word from Him. I boldly put before the Lord exactly how I felt: was this really His will for me, this constant impulse to campaign?

God made matters absolutely clear to me: "If you drop the vision I have given you, I look for another man who will accept it and do what I want." I repented of my hesitations immediately, making my decision forever. God then began to smile upon me, sending divine encouragement. I have never looked back, learning how to handle critics and criticisms by letting God Himself become my Defender. "Let them see the Lord led me by the fruit which it bears." I have trained myself to concentrate on what He wants me to do. The ministry and the results have grown, sometimes rather dramatically. Focus on God's will – and watch your life grow with increased blessings, purpose and fulfillment.

Today's Scripture

Unless the Lord builds a house, they labor in vain who build it.
(Psalm 127:1)

Daily Power!

We have only one generation to save a generation.

Today's Bible Reading

Ezekiel 45:13-25 hrough 46:1-24; I Peter 1:13-25 through 2:1-10; Psalm 119:33-48; Proverbs 28:11

Mark my Word
(for further study)

Psalm 127:1

Today's Scripture

Trust in the Lord with all your heart, and lean not to your own understanding; in all your ways acknowledge Him and He shall direct your paths.

(Proverbs 3:5)

Daily Power!

Faith is a leap into the light, not into the darkness.

Today's Bible Reading

Ezekiel 47:1-23 through 48:1-35; I Peter 2:11-25 through 3:1-7; Psalm 119:49-64; Proverbs 28:12-13

Mark my Word
(for further study)

Proverbs 3:5; Matthew 6:25-30; Hebrews 11:1; Jude 24

Leap into the Light

Every day we exercise trust in countless things, often unfamiliar and new. People, food, chairs, gadgets, everything. It is natural. We don't stand and say, "Now, do I have enough faith to get on this bus?" or "Can I sit quietly trusting this driver?" We never think of it – we just go along trusting all the way. Examining your feelings to see if you have a bit of faith lurking around in some corner of your mind is quite absurd: *"Trust in the Lord with all your heart, and lean not to your own understanding; in all your ways acknowledge Him and He shall direct your paths."* You don't really "feel" faith – at least faith and feelings don't always go together. You simply do what should be done when you know very well that you can't succeed unless God helps you: *"Now faith is the substance of things hoped for, the evidence of things not seen."*

Faith is a leap into the light, not into the darkness. It is out of the unknown into the known, out of not knowing Christ Jesus ... into knowing Him. Believing is like a child standing where it is not safe – but without any fear – because his father is waiting to catch him. He falls on purpose to be caught: *"Now to Him Who is able to keep you from stumbling, and to present you faultless before the presence of His glory with exceeding joy; to God our Savior, Who alone is wise, be glory and majesty, dominion and power, both now and forever. Amen!"*

Each of us is important to God, more than all the stars of space. He wants us to trust Him implicitly. He made us and will take pains with us. Faith allows Him to see us through until we rest in Him: *"Therefore I say to you, do not worry about your life, what you will eat or what you will drink; nor about your body, what you will put on. Is not life more than food and the body more than clothing? ... Now if God so clothes the grass of the field, which today is, and tomorrow is thrown into the oven, will He not much more clothe you, O you of little faith?"* Rest assured in God's loving provision for **you** today.

Greate than Jesus?

A breathtaking view of the Kingdom has been shown to us: *"Anyone who has faith in Me will do what I have been doing. He will do even greater things than these, because I am going to the Father."* The word for "greater" – "meizona" – does not specify what order of greatness, whether in number, quality or magnitude. This has been a problem to many Bible students. Surely nothing could outclass the miracles of Jesus in intrinsic omnipotence, such as the raising of Lazarus! But there are two senses in which someone can do greater things than Christ.

Obviously there are some works of His we could never do since He is the Son of God. He is the only Redeemer. He alone could die for the sins of the whole world. The works He referred to were works of mercy, deliverance, healing, and aid. First, there could be more numerous instances; and second, they could be spread over a wider area. Both took place as the disciples moved out in missionary travel.

For centuries, since the invention of printing and modern technology, far more vast operations can bring results impossible even for Jesus when He was localized in this village, or that village, or this town, or that town. He was physically limited – but not limited in power! He needed more hands, more voices – more extensions of Himself – for we are members of the Body of Christ. We use our arms, our hands, our feet, our mouths to spread His Gospel … but they are also His. This could only be possible through the power of the Spirit. Jesus repeated this emphatically: *"I tell you the truth, anyone who has faith in Me will do what I have been doing. He will do even greater things than these, because I am going to the Father. It is for your good* (Greek: "sympherei" meaning "expedient, advantageous) *that I am going away. Unless I go away, the Counselor will not come to you."* This is our basis for the gifts of the Spirit. Allow the Holy Spirit to use **you** today.

Today's Scripture

We take our lead from Christ, Who is the Source of everything we do. He keeps us in step with each other. His very breath and blood flow through us, nourishing us so that we will grow up healthy in God, robust in love.
(Ephesians 4:15-16; the Message)

Daily Power!

We use our arms, hands, feet, mouths to spread His Gospel … but they are also His.

Today's Bible Reading

Daniel 1:1-21 through 2:1-23; I Peter 3:8-22 through 4:1-6; Psalm 119:65-80; Proverbs 28:14

Mark my Word
(for further study)

John 14:12; 16:7; Romans 12:4-5; I Corinthians 6:15; 12:12, 18, 27; Ephesians 4:15-17; 5:30

Ancient Faith

We get what we live for, but do we live by what we get? Conditions are fantastic compared with the past. Are we fantastically more content and fulfilled? There have been fantastic people, relishing mortal existence like the finest wine, even when ignorance was profound – spiritual giants like Enoch, Abraham, and Samuel. They didn't surf the Internet, skimming across world knowledge … but below the surface, they plummeted the depths of reality. A deep understanding burned in their eyes. If we met one of these tremendous characters, we would feel inferior in the presence of greatness.

Who are in the **Honor Roll of Faith**? Abel … Enoch … Noah … Abraham … Sarah … Isaac … Jacob … Joseph … Moses … Joshua … Rahab … Gideon … Barak … Samson … Jephthah … David … Samuel … all the prophets. These were the ancients, people who knew God. They didn't use the word "faith" as a state of mind. They thought only in practical terms … such as walking with God, serving, fearing, obeying, and cleaving to Him. That is what faith is, and that is why the Bible must be our Guide every inch of the way. Today, "faith" is thought of as a possession, stacked safely somewhere in our psychological cupboard. We bring it out, dust it off and exhibit it, as occasion requires. *"Now faith is the substance of things hoped for, the evidence of things not seen. For by it the elders obtained a good testimony. By faith we understand that the worlds were framed by the Word of God, so that the things which are seen were not made of things which are visible."*

The ancients would no more go through the day without "faith" than without their clothes. It was the atmosphere they breathed, not just for the convenient moments. The world now thinks of religion as a subject or occasional practice. Sunday is given for religion. For these great men, their relationship with God was the essential quality of all their waking hours and unthinkable without Him. **You** should have that kind of faith!

Today's Scripture

The fundamental fact of existence is that this trust in God, this faith, is the firm foundation under everything that makes life worth living. It's our handle on what we can't see. The act of faith is what distinguished our ancestors, set them above the crowd.
  (Hebrews 11:1-2; the Message)

Daily Power!

Faith is the atmosphere we breathe, not just for the convenient moments.

Today's Bible Reading

Daniel 2:24-49 through 3:1-30; I Peter 4:7-19 through 5:1-14; Psalm 119:81-96; Proverbs 28:15-16

Mark my Word
(for further study)

Hebrews 11:1-40; 12:1-29

Faith of a new Kind

The world of the ancients was a perilous place. The nations had no idea how to handle sicknesses and plagues, droughts, and famines. Enemies surrounded them. But Israel learned that God was "El Shaddai" – their All-Sufficient, Protector, Deliverer, Healer, Stronghold, "Shield and Buckler." Other nations looked to their gods – to the rain god if they wanted rains, to the god of fertility for their harvests. They offered a sacrifice at their shrine as a bribe when they wanted their help. That is all the gods asked … otherwise, people forgot them. Pagans had no sustained sense of God's constant concern. Only Israel enjoyed that. In Israel, God sent the Bible prophets to assure them of His faithfulness. He was their Shepherd, and they were the sheep of His pasture. This was far beyond heathen thought. Even the greatest of the heathen – such as Socrates and Aristotle – had no such Divine awareness. Israel was the people of God. But, for example, while the Ephesians gloried in "Diana" (or "Artemis"), they were not "the people of Diana" – they just patronized her.

In the New Testament, the trust communicated by the Bible prophets continues. But it expands beyond a physical covenant, taking in more than even the prophets, who prophesied it understood. What Christ introduced embraced Life here … and hereafter – our whole moral, spiritual and psychological existence. Jesus showed us that our physical dangers were not the all-important matter, nor our material prosperity. The state of our real self – our personality or soul – was the all-important issue. The body would die, but worse would be for the soul to perish: *"And do not fear those who kill the body but cannot kill the soul. But rather fear Him Who is able to destroy both soul and body in Hell."* Ezekiel wrote: *"The soul that sins, it shall die"* – but Jesus said the soul that sins is dead already … and He comes as the Resurrection and the Life! Christ Jesus lives in **you** today!

Today's Scripture

You don't have to wait for the End. I am, right now, Resurrection and Life. The one who believes in Me, even though he or she dies, will live. And everyone who lives believing in Me does not ultimately die at all.
    (John 11:25-26; the Message)

Daily Power!

I look to God – El Shaddai – Who is my All Sufficient One.

Today's Bible Reading

*Daniel 4:1-37;
II Peter 1:1-21;
Psalm 119:97-112;
Proverbs 28:17-18*

Mark my Word
(for further study)

*Ezekiel 18:4;
Matthew 10:28;
John 11:25;
I Peter 1:10-12*

28

Today's Scripture

For God so loved the world that He gave His only begotten Son, that whoever believes in Him should not perish but have everlasting life.
(John 3:16)

Daily Power!

Faith is a process.

Today's Bible Reading

*Daniel 5:1-31;
II Peter 2:1-22;
Psalm 119:113-128;
Proverbs 28:19-20*

Mark my Word
(for further study)

*John 3:2, 16; 11:17-27;
James 2:19*

Step One, Step Two

There are various degrees of faith. We may begin with a limited vision of what to trust God for … or with only one prayer, "Oh God, help me!" I want to help you go up a kind of staircase, step by step, looking to God for an ever-wider area of your circumstances. Your faith may follow a process something like this:

First Step: Believing that something is true. James reminds those who believe in one God that the devils also believe the same thing, which is not too encouraging! Martha believed in the resurrection at the last day, but Christ wanted faith that leaped to resurrection then and there. Similarly, the Jews believed their religion was true, though it did little for them in action because it never was in action. This is still true today. Faith may be no more than agreement with a statement of truth, an intellectual assent, hardly the small change of Life's currency. Believing there is a God is not a saving faith, any more than believing there is a planet called Pluto – but it is an essential start.

Second Step: Believing a person is genuine. Nicodemus said, *"You are a Teacher come from God."* Jesus wanted a higher brand of faith than being regarded as a teacher. He talked to Nicodemus about "believing" in a new way – a way that Nicodemus had never conceived. Many believed in Jesus as Nicodemus did – as a genuine man. But admiration can turn to commitment, as there is reason to think it did in the case of Nicodemus. However believing Jesus is a good Man suffers from a fatal fallacy: if He was good, then He was not a liar, a deceiver or crazy, for He claimed to be the Son of God. He was not a good Man to claim such a thing, but a shocking blasphemer … **unless it was true**. If He was a good Man, He must have been what He said: much more than a good Man – but Christ, the Savior of the world. And He is!

These are the first two steps of faith for **you**.

Step Three, Step Four

As we mature and progress in our life-long walk of faith, we advance from childhood into adulthood: *"And I, brethren, could not speak to you as to spiritual people but as to carnal, as to babes in Christ. I fed you with milk and not with solid food; for until now you were not able to receive it."* Let us see how our faith continues to grow:

Third Step: Believing in Jesus as an inspired person, like a prophet. The disciples told Christ that was how people thought of Him, *"Some say* [You are] *John the Baptist, some Elijah, and others Jeremiah or one of the prophets."* He entered Jerusalem and, *"the multitude said, 'This is Jesus the prophet of Nazareth of Galilee.'"* They applauded Him – but Jesus, like Jeremiah, wept. They had gone so far … but not allowed Him to take them under his wing and save them. Again, we can't say He is a prophet … like saying Sir Christopher Warren was an architect. A prophet must be heard – and to **hear** Christ takes us a long, long way.

Fourth Step: Believing in God's power. In Jerusalem, everybody believed in His power. Many believed also in Christ's powers. They didn't doubt what they saw – that He had healing power, He was a miracle worker – and they even wanted to make Him King. But Christ wanted a broader faith. They believed in His physical powers … but did not place Him where He should be – as Lord and Savior. They asked Him for miracles, but He had other ideas than to gratify their love of the sensational. Their faith was only in Him as a Healer, which is worth little more than faith in a man as a doctor, driver, or even a plumber. We trust a doctor as a doctor only, not as a daily help. Christ is to be trusted for all things, not a miracle or two.

Knowing Jesus Christ in His fullness – now that's real faith!

Today's Scripture

Do not labor for the food which perishes, but for the food which endures to everlasting life, which the Son of Man will give you, because God the Father has set His seal on Him.

(John 6:27)

Daily Power!

Christ is to be trusted for all things, not a miracle or two.

Today's Bible Reading

Daniel 6:1-28;
II Peter 3:1-18;
Psalm 119:129-152;
Proverbs 28:21-22

Mark my Word
(for further study)

Matthew 6:14; 21:11;
John 2:23-25; 6:36;
I Corinthians 3:1-2

Today's Scripture

That Christ may dwell in your hearts through faith; that you, being rooted and grounded in love ... that you may be filled with all the fullness of God.

(Ephesians 3:17-19)

Daily Power!

Christ can only save what I give to Him – everything.

Today's Bible Reading

*Daniel 7:1-28;
I John 1:1-10;
Psalm 119:153-176;
Proverbs 28:23-24*

Mark my Word
(for further study)

*Psalm 27:10; 41:9;
Ephesians 4:14-15;
I Thessalonians 5:23*

Step Five, Step Six

The Apostle Paul cared very much about maturing new Christians entrusted to his teaching: *"We should no longer be children, tossed to and fro and carried about with every wind of doctrine, by the trickery of men ... but speaking the truth in love, may grow up in all things into Him Who is the Head – Christ."* As you continue in your life-long walk of faith, you will take these steps:

Step Five: Believing as trust. This turns faith into a personal relationship. We trust people, such as our parents. They know us ... we feel they won't fail us. That is the personal "faith" God wants us to place in Him. Our lives are as open to Him as if He sat in our living room. We may as well confess our sins – He knows them anyway. If we were trapped on a mountain ledge and an expert rescuer came, we would simply have to put our lives in his hands, no matter how brilliant, rich, strong, or stupid we were. That is saving faith, and Christ is our Rescuer.

Step Six: Believing in Christ. This is the real faith. We trust Christ in a way we never trust even a close friend. Friends can let us down: *"My own familiar friend in whom I trusted, which did eat of my bread, has lifted up his heel against me."* Even our own fathers may fail us" *"Though my father and my mother forsake me, the Lord will receive me."* It means surrender, letting Him take over, in every area of our lives. If He's going to keep your head above water, He's got to get a grip on you completely.

That is how Paul wanted it to be for his converts. *"The very God of peace sanctify you wholly; and ... your whole spirit and soul and body be preserved blameless unto the coming of our Lord Jesus Christ."* Christ can only save what we give to Him. Hand everything over to Him – lock, stock and barrel ... body, soul and spirit – into His total care, for all time. Then He can do something for us. He doesn't want to save us piecemeal. Satan is the only rival for that kind of possession of us, being hungry for us, wanting to "devour" us. But when you have "fullness of faith," you are God's own!

The Blood of Jesus
has been around for 2000 years.
If it is so powerful, why are there still so
many sinful people in the world?
It is like working in a soap factory.
Though you are surrounded by soap,
unless you apply the soap to your body
you are still dirty.

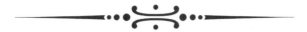

An unpreached Gospel is no Gospel at all.

Dignity is not a fruit of the Spirit,
but joy is!

When is Unbelief forgivable?

Unbelief about God can be forgiven if people are ignorant about Him. *"How can they believe in the One of Whom they have not heard?"* But **ignorance** may need forgiving. In our Western society, not hearing the Gospel is unpardonable bigotry. How can God forgive people who won't even listen after His Son died for their sins? *"Therefore we ought to give the more earnest heed to the things which we have heard, lest at any time we should let them slip ... How shall we escape if we neglect so great salvation?"* If we have "truth" without the truth of Christ, we die without truth of forgiveness.

A bishop went to a very talkative barber for a haircut. Having the churchman captive in his chair for fifteen minutes, he aggressively announced he was an unbeliever. The bishop asked the barber, "Do you read the Bible?" ... "Me, read the Bible? Of course not. I'm an unbeliever." ... "Do you read religious Christian books?" ... "You wouldn't catch me reading that rubbish. I'm an unbeliever, I told you." ... "Do you ever go to church, or listen to TV or radio about God?" ... "You bet I don't!" ... "Have you any Christian friends who tell you about their religious experiences?" ... "No, thank you!" ... "What about anybody coming from a church to talk to you?" ... "Those religion-pushers know me! They dare not even knock at my door twice!" ... The bishop waited, smiling. "You understand now?" asked the barber. "Perfectly!" answered the bishop. "I understand that you are not an unbeliever at all." ... The barber retorted, "I tell you, I believe nothing." ... The bishop answered, "You can't be an unbeliever. You don't even know what you are **not** believing. You can't disbelieve what you've never heard. I'll tell you what you are: you are a damned fool." ... The barber said, "Bishop, I'm surprised to hear you use language like that." ... The bishop replied, "I am not swearing. I'm quoting the Bible. It says, *'the fool says there is no God,'* and *'God shall send them strong delusion that they all might be damned who believe not the truth.'* You are an ignoramus about God, and a fool for not wanting to know. So you are damned already." **Know** what **you** believe!

Today's Scripture

It's crucial that we keep a firm grip on what we've heard so that we don't drift off.
(Hebrews 2:1; the Message)

Daily Power!

If we have "truth" without the truth of Christ, we die without truth of forgiveness.

Today's Bible Reading

Daniel 8:1-27;
I John 2:1-17;
Psalm 120:1-7;
Proverbs 28:25-26

Mark my Word
(for further study)

Psalm 14:1;
Romans 10:14;
II Thessalonians 2:11;
Hebrews 2:1, 3

2

God's Anointing – Man's Confirmation

God never anointed anybody twice. David was anointed of the Lord through Samuel … later, the elders of Israel anointed him a second time, thus confirming their acceptance of his kingly authority and divine anointing. Jesus was anointed by God … afterward, women poured ointment on Him, which He said was for His burial – a very special part of His service to the Father and for Mankind. *"How God anointed Jesus of Nazareth with the Holy Spirit and with power, Who went about doing good and healing all who were oppressed by the devil, for God was with Him."* Other than these examples, priests or kings only had an initial anointing at the beginning of their careers.

Some sing for a new anointing and pray for another Pentecost. But the whole concept of "another" or "new" anointing – as if the original anointing had faded away – is strange to New Testament thought on the eternal Spirit. The anointing is self-renewing – it renews us, we don't renew it. He is the Spirit of newness. *"The anointing which you have received from Him abides in you."* In the Book of Exodus, we read: *"You shall anoint them, that they may minister to Me."* II Samuel speaks of the *"shield of the mighty"* being anointed for battle, and the Book of Leviticus tells us of the anointing for sanctified service and holiness.

We can lay our hands upon our friends and pray to bring God's strength and blessing, but we must not suppose we can fill a person with the Spirit each time, assuming the enduement has died away. The Holy Spirit does not evaporate! If we are doing the work to which God has called us, the anointing rests upon us without ever diminishing. It is in the same pattern as "eternal life" – we receive it moment by moment, like a waterfall fed by a never-failing river. All that is necessary is that we release His energies by working in His Name. Swim – fully immersing yourself in the River of God today!

Today's Scripture

Rejoicing to see your good order and the steadfastness of your faith in Christ. As you therefore have received Christ Jesus the Lord, so walk in Him, rooted and built up in Him and established in the faith, as you have been taught, abounding in it with thanksgiving.
(Colossians 2:5-7)

Daily Power!

The Holy Spirit does not evaporate!

Today's Bible Reading

Daniel 9:1-27 through 11:1; I John 2:18-29 through 3:1-6; Psalm 121:1-8; Proverbs 28:27-28

Mark my Word
(for further study)

Exodus 40:15; Leviticus 8:1-13; II Samuel 1:21; Acts 10:38; Colossians 2:5-7; I John 2:27

The Gospel of the Cross

The Gospel the disciples preached as they went out was the Gospel of the Kingdom of God: the Good News that the Kingdom was close to them. But they preached it in new terms not used by John the Baptist, and only occasionally used by Jesus Himself. Their Kingdom Gospel was proclaimed in the language of Christ crucified. It was not a different Gospel, but it contained a tremendous new fact – the **vital** fact about the Kingdom of God: the Cross. When Jesus had spoken of it earlier, Peter had even tried to rebuke Him. What at first seemed outrageous to the disciples was (they later realized) the all-important mystery of the Kingdom: the self-sacrifice of the King for the Kingdom. The Kingdom is established by the titanic battle and victory of Christ. His Blood marks its foundations. Calvary is the source of the redemptive dynamic of God, the nuclear power drive of the Gospel, and of all the gifts of the Spirit.

Modern religionists are busy building Calvary bypasses. The Gospel of the Bible is caricatured as a "Gospel of gore" – as if in our world, anybody could be squeamish about blood! Roads that avoid Calvary prove to go nowhere. There are no circuitous routes. The Kingdom of God has a checkpoint and border control … and it is at the Cross. Without having been to Calvary, everybody lives a second-class existence as illegal immigrants. Passport and entry permits are repentance and faith in Christ Jesus. Then we may enter with the full privileges of citizens, no longer *"foreigners and aliens, but fellow citizens with God's people and members of God's Household."* The *"covenants of promise"* are ours. We are not beggars asking the glorified saints to send us a few scraps of help. We don't need to collect their bones, hoping some of their holiness or grace will brush off on us and stand to our credit. Believers are not bone-pickers. If we do what the apostles did, we shall get what the apostles got from the same Father, by the same Spirit, on the same terms of grace.

Today's Scripture

You are no longer strangers and foreigners, but fellow citizens with the saints and members of the Household of God, having been built on the foundation of the apostles and prophets, Jesus Christ Himself being the Chief Cornerstone.
(Ephesians 2:19-20)

Daily Power!

Calvary is the Source of the redemptive dynamic of God, the nuclear power drive of the Gospel, and of all the gifts of the Spirit.

Today's Bible Reading

Daniel 11:2-35;
I John 3:7-24;
Psalm 122:1-9;
Proverbs 29:1

Mark my Word
(for further study)

Matthew 16:22;
Ephesians 2:19

Fasting and Faith

Some say they will fast, if necessary unto death, until God answers them. That's impressive – but does this affect God? Is it a sign of their own patience that God will speak? Or are they trying to force the hand of God by a subtle spiritual threat? God does not yield to emotional pressures of any kind. It is an error to fast to twist God's arm. Fasting is just a manner of expressing our urgency, like calling on God loudly or persistently. The pagans thought that they could bring some kind of force to bear upon their gods by their exertions, bloodletting, and other efforts. But God is not like Zeus, Apollo or Baal. It is God's pleasure to **hear** His children, and they don't need to make noise or demonstration. Prayer is effective when we are participating in the work of God, especially a particular work.

Jesus taught about fasting, emphasizing the necessity of fulfilling God's command. Since the disciples' mission was to *"preach the Gospel, heal the sick, deliver the captives,"* it **was** appropriate to explain that prayer and fasting were critical elements to ministry: "[Jesus] *rebuked the unclean spirit, 'Deaf and dumb spirit, I command you, come out of him and enter him no more.' Then the spirit cried out, convulsed him greatly, and came out of him … [Then] His disciples asked Him privately, 'Why could we not cast it out?' So He said to them, 'This kind can come out by nothing but prayer and fasting.'"* Again, the **revealed** will of God was being performed – and fasting contributed to **their** focus and ability to obey, not to persuading God.

To believe God when we ask, we must know that we are heard, and that we ask according to His Word and His revealed will. Jesus said, *"Your Heavenly Father (will) give the Holy Spirit to those who ask Him"* and *"Tarry … until you are endued with power from on high."* We **should** ask for healing … for spiritual gifts … for one another … for those in the assembly who sin … and for kings and governors. These are all subsidiary requests heading up the greatest purpose of God: the world's redemption. Pray the Word to make your prayers effective.

Today's Scripture

By Your words I can see where I'm going; they throw a beam of light on my dark path.
(Psalm 119:105; the Message)

Daily Power!

Fasting helps us concentrate our focus on God – it is not to persuade Him to do "something special."

Today's Bible Reading

Daniel 11:36-45
through 12:1-13;
I John 4:1-21;
Psalm 123:1-4;
Proverbs 29:2-4

Mark my Word
(for further study)

Psalm 119:105;
Mark 9:25-29;
Luke 4:18-19;
11:13; 24:49

Not conspicuous, just changed

The anointing is not to make us as conspicuous as Joseph in his coat-of-many-colors. In a TV commercial, a young lady with a very bad cold has lost her sense of smell, and sprays herself with more and more perfume. When she opens the door to her admirer, her perfume overpowers him and knocks him down! It is human to want overwhelming power with an impact that everyone can feel. John the Baptist wore conspicuous rough clothing, and ate peculiar food – this indicated that he was a "holy prophet." Jesus did neither – He dressed inconspicuously, and ate anything set before Him. Many were awed in the presence of Jesus – but it was not by demonstrations of overwhelming power – it came as concern and love for men and women. That is why they fell down and worshiped Him.

The prophet Isaiah taught us about receiving God's anointing: *"I said, 'Woe is me, for I am undone! Because I am a man of unclean lips, and I dwell in the midst of a people of unclean lips; for my eyes have seen the King, the Lord of hosts.' Then one of the seraphim flew to me, having in his hand a live coal which he had taken with the tongs from the Altar. And he touched my mouth with it, and said, 'Behold, this has touched your lips; your iniquity is taken away and your sin purged.'"* The anointing of God **changes** us.

In ourselves, sinful and limited, we are completely unfit to become the temples of the Spirit … but we are. We wonder and worship. When that mighty Spirit takes up His abode within us, then oil, hands or anything else upon our outer flesh are only symbols of His indwelling greatness. Along with anointing, there are other symbols of the Spirit. The anointing cannot be learned as mere head knowledge, but it must enter the heart and be expressed in the life – it must "take root downward, and bear fruit upward." Allow the anointing of Christ Jesus to be a vital life-force in **you**!

Today's Scripture

And as we have borne the image of the man of dust, we shall also bear the image of the Heavenly Man.
(I Corinthians 15:49)

Daily Power!

The anointing of God changes us.

Today's Bible Reading

Hosea 1:1-11 through 3:1-5;
I John 5:1-21;
Psalm 124:1-8;
Proverbs 29:5-8

Mark my Word
(for further study)

Isaiah 6:5-7; 37:31;
I Corinthians 15:49

Today's Scripture

It stands to reason, doesn't it, that if the alive-and-present God Who raised Jesus from the dead moves into your life, He'll do the same thing in you that He did in Jesus, bringing you alive to Himself.
(Romans 8:11; the Message

Daily Power!

The Kingdom power which rested on Christ Jesus was for working signs and wonders – the same Spirit is given to those within the Kingdom of God.

Today's Bible Reading

Hosea 4:1-19 through 5:1-15; II John 1:1-13; Psalm 125:1-5; Proverbs 29:9-11

Mark my Word
(for further study)

Luke 12:32; John 1:33-34; 9:3-4; 15:5; Romans 8:11

Kingdom Power

When Jesus met a blind man, He said, *"I must work the works of Him Who sent Me while it is day."* By this He showed that the restoration of the blind was His Father's work. Kingdom mercies continued as long as Jesus was in the world. Moreover, they eventually resumed after He had gone. Jesus said to His disciples, *"The night is coming when no one can work."* He meant that soon He would be crucified, night would fall, and there would be no blind receiving their sight. He said to the disciples, *"Without Me, you can do nothing"* – and they did not for a long time. Then they received what Jesus had promised: **power** when the Holy Spirit came!

Now if the power of the Kingdom is the Holy Spirit, then Kingdom power was given to the Church on the Day of Pentecost. This is more than power and authority. In a saying of key importance, Christ announced to His followers, *"It is your Father's good pleasure to give you the Kingdom."* Believers inherit the Kingdom "lock, stock and barrel." The Kingdom power which rested on Christ Jesus was for working signs and wonders – the same Spirit is given to those within the Kingdom of God for the same Kingdom purposes. As John the Baptist revealed: *"The Man on Whom you see the Spirit come down and remain is He Who will baptize with the Holy Spirit."* The Spirit endowed Jesus and His people with the same power.

There is a difference between Christ and His followers … and it is rather noticeable! The difference is first Who He is. Those who say, "The words of Christ on our lips are the same as on Christ's lips" must remember this: it is not the words which matter, but the person who speaks them. We may be adopted sons of God, but He is the eternal and only begotten. The second difference is that the Spirit comes from Him. He is the Source. We are not sources, but channels – riverbeds through which the waters of His fullness flow. Open wide your channel–gate for Him to freely access your life.

Makers of Money – or History?

If we parallel Deborah's story in Judges with our world, who does the tribe of Dan represent? Dan is the Christian who belongs to God's family, knows what are God's claims upon him, hears God's call … but does not respond. He remains in his ship-shop when God wants him to *"seek first the Kingdom of God."* The music of the tinkling till, applause of the unconverted, or opinion of family and friends deafen him to the call of the Living God. Dan sings about *"the sweet bye-and-bye on the beautiful shore"* – but will his ship reach it, or just flounder in the Sea of Life? Can this be? Look at the wreckage of lives where people have chosen the wrong priorities. Some of the saddest people have been those who didn't keep their eyes on God, and things went terribly wrong in the end. Success turned to ashes, popularity went sour. They chose the Danite opportunities of the ship-shop … they let others follow Christ to His harvest field, or battlefield, or maybe mission field. In the end, they saw their joy and contentment turn to tragedy: *"The harvest is past, the summer is ended, and we are not saved!"*

The runner with Deborah's recruiting letter hoped for a better response as he reached the tribes of Zebulun and Naphtali. Two men were working in the fields and in the villages under the warm sun, looking forward to the end of the day and to the joy of their wives and children. They huddled around the dispatch runner to hear and consider Deborah's call to service. What should they do? There was only one choice: Go! "Praise the Lord," they shouted, "that God has anointed somebody to lead us. Let's make an end of this constant harassment from Jabin and his bandits. Thank God for Deborah! We'll back her to the hilt. Tell her we're on the way!" Zebulun and Naphtali exchanged their pruning hooks for spears. Children were hugged, weeping wives kissed, and the men marched away into the dust of battle. *"Zebulun is a people who jeopardized their lives to the point of death, Naphtali also, on the heights of the battlefield."* That's high praise … the kind of praise that **you** want to hear from God.

Today's Scripture

When leaders lead in Israel, when the people willingly offer themselves, bless the Lord!

(Judges 5:1)

Daily Power!

I am called - and God has an anointing for my calling.

Today's Bible Reading

Hosea 6:1-11 through 9:1-17;
III John 1:1-14;
Psalm 126:1-6;
Proverbs 29:12-14

Mark my Word
(for further study)

Judges 4:1-24; 5:1-31;
Jeremiah 8:20;
Matthew 6:33

8

Two Kinds of Folks

When the Israelite-Canaanite war was won, Deborah the Judge arrived at the quayside to visit Dan, asking him one withering question: *"Why did Dan remain on ships?"* Dan sat still, fingers fumbling nervously with a coin. He couldn't lift his eyes to face this Holy Spirit-anointed woman of God. Her question haunted him the rest of his life … and that question will be heard again at the Throne of God, when Dan and all the rest of us have to give account for our lives. Will Dan look at the Lord … or be too ashamed, not knowing what to answer, hanging his head in confusion? Zebulun and Naphtali didn't have Dan's eye for business. Dan made money – but Zebulun and Naphtali **made history** that day, fighting to save Israel in a battle still talked about today. They risked everything – even life itself – fighting in the high places of the field. Dan staked nothing … he never took risks. When Dan died, he was the richest man in the country, with bars of gold stacked to the ceiling. Then, as his soul was leaving his body, Dan grabbed for his gold, wanting to take it with him. The Angel of Death swept him away with a laugh: "You've made your pile, now somebody else will spend it!"

The call of God is still heard by the Zebulun and Naphtali people today, but not by the Dan people. Churches are composed of one or the other kind. The Dan people are those who consider their businesses more important than God's work, their homes more precious than Heaven for the lost, and saving money more expedient than saving souls. Any pastor will tell you who are the Dan or the Zebulun and Naphtali characters in his congregation: "It's always the same people who respond, and give, and work. If it weren't for them, this church would close." Some obey God's call at any cost, but others would not risk five cents for God. Zebulun and Naphtali died on the battleground for God's Kingdom. Jesus said, *"He who loses his life for My sake will find it … Be faithful until death, and I will give you the crown of life."* There's a nobility in that kind of dying, and even in one's readiness to give all, which we now recognize and honor on Earth. But the Lord Himself will recognize it when a glittering Crown of Life is placed upon one's head by the hand of Christ Himself. Of the Dan folk, Jesus said, *"He who finds his life will lose it."* Make **your** choice today!

Today's Scripture

Choose for yourselves this day whom you will serve.

(Joshua 24:15)

Daily Power!

Any pastor will tell you who are the Dan or the Zebulun and Naphtali characters in his congregation.

Today's Bible Reading

Hosea 10:1-15 through 14:1-0; Jude 1:1-25; Psalm 127:1-5; Proverbs 29:15-17

Mark my Word
(for further study)

Judges 4:1-24; 5:1-31; Matthew 10:39; Revelation 2:10

The Giver, not the Gift

It is absolutely necessary to learn that the Holy Spirit is "He," not "it." The Spirit is not an impersonal force or mere spiritual electricity. The anointing of God is not just power or gifts – but the Holy Spirit Himself. When people speaking with tongues first stepped into modern history, they were called "the tongues people" and similar names by many well-known British evangelicals such as Meyer, Morgan, Anderson, Scroggie, and others who were opposed to the experience. In fact, the memory of those people is still among us. They carried an impressive Godliness motivated by service, not sensation, seeking the Giver, not the gifts. They wanted to know Jesus better and be Christ-like. They did not seek power for the sake of power. Their daily desire was: "[To] *let this mind be in* [them] *which was also in Christ Jesus, Who made Himself of no reputation, taking the form of a servant and became obedient."* Many laid down their lives for God.

When Jesus healed the sick, it was not just sheer electric power He wielded … the power of His conquering love. He healed the sick by His stripes – that was the "secret wonder" of His anointing. He healed a withered arm even though it provoked men to plot against His life. He risked everything and would go to any lengths, even the Cross, for the sake of those who were suffering. Pain and the ministry of healing are strangely linked. If we are willing to know *"the fellowship of His suffering,"* then we will feel the same anointing of love that Jesus had. If we have the same heartbreaking pity that forgets self and will make any sacrifice for the afflicted as Jesus did, then we will identify with those who suffer, sharing their suffering to ease their pain. If we are *"touched with the feeling of* [their] *infirmities"* as Jesus was, and realize for ourselves what it means when it says, *"If one part suffers, every part suffers with it,"* then perhaps fewer people would go home unhealed. know nothing more profane than healing the sick in Jesus' Name to get rich or to make a name for oneself or for the gratification of wielding power. The most precious thing we can ever possess is not the gift which God gives … but He Himself. **Seek** the **giver** today.

Today's Scripture

I gave up all that inferior stuff so I could know Christ personally, experience His resurrection power, be a partner in His suffering, and go all the way with Him to death itself.
(Philippians 3:10-11; the Message)

Daily Power!

Jesus healed the sick by His stripes – the "secret wonder" of His anointing: compassion.

Today's Bible Reading

*Joel 1:1-20 through 3:1-21;
Revelation 1:1-20;
Psalm 128:1-6;
Proverbs 29:18*

Mark my Word
(for further study)

*Isaiah 53:5;
I Corinthians 12:26;
Philippians 2:5-8;
3:10-11;
Hebrews 4:15*

DECEMBER

10

The most important Job

There was once a tribe that worshipped the moon. They explained why: the moon shines at night, they said, when it is dark and we need light ... but the silly old sun shines during the day when there's plenty of light – what could be more pointless? Of course, there is light during the day because the sun shines, and there is light in America because the Gospel light shines here. But there are many places in the world where it is very dark. I guess I've been like the moon trying to bring light to the dark places of the Earth. When Paul preached in Troas all night and Eutychus fell asleep, the Bible says, *"There were many lamps in the upstairs room"* where he was talking. There are many shining lamps in America today. **You** are called to be *"shining as lights in the midst of a crooked generation,"* not *"hiding the light under a bushel."*

Some people shine intellectually and talk brilliantly. I am just an evangelist. Any brightness on my part will have to come from the Holy Spirit and the Word of God. My hope is the promise: *"Those who turn many to righteousness shall shine like the stars forever and ever."* My natural environment is a platform in a field in Africa somewhere, not a university. But as far as I am concerned, an evangelist's job is the most important in the world.

People ask what God is saying to the Church. He is saying what He has always said, *"Preach the Gospel to every creature."* If Jesus Himself were to take my place here in these last days before the final judgment, He would repeat His last words to the disciples: *"You will receive power when the Holy Spirit comes on you; and you will be My witnesses in Jerusalem, and in all Judea and Samaria and to the ends of the Earth."* Until we have done that, He has no further instructions for us. Listen well.

Today's Scripture

When the Holy Spirit comes on you, you will be able to be My witnesses in Jerusalem, all over Judea and Samaria, even to the ends of the world.
(Acts 1:8; the Message)

Daily Power!

As far as I am concerned, an evangelist's job is the most important in the world.

Today's Bible Reading

*Amos 1:1-15 through 3:1-15;
Revelation 2:1-17;
Psalm 129:1-8;
Proverbs 29:19-20*

Mark my Word
(for further study)

*Daniel 12:3;
Matthew 5:15;
Mark 4:21; 16:15;
Luke 11:33;
Acts 1:8; 20:8;
Philippians 2:15*

The Aim of the Church

It has been suggested that there should be a moratorium on bringing in more converts until the Church is fit and ready to receive them. But how can we ever hope to be fit if we stop obeying Christ? His great command is to bring in converts. Although training is vital, concentrating on our own holiness as a primary spiritual focus will never make us fit to reach others with the Gospel. Sanctification does not take place in seclusion only – holiness looks outward to the spiritually lost. Nor is it just an academic subject to be studied with a view to passing examinations or writing a thesis – it is far more than that, the very work of God Himself.

I know of no finer way to develop spirituality than to go all out to win others for Christ. When we try to reach people with the Gospel, we know that we have to be real. When church boards omit evangelism, how can we keep the Church from stagnation and sterility? If people do not see their overall purpose as winning people for Christ, they just become listeners, sermon tasters, choir critics, or leadership judges. The Church is not a restaurant for spiritual gourmets cultivating a discriminating palate for food from the pulpit – it is a canteen for workers. The primary aim of every church service – prayer meetings, Bible studies, young people's meetings, choir practice, Communion service – should be evangelistic. Why shouldn't every service be for outsiders? Especially at Communion, when the emblems of bread and wine are taken, make sure the Church is full of the godless! That cup of red wine is the greatest preacher in the world! It is the Gospel in a cup – an opportunity to invite lost sinners to accept the sacrifice of the Cross. Some churches exclude outsiders. What a lost opportunity! The precious Blood of Jesus cleanses us from all sin. If a Church has tried and failed in its attempts at evangelism, it is time for a serious evaluation of its efforts. Evangelism demands the most intensive thinking. The finance committee's job is soul-saving, not money-saving. Any surplus funds should go into the true business of the Church: saving the world. Be a dedicated soul-winner!

Today's Scripture

He Himself gave some to be apostles, some prophets, some evangelists, and some pastors and teachers, for the equipping of the saints for the work of the ministry, for the edifying of the Body of Christ.
(Ephesians 4:11-12)

Daily Power!

If people do not see their overall purpose as winning people for Christ, they just become listeners, sermon-tasters, choir critics, or leadership judges.

Today's Bible Reading

Amos 4:1-13 through 6:1-14; Revelation 2:18-29 through 3:1-6; Psalm 130:1-8; Proverbs 29:21-22

Mark my Word
(for further study)

Ephesians 4:11-16

Simple, true Faith

Faith produces an interaction between Christ and me. Believing is a relationship – not like being related to your great-aunt whom you've never met – but alive, vibrant, affecting both Christ and you. We give ourselves to Him and He gives Himself to us. We become *"partakers of the Divine nature."* The Apostle Paul used a marvelous expression: *"in Christ."* He wrote: *"If any man be **in Christ**, he is a new creature"* and *"There is therefore now no condemnation to them, which are **in Christ** Jesus."* The simplest faith in Christ has this amazing effect. It isn't some kind of algebra to find the value of X. The simplest person can believe and enjoy the same effect as the wisest.

The list of benefits of being *"in Christ"* is long! Faith in Christ brings righteousness, peace, love, obedience, assurance, unity … it makes you children of God, growing, justified, **alive** … it can cause you to take risks, speak before great men, be famous throughout the world … and much more. *"I also count all things loss for the excellence of the knowledge of Christ Jesus my Lord, for Whom I have suffered the loss of all things and count them as rubbish, **that I may gain Christ and be found in Him … that I may know Him and the power of His resurrection.**"* Paul determined these benefits were worth everything!

Jesus heard all the religious jargon of the Scribes, which ordinary people didn't appreciate. But the common people heard Jesus gladly. He talked about faith, but put it in other ways: *"Come unto Me"* … *"Love Me"* … *"Abide in Me"* … *"Eat of Me"* … *"Follow Me."* Faith is not one particular religious act. It is the transfer of responsibility for one's life to God in toto when our own resources are inadequate. It is spiritual fusion, making us one with Christ. It seems such a simple attitude … and it is. But there was no other way by which we could possibly acquire all that Christ accomplished on the cross for us. What is there greater than that in this world? **You** are saved by faith!

Today's Scripture

I gave up all that inferior stuff so I could know Christ personally.
(Philippians 3:10; the Message)

Daily Power!

Faith is the complete transfer of responsibility for one's life to God.

Today's Bible Reading

Amos 7:1-17
through 9:1-15;
Revelation 3:7-22;
Psalm 131:1-3;
Proverbs 29:23

Mark my Word
(for further study)

Romans 8:1;
II Corinthians 5:17;
Philippians 3:7-10;
II Peter 1:4

Babel reversed

Reading the Bible from the beginning, we find ourselves being told about nothing except Israel – book after book, as if God were only the God of the Jews and had limited His interests to that tiny land and small nation. But as soon as we open the New Testament, the borders melt away, and the wide world comes into view. True, Jesus did say (of His own ministry): *"I was sent only to the lost sheep of Israel."* Yet He spoke in Nazareth concerning the foreign widow helped by Elijah. His statement against racial discrimination infuriated the congregation … but He went to Canaan later, where He healed a girl who did not belong to Israel. After Christ's resurrection, the disciples retained a Jewish outlook for a long time, thinking their new faith belonged to Israel only. They even asked shortly before Christ ascended, *"Are You at this time going to restore the kingdom to Israel?"* Jesus replied, *"It is not for you to know – but you will receive power when the Holy Spirit comes on you, and you will be My witnesses … to the ends of the Earth."*

When the Holy Spirit fell, they spoke with the tongues of people from many different countries, displaying the ethnic interests of the Holy Spirit: *"Now the whole Earth had one language and one speech … The Lord confused the languages of all the Earth; and from there the Lord scattered them abroad over the face of all the Earth."* … *"And they were all filled with the Holy Spirit and began to speak with other tongues, as the Spirit gave them utterance. And there were dwelling in Jerusalem Jews, devout men, from every nation under Heaven. And when this sound occurred, the multitude came together, and were confused, because everyone heard them speak in his own language."* People had been trying to outwit God. He confused their language – so they would no longer be able to work together effectively – and scattered them over the face of the Earth. On the Day of Pentecost, He poured out His Spirit and reversed that curse: bringing knowledge of Himself, understanding of His goodness, to a great diversity of people. And He speaks **your** language too!

Today's Scripture

We hear them speaking in our own tongues the wonderful works of God.
(Acts 2:11)

Daily Power!

God revealed Himself to a great diversity of peoples and languages, bringing knowledge of Himself and an understanding of His goodness.

Today's Bible Reading

Obadiah 1:1-21;
Revelation 4:1-11;
Psalm 132:1-18;
Proverbs 29:24-25

Mark my Word
(for further study)

Genesis 11:1-9;
I Kings 17:8-24;
Matthew 15:24;
Luke 4:25-27;
Acts 1:6-8; 2:4-6, 11

Today's Scripture

The people who sat in darkness have seen a great Light; and upon those who sat in the region and shadow of death, Light has dawned.
(Matthew 4:16)

Daily Power!

There is nothing in the New Testament that says we should not preach the Gospel, and nothing to say we should not do our best to persuade folk into the Kingdom.

Today's Bible Reading

*Jonah 1:1-17
through 4:1-11;
Revelation 5:1-14;
Psalm 133:1-3;
Proverbs 29:26-27*

Mark my Word
(for further study)

Matthew 4:16; 5:14

Predestination and Evangelism

Predestination is an academic subject for high theological debate. My approach is not to get bogged down in theory … but to do the work of an evangelist. My response towards the controversy is to cut through the layers of theological concepts and step out in action. Whether people are among "the elect" or not, I want to make sure. I am not going to risk the eternal destiny of souls upon any doctrinal deductions or theories. There is nothing in the New Testament that says we should not preach the Gospel, and nothing to say we should not do our best to persuade folk into the Kingdom. So that's what I do. We shall know the truth only when we get to Heaven. If everybody I find there had been predestined – fine. I surely do not want to risk any one in Heaven saying to me, "Did you know for sure I was elected? Why didn't you preach the Gospel to me? You gambled on your ideas being right and played dice with my soul. I could have been in Hell instead of here."

Why should I, an evangelist, come to North America and "western culture"? Isn't there light there already – more than in India, Egypt or Benin? Well, there is light here. The West has the Gospel. In every town and city, on TV and radio, in the proliferation of Christian bookstores – there is light. Am I bringing light where there is already light? There is light in North America, but only because there are Christians here who shine. All the light comes from them. Jesus said, *"You are the light of the world."* So I am happy to shine with Westerners – we can always do with more light. Without Christians, night would fall on the West. The atheists, liberals and agnostics would have it the way they wanted, but they would soon reap what they sowed. Without a guiding light, there would be anarchy. **Let your light shine!**

Evangelism strenthens Nations

People say they can live decent lives without Christianity … I wonder! We can all too easily forget that the very idea of decency comes from Christianity. We can all briefly live without breathing, without food and water a bit longer, and without light for a while … but not forever. The Christian capital invested in the West by previous generations of believers will eventually be exhausted. We can't live on the spiritual capital invested by past generations – we must be wealth creators: spiritual wealth, the riches of faith. It is Christ alone Who can save, not Socrates or Plato. The condition for freedom is eternal vigilance … but vigilance alone will fail without faith in God. Freedom is a side effect of Godliness. You can't have an effect without its cause – and you can't have freedom without faith in God.

Many countries that I visit have no Christian tradition to shape their policies. It was Abraham who began a better order. He looked for a city whose Builder and Maker is God, which has foundations. A foundation reinforced with Bible-faith is what distinguishes nations … and will extinguish them if abandoned. Something like it was done in my country, Germany. Centuries of liberal and rationalistic thought and Biblical criticism diluted the Christian faith. Weak and unstable as water, it could not excel, as Jacob said about Reuben. In conditions like that, it was easy for a non-Christian regime to take over. The policies of Hitler and the Third Reich met with little moral resistance. In the 18th century, the experiment of a Christless state brought the Terror to France, with the slaughter of two-million people. Britain was spared from it mainly because of the impact of the Wesley-Whitefield revival movement. It will take at least a generation for Russia to recover from its seventy years of imposed atheism. Worse, perhaps, are the forms of Christianity, which are corrupted and mutilated beyond recognition. They devalue the Gospel by unbelieving theories, or gross superstition and idolatry. They impart no freedom because they don't have it. This cries out for full-blooded Gospel evangelism!

Today's Scripture

By an act of faith, Abraham said yes to God's call to travel to an unknown place that would become his home … Abraham did it by keeping his eye on an unseen city with real, eternal foundations – the City designed and built by God.

(Hebrews 11:8, 10; the Message)

Daily Power!

A foundation reinforced with Bible-faith is what distinguishes nations … and will extinguish them if abandoned.

Today's Bible Reading

Micah 1:1-16 through 4:1-13; Revelation 6:1-17; Psalm 134:1-3; Proverbs 30:1-4

Mark my Word
(for further study)

Genesis 49:3; Hebrews 11:8, 10

16

Today's Scripture

Abraham believed God, and it was accounted to him for righteousness.
(Romans 4:3)

Daily Power!

What is of faith is forever.

Today's Bible Reading

Micah 5:1-15
through 7:1-20;
Revelation 7:1-17;
Psalm 135:1-21;
Proverbs 30:5-6

Mark my Word
(for further study)

Romans 4:1-3

Abraham

Historians have listed the ten most world-changing battles … but it was rightly said that the greatest of them was fought in the heart of Abraham. If anyone thinks of Abraham as just a Bible character, they have not even begun to understand the world in which they live. The Bible names him 309 times – but because of his faith, his name is inscribed upon the whole of the Middle East and upon world history to this day. He was the first man noted for the "obedience of faith." His life's career was consistent with his faith. *"Abraham believed God, and it was accounted to him as righteousness."* What is of faith is forever.

Faith changes people who change the world. Abraham was the man who began the civilizing process fifteen hundred years before the Greeks and the Romans. The Pharaohs were in Egypt a thousand years before Abraham and continued another two thousand years after him, but they affected the world less than he did. The Pharaohs left no moral mark, but only cluttered the desert sands with colossal monuments to their own ego. Abraham left not one single physical trace behind him for us to see … but all our lives today – religious or not – are different because of what he was.

Abraham was not "deeply religious." He wasn't "religious" at all in our modern sense. He had no creed, no hymns, no Bible, no images, and no theology. He probably didn't really know much **about** God … but he **knew God**, personally, and very well. He walked with God. For this patriarch, God wasn't a go-to-church-once-a-week obligation, pushed into the spare corner of life – there was no church to attend. He didn't believe God just to be faithful to tradition – there was no tradition. God was his way of life. Like money, or sports, or sex is to half the world today, God was to Abraham. **You** and I should strive to have the great faith which Abraham owned!

Why believe?

Abraham didn't believe in order to save his own soul. His faith was neither a ticket for a joy ride to Heaven, nor an insurance policy to escape Hell. We don't know what he thought about such a thing as the after-life. He came from Ur of the Chaldees, and knew their pagan myths … but Abraham was starting on a new learning course. His Tutor was the Lord. The nations had developed crude and cruel superstitions for themselves – Abraham threw himself upon God. To carry on without God wasn't in his ideas, either of living – or of dying. *"By faith Abraham obeyed when he was called to go out to the place which he would received as an inheritance. And he went out, not knowing where he was going. By faith he dwelt in the land of promise as in a foreign country, dwelling in tents with Isaac and Jacob, the heirs with him of the same promise, for he waited for a city which has foundations, whose Builder and Maker is God."*

Abraham believed God for two reasons: first, he found there was a living God; second, the only sensible thing to do was to carry out what He said. His faith changed the future, but that is not why he believed. He never dreamed of any such mission. In fact, he forsook the world and got as far away as he could from the world as it was. He changed it by leaving it. He believed God simply because God was there. That must still be the most rational thing anybody can ever do.

Astronaut Neil Armstrong stepped on the moon on July 20, 1969, and said that his one small step was a giant leap for Mankind. Far bigger for Mankind was the step Abraham took when he left Ur of the Chaldees. He was the pioneer of walking by faith in God. Abraham began life in wealthy Ur of the Chaldees and then moved to Haran, still in the Fertile Crescent. After that, he sacrificed his fine dwelling for a black goat-skin tent in the wild moorland scrub of the Negeb Desert. He moved around only with his family, shepherds and cattlemen, like a Bedouin sheikh. Secretly in his heart, he nourished the ideal of a new way of life. The God of Abraham is **your** living God today!

Today's Scripture

[Abraham] waited for the city which has foundations, whose Builder and Maker is God.

(Hebrews 11:10)

Daily Power!

Abraham believed God simply because He was there.

Today's Bible Reading

Nahum 1:1-15 through 3:1-19; Revelation 8:1-13; Psalm 136:1-26; Proverbs 30:7-9

Mark my Word
(for further study)

Hebrews 11:8-10

18

God's Finger

Paul wrote to the Philippians about the beauty of Christ's humility … and then went on to mention two women who were at odds, Syntyche and Euodia. Then, with great tact, he thanked the Philippians for their recent kindness and described it as *"a sweet-smelling aroma"* – in Greek, euodia … a gentle hint to Euodia herself. The inward Spirit is seen by outward effects, physical indications of an inward and spiritual source. To desire power merely to show off is corrupting and odious, not fragrant. The real power of God only comes with the Holy Spirit, who reveals the loveliness of the Christ life and His graciousness.

Receiving the Holy Spirit and His gifts has been marred by many innovative and novel approaches. Some realignment to the Word of God is needed in this area. The gifts are not tricks, techniques or abilities we can pick up by watching others – God is pouring out His Spirit, and He does not need mere imitations of the gifts. It is not a matter of learning the correct approach and striving to obtain the gifts as prizes to be won. Gifts are not only for spiritual athletes. If they were prizes to be won, they would not be gifts. Gifts are for those in the Kingdom of God – they belong there. Israel's blessings are covenanted to the commonwealth of Israel. Christ Jesus linked wonders to the new Christian commonwealth: *"If I cast out demons with the finger of God, surely the Kingdom of God is come upon you."*

The *"finger of God"* is the Holy Spirit, as Peter tells us: *"God anointed Jesus of Nazareth with the Holy Spirit and power, and He went around healing all who were under the power of the devil."* There is no power greater than that of the Holy Spirit. That is Kingdom power, and no other power matches it. By the Spirit, He distributes His ministries to whom He chooses. Allow His finger to point **to** you and **through** you.

Today's Scripture

But if it's God's finger I'm pointing that sends the demons on their way, then God's Kingdom is here for sure.
(Luke 11:20; the Message)

Daily Power!

Spiritual gifts are not only for spiritual athletes.

Today's Bible Reading

Habakkuk 1:1-17 through 3:1-19;
Revelation 9:1-21;
Psalm 137:1-9;
Proverbs 30:10

Mark my Word
(for further study)

Luke 11:20;
Acts 10:38;
Philippians 4:2

Intellectualism

Abraham was not an intellectual, but *"the fear of the Lord is the beginning of wisdom."* Men of genius would burst upon the world scene in the distant future. They would cast their nets of thought far and wide, seeking knowledge and understanding. They would invent new ways to live and new ways to rule cities. But they were destined never to know what Abraham knew. Their searching missed the ultimate discovery: **to know God.** Paul said, *"In the wisdom of God, the world by wisdom knew not God."* Their confession of failure was carved in stone upon an altar in Athens: *"To the unknown god."*

God would never wish to be unknown. Abraham had picked up a golden key marked "faith." By it, he opened Heaven. Men of genius are as rare as icicles in summer. Abraham was not one of them. God is not the Chairman of an exclusive club for intellectuals, but He keeps His front door open for anybody. He would never deprive Himself of the love of the millions in preference to the one-in-a-million prodigy.

*"And we know that the Son of God has come and has given us an understanding, **that we may know Him** Who is true, and we are in Him Who is true, in His Son Jesus Christ. This is the true God and eternal life."*

The suggestion that we must not believe if men of intellect don't, is not a very intellectual notion. If we had to find Him via a labyrinth of learning, He would have a very small company around Him. To have the love of the vast mass of Mankind, the means had to be different. He makes Himself known to those who look up to Him in child-like hope. You don't have to be some intellectual to know and love God … you simply love Him by faith.

Today's Scripture

Whoever believes that Jesus is the Christ is born of God, and everyone who loves Him Who begot also loves Him Who is begotten of Him.
(I John 5:1)

Daily Power!

God makes Himself known to those who look up to Him in child-like hope.

Today's Bible Reading

Zephaniah 1:1-18 through 3:1-20; Revelation 10:1-11; Psalm 138:1-8; Proverbs 30:11-14

Mark my Word
(for further study)

Psalm 111:10; Acts 17:23; I Corinthians 1:21; I John 5:1, 20

DECEMBER

20

Solid Ground

Abraham learned to trust God, and it revealed to him the paths of peace. In his day, cities existed by military might, founded on blood-shed. God gave Abraham a new vision: a city of peace, whose *"Builder and Maker was God."* His eyes scanned far horizons indeed. He was the first to discern the paths of righteousness, paths "in the sea" and ways in the wilderness. The paths of righteousness and peace have been found. They are marked and known. Used or not, they can now never be forgotten but are there, freeways open for all. Many nations claim to follow them, but it is only feebly. If we traced them back, they would bring us to the tent door of Abraham, where God said to him, *"Walk before me and be perfect."*

The Book of Hebrews sums up that for which Abraham lived: *"He looked for a city which had foundations whose Builder and Maker was God."* In his day, nobody knew of any spiritual foundations. Rulers ruled only for their own benefit. Before Abraham, people's heads were vacant of any purpose or plan. Nobody knew why on Earth he or she was on Earth! Paul faced the agnostics and Stoics of Athens, saying, *"These times of ignorance God overlooked, but now commands all men everywhere to repent."* Therefore, he wrote to Timothy, *"Jesus Christ … has brought life and immortality to light through the Gospel."* Paul also talks about those who *"professing themselves to be wise … became fools."* We may live without knowing the distance to the nearest star or the secrets of the atom … but there is no real life at all without the secret of God. We are lost before we start. Agnosticism is total disaster. We either live by faith – or we don't live at all … as Jesus said, *"Whoever believes in the Son has everlasting life, but who does not believe the Son shall not see life."* Faithless life is lifeless life. Abraham knew very little about the world around him … but He knew what life was all about. God made the first man, Adam … and the first civilized man, Abraham. **Live in God!**

Today's Scripture

Therefore do not be ashamed of the testimony of our Lord ... Who has saved us and called us with a holy calling, not according to our works, but according to His own purpose and grace which was given to us in Christ Jesus before Time began.

(II Timothy 1:8-9)

Daily Power!

There is no real life without the secret of God.

Today's Bible Reading

*Haggai 1:1-15
through 2:1-23;
Revelation 11:1-19;
Psalm 139:1-24;
Proverbs 30:15-16*

Mark my Word
(for further study)

*Genesis 17:1;
John 3:36;
Acts 17:30;
Romans 1:22;
II Timothy 1:10;
Hebrews 11:10*

Mission impossible?

From the outset, the Church looked doomed, stillborn. To bring His message to the nations, Jesus had only a few ordinary local men from Galilee. None of them demonstrated any brilliance or personal qualities that would make for success. In fact, they displayed a generous share of human failings! They were as unqualified for success as men ever could be. The Jewish leaders wrote them off as ignorant and unlearned. To meet the many outstanding intellectuals of their day, or even sway the semi-barbarous masses, these lowly fishermen and outcasts of Galilee possessed not even an inkling of educational or psychological know-how. Their message seemed purposely unappealing. It had no element of intellectual wisdom, political promise or immediate social benefit. The worst part of all was that it centered on a leader from a seedy Galilean backwater town, Who ended up being executed as a common criminal. Mission impossible? Against all expectations, it became "mission accomplished"! How? They advanced with a new secret: God personally worked with them with signs and wonders. More than that, He barbed their simple words with conviction and guided them to the hearts of hearers as unerringly and powerfully as David's stone was guided to the head of Goliath. Without personal charisma, the charisma of the Spirit of God clothed them. Their "secret"? **The Holy Spirit.**

Recently, a survey of Charismatics revealed that six out of ten members had experienced a miraculous healing at some time; three out of four members experienced speaking in tongues, eighty-three percent regularly. Of even greater significance was the fact that those who spoke in tongues were the most active in evangelism. Twice as many received salvation in places where the pastor strongly stressed the Pentecostal experience. Largely because of the gifts, evangelical Christians are multiplying three times faster than the world population, with over 1.5-million full-time Christian workers. This is by far the fastest-growing faith in the world. Make **your** faith count today!

Today's Scripture

They couldn't take their eyes off them – Peter and John standing there so confident, so sure of themselves! Their fascination deepened when they realized these two were laymen with no training in Scripture or formal education. They recognized them as companions of Jesus, but with the man right before them, seeing him standing there so upright – so healed! – what could they say against that?
(Acts 4:13-14; the Message)

Daily Power!

The secret of the Apostles' "success" in evangelizing their world: the Holy Spirit.

Today's Bible Reading

*Zechariah 1:1-21;
Revelation 12:1-17
through 13:1a;
Psalm 140:1-13;
Proverbs 30:17*

Mark my Word
(for further study)

Acts 4:13-14

DECEMBER

22

Today's Scripture

For we do not have a High Priest Who cannot sympathize with our weaknesses, but was in all points tempted as we are, yet without sin.
(Hebrews 4:15)

Daily Power!

Jesus Christ was born because He wanted to be born.

Today's Bible Reading

Zechariah 2:1-13 through 3:1-10; Revelation 13:1b-18; Psalm 141:1-10; Proverbs 30:18-20

Mark my Word
(for further study)

Isaiah 9:6; 53:12; Hebrews 4:15

Family Planning

Christmas is really a birthday party, a celebration of Christ's nativity. We don't know the actual date of Jesus' birth, but it doesn't matter … 25 December is as good as any other day. If we can have national holidays for saints, battles and victories, we certainly should do a bit of rejoicing about the birth of the greatest Person ever born! The great prophet Isaiah spoke seven hundred fifty years before Christ was born – *"For unto us a Child is born, unto us a Son is given; and the government shall be upon His shoulder. And His Name will be called Wonderful, Counsellor, Mighty God, Everlasting Father, Prince of Peace"* – and they were fulfilled when Jesus came. Each Christmas, we can say, *"Unto us a son is given."* That is what Christmas is about.

And what a Son He turned out to be! Nobody else had a birth like His – and I am not just thinking of the virgin birth. Jesus Christ was born because He **wanted** to be born. Nobody else has ever chosen to be born, because people like us have never had that kind of choice! Jesus was not the result of family planning – He planned His birth Himself with the Father in Heaven. But He planned the Family of God, including its redemption by His own Blood. The Son of God knew what Life with us would be like … and yet He wanted to come to be with us. He came to a primitive home in a crude age, in a dirty and primitive village, with basic food and hard work … and knew that He would be cruelly executed. Why on Earth should He want to be on Earth and endure and suffer such a life? The answer is that He **wanted** to be our Son – just that. He was determined to join the Human Family at all costs. He called Himself by only one title: *"the Son of Man,"* identifying Himself with the Human Race. Isaiah's words, *"**Unto us** a child is born,"* express solidarity with us. Even more, Jesus went for total involvement, being *"numbered with the transgressors."* Again and again, the Bible uses two words: *"for us."* He did not choose to be born for His own benefit, for anything He could get out of it for Himself. **Everything** He was and could do was absolutely and only for His Family. He drew His very breath **for us**, for the family. He is the greatest Gift **you** have this Christmas!

What a wonderful Son!

The Gospel of Matthew begins by calling Christ the **son of David** and the **son of Abraham**. Both David and Abraham had very special sons, but they were disappointments. The **true** Son of Abraham was not Isaac – but Jesus … the **true** son of David was not Absalom or Solomon – but Jesus. This is the Son Who is not a disappointment. Fathers failed, and their sons failed also – except this Son. He came to lift the Family of Man to a new level. Jesus never needed to go to a psychologist or a counselor … He was never at the end of His tether. Jesus was never fed-up, never had a nervous breakdown, never suffered a trauma, never had a burn-out. Jesus never had to apologize, never confessed any sin or needed to repent. He met every situation with absolute poise and perfect reaction. What a Son to be proud of! We can hang on to Him. He became a Son **for us**. Because He lived like that, we can **live!** We do not just get by, scrape through, rowing hard, struggling all the way … but can sail under a full sail. With a Son like that, we can face the music even when we don't like the tune. Jesus says, *"Because I live, you will live also."* Jesus is coming back **for us**. Christ Jesus has never resigned from the Human Family – He is forever the Son of Man, born and bred here from infancy. He is due to come home anytime now – back to where He was born. What a homecoming! He loves this Family of Man, His own Family. He wants to be with us, and wants to come back to where He belongs, to the world of men and women.

The Family get-together at Christmas is a wonderful time, but it is only a picture of what is to come. When Jesus the Son comes home, what a reunion that will be! What a gathering! What a party, what feasting, what joy! Nobody who belongs there will be missing. Every born-again child of God will meet our "great elder Brother," the Son of all sons, face to face. The celebrations will go on forever. So many have forgotten about all this. They know that the Son of Man came to Earth … but think that He disappeared into the blue long ago. Christmas just keeps His memory alive. People read the Bible about Jesus and what He was like … but forget that He is coming back! He is coming for **you**!

Today's Scripture

Behold, I am coming quickly, and My reward is with Me, to give to every one according to his work. I am the Alpha and the Omega, the Beginning and the End, the First and the Last.
(Revelation 22:12)

Daily Power!

When Jesus the Son comes home, what a reunion that will be!

Today's Bible Reading

Zechariah 4:1-14 through 5:1-11;
Revelation 14:1-20;
Psalm 142:1-7;
Proverbs 30:21-23

Mark my Word
(for further study)

Matthew 1:1;
John 14:19;
Revelation 22:12

Today's Scripture

Blessed are those who do His commandments, that they may have the right to the Tree of Life, and may enter through the gates into the City.

(Revelation 22:14)

Daily Power!

We are two thousand years nearer the Second Coming now!

Today's Bible Reading

Zechariah 6:1-15 through 7:1-14; Revelation 15:1-8; Psalm 143:1-12; Proverbs 30:24-28

Mark my Word
(for further study)

Hebrews 9:28; Revelation 22:6-8, 12-14, 20

Read the Post-Script

A family received a letter from their soldier-son on duty in a foreign land. They were all busy and it was a very long letter, so they read half a page or so. They intended to sit down after work and read it all. Meanwhile someone knocked at the door and … there was their son, in person! They were astonished and said, "What are you doing here? We've just had your letter from where you were!" The son said, "Haven't you read it yet?" Well, they hadn't read as far as the post-script at the end, which said that he was coming home.

"Then he said to me, 'These words are faithful and true.' And the Lord God of the holy prophets sent His angels to show His servants the things which must shortly take place. 'Behold, I am coming quickly! Blessed is he who keeps the words of the prophecy of this Book.' Now I, John, saw and heard these things … 'And behold, I am coming quickly, and My reward is with Me, to give to every one according to his work. I am the Alpha and the Omega, the Beginning and the End, the First and the Last.' Blessed are those who do His commandments, that they may have the right to the Tree of Life, and may enter through the gates into the City."

It is time to read God's post-script in the Bible. That Great Book closes with the words of Jesus: *"Surely I am coming quickly!"* Jesus **will** come again. We have been waiting over two thousand years. People waited much longer than that the first time He came, but He did not forget to come. He will come the second time, and will not forget. As long as the Family He loves is here on Earth, He will never rest. *"To those who eagerly wait for Him, He will appear a second time."* We are two thousand nearer the Second Coming now. If the First Coming gave us the joys of Christmas, the Second Coming will bring the joys of Heaven. *"Even so, come, Lord Jesus!"* Make that **your** song today!

Luke 2:1-20

"And it came to pass in those days that a decree went out from Caesar Augustus that all the world should be registered. This census first took place while Quirinius was governing Syria. So all went to be registered, everyone to his own city. Joseph also went up from Galilee, out of the city of Nazareth, into Judea, to the city of David, which is called Bethlehem, because he was of the house and lineage of David, to be registered with Mary, his betrothed wife, who was with child. So it was, that while they were there, the days were completed for her to be delivered. And she brought forth her firstborn Son, and wrapped Him in swaddling cloths, and laid Him in a manger, because there was no room for them in the inn.

Now there were in the same country shepherds living out in the fields, keeping watch over their flocks by night. And behold, an angel of the Lord stood before them, and the glory of the Lord shone around them, and they were greatly afraid. Then the angel said to them, 'Do not be afraid, for behold, I bring you good tidings of great joy which will be to all people. For there is born to you this day in the city of David a Savior, Who is Christ the Lord. And this will be the sign to you: You will find a Babe wrapped in swaddling cloths, lying in a manger.' And suddenly there was with the angel a multitude of the Heavenly host praising God and saying: 'Glory to God in the highest, and on Earth peace, goodwill toward men!'

So it was, when the angels had gone away from them into Heaven, that the shepherds said to one another, 'Let us now go to Bethlehem and see this thing that has come to pass, which the Lord has made known to us.' And they came with haste and found Mary and Joseph, and the Babe lying in a manger.

Now when they had seen Him, they made widely known the saying which was told them concerning this Child. And all those who heard it marveled at those things which were told them by the shepherds. But Mary kept all these things and pondered them in her heart. Then the shepherds returned, glorifying and praising God for all the things that they had heard and seen, as it was told them."

Today's Scripture

And she will bring forth a Son, and you shall call His Name Jesus, for He will save His people from their sins.
(Matthew 1:21, 23)

Daily Power!

Celebrate the birth of Jesus Christ the Savior from the bottom of your heart!

Today's Bible Reading

Zechariah 8:1-23;
Revelation 16:1-21;
Psalm 144:1-15;
Proverbs 30:29-31

Mark my Word
(for further study)

Matthew 1:18-24; 2:1-18;
Luke 2:1-20

26

Today's Scripture

Turn the hearts of the fathers to the children, and the disobedient to the wisdom of the just, to make ready a people prepared for the Lord.
(Luke 1:17)

Daily Power!

Only one power on Earth can bring a fundamental alteration in us – and that is the Gospel.

Today's Bible Reading

Zechariah 9:1-17;
Revelation 17:1-18;
Psalm 145:10-21;
Proverbs 30:32

Mark my Word
(for further study)

Luke 1:17;
John 3:3, 7;
I John 2:18

"The last Time"

The theme on my heart lately is a very simple verse: *"It is the last time."* In reference to the end of a year – and even to the recent turn of the millennium – never in the experience of anyone living today has there been such a universal sense of "The End." People have mixed reactions to the end of a year – or the approach of a new millennium. Some celebrate a year's end with frantic party-going, as if to make up for a whole year of dismal living. Others fall into deep depression, realizing that another year is passing … and feeling they have little to show for it. Some optimistic people take the end of a year to set themselves new goals and resolutions for the year to come. As for millennium awareness, international leaders spent millions trying to generate optimism that AD 2000 would be the start of a wonderful new age.

As in everything else, the Christian viewpoint is different. The end of each year – and the marking of AD 2000 – keeps me on the lookout, watching for Jesus' return. It was irrational to suggest that AD 2000 would automatically affect anything at all. Time has no power or magic to create a "golden age." For that to happen, a radical change in human nature would be needed. January 1, 2000 did not turn anybody into a saint – not even for a single day. New Year's resolutions always evaporate as quickly as they were made. Health authorities in a TV program report that people are becoming overweight, warning of heart disease and other problems – so people start exercising in the New Year, but soon give up … very few people last even six months. Only one power on Earth can bring a fundamental alteration in us – and that is the Gospel. The Kingdom of God won't come because God looks at a calendar. Nicodemus came to ask Jesus about Israel being restored to the kingdom glory of the times of Solomon, but Jesus answered, *"You must be born again if you want to see the Kingdom of God."* In Greek, the word "you" is plural: Jesus meant Nicodemus **and** Israel. Getting rid of the Romans – political change – would do nothing to bring in a wonderful new order … but being born-again brings the Kingdom of God near! **You** are **in** the Kingdom of God!

Faith's final Test

God planted Abraham in an unfriendly wilderness. God also planted the Church in an unfriendly world, with the same purpose as that of Abraham. When Jesus sent out His disciples, He gave them a Divine passport into every land on Earth: *"Go into all the world and preach the Gospel to every creature."* Christ was following the will of His Father expressed to Abraham: *"I will bless you … and you will be a blessing … and in you all the nations of the Earth shall be blessed."* They could forget about saving themselves – He would look after that – their concern must be to save Mankind. The Great Commission commits us to continue Christ's mission. Concerned only with itself, the Church is purposeless in God's eyes … and harmless to Hell. Faith only operates when linked with His purposes … and the first of them is to bless all families of the Earth.

The strangest episode in Abraham's life was his call to sacrifice Isaac: *"By faith Abraham, when he was tested, offered up Isaac, and he who had received the promises offered up his only begotten son, of whom it was said, 'In Isaac your seed shall be called,' concluding that God was able to raise him up, even from the dead, from which he also received him in a figurative sense."* It might shock us that Abraham would even contemplate human sacrifice … but four thousand years distance makes it impossible for us to understand a man of his time. Human sacrifice was common, and was practiced more than three thousand years after Abraham, as in Central America. Abraham was the learner and beginner of faith in God. Spiritual lessons percolate very slowly into our human understanding.

God never meant Isaac to be sacrificed, but God tested Abraham on his own cultural level. Such a practice was then an expression of extreme religious devotion. He learned, in fact, that God wanted no offering of human blood. The purpose of this episode was the same as all God was doing with Abraham – to create a new culture in which bloodshed had no place. We are thankful that God taught Abraham a new covenant! And we are grateful that He allowed **us** to walk in the fullness of the covenant today.

Today's Scripture

Christ has redeemed us from the curse of the Law, having become a curse for us … that the blessing of Abraham might come upon the Gentiles in Christ Jesus, that we might receive the promise of the Spirit through faith.
(Galatians 3:13-14)

Daily Power!

God planted the Church in an unfriendly world … to save Mankind.

Today's Bible Reading

Zechariah 10:1-12 through 11:1-17; Revelation 18:1-24; Psalm 146:1-10; Proverbs 30:33

Mark my Word
(for further study)

Mark 16:15; Hebrews 11:17-19

Evangelism is for all Christians

No evangelist can go through life without referring to the Great Commission. That Commission – from the lips of Christ Himself – is found in varying forms in the four Gospels and in Acts. Each time, the emphasis is on the nations: the unsaved masses all over the world. Matthew wrote: *"Go therefore and make disciples of all nations."* Mark said: *"Go into all the world and preach the Gospel to every creature"* – and what happened? – *"The disciples went out and preached everywhere."* Luke wrote: *"Repentance and forgiveness of sins will be preached in His Name to all nations."* John recorded Christ's most sacred moment when He spoke to His Father: *"As You sent Me into the world, I have sent them into the world ... that the world may believe that You have sent Me."* Jesus said: *"You shall be witnesses to Me in Jerusalem, and in all Judea and Samaria, and to the end of the Earth."*

Some people regard an evangelist as a revivalist – that is, someone who gives a church a good rousing shake-up about once a year. An evangelist's job is to win people for Christ ... not to preach to sleeping Christians and revive dead churches! An evangelist's ministry is misdirected if it is aimed at the saints of God. The New Testament from Acts onwards makes evangelism the natural function of all who follow Christ. In fact, evangelism **is** following Christ, for that is what He mainly did. Evangelism is part of Christianity ... as light belongs to the sun. A believer has no option – he **must** be engaged in telling others about his faith, or in some way be involved in that business. Witnessing is the business of the Christian faith. The Church is the society for the propagation of the Gospel. In its beginnings, people joined it expecting to be witnesses, although the risks were high. All religions have their sacred obligations: Sikhs must wear a turban ... Hindus must avoid animal fats ... Moslems repeat their sacred prayer. Christian sensitivities have their roots in the sacred obligation to witness to Christ. Witnessing is an essential part of our faith. Activate that in **your** life today.

Today's Scripture

Repentance and remission of sins should be preached in His Name to all nations ... And you are witnesses of these things.

(Luke 24:47-48)

Daily Power!

An evangelist's job is to win people for Christ ... not to preach to sleeping Christians and revive dead churches!

Today's Bible Reading

Zechariah 12:1-14
through 13:1-9;
Revelation 19:1-21;
Psalm 147:1-20;
Proverbs 31:1-7

Mark my Word
(for further study)

Matthew 28:19;
Mark 16:15, 20;
Luke 24:47-48;
John 17:18-21;
Acts 1:8

Change of Focus

Even before his conversion, Paul knew that witnessing is what a believer has to do. He got into so much trouble because he did what he was supposed to do. As an apostle, he displayed a very forgivable and natural pride that God had entrusted him with the Gospel. He always speaks as if it was the most unexpected good fortune! The Church is supposed to grow – that is implicit throughout the New Testament – yet it is also explicit: *"How shall they preach unless they are sent? As it is written: 'How beautiful are the feet of those who preach the Gospel of peace, who bring glad tidings of good things.'"*

One striking difference between the Hebrew and Christian Scriptures is that the New Testament brings the world into focus. The Old Testament shuts us in to Israel's disappointing history – it narrowed and became introspective … its outlook only an "in-look" … its highest hopes were nationalistic. In the New Testament, the whole picture changes: there is bustle and excitement … men of Israel become world travelers, proclaiming the Name of the Lord everywhere. That Jesus was the One Who set them going is made clear: *"Other sheep I have which are not of this fold; them also I must bring."*

Jesus talked about shepherding and harvesting, but He also talked about fishing. One day, while taking a walk by the edge of the water, He watched fishermen at work. Simon and Andrew were casting a net. John and James were mending their nets. Some were little more than teenagers. He said, *"Follow Me, and I will make you fishers of men."* Whether they are more like sheep or fish is not important – Christ wanted to gather people to Himself. And that is still His great purpose, and should be ours too. Make that **Your** purpose today!

Today's Scripture

Scripture reassures us, "No one who trusts God like this – heart and soul – will ever regret it." It's exactly the same no matter what a person's religious background may be: the same God for all of us, acting the same incredibly generous way to everyone who calls for help. Everyone who calls, "Help, God!" gets help.
(Romans 10:11-13; the Message)

Daily Power!

Christ wants to gather people to Himself – that is still His great purpose.

Today's Bible Reading

Zechariah 14:1-21; Revelation 20:1-15; Psalm 148:1-14; Proverbs 31:8-9

Mark my Word
(for further study)

Matthew 4:19; John 10:16; Romans 10:11-15

DECEMBER

30

Today's Scripture

For the love of Christ compels us, because we judge thus: that if One died for all, then all died.
(II Corinthians 5:14)

Daily Power!

The Christian purpose is still the same: to carry the light of the Gospel into a murky world.

Today's Bible Reading

Malachi 1:1-14 through 2:1-17; Revelation 21:1-27; Psalm 149:1-9; Proverbs 30:10-24

Mark my Word
(for further study)

Luke 19:13; John 9:4; I Corinthians 7:29, 31; II Corinthians 5:14

Priorities of the Kingdom

For those who know Jesus, the passing of a year is a powerful reminder that *"the night is coming when no one can work."* Meanwhile, we follow the Lord's advice and go about our normal business *"until He comes."* Those who peruse the pages and long story of the Church of Jesus will know that whenever dark clouds have rolled across the horizon and the End has seemed imminent, it has incited men and women with faith in God to leave their firesides, and to carry the torch of Gospel hope into the cold darkness.

The small figure of the apostle Paul mingled unnoticed with the crowds on the Roman roads, a thousand beliefs in their pagan heads. They never realized that he was swinging wide the gates of history in Europe. The whole might of the empire was not able to resist him. He made converts out of the licentious devotees of the gods, and said to them, *"The time is short. From now on, those who have wives should live as if they had none; those who use the things of the world as if not engrossed in them."* He meant that because of the time limits, our priorities must be those of the Kingdom of God.

The Christian purpose is still the same: to carry the light of the Gospel into a murky world … not driven by the pursuit of glory, nor in order to count our successes, or to fill pews. The Church is not a business. Why was Paul so committed to spreading the Gospel? Because he was convinced that if Christ died for all, then **all** could live and because he was compelled by God's love. Paul – the number one evangelist – had one priority: the eternal destiny of men and women. It rose above all other interests. He made no apology for anything he did. He gave all, and expected others to do the same. Yet for centuries, the Church confined its interests to the Roman world, and not until the 8th century did notable churchmen turn their attention to "barbarians" beyond their borders, venturing with the Gospel into regions where they knew they could be martyred. **You** can change **your** world with the Gospel!

Your primary Goal

Believers of the 19ᵗʰ century believed that the 20ᵗʰ century would bring Christ back ... and they prayed for power to evangelize every tribe and nation on Earth. The prayers of those dedicated men and women **were** answered: the power of God is now exceeding everything ever known, as is evident as **Christ for all Nations** thrusts forward into the 10/40 window. Our 1998/1999 crusades won an average of one hundred thousand people for Jesus in a single crusade, and brought miracles greater than one could imagine! I continued to target for a more powerful push in the third millennium – using new means, the best that a technological age has yet produced. This is one advantage we have over earlier workers. The Harvest is ready and ripe and the New Millennium has catapulted this ministry onto a new level where we do not just see hundreds of thousands saved in one crusade, but, as was the case in Lagos, Nigeria, **one million souls** saved in one single service. God is speeding up the harvesting - *"Behold, the days come, says the Lord, that the plowman shall overtake the reaper...!"*

And there is another advantage: affluence among Christians today undreamed of a century ago. God has made wealth available – and to those who will give, He gives. Earthly conditions need Earthly means and Earthly currency. God's people can handle that ... but only Jesus can provide the power, and that is there *"more abundantly."* Some may be waiting, resting on their laurels, looking for Christ's imminent return – but we dare not do that. We must be found working in the field when He comes to take us! In his day, Paul found the whole world and the empire opposed to him, yet he said, *"I tell you, now is the time of God's favor now is the day of salvation."* If it was the *"day of salvation"* in those hostile conditions ... what is it today, with a thousand open doors and multiplied millions of open arms and hearts, precious and lovely people, ready to embrace the message of the Gospel?

Our resolve until Jesus comes again is to miss no opportunity to take the Gospel to the people who need it. As long as one person is found on Earth without the knowledge of Christ, our Lord's command remains: *"Go and preach the Gospel to every creature"* – to the last person and the very last moment. And this is what we will do. Make that **your** primary goal for the next year!

Today's Scripture

We then, as workers together with Him, also plead with you not to receive the grace of God in vain. For He says, "In an acceptable time I have heard you, and in the day of salvation I have helped you." Behold, now is the accepted time; behold, now is the day of salvation.
(II Corinthians 6:1-2)

Daily Power!

Our resolve is to miss no opportunity to take the Gospel to the people who need it.

Today's Bible Reading

Malachi 3:1-18 through 4:1-6; Revelation 22:1-21; Psalm 150:1-6; Proverbs 31:25-31

Mark my Word
(for further study)

Amos 9:13; Mark 16:15; John 10:10; II Corinthians 6:2

Chronological Index

January

January 1	God First	New Year's Day / Priorities
January 2	Reason for Living	Evangelism / Priorities
January 3	Perfectly certain	Salvation / Christian Living
January 4	Salvation is not Speculation	Salvation / Christian Living
January 5	Spiritual Need	Christian Living / Evangelism
January 6	The World's Need	Christian Living / Evangelism
January 7	Only Jesus!	Exalting Jesus Christ
January 8	Jesus never changes	Exalting Jesus Christ
January 9	The Faith Factor	Faith / Christian Power
January 10	The Faith Fuse	Faith / Christian Power
January 11	The Hands of Jesus	The Blood of Jesus / Christian Power
January 12	Jesus is real	Christian Living / Faith
January 13	God's universal Health Plan	Healing / Faith
January 14	Streams in the Desert	Holy Spirit / Christian Power
January 15	Finding God	Christian Living / God the Father
January 16	God's Identity	God the Father / Evangelism
January 17	Revival is Work	Christian Living / Revival
January 18	The silent Planet	Prayer / Christian Living
January 19	Blood different from all others	The Blood of Jesus / Christian Power
January 20	Divine Blood Type	The Blood of Jesus / Christian Power
January 21	Proven Signs	Christ's Second Coming / Priorities
January 22	Miracle Territory	Christian Living / Miracles
January 23	Miracle Conditions	Christian Living / Miracles
January 24	Sickness isn't God's Plan	Healing / Christian Living
January 25	Avoid past Mistakes	Christian Knowledge / 2nd Coming
January 26	"Even so, come, Lord Jesus!"	Christ's Second Coming / Salvation
January 27	The golden Gift	Exalting Jesus Christ / Faith
January 28	A present-tense Faith	Faith / Christian Living
January 29	Aspects of the Holy Spirit	Holy Spirit / Christian Power
January 30	God's infinite Blood	Christian Power / The Trinity
January 31	Knowing God	God the Father / Christian Living

February

March

April

May

May 1	God's lively Stones	Christian Living / Christian Power
May 2	Hardly Supermen	Christian Power / Prayer
May 3	Jonah – the reluctant Evangelist	Evangelism / Christian Teaching
May 4	Going down	Evangelism / Christian Power
May 5	Seven Rules of Prayer	Prayer / Christian Power
May 6	Perfect Wisdom	Christian Living / Prayer
May 7	Prepare your Family	Christian Living / Salvation
May 8	First Generation	Salvation / Christian Living
May 9	The Logo of God's Love	Jesus Christ / Salvation
May 10	Releasing God's Power	Jesus Christ / Christian Power
May 11	The tingling Impulse	Holy Spirit Baptism / Testimonial
May 12	When the Spirit comes	Holy Spirit Baptism / Power
May 13	Demystifying Faith	Faith / Christian Teaching
May 14	Character Test	Faith / Christian Living
May 15	Miracles and Skepticism	Christian Living / Faith
May 16	Revival is here!	Christian Living / Revival
May 17	Geared to God	Holy Spirit / Christian Power
May 18	Faith pins Hope	Faith / Christian Living
May 19	The Eye to the Unseen	Faith / Christian Power
May 20	Transforming Power	Faith / Christian Living
May 21	The Voice of Love	Jesus Christ / Christian Living
May 22	How Sin happened	Christian Living / Faith
May 23	Godly Families	Prayer / Christian Living
May 24	From Zero to Ten	Christian Power / Jesus Christ
May 25	Witnesses, not Lawyers	Faith / Christian Power
May 26	Two Gifts	Holy Spirit / Christian Living
May 27	Many Baptisms?	Holy Spirit Baptism / Power
May 28	Becoming a Child of God	Salvation / Christian Teaching
May 29	The new Way	Prayer / Christian Living
May 30	Why God spoke	Faith / Christian Living
May 31	God at Work	Christian Power / Trinity

June

June 1	Reasons for Believing?	Faith / Christian Power
June 2	Faith or Chaos?	Faith / Christian Power
June 3	Wonderful Knowledge	Evangelism / Christian Power
June 4	Truth, and the People who reflect it	Evangelism / Christian Power
June 5	"Our Father"	Prayer / Christian Power
June 6	God is unusual	Christian Power / Christian Teaching
June 7	The continual Promise	God the Father / Christian Living
June 8	He earned the Name	Holy Spirit / Christian Living
June 9	Faith is a Decision	Faith / Salvation
June 10	The Size of Faith	Faith / Christian Teaching
June 11	"Righteous Anger" and right Priorities	Christian Living / Salvation
June 12	Christ "for us"	Jesus Christ / Christian Living
June 13	Overcoming Love	Salvation / Christian Power
June 14	Power demonstrated	Salvation / Christian Living
June 15	A World Vision	Priorities / Evangelism
June 16	Evangelism is God's Initiative	Evangelism / Priorities
June 17	Low Resistance	Christian Power / Faith
June 18	Believing	Faith / Christian Power
June 19	One-Drink	Holy Spirit / Christian Power
June 20	Identified by Miracles	Christian Power / Healing
June 21	Acts Today	Power / Christian Living
June 22	God raises the Dead	Christian Power / Evangelism
June 23	No Matter where we run	Evangelism / Christian Living
June 24	True Spirit of Evangelism	Evangelism / Christian Power
June 25	Personal Presence	Christian Power / Christian Living
June 26	Pulling the Revival Trigger	Evangelism / Christian Power
June 27	The God who creates	Christian Teaching / God the Father
June 28	The good God	God the Father / Christian Living
June 29	Jonah's Problem	Evangelism / Christian Teaching
June 30	Our ultimate Objective	Evangelism / Christian Living

July

August

August 1	"This same Jesus"	Exalting Jesus Christ / Christian Living
August 2	Time to grow up!	Christian Living / Christian Power
August 3	Dynamic Power Points	Christian Power / Christian Living
August 4	"Proving" Salvation	Salvation / Christian Living
August 5	Critics don't get it	Holy Spirit / Christian Power
August 6	The Spirit's Difference	Holy Spirit / Christian Living
August 7	Ghostly Terrors	Second Coming / Christian Power
August 8	Sure of Salvation	Salvation / Christian Power
August 9	Switch on the Light!	Holy Spirit / Christian Power
August 10	Life Blood	Blood of Jesus / Christian Living
August 11	The precious Oil	Christian Living / Christian Power
August 12	Commitment	Holy Spirit / Christian Living
August 13	Only God can reveal God	God the Father / Christian Power
August 14	Divine Promises	Christian Living / Christian Power
August 15	The golden Gift of Faith	Faith / Christian Living
August 16	Faith in three Tense	Faith / Christian Power
August 17	The Source of Oil	Christian Power / Holy Spirit
August 18	Getting somewhere	Christian Living / Christian Power
August 19	Flash Flood!	Evangelism / Christian Power
August 20	Miracles characterize the Kingdom	Christian Power / Holy Spirit
August 21	His greatest Work	Evangelism / Christian Living
August 22	No Imitations	Christian Living / Christian Power
August 23	Boast only in Christ	Exalting Jesus Christ / Salvation
August 24	What a Servant!	Exalting Jesus Christ / Salvation
August 25	Power Conductors	Christian Power / Christian Living
August 26	Plugged in	Christian Power / Christian Living
August 27	The secret Side of Faith	Faith / Christian Living
August 28	Purely from the Word	Faith / Christian Teaching
August 29	Quickened by the Spirit	Holy Spirit Baptism / Christian Power
August 30	Intercession	Prayer / Christian Living
August 31	Christ-like Compassion	Prayer / Motivation

September

October

October 1	Consumed by Fire	Holy Spirit Baptism / Christian Power
October 2	Faith Breakthrough	Christian Living / Faith
October 3	Faith Giants	Faith / Christian Power
October 4	"Born Again"	Christian Power / Christian Living
October 5	My first missionary Efforts	Evangelism / Personal Testimonial
October 6	Invasion!	Evangelism / Christian Power
October 7	Natural and spiritual Laws	Faith / Christian Living
October 8	What God is saying	Christian Living / Christian Power
October 9	Evoking Thoughts of God	Christian Power / Christian Living
October 10	Nobody is a "Nobody"	God the Father / Christian Living
October 11	See and believe!	Faith / Christian Living
October 12	The Axe and the Orchestra	Christian Living / Faith
October 13	Evangelists sought!	Evangelism / Christian Living
October 14	Singleness of Heart	Evangelism / Faith
October 15	A Gospel that isn't	Christian Living / Evangelism
October 16	Marching Orders	Evangelism / Christian Living
October 17	The Authority of Christ	Exalting Jesus Christ / Christian Living
October 18	Fire comes by Faith	Holy Spirit Baptism / Christian Power
October 19	Origins of the Anointing	Holy Spirit Baptism / Christian Living
October 20	True Anointing	Christian Power / Christian Teaching
October 21	How big is Hell?	Salvation / Second Coming
October 22	Dummy Ammunition	Christian Power / Holy Spirit Baptism
October 23	"Crazy Joy"	Holy Spirit Baptism / Christian Living
October 24	Revelation in Revelation	Exalting Jesus Christ / Christian Living
October 25	Read carefully	Christian Power / Christian Living
October 26	True Faith	Faith & Prayer / Christian Living
October 27	The real Anointing	Holy Spirit Baptism / Christian Power
October 28	George Jeffreys and Me	Christian Power / Personal Testimonial
October 29	Satan's Chess Game	Christian Power / Christian Living
October 30	God's Fire in Jesus	Exalting Jesus Christ / Christian Living
October 31	Parakletos	Holy Spirit / Christian Living

November

November 1	Dead, boring Christian	Christian Living / Christian Power
November 2	The Height of human Experience	Evangelism / Christian Priorities
November 3	Live Ammunition	Evangelism / Christian Living
November 4	Eternal Purposes	Evangelism / Christian Power
November 5	Worship and Praise	Prayer / Christian Living
November 6	Faith and Knowing	Faith / Christian Living
November 7	False Faiths	Christian Living / Christian Teaching
November 8	Anointing and Appointing	Christian Living / Christian Power
November 9	Warfare Gifts	Christian Living / Evangelism
November 10	Young and Old in the last Hour	Motivation / Christian Living
November 11	Whirlwinds	Christian Power / Evangelism
November 12	The Word brings Faith	Faith / Christian Living
November 13	Faith and the Promises	Faith / Christian Living
November 14	Your last Hour	Christian Living / Motivation
November 15	Last Hour Logic	Evangelism / Christian Power
November 16	The Beauty of God	Exalting Jesus Christ / Power
November 17	Paid by the Hour	Evangelism / Christian Living
November 18	Faith Objectives	Faith / Christian Living
November 19	Swelling Power	Holy Spirit Baptism / Power
November 20	God's True Voice	Christian Living / Christian Power
November 21	Many Callings	Christian Living / Christian Power
November 22	Dan and his Ship Shops	Priorities / Evangelism
November 23	Immortal Work for Mortals	Christian Power / Christian Living
November 24	Leap into the Light	Christian Living / Christian Power
November 25	Greater than Jesus?	Holy Spirit Baptism / Power
November 26	Ancient Faith	Faith / Christian Living
November 27	Faith of a new Kind	Christian Living / Faith
November 28	Step One, Step Two	Faith / Christian Teaching
November 29	Step Three, Step Four	Faith / Christian Teaching
November 30	Step Five, Step Six	Faith / Christian Teaching

December

Topical Index
by Main Theme

Principles of Christian Living

Evangelism and Revival

God the Father

Jesus Christ

January 7	Only Jesus!	May 9	The Logo of God's Love
January 8	Jesus never changes	May 10	Releasing God's Power
January 11	The Hands of Jesus	May 21	The Voice of Love
January 19	Blood different from all others	June 12	Christ "for us"
January 20	Divine Blood Type	July 5	In one Word – Compassion
January 21	Proven Signs	July 6	Christ the Giver
January 26	"Even so, come, Lord Jesus!"	July 8	Regeneration and Resurrection
January 27	The golden Gift	July 10	God isn't who some think He is
February 8	We need a Deliverer!	July 21	Christ is our Home
February 9	Jesus the King	July 22	The Glory of the Lamb
February 25	The Acts of the King	July 24	The Cross and
February 26	The Peak of His Power		Kingdom Miracles
February 28	The true Banner	July 28	We can't escape
March 7	The Forerunner	August 1	"This same Jesus"
March 9	The new and living Way	August 7	Ghostly Terrors
March 10	The Climax of Time	August 10	Life Blood
March 12	The Mark of the Blood	August 23	Boast only in Christ
March 19	Scripture Dynamite	August 24	What a Servant!
March 20	Yesterday, Today, Forever	September 7	The Proof of Jesus
April 13	Apply the Blood	September 29	The Fire Age
April 16	"Kiss the Son"	September 30	Reunited
April 17	History in Advance	October 17	The Authority of Christ
April 19	The "impossible" Jesus	October 24	Revelation in Revelation
April 20	Our God-given Rights	October 30	God's Fire in Jesus
April 27	Jesus – God and Man	November 16	The Beauty of God
April 28	Jesus in the real World	December 26	"The last Time"

Holy Spirit

The Gifts: Salvation, Healing

Faith and Prayer

Christian Knowledge and Power

Seasonal

Scripture Index

The following Scripture References have been used throughout this Devotional, and memorization of these verses is highly recommended!

Genesis 17:7
Exodus 3:13-14; 15:26
Numbers 23:19
Joshua 24:15
Judges 5:1, 31
I Samuel 3:9
II Chronicles 7:14
Ezra 8:22
Job 19:25
Psalms 19:7-10; 33:6-9; 37:4-5; 51:7-10; 68:19-20; 86:11; 90:12, 17; 100:5; 104:13-15; 107:21-24; 119:105; 124:8; 127:1; 132:9; 139:7-10
Proverbs 3:5; 4:14-15, 18; 6:30-31
Ecclesiastes 4:9-12
Isaiah 9:6-7; 10:27; 11:10; 12:2; 40:24, 31; 43:1-3; 46:9-10; 48:16-17; 53:5; 55:6-7
Jeremiah 20:9; 29:11-13
Lamentations 3:22-23
Joel 2:28-29; 3:10
Jonah 2:9

Matthew 1:21-23; 3:11-12; 4:16, 19, 24-25; 5:13-14, 16, 45; 6:7-8, 10, 24, 33; 7:11-14; 10:8, 27-28, 38-39; 11:28-30; 16:18-19, 25; 17:20; 18:20; 19:26; 21:16; 24:13-14; 25:13; 28:18-20
Mark 1:15, 41; 6:34; 9:1, 23; 9:1; 10:27; 11:23; 12:30; 14:6-7; 15:39; 16:15, 20; 28:18-20
Luke 1:17; 4:18-19; 5:17; 6:35; 7:22-23; 9:1-2, 56; 10:20-21; 11:13, 20, 36; 15:7, 23-24; 18:1; 19:10; 21:27-28, 31; 24:47-48
John 1:1-4, 14, 29; 3:3, 6, 14-16; 4:14, 23, 34-35; 5:24, 39; 6:27, 35; 8:31-32, 36; 9:4, 31; 10:10-11, 14-18; 11:25-26, 40; 12:25-26, 32; 14:1-4, 6, 14-18, 27; 15:7-8, 14-16, 26-27; 16:7, 23-24; 17:3; 20:21-22, 29
Acts 1:7-8; 2:4, 8, 11, 38-39; 3:19; 4:13-14, 29-31; 8:16; 10:34-35, 38, 42-44; 16:31; 17:27-28; 26:18; 27:25; 28:31
Romans 1:16; 3:22-23; 4:3, 12; 5:1-4, 8-9; 6:23; 8:1-2, 11, 14, 16, 26, 28; 10:1, 10-15; 12:1-2; 14:13; 16:25-27
I Corinthians 1:18, 20-21, 23-25; 2:9; 3:1-2; 4:10; 6:20; 9:16; 12:4-7, 12, 27; 14:2, 15; 15:3, 20-22, 49
II Corinthians 2:4; 3:12; 4:6; 5:14, 21; 6:1-2, 14
Galatians 2:5-7, 20; 3:13-14; 5:25; 6:14
Ephesians 1:3, 7, 17; 2:1, 8, 13, 19-20; 3:17-19; 4:1-3, 11-13, 15-16, 32; 5:8, 18; 6:8
Philippians 1:6, 20; 2:9-11; 3:10-11, 12-14
Colossians 1:19-20; 4:17
I Thessalonians 1:2-5; 5:16-18
I Timothy 1:12; 2:1
II Timothy 1:8-9, 12
Hebrews 2:1, 4, 9; 4:15-16; 6:19-20; 7:25; 9:14, 27-28; 10:10, 19-23; 11:1, 6; 12:1, 24, 28-29; 13:5, 8
James 1:7, 17; 4:10; 5:11
I Peter 1:3, 7; 2:4-5, 9; 3:18; 4:6; 5:8-9
II Peter 1:3; 3:9
I John 1:3, 9; 2:1-3, 20; 3:14; 4:4; 5:1, 11-15
Jude 24:25
Revelation 1:5, 8; 3:20; 5:12-13; 12:11; 14:15; 22:12, 14, 17

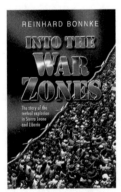

Evangelism by Fire

This best seller has spanned the globe in numerous editions. It heralds a message that fans the spark of evangelism into a blazing furnace – here lies the true heartbeat of Reinhard Bonnke. Read this 'Holy Spirit inspired' book and be motivated to reach this lost generation. It reminds us that the church of God is not a pleasure-boat, but a lifeboat; entertainers are not needed or wanted. Everyone is challenged to take their part in the saving of souls. All hands are required on deck to accomplish this gigantic task.

This book is used as an effective tool in Bible-schools, churches and fellowships around the world. Teaching materials are also available on audio and video.

Paperback, 286 pages

Evangelism by Fire – Workbook

This accompanying workbook to *Evangelism by Fire* will help you to glean a richer understanding of the great commission, and ignite a new zeal in your heart for reaching the lost. It reveals the very heart of each chapter, that you may grasp the fullness of this powerful and challenging book.

Time is running out

An extraordinary message for all Evangelists, Pastors, and spiritual Leaders.
Poignant, exhorting and uncompromising, this dramatic book combines the author's excitement for evangelism while revealing proven, effective techniques for reaching the lost. It is a resounding call to re-examine priorities, heed the call of Christ, preach the good news, and save people from hell.

Paperback, 264 pages

Faith – The Link with God's Power

Some believe that simply having faith is an entitlement to blessings and prosperity. Others believe faith in oneself is all that's needed in life. And still others contend that faith is a cosmic force that breeds superhuman, superspiritual, invincible people.
Is is none of that! Faith is not believing what you know isn't true, nor it is believing something for _____ The Bible is a book all about faith and the evidence that makes fai_____ g.
Bl_____ s being firmly set on Jesus Christ, "the author and fi_____

P_____

Mighty Manifestations

T_____ se the 'power tools' of God – the gifts of the Holy Spirit. The spiritual g_____ 12 are not given to applaud ourselves, or polish our church image, but to endorse the preaching of the Gospel. This 'back to the Bible' study will increase understanding, and energise for action. Reinhard Bonnke shows how we can be effective in using the gifts we have been given.

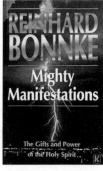

Paperback, 192 pages

Mighty Manifestations – Workbook

As you go through the exercises that have been prepared in this Study Guide, you will be led to a deeper and more intimate comprehension of the work of the Holy Spirit.

Plundering Hell to populate Heaven

Humble Beginnings

The year is 1969, the destination Maseru, Lesotho. The German preacher Reinhard Bonnke, with his wife Anni and their three children spent seven years in Maseru as missionaries. During that time, the need for more effective ways of evangelism kept burning in his soul – in a dream God showed Reinhard the vision of a "blood-washed Africa".

Stepping out in Faith

In 1974 the organization **Christ for all Nations** (CfaN), was born. Soon Reinhard led his new team to the national stadium of Botswana in the city of Gaborone to hold a city-wide Gospel Crusade. Imagine his disappointment when only one hundred people showed up. Nevertheless, he preached his heart out and amazingly, after only a few minutes, a man in the congregation jumped to his feet shouting, "I've just been healed!" Then several others shouted the same thing. The news that God was doing miracles in the stadium soon spread across the city and by the final meeting, Reinhard preached the Gospel to a packed stadium. On a return visit twelve years later, the leader of a large denomination reported that eighty percent of his current pastors were converts from that first crusade in Gaborone.

The Tents

To provide shelter from the elements, a ten thousand-seater tent was built but before long, an even larger tent was needed. The **Big Tent** seated **34,000 people** and was large enough to completely cover three football fields, with masts as high as a six-story building. It stood like an enormous combine harvester, ready to move out into the ripe harvest fields of Africa. The **Guinness Book of Records** acknowledged it as the world's largest mobile structure at that time. But soon even this huge canopy could no longer contain the masses. In Blantyre, Malawi 150,000 people attended a single meeting, more than four times the capacity of the Big Tent!

8.6 million Decisions in only twelve Months

One open-air crusade after the other was now the order of the day. In Lagos, Nigeria, a massive crowd of **1.6 million people** attended a single meeting, more than ten times the size of the Blantyre crusade. 200,000 counselors and 40,000 ushers had been trained. After the six days of the crusade, a total of over 3.4 million decision cards had been filled out by new converts and were turned over for follow-up to the 2,000 participating local churches. In addition, 80,000 pastors and Christian workers had registered for the **Fire Conference**, which has become an added dimension of each crusade. Reinhard likes to say: "In the morning they are 'taught' and in the evening they are 'caught'."

138 million Books in 140 Languages

Evangelist Bonnke has written a number of books and booklets. At present, a total of over 138 million books have been translated into 140 languages and dialects. In the industrialized world, the booklet **From Minus to Plus** has been mailed into **95 million individual homes** in 17 different countries.

Being constantly on the move, **CfaN** is faced with an endless parade of nations hungry for the Word. A complete biography of Reinhard Bonnke, "A Passion for the Gospel," is also available at your Christian bookstore or simply call the ministry office nearest you.

If you would like to learn more about CfaN, log on to the Internet and visit: www.cfan.org